Man and Forest Series
No. 6

General Editors

Klaus Seeland
Franz Schmithüsen

A joint research venture of the

Council of Cultural Growth and Cultural Relations, Cuttack

and

Chair of Forest Policy and Forest Economics, Swiss Federal Institute of Technology (ETH), Zurich

Man and Forest Series

General Editors: Klaus Seeland; Franz Schmithüsen

The Man and Forest Series consists of monographs and readers on the use and management of forests and an account of forest lifestyles in various regions of South Asia. It aims at providing the findings of an eight-year research project (1992-99) to the public. The volumes in this series are the outcome of a cross-cultural research network between the Chair of Forest Policy and Forest Economics, Swiss Federal Institute of Technology (ETH), the Deutsche Gesellschaft für Technische Zusammenarbeit (GTZ) and Non-Government as well as Government Organisations in India, Nepal and Bhutan. The series welcomes contributions covering relevant issues in the man-forest interface.

Forest Tribes of Orissa

Lifestyle and Social Conditions of Selected Orissan Tribes

Forest Tribes of Orissa

Lifestyle and Social Conditions of Selected Orissan Tribes

Vol. 2

The Kuttia Kondh

by

Mihir K. Jena
Padmini Pathi
Kamala Kumari Patnaik
Klaus Seeland

D.K. Printworld (P) Ltd.
New Delhi

Cataloging in Publication Data — DK
[Courtesy: D.K. Agencies (P) Ltd. <docinfo@dkagencies.com>]

Forest tribes of Orissa: lifestyle and social conditions of selected Orissan tribes / by Mihir K. Jena... [*et al.*].
v. 2. 23 cm. — (Man and forest series ; nos. 2, 6)
Includes bibliographical references.
Includes indexes.
Contents: v. 2. The Kuttia Kondh.
ISBN 8124601887 (set)
ISBN 8124603499 (vol. 2)

1. Orissa (India) — Scheduled tribes — Social life and customs. 2. Tribes — India — Orissa — Social life and customs. 3. Forest management — Social aspects — India — Orissa. I. Jena, Mihir K. II. Series: Man and forest series ; nos. 2, 6.

DDC 307.772 095 413 3 22

ISBN 81-246-0188-7 (set)
ISBN 81-246-0349-9 (vol. 2)

First published in India in 2006

Supported by: Tropical Ecology Support Programme (TOEB) Deutsche Gesellschaft für Technische Zusammenarbeit (GTZ)

Published and printed by:
D.K. Printworld (P) Ltd.
Regd. office : '*Sri Kunj*', F-52, Bali Nagar
New Delhi - 110 015
Phones : (011) 545-3975; 546-6019
Fax : (011) 546-5926
E-mail: dkprintworld@vsnl.net
Website: www.dkprintworld.com

Preface

HUMAN existence in subtropical forests such as those of Orissa in eastern India brings about an extraordinary richness of knowledge about trees and plants and a remarkably rich forest lore. Some of this rich knowledge has been recorded and published within this series on forests or will be done so in the subsequent years. The forests of Orissa make a world in which 63 tribes dwelled over centuries and some of them still continue to live on forest resources to a large extent. Richness of cultural life and spiritual imagination of the tribal cultures is, more often than not, combined with a deplorable poverty, sometimes persecution and often paternalism by merchants, government administrators and Forest Department officials.

This is volume 6 of the series on forests, and in this second volume of the tribal monographies within this series, the Kuttia Kondh, a Dravidian speaking ethnic group of central Orissa, is dealt with. It is a venture into their forest world that tries to approach the livelihood system of this Scheduled Tribe in an encompassing way as much as possible by using a hermeneutic method based on the fundamental ontological approach of the German philosopher Martin Heidegger. This was a daring and unusual undertaking as all Indian colleagues of our research team were academically trained and raised in a positivistic tradition of empirical social research.

The research project was conducted from 1992 until 1999 as a joint venture between the Council of Cultural Growth and Cultural Relations, based at Cuttack (Orissa), the German GTZ (Deutsche Gesellschaft für Technische Zusammenarbeit, Section *Tropenwaldforschung* and later on the Flanking Programme for Tropical Forest Research) and the Chair of Forest Policy and Forest Economics at the Swiss Federal Institute of Technology (ETH) in Zurich,

Switzerland. The latter initiated the research project and selected the location and research partners in India Except the project leader, who is a German sociologist, all other members of the research team in India were from Orissa. It consisted of an ethnobotanist who did his PhD in the wake of this research under a senior lady botanist, who particularly committed herself to the research project after retirement. Social sciences were represented by a junior lady social anthropologist, and a senior social anthropologist. Most of them are the authors of this volume. The composition of the team changed over the years, except as far as three Indian authors are concerned, who did most of the field research work more or less continuously over a period of ten years.

The institutional backing and support provided by the research partners as well as by the Forest Department of Orissa and various other government services was highly valuable and often a prerequisite for tasks that were sometimes challenging, often dangerous and always trying and hazardous to health as the climatic and hygienic conditions and the tremendous heat of the Indian summer, the remoteness of the research locations and loneliness were a burden for fieldwork. Co-operation of a development agency, academic institutions and non-governmental agencies with different cultural backgrounds, interests and aspirations was not always easy and smooth. Yet, the common goal of a long-term research in difficult natural and political environments was achieved.

The tribal population of the Kuttia Kondh of Belghar, Guchka and Gulampanga, Guma and Jhiripani, Burlubaru and Rangaparu, located in the Phulbani District of Orissa, on whose interest, goodwill and patience the field work had to count, was open to inquiry and co-operative, even if the outsiders' curiosity must have been sometimes hard to stand for them. Interviewing was mostly done with key informants and generally participant observation in everyday life provided the team with insights into local life and culture. Religion and the supernatural sphere was of particular interest to the team as it characterised the world view of the Kuttia Kondh, their values, norms and outlook on life as well as their perception and knowledge of forest and nature.

The content of this book is a compilation of contributions to the puzzle of a community in transition between an autochthonic lifestyle and fragments of modernity. After an introduction into the detailed research objectives of the project, chapter 1 gives an account of the theory and method of an epistemology based on Heidegger's thinking. Although this approach is not extensively referred to in this chapter, but only introduced in its salient features and as far as its use for anthropological fieldwork is concerned, a more elaborate treatise (Seeland 1998), although published in German only, can be consulted that has originated from this research project. A geographical description of the Kuttia Kondh landscape and forest of central Orissa, including a short historical account of this area is given in chapter 2 in order to acquaint the reader with what later on will be filled with a more detailed view of the Kuttia Kondh's perception and interpretation of their surroundings. The Kuttia Kondh society, i.e., its social structure, gender relations, institutions and patterns of coexistence with the Pano, a Scheduled Caste living in close relationship with the Kuttia Kondh in their territory, is dealt with in chapter 3. This account provides a socio-anthropological framework with particular emphasis on their lifestyle embedded in their forests. Thereafter in chapter 4 their economic rationale of subsistence, their agricultural activities, diet, barter and trade with the outside world and the socio-cultural perspectives of development are referred to. This chapter is meant to give an idea of what self-sustained living inside forests is all about and what meaning is attributed to it by the members of this tribe. Chapter 5 introduces the settlement and housing concepts of their living space and physical environment with particular reference to their religious beliefs and practices. Their sacred world-view that is looked at in its various representations is the all pervading spirit that structures everything around them and is an animated realm to them, what to outsiders seems to be unanimated biotic or abiotic environments.

The amalgam of the Kuttia Kondh's environmental perception and religious thinking is further elaborated and focussed on the sacred meaning of hills and forests within their region in chapter 6. Analogies between hills and deities as well as the description of distinct types of forests on certain parts of hills are there, where these deities are supposed to reside according to the Kuttia Kondh lore. Chapter 7 is about shifting cultivation as a local mode of production and a characteristic element in the Kuttia Kondh way of life. Shifting cultivation is at the interface of forest use and agriculture and, in practical as well as in ritual respect, a particularly relevant occupation. The conversion of forest into a temporal site for food production, including the selection of a suitable location, is a core activity of the Kuttia Kondh and an indispensable part for maintaining their cultural identity. In this regard the chapter also discusses the historical background and the political dimension of it, as it is an illegal, but more or less tolerated, way of forest use from which the tribal population is discouraged by a government policy to promote permanent agriculture in the plains. The socio-cultural aspects of plants, animals and humans are looked at in Chapter 8, including the transformation of plant and animal resources into household material objects. Besides the practical aspects of material culture which are always connected to spiritual qualities of resources and objects, the connectedness of different phenomena having a common meaning is an amazing feature of Kuttia Kondh culture, thus making it an interconnected whole, in which, for instance, hills, gods, animals and plants share the same metaphoric names. Chapter 9 is an account of religious power, magic and disease. As highlighted in the previous chapter, the spheres of society, natural environment and spirituality interact with each other and this becomes most obvious with all sorts of illness and magic. Religious festivals and events are highlights in which social and spiritual powers culminate. Based on environmental phenomena that are interpreted as good or bad omens or on the use of environmental or forest resources such as herbs, tubers or certain parts of animals to treat illnesses, the immediate surroundings are taken as general remedy or medium to inflict magic spells on fellow tribesmen and women. Social life in the forests of central Orissa and the coexistence between the tribal and non-tribal population is dealt with in Chapter 10. It is an assessment of the status of the tribal communities and a sort of future outlook on developments that are likely to happen during the present and the next decade in their settlement areas. A collection of statements made by tribal people is reflecting their situation, their anxieties and expectations of the future. The way they see themselves and the ability of their culture to survive in a rapidly changing political environment shows that most of them believe in the persistence of their traditional culture based on local knowledge of forest.

The conclusions from this account of forest life and culture of the Kuttia Kondh are mainly drawn in a socio-cultural and political way as to how a tribal community can survive under modern state forest management and social policies to unite commercial logging, maintenance of biodiversity and provision of social welfare of under-privileged people in a sustainable manner. Rendering social justice to those who live in and predominantly from the forests and ensuring distributional equality of major and minor forest produce to all members – tribal and non-tribal — of the Indian society is a challenge that asks for new political solutions at the national level. Thus, this book is not only an ethnographic account of a remote forest culture that is vanishing, but would like to be a contribution to the political discussion of what Indian forests are or could be in future.

The voluminous appendix comprises the two cosmogonic myths Kui Gaani and Kapaka Gaani in the form of a transcript and in a word by word translation in order to record these invaluable documents, and an extensive glossary of Kui terms.

Klaus Seeland
Franz Schmithüsen

Contents

Preface vii

Acknowledgements xxi

Maps xxiii

List of Figures, Tables, Maps and Photographs xxvii

Introduction 1

1. Theory and Method 15
- A Venture into the Essence of a Forest Culture 16
- The Ecosystem — A Virtual Order 20
- The Fragmentary Approach — A Holistic Methodology? 22
- Natural and Social Resources 25
- Polysemy in Context 26

2. Forest, People and their Environment in Orissa 29
- Tribal or "Primitive" Communities 32
- Semi-tribal Communities 33
- Acculturated Tribal Communities 33
- Totally Assimilated Tribals who have Acquired a Place in the Hindu Hierarchy 33
- The Natural Environment 35
- The Kuttia Kondh Area 36

Administrative Setting in the Pre-Colonial, Colonial and Independent Era 39

3. Kuttia Kondh Society **43**

The Clans 43
The Origin of Clans 45
Nondruka 46
Timaka 46
Saraka 47
Gunjika 47
Sukhbichaka 49
Sukuka 49
Mindanga 49
Andanga 49
Urlaka 50
Damanaka 50
Other Clans 50
Gender Relations and the Role of Women 54
Youth 57
The Pano 59
Informal and Formal Groups 62
Life Cycle Rituals 63
The Name Giving Ceremony: Daru Itina 64
The Menstrual Cycle 66
Marriage 67
Marriage by Elopement 67
Marriage by Capture 68
Sororate and Levirate 69
Marriage by Negotiation 69
Death 72

4. Livelihood, Economy and Development **75**

The Kuttia Kondh Agricultural Economy 75
Everyday Routine of Work 76
Agricultural Calendar 79
Nutrition (Seasonal Food Patterns) 80
Resources in Kuttia Kondh Economy 84

Village Trade and Barter 88
Inaccessibility of Forests and Deforestation as a Crisis in Resource-Use 91
Socio-economic Change and Development in the Kuttia Kondh Area 93
Perspectives on Socio-Cultural Development 96

5. The Concepts of Space, Environment and Village Settlements 99
The Environmental and Spatial Concept of the Kuttia Kondh 101
Religious Background of the Spatial Concept of the Kuttia Kondh 102
Layout of Village Settlement and Cultivated Land 103
Preconditions for a Settlement 109
Religious Sanctioning of a New Settlement Site 110
Size of Settlement 111
Change of Settlement 112
Home, Habitat and the Placement of Deities 113
House Patterns 115
House Construction 116
The Death of a House 119

6. Sacred Geography of Hills and Forests 121
Mythical Origin of Hills and Forest 121
Manang 121
Mooting 122
The Kuttia Kondh's Perception of Hills and Forest 123
Hills and Gods 124
Talabega Penu 125
Murlivali Penu 125
Bichabari Penu 125
Gunangi Penu 125
Kitangi Penu 125
Dhumamaska and Nisipidi 126
Raji Dandra Penu 126
Padekanda Penu 126

Daramaru, Tundabata & Pusarani Penu 126
Widiokadi Penu 126
Bade Gati Penu & Maunli Penu 127
Sonadueri, Pudrung & Donade Penu 127
Kamei Penu 127
Kandabada & Bakabada Penu 127
Senduroti Penu 127
Adagadi Penu 128
Sikadi Bandha Penu 128
Jindangi Penu 128
Sasadanga, Murjikeri and Katamunda Penu 128
Sechakuriaru Penu 128
Rupapata Penu 128
Achanjala and Bamanadeu Penu 129
Soru/Gati Jaka 129
Soru Tude 130
Soru Nede 131
Soru Panga (Dharani, Wango) 131
The Hills as Realms of the Gods 133
Soru Penu — the Hill God 133
The Appearance of Hill Gods in Dreams 134
Sunasella & Rupasella Penu 135
Bangeri Penu 136
Sandili Penu 136
Tambadadi & Lakuti Penu 136
Digerisoru Penu 137
Gadabali Penu 137
Dharani Penu — the Earth Goddess 137
Kama Penu & Mardi Penu 139
Kidi Penu and Gangi Penu 139
Keri Penu 140
Kutti Penu and Sandhi Penu 140
Deities Associated with the Sacred Environment of the Kuttia Kondh 141
The Great Hills of the Kuttia Kondh 141
Sapangada 141
Dimbuli Soru 145
Dera Salla/Siram Deu 147
Hati Salla (Katak Donger, Rukuni Katak) 149
Conclusion 151

7. Shifting Cultivation — Way of Life and Mode of Production **153**

Site Selection 156

Clearing the Forest 158

Crops Grown by the Kuttia Kondh 162

Zea mays L. (English: maize; KK: Pokanga) 162

Oryza sativa L. (E: rice; KK: Kulinga) 162

Panicum miliare (E: little millet; KK: Masa/Kueri) 163

Eleusine coracana (E: ragi or finger millet; KK: Mande) 163

Sorghum vulgare (E: millet; KK: Kredanga) 163

Pennisetum typhoides (E: pearl millet; KK: Arka) 163

Cajanus cajan (E: pigeon pea; KK: Kaanga) 164

Phaseolus mungo (variety-Radiatus) (E: black gram; KK: Biri) 164

Vigna indica (E: cowpea; KK: Jhudunga) 164

Ricinus communis (E: castor; KK: Kabanga) 164

Guizotia abyssinica (E: niger; KK: Tila) 165

Brassica campestris L. (E: rapeseed/mustard; KK Sorisa) 165

Dioscorea alata, L. (E: greater yam; KK Basanga) 165

Manihot esculenta, crantz (E: cassava; KK: Mara Basanga) 166

Solanum tuberosum, L. (E:potato; KK : Alu) 166

Ipomoea batatas, L. (E: sweet potato; KK: Rani Basanga) 166

Curcuma longa, L. (E: turmeric; KK: Meranga) 166

Layout of Crops in the Bagad 167

Productivity in the Swiddens — A Case Study 168

Fallow period 169

Mythical Background of Shifting Cultivation 177

Neri, Nede and Nella: a Cultural Core Configuration 179

Nella Dakina 180

Wango Dropondi 181

Bicha Supandi Dakina 181

Burlanga Kalu 182

Taka Kalu 184

Dulu Dakina 184

Policy Measures to Control Shifting Cultivation 185

8. Socio-cultural Aspects of Plants, Animals and Humans **189**

Botanical names of trees mentioned in Kui 191

Kuttia Kondh familial relations with trees and other plants 192

Jella and Palla: a Universal View of Forest Life 194

Mythical Evolution of Plants and Trees 196

Bamboo 199

Animals and Hunting Practices in Forests 200

Kdu Pata Worship 201

Hunting the Sambar 202

Animals in Dreams and Religious Belief 203

Paji (Pig) 206

Kadi and Kadinga (Cattle) 207

Poda (Buffalo) 207

Nakudi (Dog) 207

Ada (goat) and Sheep 208

Kaju (fowl) 208

Sacrifices to Satisfy the Penuni 208

Gochchi — A Plant Disease 210

Daka-Daki-Dakina 210

Saru-Siru-Soru — Linkages Between 212

Human Beings, Animals and Plants 212

Material Culture 213

Mara and Mraka 213

Intoxicants and Stimulants 214

Household Articles 219

Kitchen Equipment 219

Water Storing Articles and Eating Vessels 220

Articles to Keep Clothes 220

Sleeping Furniture 220

Storing Articles 222

Musical Instruments 222

Miscellaneous Artefacts and 223

Household Equipment 223

The Use of Prominent Tree and Plant Species 224

Achyranthes aspera, L 224

Arundo donax, L./Bambusa sp. 225

Bauhinia vahlii, wt. & Arn. 226
Bombax malabaricum, Dc. (= Bombax ceiba) 227
Cassia fistula, L. 229
Caryota urens, L. 229
Cissampelos pareira, L. Var. hirusta (Dc) Forman 230
Emblica officinalis, Gaertn 230
Ficus scandens Roxb. 230
Grewia tiliaefolia 231
Madhuka longifolia (Koenig) Mach. = (Bassia latifolia. Roxb.) 232
Mangifera indica 233
Musa paradisiaca, L. 234
Ocimum basilicum 234
Shorea robusta Gaertn. f. 235
Terminalia tomentosa (Dc) W & A 236
Thysanolaena maxima, o. ktze = (T, agrostis, Nees) 237
Xylia xylocarpa (Roxb) Jaub 237
Themda arundinacea 238
Pterocarpus marsupium (Roxb.) 238
Dalbergia sissoo 238
Eulaliopsis binata 238
Michaelia champaca L. 239
Diospyros melanoxylon Roxb. 239

9. Religion, Magic and Disease **241**
Important Religious Events 245
Puni Kalu 245
Meriah Festival (Bia Katina Dakina) 246
Badbinere 246
Dasehra Kandanga Dakina 249
Basa Dakina 249
Magic and Magician 250
Responsibilities of the Kutaka 251
Examples of the Kutaka's Power and Influence 254
Fear of Revenge Due to Marriage Disputes 254
Identifying a Thief 255
Directing Animals 255
The Concept of Disease 256
Folk Medicine 257
Spiritual Diseases 258

Natural Diseases 259
Diseases Related to Socio-Economic Relations 260
Omens and Beliefs Associated with Diseases 261
Dakandi Pdukandi 262
Wechinja 262
Doali 263
Jaka dakandi (Top-Worship) 264
Eju Penu Dakina 265
Other Diseases and Treatments 265
Herbal Medicine 266
Health Care and Traditional Medicine 267

10. Life in the Forest 271
Life in the Forest: the Tribals Non-Tribals's interface 273

Conclusion 283
Forest as World of Representations 284
Challenges for a Modern Forest Policy in a Traditional Cultural Setting 285
To Whom Do Nature and Natural Resources Belong? 287

Glossary: Important Cultural Terms of the Kuttia Kondh 297

***Appendix*-1: Kui Gaani 309**

***Appendix*-2: Kapaka Gaani 441**

Photographs 473

***Bibliography* 529**

***Index* 539**

Acknowledgement

THE authors of this book are indebted to and gratefully acknowledge the help of many colleagues and friends who have contributed to the compilation, writing and the corrections of the various forms of manuscripts and finally to the publication of the book itself. Many a helping hand worked with intrinsic motivation and deserved to be honoured for their valuable work. Those who are to be mentioned and deserve great merit in having been a substantial support to the authors at different stages of editing and making corrections are (in chronological order) Nadja Ottiger, Marielle Ebner-Rijke, Esther Thalmann, Elizabeth Wickett, Stella-Maria Hug and Till Berger.

In Orissa, it were most of all our friends and colleagues of the Council of Cultural Growth and Cultural Relations in Cuttack among whom its General Secretary, Sri Girija Bhusan Patnaik, Director of the research project on Man and Forest from 1992-1999 and his assistant, Sri Umesh Chandra Nayak who have facilitated the success of this book. A most thankful thought for the valuable contributions in field work goes to the following colleagues who have been partly members of the research team for a certain period of time: Sarita Barpanda, Abha Mishra, Sricharan Behera, and Dr. Savyasaachi.

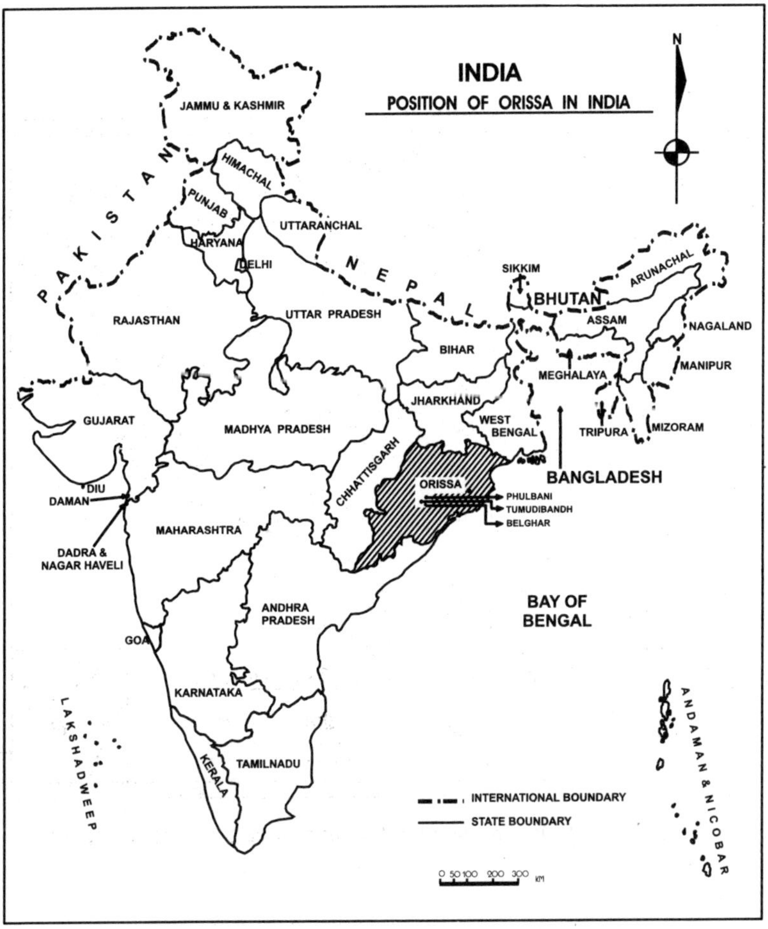

Map - 1: India, Position of Orissa in India

Map - 2: Map of Orissa showing location of district and study area

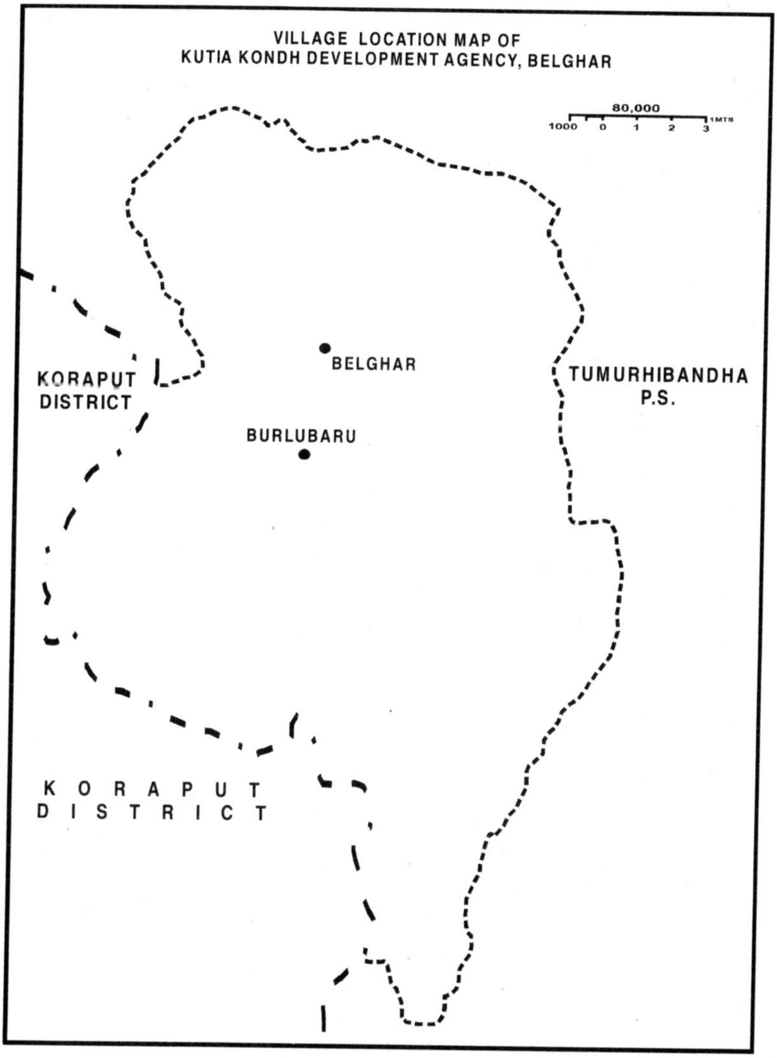

Map - 3: Village location map
of Kuttia Kondh Development Agency, Belghar

List of Figures, Tables, Maps and Photographs

Figures

Fig. 5.1: Layout of a village settlement and cultivated land.

Fig. 5.2: Diagram of a house.

Fig. 6.1: The Various Parts of a hill/mountain.

Tables

Table 1 Classification of area under forests.

Table 7.1: Plants Cultivated by the Kuttia Kondh.

Table 7.2: Plants Cultivated by the Kuttia Kondh.

Table 8.1: Folk Taxonomy of Significant Trees in Kuttia Kondh Lore.

Table 8.2: The Names of Trees Relevant to the Kuttia Kondh.

Table 8.3: Animals and Related Deities.

Maps

Map 1 India, Position of Orissa in India.

Map 2 Map of Orissa showing location of district and study area.

Map 3 Village location map of Kuttia Kondh Development Agency, Belghar.

Photographs

1. A Kuttia Kondh man climbing up a sago palm tree to collect toddy.
2. A combination of swiddens at different stages of cultivation (i) little millet on the swidden (ii) adjoined by seven years fallow land which is further continued to (left) two years fallow swidden and (right) four years fallow swidden on the same hill; and the far off hill is not cultivated for sacred purposes.
3. Two adjacent fields with the crop of alasi (*Guizotia abyssinica*) and mustard during November. The field is protected by a strong fence made of wooden logs and planks of sal. In the background, the village school is surrounded by sal and jack fruit trees.
4. In the foreground castor plants are grown on the swidden which is clearly separated from another swidden by a line of dry grasses. The background hill shows on the right side a three-year fallow swidden and an uncultivated hill top.
5. In the Kuttia Kondh habitat the elongated hill at the backdrop shows a 5 year-fallow swidden. Its foothill is marked by paddy cultivation. In between the two paddy fields tender sal trees are left for growing. In the foreground, little millet is cultivated in the swidden of another hill.
6. In the foreground near the sago palm tree terraced paddy fields and in the background the elongated hill alternately show the paddy with crops under cultivation and with fallow patches (5 years). In between the paddy field a dwarf variety of banana plantation has been grown which is surrounded by some economic trees like mango and sago palm.
7. Plain land is very precious for the Kuttia Kondh. To clear a patch of forest they do not fell big trees. Trees are girdled at the base; then the tree withers and finally the forest department fells it. The picture shows a girdled *Sal* tree.

8. A swidden plot near a 5 year-fallow forest. The swidden plot shows cultivation of little millet and pigeon pea and a watch hut where people stay to safeguard the crops.

9. Withered trees as an effect of tree girdling by the Kuttia Kondh. The plain land cultivated with alasi (*Guizotia abyssinica*).

10. Tuleni and Katani type forest — A restricted forest near the village and agricultural land due to the location of a graveyard.

11. A carefully preserved Kambani type sal forest in the Kuttia Kondh habitat near Belghar. The site is not suitable and economic to be converted to swidden plots as it would require enormous human labour to clear the patch.

12. A virgin Bamanadeu Dongar, not cleared for fear of forest deities' anger, close to the Kuttia Kondh village of Madalakuna.

13. A totally virgin forest near village Rangaparu, a Kuttia Kondh village. The forest is not cut because it is a restriction by Kulibandhu Penu. The nearby pond is named Kulibandha.

14. A scene of village Rangaparu — a typical Kuttia village, houses are arranged linearly with a long street (Rachagiri) in between. At the center, a small jackfruit tree — under which Dharani Penu is located and Karumunda is erected. Kitchen gardens are to be seen at the background of the village.

15. A distant view of Rangaparu village showing its water resource (deified) surrounding crop fields, kitchen garden, foot hill or plain lands and the uncultivated hill (because of its sacredness).

16. Entrance of village Burlubaru. Women are fetching water from the streams in the morning hours.

17. A Kuttia Kondh man and a Kuttia Kondh woman trodding little millet panicles for grains.

18. A Kuttia old man carrying siali (*Bauhinia vahlii*) for sale in the weekly market.

19. A lonely Kuttia child guarding little millet from the reach of livestock.
20. A Meriah pole in Kuttia Kondh village Rangaparu.
21. A Kuttia woman with her children returning to the village after bathing in the stream and fetching water.
22. A Kuttia Kondh woman in her kitchen garden.
23. From village to work place (forest). Kuttia women leaving for their swidden. In the background the hill closest to village Burlubaru showing virgin and fallow forest.
24. A Kuttia Kondh woman attempting to carry a pole for house building.
25. A retiring moment: Kuttia Kondh after returning from their worksites.
26. The grief of parting from her dear ones after marriage: A Kuttia young lady crying before leaving for her in-law's house.
27. Village Burlubaru: Kuttia children enjoying sweets that the grandmother bought for them from the weekly market.
28. A Kuttia Kondh man making a cow bell and winding a rope with which the bell is tied.
29. An old Kuttia Kondh lady during her swidden clearing time.
30. Cattle shed at the backyard of a Kuttia Kondh house. The quantity of wood used for making cattle sheds and fencing is to be imagined. In the background a cleared patch for swiddening is flanked by fallow lands.
31. The profile of a Kuttia house and the pigshed showing the use of wood and logs.
32. Kuttia Kondh women bringing loads of little millet from the hill to home. The crop is received by the family head. The women are usually more hardworking than the men.
33. A Kuttia man shaping a sal log for making a plough. At the background a pile set for the pigs has been constructed

utilizing a lot of wooden poles. The fence of the kitchen garden is also partly seen which is made of wooden logs.

34. Kuttia agricultural implements are mostly made out of sal wood. In view are: plough, yoke, harrow, axe, sickle, leveller.

35. Kuttia Kondh going to the weekly market.

36. Kuttia Kondh waiting to collect rice and kerosine from the mobile van of State Civil Supplies Corporation.

37. Kuttia women sharing dua (chewing tobacco) in a market place. Dua is an offering on formal and informal occasions that indicates good hospitality.

38. A market scene at Belghar. The earthen pots are purchased by Kuttia from the Pano.

39. A Kuttia Kondh girl picking up lice from her mother's head — A leisure time activity.

40. Kuttia children in village Burlubaru.

41. A successful game hunt of Sambar followed by the post hunt ritual performed by the participants with twigs of *Emblica officinalis*; *Thysanolaena maxima*, egg, rice, etc. One of the researchers is seen with a red towel.

42. Three Kuttia belles in the traditional attire in the village Burlubaru with the Bamanadeu hill in the background marked by swidden plots and fallow patches.

43. A Kuttia belle adorned with traditional costume and ornaments.

44. An old Kuttia lady carrying her grandson in front of her house.

45. A Kuttia Kondh priest with the traditional dagger.

46. A line tattoo design on the face of a Panga Kondh woman (Pangaliadu) at the Belghar market place.

47. The oldest lady called Dutali (grand mother) in Burlubaru village: The living legend of Kuttia knowledge and an important source of Kui Gaani.

48. Kuttia village deserted in the day time. When everybody leaves for the forest and swiddens, children are only left to guard the livestock and the houses.

49. Village Rangaparu: The biggest Kuttia Kondh village in Belghar area.

50. Village Burlubaru: Mother is away, so father has to look after the kids.

51. Village Burlubaru: Kuttia women sitting in front of their houses.

52. Siram Deu.

53. Field preparation for swiddening.

54. Watch-hut in a swidden.

55. Deukuda Penu.

56. Ritual for proliferation of game: Maju Penka Dakina offered to Gopal Penu performed by Kutaka (magician-astrologer). Materials used include a symbolic bamboo umbrella covered with leaves of *Bauhinia vahlii*, slippers made of *Lannea coromandelica* bark, brush sticks and leaves of *Shorea robusta* and a palanquin made of *Grewia tiliaefolia* rods.

Introduction

OVER the ages, societies have developed their notions of what forests mean to them. Whatever forests represent to the members of a particular society, they will certainly have a different relevance to what others see and understand in the domain of their own cultures. The forests of today show how people have been, and still are, dependent on them, and how they make use of, and interpret their environment. The transformation of forests that is occurring all over the world, indicates specific social needs, cultural values, and changing economic and technological processes. Forests represent a legacy, and are also a testimony of the evolution of societies and their respective perceptions of nature. Human activities have an impact on forests, that is difficult to assess, however. Some of the changes are immediate and occur in the short term, while others, and often the more important ones, are indirect, and are to be understood in historical dimensions. The spatial distribution of forests, and the degree of their transformation by humans are the result of physical conditions and of varying cultural patterns.

The United Nations Conference on Environment and Development held in Stockholm in 1972 has put forests and forestry on the international political agenda. The preparatory stages as well as the follow-up processes to this conference, represented by the work of the UN Commission on Sustainable Development, show that considerable disagreement on many issues continues to exist, in spite of a growing public awareness that forests are part of our common world-heritage. Large-scale deforestation in the tropics and sub-tropics has led to social and economic problems for many people living in these regions. The protection of forests, sustainability of uses and preservation of biodiversity are important challenges in countries like

India. The conflicts that arise are part of international controversies on social justice, self-determination and sovereignty, local political participation and democratic decision-making, as well as symptoms of the unbalanced economic development between different parts of the world.

In this context research into indigenous knowledge and the meaning of trees and forests in different cultures matters. It is necessary in order to show the many needs and values associated with forests at a given locality, as well as to show the importance of forested areas for the survival of indigenous people and their cultures. Research findings bring to light concrete facts, which result in political decisions on the utilisation of natural resources, and are a strong argument for increased efforts in protecting forested areas and considering local uses. These findings also demonstrate the confrontation between customary performances in sustainable resource management, developed from experiences and adjusted to difficult living conditions, and the development activities of modern states.

The research project on "Indigenous Knowledge of Forests" was a joint venture of the Deutsche Gesellschaft für Technische Zusammenarbeit (GTZ), the Chair of Forest Policy and Forest Economics at the Swiss Federal Institute of Technology (ETH), Zurich, and two Indian NGOs: the Council of Cultural Growth and Cultural Relations in Cuttack, Orissa and Seva Mandir in Udaipur, Rajasthan, and the Central Arid Zone Research Institute, Jodhpur in Rajasthan as Government Institution. It has generated a vast amount of data on trees and forests and what they represent for the members of two tribal societies. One tribal communitiy, the Kuttia Kondh, lives in Burlubaru near Belghar in the Phulbani District of Orissa. The other tribe, or to be more precise, two sections of the Saora tribe, the Lanja Saora and the Sudha Saora, live in the vicinity of Gunupur in Rayagada District (a part of old Koraput District). The present volume covers the Kuttia Kondh community. The monograph on the Saora will follow later on. The studies are enquiries into the worlds of these tribal communities, i.e., all aspects of material life, social and spiritual life are taken into account. The objective of three years of research was to obtain authentic data on how trees and forests are perceived by local forest dwelling communities and how appropriate forest management might be achieved with the help of indigenous knowledge. The overall objective of the project is to gather information that will enable an outside expert to understand how forests are perceived by a local population. Furthermore, it aims to provide an approach that takes into consideration the fact that every aspect of the forest dwellers' socio-cultural life is interwoven with forests and their management. For this reason, a rather broad perspective has been chosen in an effort to shed light on the whole tribal lifestyle, rather than on just those parts that appear to have a direct link with forest management in the Western sense of the term.

Investigations into the perceptions and attitudes of people and local communities with regard to the conservation of trees and forests have an increasing bearing on eco-development and policy. They provide an opportunity to acquire an improved understanding of existing management practices under specific social and cultural conditions, as well as the potential for adaptation to a changing economic environment. Forest research has to place more emphasis than it has in the past on the manifold ways humans interact with their environment. This calls for a more intensive co-operation and new forms of collaboration between the social and cultural sciences on the one hand, and established international research in applied natural sciences and forestry on the other. It also implies a more intensive exchange of ideas between researchers who emphasise the social dimensions of forestry, and those who are *ex officio* responsible for forest resource depletion, protection and development.

"Tribal advancement (as it is widely called throughout India) and poverty alleviation, predominantly among the Scheduled Castes and Scheduled Tribes", are how those schemes that interfere most with tribal life and culture have been referred to. The tribes' integration into mainstream Indian society has been an important objective of national development and social policy in the almost sixty years since independence. The state authorities consider the nation-building process to be a way of attaining or improving their legitimacy as a state that represents all inhabitants, whether they lead a traditional or a modern way of life.

The Indian Union was founded as a result of a transfer of power when the British left India in 1947. Thus, it did not undergo a process of developing a political concept of self-reliance and a culturally appropriate approach to decolonising the country, but was a transfer of power to the Indian political elite. Gandhism, which was an attempt to lead India from colonial rule towards political freedom, failed to come to terms with those who wanted to modernise India at any cost and as fast as possible. The planning commission under Prime Minister Jawaharlal Nehru designed India's first Five Year Plan with the intention of maximising the potential wealth of its abundant natural resources. India's planning economy put a radical end to what was known as the Indirect Rule of the British Raj that left large territories scarcely administered. The mobilisation of the country's natural resources was to serve the purpose of nation building (Kannan 1982:936, 938). The Indian tribes, who had been so far politically neglected, and marginal forest dwellers in the Princely States and in British India became a political factor when the Indian Constitution gave them full recognition as Scheduled Tribes. They were conceded specific rights and concessions as far as their lifestyle and cultural identity was concerned. The policy of the Government of India was at least twofold: on the one hand, the tribals would become beneficiaries of the political freedom, and have the opportunity to become members of a civil society under the auspices of the motto: "Unity in diversity". On the other hand, the tribals could not claim more rights or benefits than the Indian Constitution was prepared to give to them. The huge forests and the natural resources of the areas where they had lived for generations became an integral part of the Indian nation at the time of independence and the state was to exploit the natural wealth of the remote areas for the sake of rapid industrialisation. The policy of peaceful co-existence between the tribal and non-tribal population and the integration of the Scheduled Tribes and Scheduled Castes into a *de jure* secular society, was a *'de facto'* attempt to amalgamate them into a nation, widely dominated by Hindu values and the paramount power of bureaucracy (v. Fürer-Haimendorf 1991). This attempt, however, was largely a failure. Ten years ago, the then Commissioner for Scheduled Castes and Scheduled Tribes (Government of India), B. D. Sharma, stated in his address to the President of India:

> The situation in tribal areas is particularly disquieting. The tribal people are continuously losing command over their resources on almost all counts — pressure from more advanced people, claims by the State in utter disregard of their traditional rights, and virtually forced displacement in favour of a variety of developmental projects, big and small.
>
> — Government of India 1988: ii

With regard to the tribal resource use patterns and institutions, the post-independence concept of swaraj ("self-rule" in Hindi), which had been the core political demand in India's struggle for freedom, was widely denied to Scheduled Tribes.[1] From the days of colonial rule and beginning with India's first forest policy in 1854 and the first Forest Law in 1865, people's relationship with the forest administration was characterised by full appropriation and systematic exploitation of the forests, to which more or less liberal access had been granted before. (Government of India 1990:88ff, 105ff).

The division into village forests, protected and reserved forests was the beginning of the decline in India's natural forest wealth. Tribal people were granted limited usufructuary rights over small amounts of fuel wood, timber and non-timber forest products, so-called "minor forest produce", for their own consumption, but shifting cultivation and hunting was either legally banned or heavily restricted by the Forest Department. The expropriation of Scheduled Castes and Scheduled Tribes has increased in recent decades and has led to a situation of social unrest or political movements, aiming to achieve more power over the use and management of forest resources (Pathak 1994, Guha 1989). The importance of Non-Governmental

1. "The latent rights of the tribal people have remained non-justiciable and escaped the probe of the judicial system and its benign protection because the Executive failed to act and discharge its Constitutional obligation of adapting the formal system to the people's need rather than allowing it to supersede their institutions and customs". (Report of the Commissioner of Scheduled Castes and Scheduled Tribes, 28th report (1986-87), 1988: See also the Report of the Commissioner of Scheduled Castes and Scheduled Tribes, 29th report (1987-89), 1990:368-400 on the self-governance system of tribal society. For politically motivated tribal uprisings see Praharaj, 1988:156-177 and Areeparampil, 1992:148-174.

Organisations (NGOs) in tribal development has also steadily increased as they now act as mediators in conflicts between tribal communities, government agencies and mainstream Indian society.[2]

At the international level, a rising awareness since the early 1970s has paved the way for the development of a global rather than national perspective on use and distribution of India's forest wealth. The importance of the world's forests for the stability of the global climate, their role as carbon dioxide sinks, and their richness in biodiversity, has also had its impact on India's forests. With this change in perspective, a new dimension has emerged in the discussion on the future of forest management. The necessity of involving stakeholders in safeguarding renewable natural resources *in situ*, through local level development and participation, has been recognised as vital, and widened the scope of conservation efforts and protected area management. The social dimension of the knowledge of nature and sustainable management of natural resources has become politically inseparable from the conservation of forest. Since 1987, when the Brundtland Report on "Our Common Future" highlighted the overriding importance of sustainability in matters of environment and development, indigenous people and their knowledge have been ascribed a prominent position in the Agenda 21. (This is apart from the earlier legally binding or non-legally binding International Conventions).[3] Local perceptions of resources, resource use and management, land and the environment (Davis 1993) were increasingly acknowledged as invaluable sources of information in international scenarios of a new economic valuation of the globe's natural and cultural wealth. Taking indigenous views into account in

---

2. In 1994 a draft forest bill by the Ministry of Environment and Forests, Government of India, which was to replace the Indian Forest Act of 1927 and fell unofficially into the hands of NGOs, was heavily criticised and proposals to revise it were made through public discussions. Indian NGOs, forest dwellers and social activists have thus shown how a common effort to draft a people's forest bill gained momentum and became a socio-political movement that spread throughout India. See Fernandes, W. (ed.) 1996b.

3. IUCN Inter-Commission Task Force on Indigenous Peoples, Indigenous Peoples and Sustainability: A Call To Action. (Review draft, Dec. 1995), pp. 57-59.

→

order to contribute to development policies has been acknowledged by many development agencies as well as by most of the national and international NGOs, as partially transcending the narrow perspective of national sector policies although international policies are far from being in a position to override or bypass the limitations of national laws and strong vested economic interests.

A closer look at the development of India's forest area reveals the expropriation of communities whose subsistence is largely or entirely based on forest products.

→ **Traditional Resource Rights (selection)**

Right	Supporting Agreements: legally binding	Supporting Agreements: non legally binding
Human Rights	ICESCR, ICCPR, CDW, CERD, CG, CRC, NLs	UDHR, DDRIP, VDPA
Right of self-determination	ILO 169, ICESCR, ICCPR	DDRIP, VDPA
Collective rights	ILO 169, ICESCR, ICCPR	DDRIP, VDPA
Land and territorial rights	ILO 169, NLs	DDRIP
Right to religious freedom	ICCPR, NLs	UDHR
Right to development	ICESCR, ICCPR, ILO 169	DDHRE, DDRIP, DHRD, VDPA
Environmental integrity	CBD	RD, DDHRE
Intellectual property rights	CBD, WIPO, GATT, UPOV, NL—	
Cultural property rights	UNESCO-CCP, NLs	—
Right to protection of cultural heritage	UNESCO-WHC, NLs	UNESCO-PICC
Recognition of cultural landscapes	UNESCO-WHC	----
Recognition of customary law and practice	ILO 169, NLs	CCRIP

Table 1 shows the classification of forest types in India and their legal status over four decades.

Table 1 Classification of area under forests (thousand hectares)[4]

Category	1950-51	1960-61	1970-71	1979-80	1985-86
I Forest types					
(a) Merchantable	58,460	52,701	47,654	56,493	49,246
(b) Inaccessible	13,343	15,289	19,426	16,042	25,981
II Legal status					
(a) Reserved	34,405	31,631	31,798	37,252	40,612
(b) Protected	11,793	20,355	20,444	22,537	21,509
(c) Unclassified	25,570	15,069	12,946	10,558	13,107

As per definition of the Indian Forest Department, area under forest is defined as land where tree cover/*canopy cover amounts to more than 10 per cent/hectare.

Since the 1950s, the first decade after India's independence, forest cover has increased by 3.4 M. ha (from 71.8 M. ha in 1950/51 to 75.2 M. ha in 1985/86) and the Reserved Forest has . . . increased by 17 per cent. This increase in reserved area has come about by reclassifying protected and unclassified forests.

— Chakraborty 1995:228.[5]

4. Source: Agarawala 1989 (recte 1990, 2nd ed.), India's Forests. Department of Environment, Government of India, 1987, *cit.* by Chakraborty, M., An analysis of the causes of deforestation in India. In: Brown, K. and D.W. Pearce, (eds.), The Causes of Tropical Deforestation. London: UCL, 1995 (2nd ed. publ. in India by OUP & IBH Publ.), p. 228. Only the categories, forest types and legal status are shown here.

5. The Forest Conservation Act (FCA) 1980, which replaced the Forest Act of 1927, brought about an ambiguous situation with respect to the enactment of power to the classification and use of forestland. Pathak (1994:58) states: "The Act provided that no "forestland" can be "de-reserved" or put to non-forest use without the permission of the Central government. The meaning of de-reserving forestland was clear. Reserved forests are "de-reserved" through a notification of the state government. →

Chakraborty, however, fails to give a plausible explanation as to how and why this reclassification took place. Unclassified forest, a category into which community or village forests and small forests owned by local people fall, has either been converted into arable land or Protected Forest where tribal people have concessions to use certain forest products, mainly for their own consumption. In the 1970s, Reserved Forests increased by 10 per cent and Unclassified Forests by roughly 30 per cent, whereas Protected Forest decreased by 0.5 per cent. Inaccessible forest has increased by 10 M. ha within a period of seven years while commercial forest has declined by almost 7 M. ha. It seems that in the early 1980s a substantial amount of forest, previously categorised as commercially exploitable, was either found in areas that would have been too expensive or impossible to open up, or found within areas declared Protected Forest. An increased percentage of degraded forest would explain the drastic rise in Unclassified Forest area in the 1980s while the remarkable rise in Reserved Forests may have been due to the transfer of valuable timber forest from Protected Forests to this category, possibly through exchange of forest land between the categories, "Reserved and Unclassified Forest". Furthermore, it is claimed that the area under forest has increased by 26.7 M. ha and the net area planted with trees increased by 21.9 M. ha from 1950 until 1985, although India's territory grew by 20 M. ha in this period through the absorption of Goa and Sikkim into the Indian Union, and the reduction in uncultivable land is claimed to have amounted to 28.5 M. ha.[6] Considering that

→ However, the meaning of putting forestland to non-forest use was unclear, at least unclear enough for the states to ignore the Act itself. The states continued to transfer forests to raise tea, coffee and rubber plantations based on the interpretation that raising such vegetation is forest use. The transfer of forestland to plantations was one of the state government's domain of favouring the regional capital. The states interpreted non-forest use as raising structures or practising cultivation. These practices were subsequently opposed by the Central government and, including shifting cultivation, strictly prohibited. The weaknesses of the FCA 1980, as, for instance, forestland was not defined, led to an amendment of the Act in 1988.

6. According to Agarwala 1989, CSO 1989 the reduction of uncultivable land comprises of "area not available for cultivation" (7 Mio ha), "other uncultivable land excluding fallow land" (18.3 Mio ha) and "fallow land" (3.2 Mio. ha) cf. Chakraborty 1996:228f.

remote sensing data puts India's forest cover at 64 M. ha and there was an estimated annual deforestation rate of 48,000 ha during the period 1983-87 (World Bank 1991), the forest increment figures become very doubtful. By shifting areas of forest to different categories in order to maintain the overall forest size, without referring to the quality of the respective forest and land, it would appear that reclassification has become a strategic means to restructure areas under the Forest Department's jurisdiction.[7] Furthermore, there is often only a *de jure* difference between severely degraded forest land (i.e., where there are no longer any trees) and uncultivable land.

An incremental increase in forest cover (whether statistically reliable, or a strategic rather than accurate assessment of resources) and at the same time, an increase in areas of deforestation and impoverishment of dwindling forest resources is not an inherent contradiction. Since 1950, India's population has more than tripled and the pressure on forests and forest products has certainly increased over the last sixty years.[8] The classification of forests and the re-allotment of forested land to the various categories by demarcation enable the forest service to maintain productive forests for timber production. Timber production in India's forests, however, is of decreasing importance, although India is importing timber and other forest products (Poffenberger 1996:270). "In 1986, more than 87 per cent of all wood used nation-wide was consumed as fuel" (*ibid.*) and this is in addition to fuel wood used for cooking and large amounts of wood required in cremation. Own-consumption by local communities and need for industrial supply have opposing and contrary objectives with respect to timber growth and the use of non-timber forest products. "Unregulated use" of any product in the forest, from the Forest Department's point of view, is ambiguous as far as its social impact is concerned. A tribal economy, as a self-sustained configuration of linkages between its subsistent units, i.e., foraging,

---

7. 95.7 per cent of India's forests are owned by the state.
8. Likewise the "bovine population in India has increased by 31 per cent over the past thirty-five years from 198 million in 1951 to 259 million in 1987. Similarly, sheep and goat population pressures have expanded over 200 per cent from 47 to 144 million during the same period". (Lal, J.B., 1992:44).

swidden, or sedentary agriculture, represents a local lifestyle and a form of *in situ* conservation of transitional livelihood patterns. Social sustainability is re-inforced through use of a wide range of locally available items such as bamboo, grass, flowers, leaves, tubers, bark, mushrooms, etc., processed mainly by tribal people in rural areas. Sale of these products adds to the income of the Scheduled Caste and Scheduled Tribes. The forest, as a whole, is the life-world of the tribals. In addition to its immediate use value for timber production, this has more of an option value and an existence value, with respect to the preservation of a habitat for flora and fauna species, its ecological functions, (viz. adopting measures to prevent soil erosion and retain soil moisture) and the positive impact these practices have had on the climatic conditions of the respective area. The tribal forest economy is a complex form of subsistence by which people organise their communities to survive times of increasing scarcity and to withstand the growing number of obstacles and adverse impacts that threaten their independence and cultural integrity. The protection of their habitat is in itself a means of maintaining their cultural identity. Their ancestors still exert their influence on them as spiritual powers. Wherever a local tribal subsistence community has managed to avoid becoming a client of a patronising state agency, this can be taken as an indicator that survival is still possible even in a so-called underdeveloped environment with many natural and even more administrational limitations that make it difficult to earn a meagre living.

The indigenous knowledge of forests is, thus, a means to survive during times of environmental degradation and transition towards modernism in which a stratified, mainstream society is taking over, as many of the tasks undertaken are structured at the local level, thus creating a simpler and more effective system. Decisions that favour the survival of a tribal community in a local environment have to be matched by adequate political backing of the community's ability to manage their local resources. Restricted access to the social and political institutions of the non-tribal mainstream society, and limited access to essential forest resources, make indigenous knowledge the last stronghold of tribal survival in their ecosystem, for they are neither compelled to adopt middle class values nor "economic development". Instead of giving consideration to improving their local survival and wellbeing by upgrading their self-help-capacities, in times of political deregulation, many economic development objectives to uplift marginal people and the rural poor have fallen by the board.

Indigenous knowledge about forests is something the younger generation, in particular, is losing interest in, although it plays a vital role in the forest dwellers' subsistence economy. The attraction of worlds outside the forest is evident if one considers the temptations of modern lifestyles and the amenities that big metropolises seem to offer to migrants from rural areas. Whether the forest world is, or continues to be, attractive in the long run will mainly depend upon the prospects of survival in forest environments. The political recognition of tribal usufructuary rights and entitlements to share in the wealth of the forest with the non-tribal neighbouring population will be one of the prerequisites that will enable forest dwellers to continue to live their lives in the habitat they know. In the wake of divergent interests at the regional, national and international policy level, the need to focus on conservation and development issues at the local level, and to consider the social impact of forest use and management restrictions in terms of biodiversity conservation policies, have become the overriding factors. The importance of high value timber production in natural forest is declining. Only by increasing the productivity of anthropogenic forests and through agro-forestry can India's ever increasing demand for industrial timber, pulp and plywood be satisfied, and its natural forest wealth safeguarded. Thus, the segregation and classification of natural forests as a distinct habitat of indigenous human, plant and animal communities has become more of a social and political issue than one traditionally dealing with forestry. Areas of timber production and the supply of non-timber forest products will have to be distinguished, in the long run, from areas to be conserved for their biodiversity and the cultural survival of forest dwellers in India's natural forests. Safeguarding the natural surroundings and knowledge of forest resource use amongst indigenous peoples contributes to preservation of culture. The principle of subsidiarity requires that the sustainable use and management of forests, if achievable at the local and regional level, need not be taken up at the national level. Subsidiarity, however, particularly in the wake of deregulation policies, may adequately tackle natural and cultural conservation issues and those of local resource supplies but leaves open political questions of tribal empowerment and self-determination through self-regulation. Although it is often claimed by forest officials and administrators that local forest dwelling communities contribute substantially to the degradation of their forests[9], it is a fact that they are the only ones who have a personal stake in conserving their environment and livelihood gained from the forest.

Since the United Nations Conference on Human Environment in Stockholm in 1972, increasing global concern for the protection of the natural human environment to secure agricultural production has found its way into India's Sixth Five Year Plan. Conservationist ethics combined with a rising national consciousness and demand for an environmental protection policy have come to shed more light on the role of forest dwelling communities, their knowledge and social institutions in the use, management and conservation of renewable forest resources. Twenty years later, at the United Nations Conference on Environment and Development in Rio de Janeiro in 1992, two important documents were formulated which acknowledged indigenous people and their local traditional knowledge as important actors in combating deforestation.[10]

---

9. The National Commission on Agriculture (NCA) in the 1970s strongly supported the vision that forest dwellers should pay for the forest products they use, and even better should grow their own renewable resources with the help of the Social Forestry programme. The NCA suggested the need to focus on scientific forestry in order to meet the requirements of industrial production (see Pathak 1994:24, 28 and Kannan 1982:937f.).

10. Firstly, indigenous people and forest dwellers are explicitly mentioned in the principles 2d; 5; 9b and 13d of the Non-Legally Binding Authoritative Statement of Principles for a Global Consensus on the Management, Conservation and Sustainable Development of all Types of Forests, June 16, 1992. Secondly, chapter 11 of Agenda 21 (Combating Deforestation) refers to local communities and indigenous people under chapter 11.4b; 11.14, 11.14b, 11.14i; 11.15d.

The transfer of knowledge of these important international declarations to the national political arena is often hampered by strong commercial interests, however, resulting in the overexploitation of resources. The survival of tribal communities, and of endangered animal and plant species, is threatened by a locally extractive but de-linked economy that widely ignores the principles of biological and social stability. Economic activities oriented towards distant markets are likely to transcend the capacities of production and biological regeneration at the local level. As local habitats become increasingly threatened, their value within a worldwide agenda for environmental preservation becomes even more obvious.

An inquiry into the world of a tribal community of Orissa means to explore a society closely interlinked to the natural and spiritual space that constitutes its habitat. The Kuttia Kondh as a sub-section of the Kondh, the largest tribal group of Orissa, is an example of how a community copes with the challenges of environmental stress and massive exposure to non-tribal cultural values and modernity. The social changes that have been wrought, as with so many other tribal communities all over India and the world, would perhaps have passed unnoticed by the outside world if their forest habitat had not raised the attention of researchers, interested in obtaining a detailed account of their forest world. This book documents the findings of a research venture that advocates a serious reappraisal of the role indigenous communities can play in conservation of forest resources.

1

Theory and Method

THEORIES may not always be true, but they are indispensable in attempting to approximate the truth. The meaning of truth in cross-cultural research is predominantly a question of theory of what can be compared between different configurations where nature and culture fuse into locally unique amalgams in time. Finding a methodology that is both appropriate and able to shed light on these amalgams is the challenge in cross-cultural investigations. Moreover, cross-cultural research is an encounter with societies, other than one's own, to engage in the decision-making process that revolves around the use and management of environments. Such enquiries are important to societies other than just those who inhabit them. An epistemology of the meaning and perception of natural and socio-cultural phenomena is indispensable if one is to reveal something about the validity of notions concerning natural or social phenomena in a particular setting. Whether these different complex phenomena may be compared as cultures; or even be denoted as the same, or similar, is a matter of profound theoretical debate and research.

Natural settings are all distinct due to the fact that they are unique locations (Greek: *topoi*) within a geographical network that enables us to identify any place on earth by its latitudinal and longitudinal points. There is no space without landscape and no landscape inhabited by man without cultural features. Landscape is, in fact, a space that has been shaped by one or more cultures by virtue of the ways the indigenous flora and fauna are used in the region, for example, in the domestication of animals. There is very little space on earth where nature is to be found where humans have not shaped the face of even the most remote biospheres of the world.[1] As a generalisation, therefore, one may assume that there is no space without a cultural identity and so an indigenous perception of space will always be informed by the particular culture, just as the outsiders' perception of 'the other' will be influenced by one's own notion of culture.

A Venture into the Essence of a Forest Culture

A hermeneutic methodology was chosen for this enquiry into the life-world of the Kuttia Kondh, based on an ontological premise that nature and culture makes up an inseparable and encompassing life-world, and aimed at a comprehensive understanding of these complementary points of reference. It was assumed that the findings themselves would begin to reveal relevant topics, and, ultimately the focus of research. The significance of a forest is visible in the way in which it is perceived within a culture. Over the ages, societies have developed their notions of what forests mean to them. The significance of a forest differs between societies whose members' perceptions of it may vary, and for whom it has a different relevance within the dimensions of their own cultures. The forests of today show that people have been, and still are, dependent on them, and how they make use of, and interpret their environment, in terms of survival and social advancement. The transformation of forest vegetation indicates specific social needs, cultural values, and changing economic and technological processes. Forests represent a legacy; they are a testimony to the evolution of societies and their respective perceptions and appropriations of nature. The significance of trees and forests can only be revealed by understanding these perceptions and the modes of appropriation developed by a culture.

Although it is clear that human activity influences forests, its impact is difficult to assess. Some of the changes are immediate and occur in the short term. Others, and often the more important ones, are indirect and need to be understood in their historical dimensions. The spatial distribution of forests, and the degree of their transformation by man

---

1. See Ballée 1989:2: With respect to the rainforests of the Amazon he emphasises in particular his rejection of "the nature/culture dichotomy, as scientists in all areas of Amazonian studies have employed it to date".

are the result of physical conditions and varying cultural patterns. This applies to forests that have been intensively used over centuries, but also to forests that still appear to be in a natural state. They may have been spared from human intervention due to physical inaccessibility and economic considerations, or because they represent a society's particular spiritual values. The border between intensively used forests and those showing little or no trace of human interference reflects social rules, economic options and political decisions. In this respect, all forests, including those that we still consider to be natural, are cultural phenomena. Taken from this aspect, the constitution of an indigenous culture is a mode of appropriation of physical and biological elements in a local natural setting, and its transformation into cultural livelihood patterns. This "ecological hermeneutics" is based on the background of the theoretical concept developed by E. Husserl's phenomenology in its transformation into fundamental ontology by M. Heidegger (Seeland 1998). J. L. Mehta (1970, 1976, 1987), whose thinking is intensively based on Heidegger's philosophy has worked extensively on analogies in the Indian philosophical tradition.

In an Indian context, applied hermeneutics in the field of environmental studies is rare. The legacy of empiricism and positivism has a long-standing tradition within social anthropological research in India. Breaking through the methodological "crust" of quantitative research methods and classical methods of field research, participatory observation and rapid rural appraisal, the intention was to try out a research method that promised to be more appropriate in investigating a forest dwelling tribe's life-world. The necessity to interpret the natural environment, its symbols, natural phenomena such as plant occurrence and animal behaviour, weather and fertility, makes the tribal world a suitable realm for hermeneutic investigation. Interconnected as all phenomena are within the natural world of the forest, a place where tribal people are exposed to the hardships of life in a wilderness, all natural and social phenomena are multi-referential and are representations of the natural and supernatural powers to which social and cultural life must respond in order to survive.

Vedic tradition, particularly the hymns of the *Rigveda*, originating from an early Indian forest culture, comprises texts on natural phenomena that have been a matter for hermeneutic interpretation throughout the ages. Tribal lore and myths still continue to add to this legacy by probing and interpreting the abode of divine nature. One major challenge of a methodological venture into the life-world of an Indian tribe was to come forward with a concept that could adequately grasp the essential notions of its socio-cultural values and its outlook on life, the authority to be interpreted in this hermeneutic way, defined as the amalgam of nature and the supernatural that makes up the "nature/culture continuum" of the tribal life-world. This approach explicitly avoids the dichotomy of nature vs. culture, (Ellen/Fukui 1996; Seeland 1998) a claim based on previous pilot field research, that there is no such Western theoretical concept to be found in the whole of the Indian tribal world. The preference for a nature/culture "continuum", instead, refers to the presumption that phenomena reveal their multiple meanings, all of which can be both natural and cultural. Tribal culture is the result of processes that involve appropriation by the tribe of the natural and social environment, and in the end, a distinct form of environmental decision-making. Hermeneutics, thus, means the interpretation of structured observations, narratives, and interviews about people's life experience, knowledge of plant-man-animal relationships, and their symbolic interconnectedness. No preconceived notions of what a tree or forest, a plant or an animal might be were used at the beginning of fieldwork. The hermeneutic approach is based on disclosure by informants of what the phenomena are, and in the context of Kuttia Kondh culture, it was expected that these disclosures would become self-referential. Through these recurring self-referential or intra-cultural analogies (Caietan 1959), it was expected that the main constructs of Kuttia Kondh culture would appear and reveal themselves, and they did, again and again, in different contexts, thus enabling the investigator to gain insights into their 'cultural reality'. Recurrence of analogous phenomena in different spheres of life were taken as referential links from which the fragments, collected in a more or less arbitrary research approach, could be pieced together. This method was an attempt to construct an endemic view of life-worlds in the forest.

Similar phenomena in the spheres of landscape, animal and plant world and the human life-world were found to have analogous names. In fact, sometimes, a common term denoted more than one thing in totally different contexts. Parallel use of names and of metaphors to bridge realms otherwise perceived as separate and distinct to a Western scientific perception reflect the fact that these entities were perceived as part of a unified body of objects, inseparably linked in a forest tribe's everyday life. Resources, for instance, were not merely understood in their function as part of material culture or as important raw materials for people's sustenance but also as part of a broader social, spiritual and technical system. The genealogy of plants in the Kuttia Kondh folk taxonomy, where trees marry each other (Parkin 1997) and people become offspring who marry trees again, is one prominent example for these intertwining realms. Gods, goddesses and ancestors are associated with distinct places in the ritual landscape and sacred geography of the Kuttia Kondh universe, furthermore, and are all related to the Kuttia myth of origin. The plant names and their uses in relation to their mythical meaning show their significance to the "mind" of the forest landscape they are living in. This is due, as Ingold (1996:134) suggests, referring to Scott (1989:195) to the fact that "It is the creative unfolding of a total field of relations within which beings emerge and take on the particular forms that they do – humans as humans. . . and so — each in relation to the others". These relations focus on a concept of life that mirrors a significant aspect of the Kuttia Kondh environment. Social actions represent natural phenomena and become visible in the surrounding environment.

A more comprehensive picture of the Kuttia Kondh life-world was obtained after fieldwork had reached a certain saturation point and little new data was being acquired, once key esoteric knowledge acquired by the team had been shared with researchers who had been doing fieldwork for more than one year in the Burlubaru area. This "esoteric" knowledge had been recorded in interviews with a few key informants, a herbalist, shaman and a spiritual healer, mostly religious specialists. These findings are necessarily fragmentary though it is evident that virtuosity and competence in supernatural matters are important to the realm of esoteric knowledge these religious practitioners of the Kuttia Kondh inhabit.

The Ecosystem — A Virtual Order

The historian Donald Worster (1993:37) makes an interesting comment on the consequences of dividing nature and culture: " . . . it is a completely arbitrary act to put nature and culture into separate categories, requiring rigidly separate methods of analysis". The methodological separation gives rise to the question of whether there are integral theoretical models that might permit one to apply the same, or similar, methods to both categories. An attempt was made to establish a theoretical foundation by linking nature and culture in a common reference model: the *ecosystem*. Worster claims the ecologist A.G. Tansley to be the founder of the "ecosystem" concept (Worster 1993:175ff). When he introduced the term in 1935 he regarded it as a necessary act of isolating the large interacting whole of the universe for the sake of scientific study (Tansley 1935:299f.). The background for Tansley's reductionist position lies in his criticism of "wholes" which are described as "organisms". He prefers to call them "systems" for the simple reason that "organism" is a term that is already being used for an individual biotic unit. He even extends the term "ecosystem" to a concept of anthropogenic ecosystems to differentiate between man-made environments and those devoid of human interference. Man as an ecological factor enters the discussion of advanced biological and organic philosophical theories in the 1930s and 40s. The Austrian biologist Ludwig von Bertalanffy (1949) and the German philosophers Hans Driesch and Helmuth Plessner[2] have advanced theories that the position of human beings within a natural and cultural environment should be regarded in a holistic way. Organic and holistic theories were then among the challenging ideas and visions of this period evinced by scholars trying to overcome "particularistic" views. In American cultural anthropology A.L. Kroeber published an

2. Driesch, H., Der Mensch und die Welt. Zürich: Rascher, 2nd ed., 1945 (1st ed. 1928). See also one of Driesch's major works "Philosophie des Organischen" 1909. H. Plessner published his *opus magnum* "Die Stufen des Organischen und der Mensch" as well in 1928.

essay in 1917 on "The Superorganic" and was thus among the pioneers of this topic which became a major issue in the philosophy of culture in the twentieth century. F. Boas, another founding father of cultural anthropology in the United States at the beginning of this century, was a physicist-turned-anthropologist who wanted to avoid applying the methodology of the empirical natural sciences to the humanities, claiming them to be particularistic and not appropriate for the study of man (see Horigan 1988:15ff). He attempted to develop an independent methodology as a result.

Tansley's retreat to the ecosystem concept leaves most of the core questions of the contemporary discussion open. Taking complex phenomena such as climax vegetation or plant succession, for example, each in turn constitutes an environment that Tansley would call a *biome,* subject to change and development culminating in systems in a state of equilibrium. This, he claims, gives them their methodological value:

> The fundamental concept according to which the biome may be considered together with all the effective inorganic factors of its environment is the *ecosystem*, which is a particular category among the physical systems that make up the universe.
>
> — *op. cit.*: 306

The theory of ecosystems, irrespective of whether they are considered to be "open" or "closed" systems, has the great advantage that no dogma has been established that makes the ecosystem more than it is claimed to be, i.e., interconnected components within a physical universe. Proponents do not question what an ecosystem is, or what it means, and perhaps this is the dogma behind the theory of ecosystems. Apart from the basic concept that an ecosystem links organic and inorganic components, it claims no ultimately speculative notions of what the concept stands for. Its ability to act as an intermediary is the most important. This rudimentary attempt to order nature and culture with the help of a mental concept has been a bid to dissect order from meaning what the "philosophic organicists" had tried to unite and what the "scientific organicists" like F. E. Clements and J. Phillips,[3] against whose positions Tansley argues, understood to be an "organism" or a "biotic community". Ecosystems as a virtual concept may be devoid of social meaning, but the social world in which they are embedded attributes a meaning to them and integrates them into larger socio-cultural units. Ecosystems are, in this sense, more of a popular than scientific notion of order in different sections of the universe. The idea of an ecosystem supposes that there is interaction according to the inherent logic of all elements known to-date and are all part of a commonly functioning configuration of biotic and abiotic factors. Whether there are ecosystems in a purely physical sense, i.e., apart from the social and cultural act of taking ecosystems as realistic representations of what happens in the universe, is ultimately irrelevant in this context. Ecosystems are not distinct units but segregated configurations that relate to each other in some way. They are heuristic models of self-contained structures and processes that define them, e.g. water, soil, air, forest, etc. Ecosystems are fragments of a supposedly larger whole rather than "closed" systems.

The Fragmentary Approach — A Holistic Methodology?

Any methodology is tailored as far as possible to the queries raised by a theory. Consequently, a theory that aims to cover innumerable possible interactions within the universe has to take the entire Being into account. In this respect only an ontological theory could provide authentic records of interactions that are perceived as ecological, because it involves the most all-encompassing and holographic representation of Being. Only a hermeneutic methodology can make the necessary enquiries into the world of a certain culture which claims their representation of Being as reality. Configurations of things, living beings and events, which are somehow interconnected in the world making up a particular culture, are such holographic fragmentations.

---

3. Clements, F.E., The relict method in dynamic ecology. Journal of Ecology 22 (1934), pp. 39-68. Phillips, J., The biotic community. Journal of Ecology 19 (1931) pp. 1-24; Phillips, J., Succession, development, the climax and the complex organism: an analysis of concepts. Part I. Journal of Ecology 22 (1934) pp. 554-571; Part II. Journal of Ecology 23 (1935) pp. 210-246; Part III. Journal of Ecology 23 (1935), pp. 488-508.

The entire cultural set-up can never be grasped in its totality but rather, through these fragmentary aspects.

The connectedness of a scope of cultural representations may be fixed in a single fragment even if a number of the dimensions of its complex structure remain untouched. Empirical research activates the fragmentary elements of a structure, so pointing to elements in other fragments that it refers to. Research findings are obtained by reconstructing the larger units or the universal whole to which certain aspects are linked. The puzzle of reality, and its reconstruction in the process of research, aims at selecting subject-oriented spheres that have a common orientation or practical nexus. Within this puzzle, fragments are complementary elements due to their analogous structural patterns, and their disposition to contribute to the reconstruction of their common background, i.e., the layout of culture. Intimacy, among all aspects of a culture, is the underlying assumption and a rationale to make this methodological approach work. For example, kinship relations among plants, animals and material objects hint to the larger complex of the human kinship system and the even larger relationship between these two spheres and the worlds of the ancestors and deities. At times, a plant can be an ancestor, a relative, a deity or simply a plant.

It is, indeed, a hermeneutic methodology because different spheres of life and different aspects of culture bear the same mode of appropriation of things and enact the particular life-style that make the world of a culture. All that claims meaning and common sense in a culture is thus represented by the multiple dimensions and issues that matter to it. The more closely a culture's fragmentary set up is investigated, the more analogies there are which constitute a hermeneutic circle of references. However, they are far from being a system or ecosystem. A clearly defined rationality that can be called a system may not be obvious and it is primarily the view of the concerned culture itself that puts together the elements of what sometimes seems to be a confusing puzzle. To avoid all the explicit and implicit connotations of a system, this research project has rejected the term "system" and refrained from considering it in terms of an organic or systemic whole to be investigated. A fragmentary methodology tries to evade systemic and systematic positivism by not taking for granted the notion that surface phenomena that conform to a Western classification of nature, space and time, are inter-culturally valid. Fragments within the framework of a hermeneutic methodology are representations of culturally meaningful aspects in any part of cultural life. The documentation and attempt to understand social and natural configurations as a representation of a characteristic and indivisible, contemporary socio-cultural universe in this natural space, is an enquiry into a social world.

Yet, in practical terms what is the purpose of reading fragments as findings that fuse into a larger cultural whole, an ontological entity? "Reading" fragments means that one enters into an environment where the mode of appropriation characteristic to that culture is performed by its members, at a given time, in a commonly accepted and sanctioned manner. The general use and management of resources and of the forest in particular, for instance, would be such a mode of appropriation. Becoming a social being is a cultural process. It means much more than being social with fellow members of a society. It may mean to coexist, to validate and even to understand a fellow being through a negotiable perception and a common use of one's surroundings. Fragments have aspects of more than just one socio-cultural configuration. For instance, hunting has a gendered aspect, and economic, ritual and spiritual aspects when linked to social interaction. Fragments are interconnected by ubiquitous elements such as symbols and style in material culture, etc. and these make up patterns of culture. Strictly speaking there is no "man-environment-interaction", because such an interaction would require one to perceive man and environment as distinct and separate units that empirically they are not. Both man and his surroundings are already complex and permanently interacting configurations. To constitute them as heuristic and analyse one's interaction with another would mean construction of a pleonasm.

Another question in this context is, if we assume that there are distinct and separate elemental units within the environment, what propels these beings or things to interact in a common, natural and, moreover, social world?

Natural and Social Resources

Complex configurations, like people acting in their genuine environments, evolve from a complex network of interrelations. Plants, animals and human beings are interrelated from the very beginning, the point at which they evolve and become part of a particular habitat. Interactions create mutual interrelations and multiple dependencies. The natural phenomenon originates from its being-in-the-world, thus acquiring a social meaning by putting something into an already existing social context. This process contributes to the development of culture.

Strictly speaking, there are no *natural* resources (Seeland, 1997). They are natural in the sense that they are part of a naturally growing and perhaps renewable natural wealth, but from the perspective of management of natural phenomena, it is the social life of that resource that determines its use within the economy of a society. Natural phenomena are social resources, because the economic and political reasoning (and the spirit and ethics of a particular time) that determine their appropriation and cultural meaning, cannot be anything other than socio-cultural. Economic value derives from social and cultural values so that any natural phenomenon may be considered as a social resource. Moreover, social resources are appropriated largely by society as a whole, although they can be owned by social units such as families or individuals. The usage value of certain phenomena can sometimes be bigger or smaller than their option value, or value of existence. In any case, they are esteemed resources which are of principal interest to a society, irrespective of whether they are useful to it at a given time, or abandoned or spared from use at another time by the same society. Social resources are formed through a common cultural consensus whereby people make use of natural resources, and this very consensus is a representation of the socio-cultural societal whole. Thus, natural resources are more than just practical assets. They have a symbolic dimension, and help to constitute a social life of production and consumption of products and services. Social resources structure interaction and exchange between members of the same or different communities. Shifting cultivation, for example, is, thus, perhaps more important as a social resource than a practice perpetuated for its value in subsistence, since by following their age-old lifestyle pattern in its practice, the Kuttia Kondh do succeed in distinguishing themselves from the Hindu society that surrounds them and at the same time, manage to re-inforce their cultural identity.

Polysemy in Context

In principle, a modern natural science approach aims to construct a comprehensive vision by detecting all species on earth and proceeding with their systematic classification according to a scientific pattern, claimed to be valid for all species irrespective of their cultural appropriation. Strictly speaking, this perspective should generate botanical or anthropological data, rather than ethnobiological *data*, but in fact, they are merged into an ethnobiological paradigm. Within this paradigm, taxonomic terms might be, and often are, polysemous and might not easily be categorised by a scientific theory of classification (see Ellen 1993:215-226). It is the process of research itself that produces biological data in the strict sense, whereas research into the context of cultural appropriation does not necessarily distinguish between plants, animals or ancestral spirits: indeed, local people believe that the latter can be manifested as plant or animal, or perhaps both.

Ethno-biological phenomena are configurations of contexts that may have manifold meanings. Ethno-biological configurations are neither authentic accounts from the emic point of view of the concerned culture, nor simply one-dimensional or scientific data that can be analysed. It is the ethno-biological paradigm that makes up a distinct culture because it takes into account all forms of life which are perceived by a culture to form an interconnected whole. As there is no ethno-biological *data*, there are, for instance, no living species to be found *in* the entity we call “forest”. The forest *itself* is a virtual configuration of meaningful cultural appropriations that appear as *nature*, but in fact exist only in their cultural representation (Duncan and Ley 1997). How do people of a certain locality recognise and become acquainted with their surroundings?

An ethno-biological enquiry into a people’s world as being the entire set up of its cultural appropriations must try to establish what motivates these people to convert the surroundings, in which they live, into a cultural sphere. This enquiry goes far beyond the reconstruction of a process of classification to discover the origins of nomenclature of certain species. There are at least four plausible explanations of how societies have developed their nomenclature: either by expansion of reference, by restriction of reference, by the use of metaphors or by description (Atran 1993, Gerber 1997:4-6). An inherently human tendency is to compare similarities between previously known phenomena, and new phenomena either being observed and in the process of becoming known. A discriminatory distinction, thus, evolves from a comparison of new phenomena in a local dweller's surroundings, with those he has already observed. It is often disputed whether imagination or experience may have cognitive priority in the primordial acquisition of knowledge. It is widely accepted, however, that metaphors matter a great deal in this process (Barnes and Duncan 1992). It is the metaphor that inflects a previously unknown thing as a *new* object of interest amidst a partly ordered and structured environment with attributes that will fit into what is known to-date as one's own culture. Paul Ricoeur (1986) claims, for instance, that common everyday language is a "sunken metaphor" which can only rarely be traced to its origins. In this way, forest-dwelling communities perceive and order their culture from their forest environment. The role of the metaphor is to denote a so far unknown thing with a name that is already used for one or more other items in this culture. Its application 'out of context' broadens the scope of what is potentially to be known by transferring a term into another context.

We can assume that the degree to which, what may be called "knowledge of forests", is perceived as globally relevant to all cultures and societies, does vary, both in its scope and depth. Different world-views and traditions at different stages of economic and technological development reflect what the term "forest" and "knowledge of forests" means to those who share a common culture. This kind of knowledge is more than technical, i.e., botanical knowledge, hunting skills, how to harvest wood or the use of non-timber products means more than the knowledge of the disciplines that come under the Western tradition of forestry sciences; it is an applied social science approach.

2

Forest, People and their Environment in Orissa

THE Kuttia Kondh is one of the 62 tribes of Orissa in eastern India(The 63rd tribe has been identified by the anthropologists but it is yet to appear in government records). Orissa belongs to the "tribal belt" extending from the western to the eastern part of central India: a broad strip of *sal*, teak and acacia forests transecting the subcontinent from Gujarat to Bengal, inhabited by a large part of India's 60-80 million tribal people (Poffenberger 1986:28). Their geographical distribution in Orissa is uneven, but predominantly they inhabit the hilly areas of the hinterland. The coastal districts and the plains (Balasore, Cuttack, Puri) show low percentages of tribal population, whereas districts such as Koraput, Mayurbhanj, Sundergarh, Sambalpur, Keonjhar, Phulbani and Kalahandi covering the Eastern Ghats stretching in a north-south-westernly direction have a higher percentage.

In 1982/83 (provisional figures, Agarwala 1990:7) the forest area of Orissa comprised 6,64 M ha[1] whereas it had been 5,996 M ha in 1981 (*ibid*: 23). Out of these, 2,504 M ha were "Reserved" and 3,491 M ha were "Protected Forest". "Unclassified Forest" comprised 1,000 ha only. In Phulbani District where the majority of the Kuttia Kondh live and whose relationship with the forest is investigated in this volume, the forest covers an area of 6,474 sq km or about 58 percent of the district's area. 39 percent of the total population of 717,280 (cf 1981 Census) are tribals and the rural population makes up almost 95 percent of Phulbani that is largely

1. The net sown area is 6,13 million ha.

dominated by a forest plus agriculture-based economy (Kant *et al.* 1991:35). The Kuttia Kondh, the largest among the Scheduled Tribes of Orissa, make up 17.5 percent of its tribal population, or 989,342 people respectively according to the 1981 Census.

The majority of the Kuttia Kondh inhabits the south-eastern part of the Phulbani District while some communities have settled in the Kalahandi District near the western boundary of Phulbani and in the Koraput District, south and south-west of their homelands. Before focussing on the society, economy and culture of the Kuttia Kondh, a brief discussion of the concept of "tribe" in the Indian context is necessary. In order to clarify the terms and concepts used to describe Indian society, a rough distinction may be made between the use of the term "tribe" or "tribal" by the administrative and political spheres of contemporary India on the one hand, and its use as a scientific concept, especially by social anthropologists, historians and other social scientists, on the other hand.[2]

Since 1951 the Indian Government has launched a series of schemes in order to consider and raise the specific living conditions of Scheduled Tribes.[3] Scheduled Tribes as well as Scheduled Castes[4] and "Other Backward Classes" are considered to be vulnerable and socially, economically and politically marginalized communities. Poor infrastructure in tribal areas, poor economic conditions and health, a

---

2. In the Indian politico-administrative context, the term "tribe" usually refers to the administrative category of "Scheduled Tribe" and has a precise juridical definition: Scheduled Tribes are communities who have been enlisted as Scheduled Tribes, in accordance with the provisions of Article 342 of the Constitution of India. They are identified by the list of Scheduled Tribes to be found in the "Scheduled Castes and Scheduled Tribes Lists Modification Order". This category together with the category of "Scheduled Castes" and "Other Backward Classes" has been created by the Indian Government in order to provide special safeguards and more effective protection to population groups defined as belonging to "Backward Communities". However, the Indian Constitution does not state explicitly how a "tribe" is recognised and by what criteria it may be distinguished from caste.

3. For a Review of Tribal Development Programmes in Phulbani District of Orissa see Tripathy 1989.

4. Most of them are "Untouchables", they call themselves "Dalits". (see Fernandes 1996).

very low literacy rate and little political representation at all levels are some of the general features attributed to tribal communities.

Although there are some marked differences between tribes and castes, particularly as far as legal provisions of land ownership and reservation policy are concerned, processes of change, acculturation and assimilation may integrate some of the educated sections of the tribes into mainstream society where norms will be shaped by modern middle class values.[5] The similarities between Indian tribes and lower Indian castes have led to the development of the "tribe-caste continuum" concept by some social scientists (Sachchianand 1987:43), putting caste and tribe at the opposite ends of the same social continuum (Oberdiek 1991:109).

Based on the definitions and classifications, a rough typology can help to classify the position of the Kuttia Kondh[6]:

1. Hunter gatherers: Only a very small minority of Indian tribes still depends solely on hunting, fishing and gathering and deriving their livelihood exclusively from local resources. A few hunter and gatherer tribes have developed a symbiotic relationship with peasant communities in their vicinity, exchanging forest products for agricultural produce or other commodities not available in the forest.

2. Shifting cultivators: a number of tribal communities living in the hills and forests depend principally on slash and burn cultivation. Axes, hoes and digging sticks and sometimes animal-drawn ploughs are the implements used for tilling the soil. Land for shifting cultivation is usually controlled and allocated by the village community. The agricultural produce from swidden farming is largely used for subsistence needs. However, some tribes grow cash crops on their swiddens. Shifting cultivation may involve the shifting of the settlements.

---

5. An early post independence and competent view on these phenomena was given by Roy Burman, 1959.

6. See, e.g., Patnaik N., 1996: 9ff. and Oberdiek 1989:103-105 referring to D.N. Majumdar, Elwin, Vidyarthi and Rai as well as to the classification of tribes of the Tribal Welfare Committee.

3. Peasants: there are tribal communities practising settled agriculture by means of cattle and plough and other methods of intensified farming like terrace cultivation and irrigation. Mostly tribal peasants are settled in valleys and plains with increasing contact with non-tribal communities.
4. Artisans: for some tribal communities, increased contact with non-tribal peasant communities has resulted in the development of specialized occupations like basket making, iron work, weaving, etc.
5. Nomadic groups: there are cattle and buffalo herders and shepherds of tribal origin in various parts of India. Other nomadic tribes are traders who transport merchandise from place to place with the help of pack animals. But with the development of road communication and modern transport systems these nomadic groups face serious problems to keep their way of life.
6. Industrial workers: in industries, mining operations, and river valley development projects, tribal people are employed for unskilled and poorly paid work, mostly working under contractors who exploit them. Such work may result in temporary or permanent migration to urban, industrial and mining areas. But industrialisation, mining and urbanization often develop in tribal areas with quite deleterious effects on the local tribal population.

When dividing the tribal communities according to their patterns of life, or the degree of assimilation to mainstream society, four categories emerge which are linked more or less directly to economic livelihood (Oberdiek 1991: 104), namely:

Tribal or "Primitive" Communities

They confine themselves to their original habitats (mostly hilly and forested areas) and live a distinctively isolated lifestyle. Geographical isolation in general supports a traditional tribal lifestyle. Most hunter-gatherer communities as well as tribal communities who depend mainly on shifting cultivation using hoes are considered to belong to that group of "primitive" tribal people. The influence of Hindu culture on such communities is considered to be rather weak. Although their livelihood does not entirely rely on shifting cultivation, the Kuttia Kondh may be classified in this category.

Semi-tribal Communities

These are tribals who have settled down more or less in rural areas and have taken up the technique of plough cultivation. They may live in homogenous tribal villages or in mixed villages of tribals and non-tribals. In these situations, a blending of their own cultural traditions with the traditions of neighbouring Hindu peoples usually takes place. Kondh tribes living in the plains may belong to this category.

Acculturated Tribal Communities

These tribals have migrated to urban or semi-urban areas and are engaged in "modern" occupations in industries. As a result, many have adopted traits and culture of the mainstream population to a considerable degree.

Totally Assimilated Tribals who have Acquired a Place in the Hindu Hierarchy

Aborigines or Adivasi,[7] as they are usually known in India, belong to different races and are assigned linguistically to the Munda, Sino-Tibetan, Dravidian and Indo-Aryan speaking groups. Only two large linguistic groups have retained their original language, those speaking Munda and Sino-Tibetan. By far the largest part of the tribal population of India does not speak their indigenous language anymore: they have adopted either Indo-Aryan or Dravidian languages (Fuchs 1973: 40). The Kuttia Kondh, being a culturally distinct subgroup of the Kondh tribe, speak a Dravidian language, the second important language family in India. The Dravidian group forms a solid block in South India as it includes four great literary languages (Tamil, Malayalam, Kannada and Telugu) and a number of less current languages (*ibid*: 42).

---

7. Adi means "first", Vasi means "inhabitant" in Sanskrit.

Cultural similarities support the theory that the Dravidian-speaking tribes in the north-east region of central India (Bihar, Chhattisgarh, Jharkhand, Madhya Pradesh and Orissa) had originally lived in south India. The traditions of the Gond, Khond (sic) and Kolam, e.g., indicate ancestral connections with the south.[8]

The Dravidian language spoken by the Kondh is Kui, which resembles Telugu, Tamil and Kannada in grammar, but not Oriya, the Indo-Aryan language spoken and written by their non-tribal neighbours (Boal 1984: 5). Notwithstanding their common language, the Kondh are subdivided into several sub-divisions, differing in various respects. One main distinction can be made between the hill section (consisting of the Kuttia Kondh and Dongria Kondh (Jena et al. 2002)) and the plains section, again divided into various endogamous groups. A general feature of the hill section, compared to the plains, is a lesser degree of acculturation to mainstream Hindu society.

The Kuttia Kondh identify themselves in the Kui language group as *Kuenja* or *Kuiladu*, the suffix *-enja* and *-adu* referring to male and female persons respectively. Not only the Kuttia Kondh but members of many other sub-groups of the Kondh tribe use these Kui terms for self-identification. Only when using the Oriya language do the Kuttia Kondh define themselves as "*Kondho*" or "*Kuttia Kondho*". According to Niggemeyer, the "Kuttia Kondh" have been given this name by Oriya-speaking non-tribals and the name does not refer to the origin of the term "Kondh" (Niggemeyer 1964: 11). Two Oriya words, "*kuto*" and "*kuti*", offer an explanation: *kuto* means "mountain" and "*kuti*", hut. The Kuttia Kondh distinguish themselves from other Kondh groups in that they have a specific way of constructing their houses, namely that the floor of their mud-walled thatched houses is situated about two feet below the village road.

According to Bates (1995:118), it is a generic term given to various *adivasi* communities in Orissa, "*konda*" meaning "low hills"

---

8. Fuchs 1973: 31 and 33: "Racially, the Dravida-speaking tribes who had migrated towards central India and further north may belong to the so-called Proto-Australoids or Veddids, as Guha and Eickstedt call them. [...] The date of this northward migration is uncertain, but it cannot have taken place much before 500 BC".

in Telugu. He claims that as time went on, tribal people started to use this foreign word to describe themselves in communicating with foreigners. It is not clear, however, how the Telugu term "*konda*" meaning "low hills" entered the Indo-Aryan language, Oriya, or if there is an authentic Oriya term "*Kond*" meaning something different. Fuchs mentions the Telugu term "*konda*" (that he translates as "hill") as the etymological root of the name for the *Gond* tribe, another tribal group of central India.

The Natural Environment

Orissa is situated on the east coast of India and extends from 17°49' to 22°34' north, and from 81°27' to 87°29' east, with a total area of 155,770 sq. km. Surrounded by West Bengal, Jharkhand and Bihar on the north, Andhra Pradesh on the south, the Bay of Bengal on the east and Madhya Pradesh and Chhattisgarh on the west, Orissa can be roughly divided into four zones according to its physical features and agro-climatic conditions: (1) the northern plateau constituting 23% of the state's total geographical area, (2) the central tableland constituting another 23%, (3) the Eastern Ghats running along the length of the state then merging with the Chotanagpur plateau and constituting 36% of Orissa's landmass and (4) the coastal plains making up the remaining 18%. 40% of the land in Orissa is cultivated, 40% is forested and the remaining 20% is grazing land, cultivable land and wasteland, townships, industries etc. (Fernandes et al. 1988: 14-15). Although situated on the seacoast with a shoreline of about 500 km, the bulk of the State is hilly and mountainous. Orissa has a tropical monsoon climate with erratic distribution of rainfall, often resulting in floods, droughts and is often affected by cyclones. The relatively high percentage of forest figuring in official documents actually comes down to approximately 20% of land under tree cover, as satellite imageries have shown. The main types of forests are dry deciduous (approximately 50%) and moist deciduous (approximately 30%) with the remaining 20% consisting of various types of forest cover such as semi-evergreen, littoral forest and tidal swamp forest, though the predominant type of forest cover is dry and moist *sal (Shorea robusta)* (ibid.).

The different sections of the Kondh inhabit the Kondh Hills forming part of the Eastern Ghats, bounded on the north by the Mahanadi river and on the west, by its large tributary, the river Tel.

> To the south and west the wild country continues into the area inhabited by the Saoras and other tribes, but in the east and north, the hills drop precipitously to the coastal plains of Orissa. Thus the area forms a rough rhombus consisting of a plateau about 2,000 feet above sea level broken by innumerable mountain ranges rising generally to 3,500 feet and above 4,000 feet in the southwest. To stand at any point within that rhombus is to be surrounded on every side by a complexity of hills great and small, near and far, blocking the valleys and over-shadowing the footpaths which pass over saddles from one valley to another.
>
> — Boal 1984: 6

Such natural and geographical conditions have favoured a spatial isolation of the Kuttia Kondh. Niggemeyer describes their land as a classical area of retreat with fortress-like characteristics in the early 1960s.

The Kuttia Kondh Area

This research work was conducted amongst the Kuttia Kondh residing in and around Belghar. Belghar lies at an elevation of 2255 feet above sea level within 19.45' to 20.5' N (latitude) and 80.30' to 83.45'E (longitude).[9] The annual maximum temperature is 45° C and the minimum temperature 6° C. The average annual rainfall amounts to 1680 mm, with 86 rainy days in a year.

The people of three village Panchayats, namely Belghar, Guma and Jhiripani, acted as informants in this research venture. However, the base villages chosen for this study were Burlubaru and Rangaparu, big villages that are quite developed in comparison to others such as Kinadi, a big village in the remote pocket where life is still very traditional. All these villages (in Hindi, *gram*) are located in Belghar Gram Panchayat. The Kuttia Kondh Development Agency (KKDA)

---

9. Source: Forest Range Office, Belghar.

at Belghar covers 68 villages out of which 36 villages are in Belghar Gram Panchayat and 32 villages are in Guma Gram Panchayat.

Belghar is part of Tumudibandh block of Balliguda subdivision in the newly formed Kondhamal District of Orissa. It is connected by bus with Bhubaneswar. Tumudibandh is a junction from where one road goes to Bhawanipatna and another to Muniguda, at which point the road bifurcates again towards Bhawanipatna and Rayagada. Tumudibandh is roughly 80 km from the district headquarters of Phulbani while Belghar is 28 km from Tumudibandh.

Belghar has a sound infrastructure of institutions run by government services such as a Forest Range Office, a Revenue Bungalow, a Forest Rest House, an Additional Primary Health Centre, a bank (the "Kalahandi Anchalika Gramya Bank"), an office of LAMPCS ("Large-sized Agricultural Multipurpose Co-operative Society"), a Police Station, an office of the Junior Agricultural Officer, a veterinary dispensary, a residential school having educational provision till matriculation, a collection centre of AMCS (Agency Marketing Co-operative Society) and the Kuttia Kondh Development Agency. Non-Governmental organisations located in the area are AWARE (Belghar), and Utkal Navjeevan Mandal having offices in Burlubaru, Dupii and Rangaparu. The Kuttia Kondh Development Agency started working in the area in June 1978.

The climate in the Kondh Hills is more extreme than in the plains of Orissa. The cold and dry season starts approximately in November and ends in February. It is followed by an increasingly hot season that lasts until mid-June. But in April or May the first storms announce the arrival of the heavy south-west monsoon lasting from mid-June until October. The average rainfall during monsoon is more than one inch per day. A delayed or scanty south-west monsoon can induce famine like conditions quite soon. A light north-east monsoon sometimes follows the south-west monsoon. The temperature may approach the freezing point in the coldest nights of December, but in May the temperature may rise to 43° C (Boal 1984: 10).

The soil in the fields of the Kuttia Kondh consists of red laterite that becomes hard and cracked during the dry season and can be worked only after it has been softened by the rain. One of the characteristic features of the Kondh Hills is the dense mixed forest cover on the eastern slopes. In the west and the south, trees and hanging-creepers reach great heights, while in the north, mixed forest is frequently replaced by bamboo (ibid: 6). In his ethnographic study about the Kuttia Kondh, Niggemeyer (1964) describes the area as densely covered by tropical forest, but mentions that formations of primeval forest can only be found in marginal areas, on the tops of the hills and in the border lands of village communities. More characteristic for the landscape is the secondary scrub-jungle dominating the areas used by the Kuttia for shifting cultivation, areas that will be abandoned for years till the next agricultural cycle.

One of the dominant species of the forests in the Kondh Hills is *sal (Shorea robusta)*, greatly esteemed by the Kuttia Kondh because of its manifold uses in their everyday life and its religious and ritual significance. But *sal* has also a commercial value and Niggemeyer gives an account on how the Forest Department together with contractors started to exploit stands of *sal* trees in the Kuttia Kondh settlement area around Belghar in the 1950s. He mentions the endeavours of the foresters to restrain the Kuttia Kondh from felling *sal* trees on their shifting cultivation plots (Niggemeyer 1964: 13).

Mango trees (*Mangifera indica)* are another widely distributed species of great importance in the economic and cultural life of the Kuttia Kondh. Bamboo is common, although there are few extensive bamboo stands in the area of the Kuttia Kondh. A great variety of other trees like the *mahula* tree (*Bassia latifolia* or *Madhuka longifolia),* the Indian *sago* palm (*Caryota urens),* and the *siali* creeper (*Bauhinia vahlii*) are used by the Kuttia Kondh. In addition, the jungle yields grass, rushes, leaves, bark, edible roots and berries, to name just a few of the other valuable forest products contributing to the living of the Kuttia Kondh.

Niggemeyer (1964:13) describes the Kuttia Kondh highland with its dense forests, numerous perennial rivulets and small rivers as an area of retreat for animals such as elephants, leopards, bears, wild boars, snakes, peacocks, monkeys, deers and on occasion, Royal Bengal tigers. The fauna of the forest may be regarded as much a liability as an asset for the Kuttia Kondh; some of the animals may be dangerous for people passing through the jungle or they may even enter settlements, causing huge damages to fields and crops and resulting in hunger for the cultivators.

Hunting is an important tradition of the Kuttia Kondh society. It provides not only highly valued meat, but is also part of the socially and culturally valued activities. Animals have manifold significance in the religious and ritual life of the Kuttia Kondh. By sheltering both flora and fauna, the Kondh Hills embrace the elements that contribute to the cultural life of the forest dwelling communities. With the degradation of the forests, the forest fauna is diminishing, however, and whereas Niggemeyer in the fifties of the last century speaks of the Kuttia Kondh environment as a "paradise" for wild animals, this paradise has become severely endangered in the meantime.

Administrative Setting in the Pre-Colonial, Colonial and Independent Era

Detailed knowledge about the pre-colonial political setting of the Kondh area, either pertaining to conditions at a micro-level, or in the wider political arena, is scanty. But with some certainty, the image of pre-colonial tribal societies, living as isolated communities in their forests, fully autonomous within the political sphere does not stand up to scrutiny in the centuries before British colonisation. The population of the Kondh area, as well as those of other tribal areas in Orissa, were dependents, albeit loosely, of small principalities of the coastal plains. The Rajas of these princely states governed their hinterlands with the help of local representatives although their hold on far distant, hilly and barely accessible areas should not be overestimated. For different reasons, the tribal communities in the Kondh Hills most probably enjoyed a much higher degree of local political autonomy, during, rather than after, colonial times (Cobden-Ramsay 1982, Praharaj 1988, Padel 1995).

After the introduction of the Anglo-Indian administration in the Kondh Hills by the middle of the nineteenth century, the Kui-speaking peoples lived under three separate authorities. The Kondhmal sub-division in the north was administered from Angul, the Balliguda sub-division south of Kondhmal had come under the authority of a British Collector, and a part of Gomsuur (Ghumusar), situated in the hill-tracts, was administered by an Indian Deputy-Collector.

The Kuttia Kondh land was part of the Balliguda sub-division belonging to Ganjam District. This district was then part of the Madras Presidency and the whole Kondh region was known as the Hill-Tracts-Agency. The Collectors of the subdivisons exercised special powers as Agents to the Governor. They were responsible both for the civil and criminal jurisdiction, with the possibility of further appeal to the High Court and the Governor-in-Council (Boal 1984: 10). The historical reasons for this procedure go back to the British policy of abolishing the practice of human sacrifice, discovered in the beginning of the 19th century in the Kondh Hills (MacPherson 1846, 1852, Padel 1995).[10]

Based on the British colonial policy of "Indirect Rule", Zamindars acted under the Collectors. These Oriya chiefs received fixed amounts of money from "*muta* heads" (Oriya headmen) of a so-called "*muta*" (a small area including its villages). The *muta* head, which was a hereditary office, was responsible for collection of the tribute levied on each village and for law and order in the *muta* (Boal: *ibid*). In areas with a tighter control on the hierarchies of public administration, the power of the *muta* was quite limited, but in isolated areas like the Kuttia Kondh land, the *muta* heads (called locally *patro*) exerted their influence on the local tribal communities even some years after Independence.

Niggemeyer describes how in the 1950s Kuttia Kondh people perceived their *patro* as a person of authority who might ask them to work without compensation, whom they had to obey, and who would have a say in settling village disputes. With the reorganisation of the Indian administration, the institution of muta disappeared. The Balliguda sub-division, as one of the three sub-divisions of Phulbani District, was divided into several Panchayat districts, and equipped with the organs of local self-government.

---

10. For human sacrifices in the Kondhmals and its social and political implications see for instance Boal 1984: 36ff. and Padel 1995.

The administration of Orissa State is structured into four levels: state, zone, district and the Gram Panchayat (village government) made up of political personnel and government employees. The Governor as the head of the state and appointed by the Government of India is followed by the elected Chief Minister, one or two Deputy Chief Ministers, Ministers and Ministers of State. The top position of the higher administration at the State level is the Chief Secretary and the Additional Chief Secretary, the Development Commissioner and the Board of Revenue. From here the hierarchy is split up into two lines of government servants, one under a Member, Board of Revenue and another one under the Additional Chief Secretary and Development Commissioner. Under the Member, Board of Revenue, there are Revenue Divisional Commissioners who are the administrators at the zonal level, followed down the hierarchy by the District Magistrate and Collector. Further down the administrative ladder are the Additional District Magistrate, Sub-Collector (Sub-Divisional Officer), Tehsildar and Block Development Officer. Down the other line, under the Additional Chief Secretary and Development Commissioner, come the Commissioner-cum-Secretary, Secretary, Additional Secretary, Joint Secretary, Deputy Secretary, Departmental Directors and Departmental Deputy Directors.

With the change in the Panchayati Raj system, and the reforms in local self- government, a new administrational hierarchy is being formed through a process that has been implemented since 1996. The local self-government is headed by the chairman of the Zilla Parishad who is elected by its members and working under the District Magistrate and Collector. Under the chairman of the Zilla Parishad comes the Project Director of the District Rural Development Agency, followed by the Block Development Officers. In local self-government there is another political hierarchy operating under the Block Development Officer. At the Gram Panchayat level, the chairman of the Panchayat Samiti heads the Panchayat Samiti, assisted by his subordinates, the Sarpanch and Samiti Savya, followed by the Naib Sarpanch and finally the ward member.

3

Kuttia Kondh Society

The Clans

Clan organization is an important feature of Kuttia Kondh society although according to Niggemeyer, the significance of belonging to a village community in many domains of everyday life outweighs that of clan membership.[1] He claims that the Kuttia Kondh clans used to live in separate villages in the past.[2] But in the course of time, these homogenous clan villages split up and clan members dispersed into several villages. Today, village communities are composed of families of different clans, although in many cases a dominant clan may be found within the village community. In the 1950s, villages with the same dominating clan used to be adjacent, according to Niggemeyer but the continual mixing of clans within the villages has resulted in profound consequences to existing marriage rules. In those days, the rule of village exogamy, once identical with the rule of clan exogamy, was still maintained, Niggemeyer says. As a result, members of the same village were not allowed to marry even if they belonged to different clans since they regarded each other as sisters and brothers. This kind of real or perceived kinship of members of the same village community is reflected in the rule that boys and girls from the same village do not normally dance together. There are occasional cases of marriage between a boy and a girl of the same village, but in that

1. Niggemeyer 1964: 45. A detailed investigation on Kuttia Kondh clan structures does not exist. A study of Kondh clan structures is given by F.G. Bailey (1960) for the Kondh village Baderi and its surrounding area.

2. This perspective of homogenous clan villages implies that unmarried wives belonging to other clans are not counted. A wife keeps her own clan identity, i.e., membership to the clan of her father. But her children belong to the clan of their father.

case one spouse must be from *jani* clan and the other from *majhi* clan.

Originally, clans were not only territorial units inhabiting separate villages, but also cultural units. Niggemeyer describes how in mixed villages only the main clan, once the only clan, had its religious centre in the form of deified stones (*Dharani vali*) in the centre of the village. Members of other clans have their *Dharani vali* in the village where they originated and where their clan is the biggest, although they have the right to live and work in the village of their actual residence (Niggemeyer 1964:48). However, there are still some village ceremonies to which non-members of the main clan are excluded. In other ceremonies, all villagers participate, but villagers not belonging to the main clan usually visit the villages of their clan in order to celebrate the same ceremony there.

In the area of investigation 33 different clans were recorded, but the total number of clans for the whole Kuttia Kondh area is unknown.[3] The origin of the clans and the meaning of their names cannot be clarified in all cases. Some clans are named after geographical designations, indicating the origin of the clan ancestor. Members of other clans tell mythical stories about the way their clan got its name invoking animals, plants, trees and or inanimate objects from the Kuttia Kondh's natural environment. In a few clans, Niggemeyer recognises signs of totemic representations, but only in one case did he receive information about totemic taboos. In his opinion, there is no reason to suggest that all Kuttia Kondh clans once were totemic (ibid: 48).

A few objects of Kuttia Kondh material culture like an axe or a specific pot may also be connected to a clan's origin. A considerable part of the clan mythology refers to the Kuttia Kondh myth of origin and explains how and under what circumstances the different clans originated. Stories about clan origin are subject to local variation, and members of the same clan may tell different stories about the origin of their clan. From a historical perspective, the meaning and importance of the clan as an organising principle of Kuttia Kondh life

3. Niggemeyer (1964: 45) found 14 clan names during his research in the central settlement area of the Kuttia Kondh.

is diminishing. Clan organization still matters as a way of regulating matrimonial affairs, but for many other social, economical, political and ritual activities, the village community that consists of members from different clans, is the most important social unit.

The Origin of Clans

The origin of the Kuttia Kondh society is described in their cosmogonical myth, *Kui Gaani* (see Appendix). It tells about human beings who existed in the underworld of the earth, and their division into different groups. The text says *"Atpa bicha lega atpa jaralega"* which means "eight seeds like eight seeds". Being a metaphor, *atpa* means many types and the seeds stand for human beings, different groups of people or clans, not only the Kuttia Kondh, but all people on earth as well. *Bicha* and *jara* are synonyms and both mean "seeds". The literal meaning of the term *atpa* is 'light' but in the above context, it should be translated as "variety" or "types" or "mixture". Thus *atpa bicha lega* implies that the Kuttia Kondh people have emerged like different varieties of seeds. Just as different types of crops are grown in a mixed cropping system in shifting cultivation, the different sub-groups of people who once lived in the underground, later on emerged from Sapangada, the cosmic hole. These *atpa bicha* or the sub-groups of society correspond to the clans. Each clan has a name, and is believed to have a set of the following characteristics, a common origin, a common belief, common thoughts, etc. Although the members of all clans have taken up similar practices of earning their livelihood, they differ with regard to their origin.

The Kuttia Kondh believe that 33 main clans have emerged from Sapangada and several others have derived from those. In a sample survey in several villages, the following 27 clans were recorded: Nondruka, Timaka, Saraka, Gunjika, Sukubichaka, Andanga, Mindanga, Urlaka, Bandalaka/Bandanaka, Damanaka, Rodomika, Sukunga/Sukuka, Prepanga, Sunamudanga, Pangranga, Shidanja, Kamralinga, Dulaka, Bidraka, Sakadaka, Garanka, Padanujenga, Bolibuka, Padanaka, Bangruka, Polubaka and Duduka. It is a common belief amongst the Kuttia Kondh that the Nondruka and Timaka clans were the first to have emerged from the Sapangada hole and some legends hold that the Timaka followed the Nondruka.

Nondruka

According to a Kuttia Kondh legend, the members of the Nondruka clan had a giant and massive body, long ears and big eyes. Nerandali, the supreme goddess, was surprised to see people with such a body and at first wanted them to be priests. But she was upset to see them and angrily cursed them to survive by eating their own bodies. She drove them away from Sapangada.

Another legend associated with the origin of the Nondruka clan states that they were born from the earth under Sapangada. Three pairs of male and female folk formed this clan, i.e., they were born first. The three males are Rake Majhi, Gurpa Majhi and Rayara Majhi and three females known as Raniadu, Bendiadu and Kumari. The three males and three females formed three couples, viz., Raniadu-Rake, Bendiadu-Gurpa and Kumari-Rayara. They all settled in Sussabata after they had been driven away from Sapangada for eating buffalo intestines. According to both legends, the Nondruka clan originated from Sapangada, but neither of the legends mentions anything about the meaning of Nondruka or the etymology of the name.

Timaka

There are two different myths regarding the origin of the Timaka clan. The Kuttia Kondh myth suggests that Nerandali desired to give birth to the Timaka, who lived underground. She decided to find a way out for the Timaka that should be different from that of the Nondruka. In the dark underground, Nerandali searched for a way and eventually the Timaka, having covered a long path to reach Knehelpanga and Damanpanga, were born from *terka,* i.e., bamboo shoots. Nerandali wanted to be given offerings by the Timaka and so they became the priest clan, being the first to get crop seeds from Nerandali.[4]

There is a different legend about the origin of the Timaka, told by the Lake Majhi of Rangaparu village. According to this legend, trees, plants and animals emerged, along with the Kuttia Kondh,

4. The legend was told by Badu Pujari, son of late Priti Pujari of the village Kranja.

from the Sapangada hole. One of the emerging buffaloes wanted to eat up everyone and everything, but some people killed the buffalo. The buffalo fell down covering half of the Sapangada hole. From the covered part of the hole grew bamboo shoots called *terka*. One woman took the shoots and kept them in a bamboo basket *(mani kapa)*. The following day, the *Kutaka* announced that the bamboo shoots were their fellow beings. The women then covered the basket for seven days after which members of the Timaka clan developed from the bamboo shoots. Thus, both tales agree that the Timaka clan was born from *terka*, (i.e., bamboo shoots) although at different places and under different circumstances.

Saraka

Like the Nondruka and Timaka clans, the Saraka clan was also born from the Sapangada hole. Once, the myth says, there was a meeting of all the people living under Sapangada. Bamboo mats were spread on the ground for the people and all of them sat down on the bamboo mats before the people of the Saraka clan came. As the members of the Saraka clan came in droves, not enough bamboo mats could be offered to them so that they had to sit on the bare ground. Consequently, there are two opinions regarding the meaning of Saraka. One argues that their name means they were left out, the other holds that they were called Saraka due to their large number. The literal meaning of *saraka* is surplus (see also Niggemeyer 1964: 46).

Gunjika

A legend told by the Lake Majhi of Rangaparu village about the origin of the Gunjika clan says that its members were born by a golden ring. To the north of Tumudibandh there lived a man called Kango. His sister was married to a man of a far-off village. When her husband died, Kango's sister returned with her son to live with her brother. There were only a few people living in Kango's village and he wanted more people to settle in his village. He planted *loki* (*Lageneria vulgaris*), a creeper, in local Oriya known as *lau* in his swidden field. But Kango got only one fruit from his plant. He took care of the plant and the fruit and did not allow anybody to touch either. His young nephew, his sister's son *Bhanja*, was curious to know why he was not allowed by his *mama* (maternal uncle) to go near the plant and the fruit. One night he got the chance and quietly went near the fruit and heard some sounds coming out of it. He took a *lohakila* (iron pin) from his hair and pricked the fruit. There were many people inside the fruit who were killed when the iron pin was pricked deep into the fruit.

As usual, Kango visited his field the next morning. He went near the fruit and surprisingly, heard no sound emanating from it. He took a closer look and found that an iron pin had pierced it, killing many people inside. He got terribly angry and took an oath to take vengeance on the culprit for killing people inside the fruit. He returned to his village with a heavy heart and announced to everybody that he was going to the blacksmith (*lohrasal*) to get some iron implements for working his *podu* field. He maintained that he had got something made of iron that might be melted down by the *lohrasal and* asked if anybody was willing to accompany him. He was convinced that the culprit who had killed the people by piercing the iron pin would take an interest in knowing more about that material of which many things could be made. Luckily for him, *Bhanja* agreed to go with him. Kango became convinced that it had been *Bhanja* who had killed the people in the *lau* and was relieved to have found the culprit, but felt sad that it had been he. As he had already taken the vow to kill the person who had killed his people, he had to take *Bhanja* with him.

Kango picked up his *luha bilu* (bow) and *luha ambu* (arrow) and his sister packed some food for her son and her brother. After walking a long distance his nephew felt hungry. Both the uncle and the nephew sat down to eat and then they wanted to drink water. Kango asked his nephew to climb up a tree to see if water was available anywhere. The nephew climbed up the tree to spot water. When he was halfway up, Kango shot him with his arrow and *Bhanja* fell down dead. Kango left him to the wild beasts and proceeded with his work. When he had finished, he returned home where his sister asked him about her son. Kango told her that he had killed him. Kango's sister cried loudly and went out in search of her son's dead body. But all she found was a gold ring at the spot where her son had been shot dead. She kept it as a reminder of her son and went about her work. She kept the ring in her waist but it slipped down. Then she knotted the ring within her upper cloth from where it also fell down. She then placed it in her hair *(kapoli)* but it did not stay there either. Finally she kept it in her mouth from where it slipped into her stomach. She became pregnant and gave birth to a son who founded the Gunjika clan.

According to another myth told about the origin of the Gunjika clan its members were born from a *tumba* ring, (i.e., from the ring of a gourd). The *tumba* ring was made out of gourd of *anka* (a wild variety of *Lagenaria vulgaris* that is shaped at one end like a cylindrical shaft that tapers towards the pedicil while the other end is bulbous). The gourd was perfectly dried and a mouth cut side ways to be used as a spoon. This is also called *tumba.* Thus the people who came out from the mouth of the *anka* fruit are called Gunjika. The literal meaning of *gunjika* is ring.

Sukhbichaka

Members of this clan were born by a squirrel (*Sukhubichaka* means squirrel).

Sukuka

Members of this clan came out from the nest of a mouse.

Mindanga

Members of this clan were born by a fish. According to a legend associated with this clan there was once a man who went to catch fish (*minu*) at a water ghat. He caught a big fish. When he was about to cut it, he heard some sound coming from its stomach. With great care he cut the stomach of the fish and surprisingly a man came out of it. Because the man was born by a fish (*minu*) he was given the name Mindanga.

Andanga

The origin of this clan is associated with the pig (*paji*). The members of the clan also originated from the Sapangada hole. Because the mother of other members of the clan drank pigs' milk (*tudu*), the members of the clan became known as Andanga.

Urlaka

Members of this clan claim their origin from a plant called *"urla"* which is called *daskerenta* (*Barleria cristata*) in Oriya. According to the cosmogonical myth of the Kuttia, the *urla* plant was born from the lungs of the mythical sambar (*Cervus unicolor*). Due to their origin from the *urla* plant, the clan is called Urlaka.

Damanaka

This clan owes its origin to *daman mara* (*Grewia tiliaefolia*). It is believed that at one time, the forests and trees were owned by members of this clan. Other clans also believe that the first being of the Damanaka clan has to be invoked and consulted before cutting trees to prepare a new plot for shifting cultivation.

Other Clans

Sunamudanga clan, like the Gunjika, claims its origin from a golden ring, the Bandanaka clan from a *bandhan* tree (*Xylia xylocarpa*), the Kamralinga clan from *lohra sal,* the blacksmith's workshop, and the Garanka from *Gara,* i.e., a brass pot used for storing water. The origin of Shidanja, Dulaka, Sakadaka, Rodomika, Prepanga, Pangranga, Bidraka, Padanujanga, Bolibuka, Padanaka, Bangaruka, Polubuka and Duduka could not be traced. There are a number of clans about whose cosmogonical origin the Kuttia Kondh around Belghar area have no knowledge, since after being born from Sapangada, they believe that they lived in different areas separated from the others. There are several clans of which a few members reside in Belghar, some in the Kotagarh area and some in the Chandrapur area and as a result they are unable to know all the clans of the Kuttia Kondh.[5] The following 12 clans have been recorded based on information from people in the Belghar area about clans they know. However, the research team has not met any member of these clans:

5. Lochan *jani* of Burlubaru village, a major informant, reported that people also change the names of their clans in the course of time. He gave examples of some other clans that he knew from their myth. But the authenticity of this information could not be checked.

1. Pangalienja: they come from a hill base (*panga*).
2. Sanderlienja: there is no information about the origin of members of this clan.
3. Diatrelu: Members of this clan emerged from *Diatrelu*, a fruit called *anka* (*Lagenaria vulgaris*). It is held that pounded rice was kept in a *dia*, i.e. the gourd of *anka*. The gourd burst and thus members of the Diatrelu clan were born.
4. Talajetinga: Members of this clan were born from hair knots (*talajeting*).
5. Pajibandi: Members of this clan were born from an earthenware pot from which pigs were fed. The earthen pot burst and Argadi Majhi (who was the first member of the Pajibandi clan) was born.
6. Wisangurada/Wisanga: The clan claims its origin from an old axe. The flat end of the axe became smaller after continuous use. Members of the clan were born from such an axe (*wisang*) and when they emerged they carried such an axe in their hands.
7. Makapuju/Atarnaka: The clan members were born by *makapuju*, i.e., flower of maize (*Zea mays*). As many as there are corn seeds in an ear of maize, the identical number of human beings was born from this maize.
8. Suidedhinja: The clan originated from *suidedhi*, i.e., a vertical pole placed at a particular place for construction of a house.
9. Sarasambu: Members of this clan were given birth by *sarasambu*, the seeds of taro (*Colocasia esculenta*).
10. Wikajudanja: The clan originated from wikajuda, i.e. from a bundle of *wika* grass (*Themda arundinacea*), that is used for thatching.
11. Meragundanja: The members of this clan originate from *meragunda*, the turmeric powder sprinkled in the place of the *Meriah* festival. The first of this clan was Bandan *majhi*.

12. Bangura: Little is known about the origin of this clan.

In the evolution of the clan system, the Timaka clan is regarded as the first-born clan of Kuttia society even though the Nondruka clan claims to have originated earlier. However, as the Nondruka clan was driven away from Sapangada, the Timaka clan is regarded as first, and in terms of social stratification, members of the Timaka clan are seen as superior. They are given the responsibility to perform the religious rites for the society. The members of other clans may also hold the position of a village priest, but to worship at Sapangada the priest must be from the *pujara* group.[6] Since the Kuttia Kondh originate from Sapangada, a special worship is organised in honour of Sapangada in *Chaita lanju* (March-April) every year. The worship of Sapangada is organised by a special priest called Sapangada Pujara. The Sapangada Pujara is responsible for the religious ceremonies offered to Sapangada Penu (sing. *penu*, pl. *penuni*) and without him the act of worship and sacrifice cannot take place. Other priests may assist only. Due to his association with Sapangada Penu the status of the *pujara* is superior to *jani* and *majhi*. During field investigations in the Kuttia villages around Belghar, only one *Pujara* family was found in the village Kranja near Sapangada. For many generations, men from the same family worshipped the Sapangada Penu that it became a hereditary right of that family for one of them to act as Sapangada Pujara. No other remarkable status is given to the *Pujara* family.

The political headman of a village is called "*majhi*". The *majhi* is a position given to a person from the *majhi* group (the *majhi* and *jani* live in two opposing rows of houses in a village). In case of individual disputes, family conflicts, group rivalry, and inter-village rivalry, it is the *majhi*'s responsibility to solve the problem. Whether it concerns the selection of a new hill for swidden, or the fixing of a day for a community festival, the *majhi* takes the decision in consultation with the *jani*, the priest of a village. A person with a *majhi* surname, but working as a *jani*, is regarded as a *jani* in the social hierarchy, yet

---

6. A worship is offered at Sapangada at an interval of 3-4 years.

lives in the *majhi* row. As far as decisions on fixing days to celebrate rituals and festivals are concerned (fixed for every year), the *jani* takes the decision with or without consulting the *majhi* (political head). Any person who gets some sort of divine blessing may act as priest, so a priest may come from the *jani* or the *majhi* group. The following description is about the history of the *majhi* group and how it took over the political representation of a village.[7]

It has been mentioned that the Nondruka clan descended from three couples. It is probable that the *majhi* group split off from the Nondruka clan, the latter having been boycotted by other Kuttia Kondh clans. The Kuianka's explanation is that the *majhi*s who descended from the Nondruka clan were powerful because of their physical strength, and dominated others. Thus, the *majhi* held supremacy and exercised power in society that they maintained until today. However, people bearing the Majhi surname also come from other clans. Examples are Argadi Majhi of the Pajibandi clan (Paji-pig, *bandi* — earthenware pot) and Bandan Majhi of the Meragunda (*mera* = turmeric, *gunda* = powder) clan. But Argudi Majhi and Bandan Majhi do not hold the same status as other majhis because the Pajibandi and the Meragunda clan are considered to be inferior to clans such as Timaka or Saraka. The Timaka clan, responsible for the religious activities of Nerandali, claims its superiority over all other clans on the grounds that they were blessed with divine power.

Nowadays, the Saraka clan dominates and the number of their members is so large that not enough bamboo mats could be offered to them to sit on. The Saraka clan outnumbers other clans by far and so creates the impression that Kuttia society is mainly composed of people from the Saraka clan. Its members are considered as the main group within the Kuttia Kondh society even though the Damanaka clan claims superiority as former owner of the hills and forests, the main resource of the Kuttia Kondh society.

---

7. For Niggemeyer's account on the *jani* see 1964:102, 158ff, 182, 185 and on the male *kutaka*: 1964: 51, 56, 60, 119, 130, 147, 149, 154, 156, 159ff, 179f, 182ff and on the female: 163; on the relationship *jani-kutaka*: 163ff.

The other central figure in Kuttia Kondh religious life is the *kutaka*, the shaman and medicine man and sometime astrologer, sorcerer and magician. As an astrologer, he predicts future events, performs and interprets oracles. As a medicine man, he recognises the deities and spirits who cause diseases and epidemics and knows how to deal with them. By falling into trance he communicates with them; by using techniques of witchcraft he may cure sick people. He is attributed with magical power and said to be able to transform himself into a tiger. Although the *kutaka* is believed to be equipped with some highly feared skills, he is supposed to act for the welfare of the village community and its individual members. He co-operates with the *majhi* and *jani* in that he suggests actions be done by them to restore order in the Kuttia Kondh world and in most cases, his suggestions are taken seriously. Whereas the *jani* is responsible for the "normal" way of the Kuttia Kondh world, the *kutaka* deals with the negative forces that interrupt normality, presenting themselves in the form of unforeseen and inauspicious events, diseases, abnormal deaths, etc.[8] A new *kutaka* is chosen by deities in dreams and the position is not restricted to any specific clan. Not every village has its own *kutaka,* but some villages may have more than one.[9] The *majhi,* the *jani* and the *kutaka,* besides having their specific duties, are mainly working as peasants on their land.

Gender Relations and the Role of Women

In contrast to the stratified Hindu caste society, tribal communities like the Kuttia Kondh are often claimed to be more egalitarian insofar as gender relations are concerned. Although gender inequality in the Kuttia Kondh society is in no way as pronounced as in Hindu society, there are indicators of unequal male and female status. Yet it

8. While *jani* is the person who performs most of the routine religious activities of the society, the *kutaka* sits with *jani* for bigger religious activities like Meriah-festival, Bad-binere and Pani kalu. Perfomances in which bigger sacrifices are executed, the *kutaka* is desired to be with the *jani*.

9. There are claims that women act as shamans. Niggemeyer (1964:163) heard of female *kutaka* in the mid 1950s, but could not collect much data on them.

is difficult to judge the general status of males and females in Kuttia Kondh society because the status of an individual often depends upon the context. In the public sphere, Kuttia Kondh men formally rank above women. Affairs that concern the whole village, (i.e., the moving of the village settlement, or the preparation of new swiddens) are mainly regulated by family heads in consultation with the political and religious headmen. However, it is difficult to judge to what extent women influence men's decisions informally. All major rituals are performed by male priests and/or male shamans and healers. Nevertheless, the religious world of the Kuttia Kondh is inhabited by many female deities and both Nerandali and the earth goddess, Dharani Penu, are female and of great importance.[10] In their myth of origin, women were created before men and it was Nerandali, who gave birth to them. It was also Nerandali, who decided that it was necessary to have males in order to perform certain tasks and activities in society. At the same time she is characterised as a responsible woman concerned with the wellbeing of all people she had once given birth to.

Whereas public life is male-oriented, most activities in everyday life take place within the family and the household. Here patrilineal kinship organization and patrilocal or virilocal residence patterns are expressions of male-oriented structures. Although men formally are the heads of families, the relationship between husband and wife in the private domain is characterized by co-operation rather than by subordination. Important family matters like the marriage of their children involve the mothers as well as the fathers of the bride and groom. The gender-based division of labour allocates certain activities to men and others to women, but there is work performed by both. Besides bearing the vital task of child-rearing, women have to do all the household chores such as fetching water, cleaning the house and utensils, cooking and carrying food for the male members working in the field, taking care of the livestock, making house walls by kneading mud, etc. Apart from these responsibilities, women make a major contribution to the subsistence of their family by working on the farms and collecting various forest products.

10. Niggemeyer calls it *Bangu Pinnu*.

In contrast to the present-day Hindu society, Kuttia Kondh men have to pay a bride price as an acknowledgement of the "economic value" of female labour. Child socialisation within the family focuses on gender-specific activities, norms and values. "Learning by doing", daughters are taught by their mothers and elder sisters, and sons by their fathers and elder brothers. The social position of men and women not only depends on their sex, but also on their age and situation within the life cycle. Both elder men and women have to be respected by the younger generation regardless of their sex. Married men and women acquire a higher social status than unmarried men or women. However, the status of a newly married woman living in her parents-in-law's household and her husband's village is ambiguous. A newly married woman (*kudua)* is cordially accepted by her parents-in-law but is not allowed to move outside for a period and she must show obeisance to the parents-in-law and other in-laws in the traditional fashion. For the first fifteen days in her in-law's house, she is not given the work of cooking, fetching water from the stream or cleaning the goat pens and pigstys. She may serve food to others and, may involve herself with other women members of the family to pound rice. When she becomes familiar with the members of the family and the neighbours, she has to start cooking, fetching water, doing agricultural work, pounding rice herself, etc. Her efficiency in domestic and agricultural work is important with regard to her status in the family as well as in society. She gets a great deal of love and affection from her parents-in-law when she proves herself capable and efficient in domestic and agricultural work as this means that the bride price which the parents-in-law had to pay for their son's wife is negligible compared to the labour the woman contributes to the family.

Often the woman's opinion is not taken into consideration in household affairs, generally decided by her father-in-law, mother-in-law and their sons. A married woman tries to abide by the customs and traditions of the society and if she in any way violates the social norms, she receives hard punishment from her husband and in-laws. After coming to the husband's house, she carries out most of the household work though helped by her sisters-in-law and mother-in-law. Many restrictions are imposed upon her, e.g., she is not allowed to wear flowers in her hair, and she is bound to respect elderly people in the husband's village. She is prohibited from taking buffalo meat and sometimes also pork. She is not allowed to attend a common feast in the village. In festivals like *Panikalu*, *Burlanga Dakina*, and the *Meriah* festival and occasional ceremonial affairs like marriages and death rituals, the Kuttia Kondh put on feasts. During the feast, men and women both sit together to eat except for recently married women who are not allowed to sit with the others. Her share of food is sent to her to be eaten in her parents-in-law's house. She is not allowed to participate in a group dance in her husband's village.

On the delivery of her first child, the social status of a woman goes up since motherhood is of central importance in the Kuttia Kondh society and regarded as the crux of female identity. Barren women suffer from social discrimination and may be treated unjustly by their parents-in-law or husband. The husband of a barren wife may leave her or take a second wife. To see or meet a barren woman while going out in order to do an important work is regarded as an inauspicious omen. A barren woman is not allowed to participate in name-giving ceremonies, as she is believed to "put her evil eye" on the child and to cause misfortune in this way.

Youth

There are no special rites for either boys or girls to mark their change in status from children to mature members of society capable of sexual activity and marriage. But after reaching the age of puberty they start to sleep in dormitories and as peer groups, perform some common economic and social activities. The institutionalised visiting of peer groups of the opposite sex and of other villages is the preparation for marriage matters. Singing and dancing is an important part of the cultural life of the youth, but as long as they are not married, young boys and girls in many respects are still under the authority of their parents, living and working in the context of the family and household, and performing the required tasks in accordance with their sex, age and capabilities.

When the youth "dormitories" developed in the past, they were not simply meant as separate sleeping places, but thought to unite the power of youth and serve as a source of co-operative labour for use by the community. The youth in the dormitories maintained a specific way of life, oriented towards the exchange as well as development of their individual talents in song and music, learning the myths about their society, and their dance traditions. These artistic elements have not only helped to develop an awareness of social values and of the cultural meaning of daily life, but have also facilitated processes of socialisation and enculturation. The recent plight of dormitories has thus contributed to a tightening of the scope for socialisation and dimmed the chances for continuity within Kuttia Kondh culture.

In Kuttia Kondh villages, youth dormitories (*karambara*) are built separately for boys and girls. They are usually at the end of the village. When boys from another village come for a visit, the young girls of the host village act as hostesses, cooking for them, singing and dancing with them. When young women arrive on a visit, the young boys do the same. In Kuttia communities, a guest is a person from another village who visits and stays there for the night. After the guest is provided with food and drinks, the youth of the opposite sex sing songs. The act of singing songs while encircling the person, is an indication that the youth wants the guest to dance and sing with them. The guest is then bound to accept the invitation. Songs and dances are accompanied by instruments called *laudi*. Kuttia songs in dormitories usually recollect myths and legends or have religious themes.

Gifts are exchanged between the visiting youth and the youth of the host village. The gifts that are exchanged are mostly *Mahuli* liquor or a cock or a hen. Usually the youth of the host village give liquor and a cock or one of the two things as a token of friendship, and also as a token of gratitude, for the guest spent the night dancing and singing with the youth of the host village. Similarly, when the youth of the host village visits the guest's village, the guest in turn gives money or liquor bottles. Sometimes other gifts, such as ornaments, are exchanged.

Youth groups show a strong sense of comradeship. For example, if anyone, host or guest, has an attack of fever or any other sickness, all music stops as it might increase the sadness of the guest or host. There is a period of total mourning if someone young in the village dies. The mourning continues for a month.

Gradually, Kuttia youth are departing from tradition mainly due to modernisation and the influence of other cultures. This study has shown that Kuttia youth have been passing through a phase of transition in an attempt to mirror the culture of caste people in their neighbourhood. The culture of modern cinema has a strong impact on the Kuttia youth (both boys and girls) and cinema songs may replace the traditional myths, songs, riddles, and tales.

The Pano

The Pano who are low caste Hindus have an ambivalent position in Kuttia Kondh society as they are attributed a low status by the Kuttia Kondh even though they are in a stronger economic position due to their central role as middlemen and moneylenders. The Kuttia Kondh are highly dependent on them and often find themselves in a state of indebtedness. The Pano are a minority[11] living in the native place of the Kuttia Kondh. To a certain extent, they recognise them as landholders. Although the relationship between the Kuttia Kondh and the Pano is generally described as exploitative, it should be more accurately described as a relationship of interdependence.

There is not much historical data about the Pano and the beginning of their relationship with the Kuttia Kondh. Bailey suggests that the Pano might have established their position in the Kuttia Kondh area even before the first wave of Oriya settlers who started to immigrate there more than 300 years ago (Niggemeyer 1964:16). Today, the Pano are the largest non-tribal community living with the Kuttia Kondh. They trade in *sal*, dry fish, tobacco leaves, earthen pots, clothes, etc. and exchange these articles for natural produce. Although this kind of barter still exists, cash has gained in importance and the Kuttia Kondh now get articles from the Pano which include modern industrial products.

---

11. The ratio of Pano villages to Kuttia Kondh villages on an average is one to ten.

Another central item the Kuttia Kondh get from the Pano is *mahula* liquor. Although they know how to produce it from the flowers of the *mahula* tree, the local production is not sufficient for their needs. For a long time the Kuttia Kondh did not go to the market, but acquired the articles they needed through the Pano visiting their remote villages. The Pano also procured animals to be sacrificed during the numerous religious ceremonies of the Kuttia Kondh. Before the abolition of human sacrifice in the Kuttia Kondh area by the British in the 19th century, they helped them with the provision of human victims. But the relationship between the Kuttia Kondh and the Pano should not be reduced to an economic dimension only as the division of labour between the Kuttia Kondh as agricultural producers and the Pano as small merchants and their interdependence find cultural expression in the myths explaining the origin of their specific relationship.[12]

In spite of century-old contacts, the Kuttia Kondh and the Pano have never moved closer to each other at the social level. The Kuttia Kondh dominate the Pano and provide services on almost all socio-cultural occasions of the village. In day-to-day interaction, the Kuttia Kondh usually address a male Pano (elderly person) as *mama,* the

---

12. There is a legend to say that the Kuttia Kondh and Pano are brothers. This is as per their myth of origin described in *Kui Gaani*. According to the myth, both of them came out of Sapangada as Kuttia Kondh, but as one of them ate pig intestines, he became Pano. There is another story telling about the simultaneous and common origin of the Kondh and the Pano: in the mountains of Darmadadi near Dasingbadi in the southern part of the Kuttia Kondh region, in the midst of the thickest jungle stood a bamboo bush having only two tall shoots. Amidst torrential rains, by the action of the wind and with the fasting of *Bura penu,* these two bamboo shoots broke one after the other and from inside the shoots came first the Kondh followed by the Pano. The former became the King and the latter the minister, giving rise to the saying "Kondh *raja* (King) and Pano *mantri* (Minister)" since time immemorial. The first two creatures born were males and had to wait till two females, through a similar act of *Bura penu*_were born on the same mountain. In the following year they were married to give birth to the human race. Another legend states that the Pano and the Kondh came out of two eggs laid by a serpent on the same mountain. Out of these legends, the first one relates that *doms* came with the Pano from the underground with the former being followed by the latter. But the persons who ate pig's intestine (*paji knahanga*) became the *doms* has not been mentioned in the myth. The other legends do not suit the Kuttia Kondh's feeling about the *doms*.

Kuttia term for maternal uncle. In Kuttia kinship, the *mama* plays a central role within consanguineous groups. He is a person not to be joked about, and is a respected person in the family, able to advise and even command others. It seems that such a term is hardly suitable to be used by a Kuttia Kondh to address a Pano, as the Pano are inferior in status and mostly looked down upon. The Kuttia people explain this by saying that a Kuttia man can marry a Pano girl whereas the reverse is impossible. Concerning their ceremonies, the Kuttia ask the Pano for suggestions (this is, in fact, the role played by the Kuttia Kondh maternal uncle). Thus, the term *"mama"* is associated with a dual context and meaning by the Kuttia Kondh. It would not be tolerated if a Pano addressed a Kuttia male as *"mama"*. On the whole, the term *"mama"* has thus become a crucial term re-inforcing the lower social status of the Pano, on the one hand, and the close interaction between the two communities on the other. The contact between the two neighbouring communities had led to the establishment of symbolic kinship, although intermarriage between the two communities is not practised and symbolic kinship relations always attribute a lower social status to the Pano. A Pano may never enter the house of a Kuttia Kondh, whereas a Kuttia Kondh may enter a Pano house at any time. The Pano are tolerated by the Kuttia Kondh as they are aware that the Pano provide them with daily useful articles, ready-made foodstuff, liquors etc. Furthermore, the presence of the Pano community prevents further large-scale exploitation of the Kuttia Kondh by foreign traders, and at the same time, the Pano secure their own commercial interests.

The majority of the Pano does not live in Kuttia Kondh villages. Rather, the Pano have their own settlements or stay in Oriya villages, together with people belonging to other Hindu castes. Only a few Pano families live within Kuttia Kondh housing communities and there they are often marginalised, performing low-status services for the villagers. Usually, these people belong to the lowest strata of the Pano community, having failed in business or having been excluded from their own Pano community for some reason. Whereas in earlier times, the Pano-Kuttia Kondh interdependence was a more or less balanced one, the contemporary situation is different. Due to their knowledge of the Oriya language and their role as "brokers" between the Kuttia Kondh and mainstream Hindu society, and due to the growing influence of Hindu society on the life of the Kuttia Kondh, the Pano are gaining more and more power and their education is superior, an aspect that enables them to obtain government jobs, to profit from development programmes and projects, and even to obtain land from the Kuttia Kondh.

Informal and Formal Groups

The Kuttia Kondh's social life in the village and beyond is not only based on kinship relations, but also on associations and institutions. Such formal groups arise from certain social events and on the basis of specific social relations. Formal groups may be organised for the pursuit of a common interest. During rituals or ceremonial events,[13] the village priest, the astrologer and their assistants form a professional group united in the common interest and task. Peer groups are another type of formal groups in Kuttia Kondh society. The children, the youth, elder and old people constitute different groups for different purposes. Neighbourhood relations of Kuttia Kondh come under both formal and informal grouping. In most cases it is an informal grouping, for neighbours are often related. As stated earlier, a son lives independently and separately from his parents after marriage. He builds his house in the space available adjacent to the parent's house. In this case, the relation between two neighbours and members of such families is regarded as informal. On the other hand, it is regarded as formal if neighbouring families are neither consanguinal nor affinal. Within informal groups and in formal neighbourhood relations, items like food and other things are exchanged and whether the relation be formal or informal, there is a sense of understanding and mutual help between neighbours.

In the case of community rituals and festivals or personal ceremonial events there are different sets of formal and informal groupings. For example, in a death ritual when relatives come to the dead person's village, they form an informal group whereas the villagers accompanying the dead person's relatives are considered a

---

13. All ceremonies involve rituals, but all rituals may not be ceremonies. Thus ritual is organised both at the individual and group level whereas ceremonies are group performances.

formal group. At work, men and women form formal groups to discuss various aspects of agricultural activities.

Life Cycle Rituals

Birth is an important social event and everyone in the village rejoices in the birth of a child, be it a girl or a boy, though the pleasure is greater if the child is a girl. Girls enjoy greater esteem as females play an important role in the household and in agriculture, thus contributing to the livelihood of the family.

A child is born through the blessings of a god who is a representation of a *dukeli*, i.e., an ancestral spirit, and in this way, a birth acts to strengthen the bonds between parents and their relations.

During pregnancy, a woman is not given as much importance as after delivery. As soon as a pregnant woman suffers from labour pain, she is taken to the rear of the house or the *jaka kuda*, the small hut where women stay during their menstrual cycle. The birthing house is very unhygienic as the animal sheds are adjacent to it. An experienced mother remains with the pregnant woman to help her during delivery, but in case of difficulties the woman is not taken to a local health centre. Instead, people go and ask the doctor or pharmacist to come and examine the woman. After childbirth, the woman assisting the mother cuts the umbilical cord with a knife and the father buries the placenta in a deep hole in the back of the house. Smoke from burning resin is wafted over mother and child to drive away the mosquitoes. The mother gets something hot to drink and in order to keep the baby and the mother warm, a burning charcoal pot is placed nearby. Both father and mother are considered impure in the moments after the child's birth. The father is impure till the umbilical cord with the placenta is released. When this happens, the baby is given a bath with warm water and turmeric paste or *neem* leaves (*Azadirachta indica*) boiled in water.

The mother is considered impure for one month after the date of delivery. She does not cook or move around in front of the house. It is believed that if the mother comes out of the house to move around the premises before one month since the day of the delivery has passed, Dharani Penu feels disturbed.

Unless a *puja* is performed, neither mother nor child will be accepted by the community. The *puja* is offered to the ancestors, the *jendabenja-kadenja and* serves to thank the ancestors for their rebirth into society. Performed by the priest, the *puja* is offered to Elu Penu with Linga Penu, considered the authority on birth. After that, the whole village is offered a feast. If the parents of the newborn are financially sound, a large quantity of rice is cooked in the parent's house and a leaf cup, filled with cooked rice is sent to each household in the village.

The Name Giving Ceremony: Daru Itina

As the Kuttia Kondh believe that the child is born from their ancestors, during the name giving ceremony the priest invokes all ancestors to tell him which ancestor was born in the house. The priest traces back up to three generations in order to find out who amongst the dead has been reborn, which in most cases is the paternal grandfather or the great-grandfather's spirit.

A *semul* (*Bombax malabaricum*) pole is worshipped at the time of giving the child a name. The ceremony is called *"dukeli dakina"* to indicate the worship of *dukeli,* i.e., the ancestral being that lives as a spirit or ghost in the outer space of the village. Usually a child is given a name by the age of three years.[14] For the first child, the Kuttia Kondh perform a great sacrificial offering. The animal chosen for the sacrifice is usually a pig or a buffalo in case of a boy, and a cow or buffalo in case of a girl. The child is made to sit on the back of the pig or buffalo kept tied to the *semul* pole. People then put some rice and turmeric powder on the back of the buffalo where the child is obliged to sit. This animal, which is to be sacrificed, is then taken around the village with the child on its back. Afterwards, some rice is put on the buffalo's head between its horns, followed by a cock. It is to be sacrificed after the buffalo is made to eat the rice. The priest then gives a hard stroke with the sharp end of an axe on the buffalo's head to sacrifice the buffalo in the name of Linga Penu, and the

14. Details of the *puja* performance are described with the *semul* tree (*Bombax malabaricum*) in this book's chapter on "Socio-cultural aspects of plants, animals and humans".

ancestral spirit who has been "reborn". The buffalo's blood, then mixed with the rice, is taken and smeared on the forehead of the child (the sacrificed buffalo is meant for both Linga Penu and *dukeli*) and a ritual is performed inside the house of the child. There, a cock is sacrificed in the name of Elu Penu.

After this act of worship, the priest announces the name of the child that he has gleaned (during the ritual) from the *dukeli* (or ancestral being) who has been "reborn". The name of the ancestral spirit is transferred to the child. On the same day, the nose and the ears of the child are pierced by its grandmother: she first touches the places to be pierced with a *semul* thorn, and then pierces with the thorn of a *bael* tree or a pointed brass wire.

At the time of invoking the ancestral spirits, the priest (*jani*) chants to invite the ancestral spirits and the home deity to the spot where the worship is being organized:

"Raniadu Bendi adu	"Queen (the ancestral-mythical woman)
Pusarani, Batarani	(synonyms of the Queen)
Daene wedasila daene lanjusila	Under sunless under moonless
Udurengad penarengad satenje	Udurengad *Penarengad* died
Mara ai dadi aai Satenje	Trees came, branches came, died
Kueni Sapangadata	Over Sapangada
si daki kitkitere	This *puja* is being given
Ye daka Ye kitka amu	This *puja*, this rice, we
Geau kadi siamu	Telling like, giving
Aku Pemba satenje	Grandfather (maternal), Uncle (elder to father) died.
Ye daka Ye kitka	This *puja*, this rice
Amu sandipadi kadimanamu	We step wise doing like
Ye gaani Ye kabba	This song this chant
Amu 'jendabenja-kadenja bihitenje	We, (our) ancestors, finished
Ye sandhi Ye padi kadimanamu	This step this way doing

Memu Anganju likanju	We seniors, juniors
Ajananga Sandipadi Kadimai	Like this stepwise doing
Sapangada sarchangada bamu	Sapangada Sarchangada come
Ranipalu Bendipalu bamu	*Ranipalu Bendipalu* come
Sorugada arapimai	Hill hole offering
Lingajanani gaisi Alek	Birth for, bondage for *Judek Gaisi*
Daru pada Ekalpimai"	Offering (asper) established"

These lines give appeal to the invoked deities and the priest calls out their names (*Pusarani-Batarani*, *Raniadu-Bendiadu*) so recalling the first life under earth where there were no sun and moon. When everybody came to live on the earth, *udurengad* and *penarengad*, the mythical heroes died and the plants and trees also died, so stressing the mortal nature of life on earth. Then the priest says that this ritual was done for the dead and this *puja* offered by the ancestors (the term *jendabenja-kadenja* means ancestors). The names of the ancestors are not mentioned because they are taboo. The ritual ends with a common feast with meat of the sacrificed animal.

The Menstrual Cycle

Kuttia Kondh girls' puberty is associated with a number of taboos, of which one of the most important is the first menstruation (*jaka aate*). It is an occasion of joy amongst the women because it is a sign of fecundity. Immediately after the first menstruation, the young girl is taken for a bath by an old woman from the village and the girl is anointed with turmeric paste and oil. She takes another bath and after that a new set of clothes is given to her and she is taken to the backroom of a house or to the *jaka kuda*. There she stays for seven days until her cycle is over. By then, all the women will have rice prepared for the feast to celebrate the girl's puberty. During her seven-day confinement in the *jaka kuda*, the girl receives food given to her by others on plates fashioned from leaves. Menstruating women, married or unmarried, are avoided by everybody and are restricted to the houses where their family members live. A menstruating woman does not use or touch other people's dresses. Nobody even accepts a glass of water from her. She lives in the *jaka kuda* or in the house to the rear during her menstruation period. Food is served to her by her mother-in-law or sister-in-law, and separate eating vessels are used. She is not allowed to put her clothes at places where there is a possibility of children touching them. Usually after four days, the woman takes a bath, washes all her clothes and returns to her house. People do not consider it as auspicious to see the face of a menstruating woman when going off for an important job, and menstruating women are not allowed to attend rituals or acts of worship.

Menstruation remains associated with certain rules of behaviour, after puberty as well. During this period, whether married or not, the woman is not allowed to cook. Moreover, she has to go for work by the path behind the house, in order not to enter the front part of the house where *dharani* is established. She is not allowed to sweep the cattle shed, nor to touch the plough. All male family members are to be avoided, and a married woman does not sleep with her husband during her menstrual period, in particular. Deviations from the rules result in misfortune and the gods will have to be appeased by making sacrifices.

Marriage

While dealing with the life of tribals it is necessary to mention the different types of marriage (*sedi*) in Kuttia Kondh society. Marriage is an important aspect of the life cycle for it is the basis of many relationships with other members of the community. For the Kuttia Kondh, marriage does not only concern the relationship between two persons, but forms the inter-familial relationship. In Kuttia Kondh society, different types of marriages exist.

Marriage by Elopement

This is a type of marriage in which a young boy and a young girl first fall in love. By mutual agreement, they decide when and how to marry. A plan is conceived and, as soon as an opportunity arises, they both leave the village without telling anyone. The opportunity is usually given during community ceremonial events. The boy leads the girl to a place he has arranged to stay for some days. They remain hidden there from their friends, relatives and villagers, and after a few days of conjugal life, they request their parents to agree to their marriage. At that point, the parents organise their wedding with the usual amount of giving and taking presents.

Marriage by Capture

In this type of marriage, a young boy decides to marry a girl of his choice with whom he has fallen in love. He then tells the girl about his desire. If the girl reacts favourably, keeps quiet or answers through one of her very intimate friends, then the matter is fixed. The boy and the girl may meet secretly. This may lead to cohabitation. However, if the boy and the girl feel that their parents will not agree to their marriage, they decide to marry by capture. The boy seeks the help of his intimate friends for the purpose and tells them all about the girl and his affair with her. He informs his friends that he wants to snatch the girl from her parents. When his friends agree to help him, he fixes the time and day of capture. He may or may not inform his girl friend instantly. At that point, the boy waits for a chance to execute the plan to capture the girl. They await a community ceremonial event or the weekly market, when there is opportunity to take the girl and to run away with her. This act is opposed by the girl's friends and a fight may take place between the boy's and the girl's friends. Since the groom's group is prepared and has anticipated the fight, they are usually successful in taking away the girl to a secret place. There the groom waits for the girl. During the fight between the two groups, the police do not interfere since it is a traditional form of marriage in Kuttia Kondh society. After the fight, the boys on the girl's side try to locate the girl of their village. But usually, before the boys of the girl's side reach her, the groom and the bride will have cohabited at least once, thus rendering immaterial anything the boys from the girl's village might do. If, however, the boys on the girl's side are able to locate the girl before they had sexual intercourse, she is taken back. The boy then waits for another chance.

Sometimes during the fight between the two groups, weapons are used and severe injuries are not uncommon. After a marriage by capture has occurred, the father of the girl invites the boy's friends for a feast to finalise the marriage. Before that, however, the groom has to pay a fine. After that the marriage is organised. This type of marriage is more common in the Kuttia Kondh society than any other type of marriage.

Sororate and Levirate

This is the preferred kind of marriage for a widow or widower. The younger brother of the woman's husband is the first man to be considered in marriage to the wife of his deceased elder brother. Similarly a wife's younger sister is considered appropriate for marriage to her brother-in-law after her elder sister dies. This type of marriage does not involve a bride price. However, if a husband's younger brother does not agree to marry his sister-in-law and any other man is interested in marrying the widow, the interested person will have to give gifts to the widow's parents as well as to the family of the widow's former husband.

Marriage by Negotiation

This is the gentlest form of marriage in Kuttia Kondh society, but the process of marriage in this way takes a long time, since the actual wedding takes place long after it has been arranged. The process begins when male and female family members of the bridegroom go to the bride's house with rice and liquor, offered to the father of the girl. The gift indicates that the guests have come with a proposal for marriage. If rice and liquor are accepted by the girl's father, an agreement has been reached. A girl is considered a bride after her parents agree upon the bride price. The giving of the bride price money may take many years and the amount may be paid by instalments. There are cases in which it takes 10 years to pay the bride price.

There is a period of transition between this first agreement and the marriage during which different events may happen. During that period the negotiation may break down. If the negotiations are abandoned by the girl's side, all the money and gifts received as bride price are returned. On the other hand, if the negotiations are abandoned by the boy's party, they will not get the gifts back, but the money must be returned by the girl's parents.

After the bride price has been paid, the two parties meet and the boy's parents decide about the date of marriage. On that day the boy along with his friends and other village members usually comes to the girl's village, which, however, is not compulsory. If they come, they are welcomed with *mahula* liquor and a feast is arranged for them. The boy's father and the girl's father sit next to each other and ceremonially eat the buffalo meat, for buffalo meat makes them *samdhi*.[15] According to traditional beliefs, they cannot become *samdhi* without eating buffalo meat. After all that, the young boys and girls of both villages sing and dance. While the singing and dancing is going on, the girl is taken to a different house. Before she is dressed, she is taken for a bath. There, the bride is adorned with ornaments by her friends, in the traditional fashion, so that she will be ready to go off with her husband's parents and villagers in the afternoon. The girl wears a saree or two-piece, but no blouse. Her chest is covered with beads, *kagada* (a round aluminium ring worn around the neck) bangles on her wrists, hairpins or *kapoli* (hair knot) and a number of combs in her hair. The *jani* of the girl's village and of her in-law's village bless the girl and also the boy if he is present. The girl is taken to all elders and friends to get their blessings. Then she starts crying and her friends and relatives cry with her. Before leaving the village she is again blessed by the *jani* at the outskirts of the village. The *jani* spits on the girl's head to avoid the evil eye and uses *tolo*, oil extracted out of *mahula* (*Madhuka longifolia*) fruits to massage her head. By invoking all the deities he blesses her. Then the girl is led out of the village where a *sal* tree (*Shorea robusta*) has been chopped down about ten feet away. There, a game is played together with the female groups of both the bride's and the groom's village, including a lot of singing and dancing. After this, the girl goes with the people of the groom's village. Together with the girl, the parents send a buffalo, clothes, rice and liquor to the groom's house. The buffalo is meant for a common feast for the groom's villagers. The bride's family also sends gifts for the bride's younger in-laws. The gifts depend upon the income of the bride's household. The bride price the bride's father has received in exchange for the bride has to be repaid if the bride

15. The term *samdhi* means : the most important guest.

refuses to stay with her husband or disgraces herself. Intra-clan marriage is considered incestuous. Even marrying within a village is considered to be incestuous, because the boys and girls of the village are considered as brothers and sisters though nowadays, this attitude is changing and there are girls and boys of different clans living in the same villages who marry each other.

During the first eight days of the girl's stay at her husband's house, she is kept in a separate room. Husband and wife are not allowed to meet each other or cohabit during that period. On the eighth day, after the marriage, the bride's parents and friends as well as other village people come to take the bride back to her village. *Mahula* liquor is served to the guests as well as *katul*. If *salap* (*Caryota urens*) toddy is available, guests are escorted to the *madangabasa*. If the groom's house is a long way from the bride's home, the guests take shelter at the groom's village for the night. The next day, the girl is made ready to be sent to her own village with her parents and other people. The girl is dressed up according to tradition and walks with her head bent and her palms beneath her lower jaw. This is regarded as the traditional veil. Before leaving the groom's village the girl is blessed by the elderly people and *jani*. They bless her in order to save her from evil spirits, wild beasts, etc.

The villagers of the girl's village and her parents are given a buffalo for a common feast in the girl's village. As the girl, after marriage, at first lives with her parents, her husband will visit his wife there. In fact, the first cohabitation between wife and husband takes place in the wife's village. According to tradition, the girl will not return to her husband's village till she is pregnant. Only then does she leave her parents to live in her husband's house.

Nowadays, girls try to avoid their husband's home in order to escape from bearing responsibility and from working hard in the husband's fields since the earnings from them become his. They prefer to stay in their own village for as long a time as possible to cultivate their own fields. This enables them to save money that they can spend on amenities for themselves. That is why they play hide and seek with their husbands lest they become pregnant and have to move to the husband's house. During their stay in their native village, married women may be involved in sexual affairs with other young men of their village but do not like their husbands to do the same.

In some cases the girl is not happy with her parents' decision to marry a man of their choice. But the Kuttia Kondh are bound to their promises. Once they have accepted the bride price, they will definitely give their daughter to the man from whose parents the bride price has been received. In order to save her parents' prestige, a girl usually agrees with the marriage arranged by them. The only alternative might be that the girl is captured by some other young man for love. But such cases are very rare and the girl may feel the dilemma of neither being able to betray her father, nor being able to go with another young man for fear that her parents and her new husband may be harmed by witchcraft organised by the first groom and his relatives.

Death

The corpse of a Kuttia Kondh is generally cremated with the exception of pregnant women who die during childbirth or babies less than a month old who are usually buried. The personal belongings of the dead are cremated along with them. The Kuttia Kondh observe restrictions due to death pollution for three days. After rendering their sympathy to the bereaved family, the mourners bathe in the stream with a paste of mango twigs. The bereaved family does not cook for these three days, as food is provided by other villagers.

The deceased is covered with a cloth and his kin and relatives are informed immediately. They come to express their sympathy and are offered food by other members of the village. They may bring some *kueri,* i.e., little millet (*Panicum miliare*) and cook it. This is compulsory only for the daughters and sisters of the deceased. The corpse is kept for a last look by close relatives for 10 to 12 hours. Then it is carried on a bier prepared out of bamboo to the *tuleni,* i.e. the graveyard. A *kadeli* (cot) may be used instead of a bamboo bier. In the *tuleni*, the body is either cremated or buried. The *jani* first puts earth on the dead body (if it is to be buried) or adds fire to the body, if it is to be cremated. The men who have brought the dead body break twigs from trees nearby and each of them puts one twig on the corpse, no matter whether it is buried or cremated. Before burying or cremating a deceased, the corpse is anointed with oil and turmeric paste. Then everyone leaves the place, takes a bath and washes his clothes. For three days, the *jani* goes to the place where the dead was buried or cremated and offers food to *duma* or *dukeli,* i.e. the spirit. Women never enter the *tuleni* at the time of a death ritual. Death rituals are usually organised in the village on any day between the third and the seventh day after death. They are called *dasah.* On the day the ritual is performed (which is called the *dadi),* the departed soul is appeased by the *jani* with the help of the *kutaka* by performing the ritual and sacrificing the animals brought by everyone. On that day all the old earthen pots are kept aside and rice is cooked in new pots.

The relatives of the dead, particularly the in-laws, and among them daughters and sisters send animals and little millet for the *dasah* feast. The village people also contribute some millet in proportion to their wealth. The animals sent by the relatives are cut into two symmetrical halves. One half is sent back to the relatives who gave it. The other half is slashed and cooked in new earthen pots. *Mahuli* liquor as well as *salap* are brought and offered to all guests and villagers. All ancestors and the spirit of the deceased are offered food and drink on that day.

4

Livelihood, Economy and Development

The Kuttia Kondh Agricultural Economy

Shifting cultivation is the mainstay of the Kuttia Kondh economy. Cleared forest patches are cultivated for two to three years followed by a fallow period of several years to allow the natural vegetation to recover. In Kui language, this agricultural technique is called *nella kama*.[1] On their swiddens, the Kuttia Kondh grow more than twenty different kinds of crops in a mixed cropping system. Settled agriculture in the form of irrigated paddy cultivation is also practised, but due to scarcity of suitable land, it contributes little to their subsistence. Gardens in or near to the villages supply additional crops. The Kuttia Kondh keep livestock such as cattle, buffalo, goats, pigs and poultry.

Besides shifting and settled cultivation, the gathering of a wide range of forest products is of eminent importance. It bridges food gaps that increase towards the end of the summer and beginning of the rainy season before the harvest of the cultivated crops begins. Today hunting only adds little to the livelihood of the Kuttia Kondh, although it probably was of much more importance in earlier times. Yet hunting is still highly appreciated and replete with cultural meaning to the Kuttia Kondh. While hunting in groups, the participants divide themselves into smaller groups to encircle the forest. In the middle of the forest, the gun-bearing men are situated. Animals killed by this kind of group hunting are distributed among the participants. The man shooting the game, and the *majhi*, are given the largest shares.

1. Other synonymous terms are *dongar chasa*, *bagada chasa*, *gudia chasa* refers to irrigation.

The Kuttia Kondh are reputed to have a great deal of pride and self-respect, a trait which makes them reluctant to work for or serve "foreigners". Daily wage labour is hardly ever engaged in by the Kuttia Kondh, but to get some additional income they may occasionally work as wage labourers for other peasants, government agencies such as the Forest Department, or for private contractors. There is little occupational specialisation within Kuttia Kondh society. With a few exceptions, most are shifting cultivators, and besides the division of labour by sex and age, and the role of the political and religious headmen, there is no other notable division of labour. This is not to say that there are no specialists in the Kuttia Kondh society nor that capacities and knowledge are homogenously distributed within the community, however.

Manpower is the chief input in almost all work, and everybody contributes according to his or her physical capacity, either in joint labour projects or in work performed at the household level. Co-operative labour beyond the household level is provided by the Kuttia Kondh for the clearing of new swiddens and the harvesting of paddies and other crops cultivated in the plains. For agricultural operations, a person may seek the help of several people from different families for one day and is bound to serve them for one day each on reciprocity. Co-operative labour is also organised for house construction, digging a well or a water pool, and for performing different religious ceremonies and festivities concerning the village community. It increases efficiency and helps to handle activities according to the agricultural calendar. Thus, co-operative labour stands as a symbol of unity in Kuttia Kondh society. To refuse work for others in exchange for having been helped by others is punished by social isolation or by formal punishment by the *majhi* in a village meeting.

Co-operative labour facilities are not open to local Pano people as they are regarded as inferior. On the other hand, the Kuttia Kondh people sometimes employ Pano labourers.

Everyday Routine of Work

For the Kuttia Kondh, the day is divided into eight phases. They are called "*kaju gnepata*", i.e., when the cock crows, followed by the morning called "*laesi*". The midday is called "*gauat*" or "*madeni*", the afternoon is known as "*mileni weda*" and dusk, "*andhar jum jum*". Evening is called "*mileni*" and night, "*la-angi*". Midnight is called "*tudekena*". Daytime is measured by the sun's movement. To know the time during the day people ask "*icheke weda*?" which literally means "how much sun?" For the time at night, they ask, "*icheke La-angi*?" which literally means "how much darkness?" Light and dark are described in one term "*la-angi*" (night). For the Kuttia, daily life begins in the morning with *kaju gnepata* and the night begins immediately after *mileni* when darkness gets the upper hand. The period from *la-angi* to *ujali* (night to dawn) is the time for rest.

Agricultural work in the Kuttia Kondh society varies with the seasons, is very taxing and is extremely labour-intensive. Daily routines of work at home and in the fields are marked by a gender division of labour. For a Kuttia Kondh woman, the morning starts with "*kaju gnepata*" and sometimes even earlier if there is a lot of work or if there are guests at home. She pounds paddy, millet, *jowar*, etc., for the early breakfast, lunch and dinner. After pounding rice or other grains, she starts cooking. During the time the food is being cooked, Kuttia Kondh women sweep the house, fetch water, clean up the front yard and the courtyard as well as the cattle sheds. When the food is ready, they serve all the family members. They keep some food aside to carry it to the fields where they work with the males. Women do a lot of work in the field, have their food by *madeni*, i.e., midday, and after some rest start working again till dusk. Sometimes women also go to collect fruits and edible leaves for their households. When returning from the fields the women take a bath and also bathe their children. They return to their homes, carrying a load of fuelwood on their heads, and continue with their household work till evening. They also fetch water for use during the night and for the next morning. Women may also pound rice and millet if there is time in the evening. After that they cook and clean the house. They spread the grains needed for the next day on the loft above the fireplace to dry and prepare the beds for all members of the family. If not too tired, a woman gossips with her husband and children for some time and then drops off to sleep.

The Kuttia Kondh men rise later than the women. If *salap* toddy is available (in winter and early summer) they gather under *salap* trees (Caryota urens) to drink toddy. When they do not go to the toddy drinking place, locally known as *madangbasa*, they leave the house either to tend their vegetable plots or for other agricultural work. In the rainy season they usually sit on their verandah, light country cigars called "*tapari*" made of tobacco leaves (*Nicotiana tobaccum*) and relax. If they do not have any work outside, they do work around their homes, such as constructing houses, making agricultural implements, etc. On leisure days, they make plans about what to do and when to do it. In early summer periods, after having had something to eat, the male members leave for the *nella kama* to slash and burn trees in forests and hills for preparing swidden plots. They work in the fields till noon and then have a small meal, usually gruel, and rest for some time. After that they continue work till about 4 o'clock in the afternoon. If available nearby, they take toddy in-between. On their way back the men sometimes collect firewood. Then they have a bath and may proceed to *madangbasa* for an evening drink or if somebody has rice fields or vegetable plots they go and work there for a few hours before taking a drink. At about 6 to 7 o'clock they have another meal and then again sit together gossiping for a few hours. In winter a small fire is lit to warm them. Then they go to bed.

On the occasion of social events, the work pattern of the men necessarily alters as they then have to do work in the village. At leisure times, or at times when the females in the families are busy with other work, the men look after the children. Everyone in the family contributes to the household duties according to his or her capacity, age and gender. Children take the goats to the grass fields or into the forests for grazing. The work done by the youth resembles the male and female patterns described above (only that singing and dancing are included in the routine). Young girls help their mothers in performing female tasks while boys support their fathers. It is rare to see somebody sitting idle. Old people unable to do heavy work are watching the rice fields or shelling seeds, breaking castor pods, etc.

Agricultural Calendar

The work schedule of the Kuttia Kondh follows the annual agricultural cycle and agricultural work is divided according to the twelve calendar months. The names of the months resemble the names given to the months in Oriya. Month in Kui language is "*lanju*" which also means moon. Their agricultural calendar has three seasons, denominated as "*weda lanju*", "*piju lanju*" and "*peni lanju*" which refer to summer, rainy and winter season, respectively. "*Weda*" stands for sun, "*piju*" for rain and "*peni*" means winter. The different types of agricultural work are structured by changing conditions of climate and vegetation.

The preparation of hill plots for swiddening starts during the month *Phagun lanju* (February to March). Men cut trees and remove rocks while women cut and clear bushes, collecting them in one place. The children help their parents if required. After that the cleared fields are left to dry for one to two months. By the end of April or early May, the slashings are burnt. During *Chaita lanju* (March to April) the forest floor is completely cleared and *Baisaka lanju* (April to May) is also spent on cleaning. Then the field is hoed and after the first shower the seeds are sown. The Kuttia Kondh look after their fields besides going to the jungle to collect fruits, edible leaves etc. April to May and May to June (*Jyestha lanju*) are periods when minor forest produce abounds. Produces like mango (*Mangifera indica*), flowers of the *mahula* tree (*Madhuca longifolia/Bassia latifolia*), thatching grass (*Eulaliopsis binata* or *Themda arundinacea*), tamarind (*Tamarindus indica*), seeds of *sal* (*Shorea robusta*) are collected by men and women and sold in the market. During the month of *Jyestha lanju* (May to June), weeding starts and continues till *Asad lanju* (June to July). By the end of July or August (*Sravan lanju*), the harvesting of the early millet starts. Although sown at the same time, the different crops on the swiddens mature at different times and thus, the harvesting is carried out till the month of January.

The available paddy lands are cultivated in June to July and harvested in *Margasira lanju* (November to December). After the rainy season, around August to October (*Bhadrab lanju* and *Aswin lanju*), the Kuttia Kondh cultivate winter vegetables such as mustard (*Brassica campestris*) and *niger* (*Guizotia abyssinica*). The staple crops are harvested in *Pusa lanju* (December to January) or *Magha lanju* (January to February). *Kartik lanju* or *Dassera lanju* (October to November) is spent with harvesting the swidden plots. By the end of *Magha lanju* (January to February), the harvesting of the fields is finished. The hunting season starts in the summer months (from March to May or August to September), when the men have time to go to the jungle because the harvest is over. The forests look less dense then because the deciduous trees have shed their leaves. There may be hunting expeditions at other times but the period after harvesting is preferred.

Nutrition (Seasonal Food Patterns)

Cereals, pulses, meat of fowl and goat are the main food of the Kuttia Kondh. Among vegetables and tubers, yam (*Dioscorea sp.*) is particularly preferred. According to their food habits, little millet, finger millet, cowpea, pigeon pea and yam cultivated in the swiddens are of importance to the Kuttia Kondh. The Kuttia Kondh are very fond of gruel. The principal food is gruel made either out of millet *mande*, i.e., finger millet (*Eleusine coracana*), flour with little millet (*Panicum miliare*), *jana* (*Sorghum vulgare*) with some paddy and seasonal vegetables, or of rice (*Oryza sativa*). Raw rice is called *pranga*, and cooked rice, called *bidi*.

Cooked rice is not a common dish throughout the year. Rice is only prepared when the paddies are harvested. On rare occasions, the Kuttia Kondh purchase rice in the market; however, rice is not given priority in the food habits of the Kuttia Kondh in comparison with other cereals and millets harvested in their swiddens. Paddy is harvested, immediately pounded, cooked and eaten.

In the early morning when the cock crows, the women start pounding rice with mortar (*seni*) and pestle (*kutani*). Some pounded rice is kept for the evening, since otherwise the women will have to pound rice again. After having separated the husks from the rice with a winnow, the rice is cooked, and seeds of cowpea (*Phaseolus multiflorus*), *kredanga* (*Cajanus cajan*), *biri* (*Phaseolus vulgaris*), mungo (*Phaseolus mungo*) or any other pulses available, such as the seeds of *jata* or carpet legume (*Lablab purpurens*), are usually mixed with rice. Very rarely is salt used to add flavour to the rice, though sometimes, turmeric powder is added.

The paddies are harvested in winter and sometimes the Kuttia Kondh do not consume all the rice right after the harvest, but keep a large part for the lean period. The lean period starts in *Jyestha lanju* (May to June) and lasts till August when the little millet (*Panicum miliare*) and maize are mature. It is a precarious time for the Kuttia Kondh as they live on the rice stocked earlier and on finger millet (*Eleusine coracana*) from which they prepare gruel. But that is not adequate food for adult working people. Whereas the children are given the required quantity of gruel, old people do not have enough food. To supplement their diet, the Kuttia Kondh search for mango kernels, sago, wild and cultivated tubers (*Basanga*) plus spinach in the forests, kitchen gardens and paddy fields. Apart from that, dry maize, cowpea and bamboo shoots adds substantially to their diet. It is not uncommon for Kuttia families to suffer from hunger during the lean period and diseases are rife as a result of malnutrition.

In the rainy season, the Kuttia Kondh depend on bamboo shoots called *terka* in Kui. The Kuttia women and men go long distances to collect *terka*. The bamboo shoots are cut into fine chips. These chips are first ground and then squeezed to remove water. Then they are ground again, and put into hot water. After some time, rice is added to the *terka* and when it is cooked, the water is removed. The preparation is called *terka bidi*. *Terka* is sometimes also cooked without mixing with rice. If the water is not removed from the pot, the *terka* preparation is called *terka jada*, i.e. *terka* gruel. *Terka* is also used to prepare another dish called *kanji* or *terka jau*: fine chips of bamboo shoots, cooked with pulses or vegetables. Towards the end of the rainy season, the maize matures in the shifting fields and this saves the people from hunger or even starvation. Therefore, mango kernels, tubers, roots and bamboo shoots are a boon to the Kuttia Kondh during this period.

The late rainy season and the whole winter are the optimal seasons for the Kuttia Kondh because it is the time when the crops are harvested, and they get enough nourishment. In the podu fields, various crops mature at different times: e.g., finger millet (*Eleusine coracana*), little millet (*Panicum miliare*), cowpea (*Phaseolus multiflorus*), paddy, vegetables like pumpkin, banana, cucumber, bottle gourd (*Lagenaria vulgaris*), and beans. The Kuttia Kondh cook *masa bidi* (millet rice) and *kuli bidi* (paddy rice) with various types of *jau* (curry). Besides, the availability of plenty of sago palm (*Caryota urens*) and date palm (*Phoenix sylvestris*) toddy keep the Kuttia Kondh in good health. There is plenty of food in the village and in the podu fields. During the winter, gruel is rarely prepared. The Kuttia Kondh enjoy tasty dishes with produce from their swiddens, such as tubers called *basanga* in Kui and *kanda* in Oriya, important components of their diet in winter. Some of these varieties grow in the forest in addition to being cultivated in the fields. The larger varieties are exclusively cultivated on swidden plots together with other crops. Among all the types of tubers, *Dioscorea* species,(*D. alate, D. belophylla, D. bulbifera, D. glabra, D. oppositifolia, D. pentaphylla, D. wallichii*) yams are dominant. *D. alate* is the most often cultivated. They are called *kuna basanga, supka basanga, kui basanga, napanga, pati basanga, nangal kanda* and *kanda basanga.* Other tubers are *rani basanga*, i.e., sweet potato (*Ipomoea batatas*), *mara basanga*, i.e., tapioca (or Cassava, *Manihot esculenta*) and *sarubasanga,* i.e., taro (*Colocasia indica*). Besides these, there are a number of tubers that could not be identified botanically (*talanka basa*, *loari basa*, *katka basanga*, *poandaka*, *acha basa*, *kuna basa, potinga basa, kakaroka basanga,* etc.). Herbs also are an important component of their food intake, e.g., *Alternanthera sessilis* (*modaranga kucha*) found at water points, plus different species of *Amaranthus* (*khada*), *Bauhinia purpurea* (*barada kucha*), *Benincasa hispida* (ash gourd, *pita kucha*), *Cassia tora* (*chakda kucha*), *Celosia argentea* (quail grass, *nahga kucha*), *Cleome gysnandra* (*kamban sarcha kucha*), *Coccinica indica* (*torda kucha*), *Commelina benghalensis* (*kena kucha*), *Indigofera cassioides* (*girli kucha*), *Allmania nodiflora* (local name unidentified) *Alocacia indica* (*saru kucha*), *Leucas aspera* (*gassa kucha*), etc., all of which are wild species most commonly cooked as a kind of spinach.

Among the cultivated varieties, the leaves of *Cucurbita moschata* (*kumda kucha*), *Amaranthus oleraceous* (*kosila kucha*), *Phaseolus multiflorus* (*jhudunga kucha*) *and Brassica campestris* (*sarcha kucha,* i.e., mustard spinach) are most important.

During the rainy season (from May till August), many varieties of mushrooms are also eaten by the Kuttia Kondh. They are called *kutka* in Kui language. Some of them are: 1. *vigur kutka.* 2. *kambal kutka.* 3. *madag kutka.* 4. *gacha kutka.* 5. *luga kutka.* 6. *singmorna kutka.* 7. *vada kutka.* 8. *maska kutka.* 9. *puchu kutka.* 10. *jaranpatar kutka.* 11. *krusu kutka.* 12. *sakar kutka.* 13. *patar kutka.* 14. *para kutka.*

Many other varieties, such as wild banana flowers, piths of the sago palm (*Caryota urens*), piths of the banana plant (*Musa paradisiaca*), young jackfruit (*Artocarpus heterophyllus*), papaya (*Carica papaya*), and *muniga* (*Moringa oleifera*) are also eaten by the Kuttia Kondh.

To sum up, the Kuttia Kondh maintain their livelihood with produce from shifting cultivation and settled agriculture. Produce from agriculture, both from hill land agriculture and plain land agriculture, forms the backbone of their economy and livelihood. One part of the crop is consumed by the Kuttia Kondh while another part is sold or bartered. Paddy cultivation does not contribute substantially to their subsistence economy, as the yield from paddy fields is not sufficient to provide for the household needs for the whole year. The yield from paddy fields is less than that from the swidden plots. The Kuttia Kondh do not have many irrigated paddy fields and therefore, depend upon dry land cultivation (from which they actually produce more).

In swidden plots, the Kuttia Kondh grow about twenty or more different types of crops in a mixed-cropping system. Many varieties are not meant for household consumption but are sold for money in the market to purchase other things. The sale of mustard and til (sesame, *Sesamum indicum*), both winter crops, yields some cash income, although not enough to meet their needs. Little millet, finger millet, jowar, and sorghum are never sold, because they are important components of their self-sufficiency in food supply. Vegetable cultivation gives a reasonable return for the labour in terms of money.

Families who have able-bodied members and possess land that can be irrigated, can benefit from the sale of vegetables. The Kuttia Kondh also depend upon their livestock to ensure some income and sell it when they are in a crisis.

Resources in Kuttia Kondh Economy

A resource is any part of a human being's physical or social environment or an aspect of landscape, living or inanimate. The resources that have traditionally met the demands of human beings for food, clothing and shelter have always been subject to identification and denomination. How resources are defined, and how they are used varies among different communities. The Kuttia Kondh do not have a term equivalent to the Western term "resource". For them a resource is something which is presented for their use (*kama aate or kama aatati*), i.e., "something which has to be worked on" and "gives" (*si-eete*). The Kuttia Kondh perceive nature as comprising *tana* (earth), *vira* (soil), *mara* (tree), *kambani* (forest), *soru* (hills), *kadi* (cattle), *karu* (buffalo) and *weda* (sun). The latter is considered to be one of the most useful resources, and their origins are described in the tribe's myths (Srivastava 1972: 37f.).

Traditionally, the Kuttia Kondh have hunted animals and collected fruit and roots in the forest. While wandering through the forests, they began to associate different kinds of food with different landscapes and these, as the source of particular foods. They claimed that their ancestors had lived in a certain place until the food supply had been exhausted, whereupon they moved to another location. Long ago, when the tribe led a more nomadic (*treyenja*) existence, the roots that they gathered from the forest, made up an important part of their nourishment. The hill known as Dimbuli Soru was their food base then. The Kuttia Kondh believe that on the hill land, the Soru Penu of Dimbuli cultivated the same varieties of crops as those grown by the Kuttia Kondh today. The word *basa* can mean both "place" and "tuber" and has this double meaning. Tubers play an important role in the food pattern of the Kuttia Kondh and the use of tubers has been traced back to mythical origins of the Kuttia Kondh. They are considered the tribes' first food source. In this case, *basa* can also be used metaphorically to refer to the Kuttia Kondh's first food.

The Kuttia Kondh perceive rain, wind, vegetation, animals, and the earth itself as their most important resources, and identify their origin by naming the source, often according to the physical characteristics of a place. For example, a hill may be named according to a tree species that once grew or still grows in the area. Pijubangeri is a hill that is associated with rain (*piju*), while Bidibangeri is a hill associated with the wind (*bidi*). The name of the hill Titigada-Bajargada refers to the plentiful wildlife in the area. Similarly, forests or patches of forest are generally named according to the types of vegetation and wildlife found there.

The Kuttia Kondh believe that the two main perennial streams known as *Gunjinanu* and *Mahananu* are their oldest sources of water. Dharani Penu is the all-powerful earth goddess who is the authority of the land where the Kuttia live. The Kuttia Kondh believe that the goddess controls their lives and those of other beings inhabiting the earth, and that the blood (*Neri*) flowing in the body of an animal or human being is a gift from Dharani Penu. Therefore, the goddess is worshipped and offered blood in sacrifices.

In fact, the Kuttia Kondh appropriate nature through their cultural traditions. Their religious culture emphasises the supreme power of gods (penu) inherent in various parts of the landscape. The landscape in its entirety is called *dharani*, while the components or fragments of that landscape, such as the settlement sites and the cultivation areas are identified by their own names and by their own penus, which are fragmentations of the principal Dharani Penu. This penu refers to nature as a whole, and society known as grudu. Nature is seen as a collection of different landscapes associated with different *penuni*. Thus, the penu is the resource base, invoked and worshipped as part of religious rituals performed before the resources of particular places are utilised.[2] Being a forest dwelling community, the Kuttia

---

2. A. Salmond hints at a similar meaning of landscape in the Maori culture of New Zealand by claiming ". . . knowledge is a landscape" (1982:67) Further on she states: ". . . stories are told of how ancestors claimed territory, naming landmarks after parts of their bodies; how they travelled across that territory, leaving names behind them . . ., and most of the names evoke ancestral histories. . . . One could argue that Maori talk →

Kondh have developed strong social and spiritual ties with forests, regarding them as their brothers and ancestors. There are kinship relations associated with forests and other aspects of the landscape. The forest can, therefore, be seen as a socially meaningful resource. The entire process of socialisation of the people is aimed at becoming a part of the forests, hills, valleys, and plateau around them.

The Kuttia Kondh, in common with many other tribal societies, generally perceive women as producers and men as dependants. In addition to their daily work in the household, women are invaluable contributors to agricultural production as they undertake most of the labour. The Kuttia Kondh possess a remarkably well co-ordinated management pattern. Management, raw materials, manpower and the necessary tools and equipment are essential for manufacturing, production or maintenance. The Kuttia Kondh do not have a term comparable to the Western term "management". However, they have certain terms that they use either directly or indirectly with regard to various aspects of "management". Some of these terms are *dapakandi, itautimena, nehisapa itina, ninipani,* or *nipandi*, which will be described later in relation to various production and maintenance practices of the Kuttia Kondh.

The Kuttia Kondh perceive management and production as two different processes. As regards the production process a great number of factors is taken into account. Resources have both a social and a cultural meaning to the Kuttia Kondh and they are equally important. The social meaning of a resource refers to its regular use in the social life of the Kuttia Kondh, in their daily activities and by fulfilling their every day needs. Most Kuttia Kondh people are aware of the social aspect of a particular resource, but awareness of its cultural aspect is limited to those who are associated with religious rituals.

→ about knowledge is more in keeping with an interpretive, dialogical approach to anthropology than our own spatial metaphors. The "landscape" account presents the anthropologist as a detached intelligence, working to domesticate and master an objectified world, whereas in Maori thinking, truth is always contingent upon situational factors, knowledge claims are tied to power, the environment has a right of reply and one is vulnerable to its rebuttals". (1982:84f.).

The inputs for the production process include manpower (*maane*) (the most important) seeds (*bicha*)[3], knowledge, skill, and of course, agricultural implements. As part of the process, seeds (*bicha*), the most important raw materials, are sown to produce crops.[4] This basic seed input produces an output of many seeds (*penka*) from the fruit (*padasi*). The terms *bicha* and penka both mean seed, they distinguish between the seed as input (*bicha*) and the seed as output (*penka*), while the conversion of *bicha* to *penka* is the core of the Kuttia Kondh's economic reasoning: a *bicha* can be a *pan-no*[5] if it is harvested for consumption, while a *pan-no* can be a *bicha,* if it is sown with the intention of producing a crop. *Bicha* need some sort of treatment (*ita utimena*) before it is sown. The *ita utimena* depends upon how carefully *bicha* has been stored (*sapa itina*).[6] The Kuttia Kondh keep the seeds in containers made of hay and bamboo in which they put *began mara* (*Vitex nigundo*) leaves which act as an

---

3. *Bicha* also denotes the material object and its production. The Kuttia Kondh believe that all that exists is a product of work. Its visible aspect is a product of work and the invisible aspect is its shadow, the process of production. *Bicha* is further perceived to take on the form of contagious pox diseases. The ambivalence in the definition of *bicha* as a process of production and destruction (as the pox is harmful to the Kuttia Kondh) shows that 'becoming' and "perishing" are contrasting aspects of a continuum.

4. A Kuttia Kondh once said, "*Mehanangani budhi ate*" meaning "knowledge follows from long observation", and cited the germination of a seed as an example. A seed does not germinate if it is kept in the house or planted on dry land. It will only germinate if it rains on the land or if the seed is planted on wet land. When a seed matures into a plant or tree it will not flower or bear fruit if it is not exposed to the sun. The seeds, water, sun and any other materials that were instrumental in encouraging the seed's germination are necessary for life and are therefore considered to be resources. "*Aaga kata*" is the precursor of all that is now a resource in the Kuttia Kondh understanding. According to their myths the trees, plants, forests and hills were created to beautify nature. Seeds are known as *bicha* or *jara* and are claimed to have been the first resource to be brought from beneath the earth through the Sapangada hole. The *bicha* are the seeds sown on the fields that will eventually produce a crop. The seeds are symbolic of the regenerative and reproductive capacity of the resource.

5. The term *bicha* is both singular and plural, while the singular of *penka* is *pan-no*.

insect repellent. The seeds are kept in places with low humidity and this prevents them from germinating before they are sown. Yet, before the seeds are taken to the field, they are put in a humid or wet place to germinate and grow.

When the crops reach maturity they need to be harvested before the seeds and fruits fall to the ground. Family members transport the crops from the field to the house, where they are stored. Further maintenance is required for the preservation (*nehi sapa itina*) and conservation (*ninipani* or *nipandi*) of the crop in the houses. *Dapkandi* is the term used for processing crops at the household level. An important aspect of the management of crop production is careful timing as crops grown on swiddens and on dry land depend upon rain for their growth and survival. Therefore, crops may fail if cultivation does not begin at the appropriate time.

The Kuttia Kondh believe that shifting cultivation maximises the potential of the land. By practising multiple cropping on the hill slopes they can provide themselves with different foods at different times throughout the year and this strategy makes their economy self-sufficient. The land is left fallow for a number of years, a practice that ensures that soil fertility is not depleted and that the forest can regenerate. A specified man-to-land-ratio is generally maintained. The size of the cultivated area depends upon the number of members in a family, but they never clear more land than they are able to cultivate.

Village Trade and Barter

During the early summer season, during the time when the fields are prepared for cultivating crops on swiddens, the Kuttia Kondh collect minor forest produce which they sell in the market to get some cash. But the income from the collection and sale of minor forest produce is negligible. So they suffer from perpetual economic crises although it seems that the quantity they produce, harvest and collect is sufficient to meet a family's needs. There is, however, the problem of ruthless exploitation by local Pano people. The Kuttia Kondh become indebted as a result of this exploitation by the non-tribal people. Other factors that are often associated with their poor economy are the current village marketing and barter systems, and exploitation derived from an economically unfavourable loan system. The Kuttia Kondh are subject to large scale exploitation by the traders who advance them money and then collect the crops at harvest time when the price is extremely low and a fraction of the value at other times. (Fernandes *et al.* 1988) The Kuttia Kondh are in need of cash loans for their costly birth, marriage or death ceremonies, and as a result of a poor yield or illness. Usually such loans are given by their own kin or by members of their own community. The interest rate is 100% p.a., but if somebody is unable to return the loan within one year, he may return it in the following years without incurring additional interest.

In the past, the Kuttia Kondh took more loans in the form of crops from people of their own community. But this system is slowly and steadily changing because the tribal people who produce more, sell their surplus in the market after keeping a major part for their own consumption. Those Kuttia Kondh in need of money, go to the Pano or *sahukar* (the non-tribal money-lender) to ask for a loan and are charged even higher rates of interest. The payback of these loans may be in kind, i.e., agricultural products, but of course, the person in debt is trading back his goods at a very low price. And as a result, once a Kuttia Kondh has asked for a loan, it is rare for him to free himself from the clutches of the Pano or the *sahukar*.

As already mentioned, the Pano, historically, were the first tradesmen to enter the isolated Kuttia Kondh area and engage in barter. They brought salt and dry fish, and later on, ready-made food items, matches, country cigars, biscuits, clothes, ornaments and other things not produced by the Kuttia Kondh. Traditionally, the Pano were the liquor suppliers to the Kuttia Kondh. Even today the barter system is still continuing in the Kuttia Kondh villages though nowadays they are aware of weight and measurement systems. The barter system prevails especially during the harvesting period of the Kuttia Kondh and the Pano use it to exploit the Kuttia Kondh.[7] The crops that the

6. *Nehisapa itina* literally means "well preserved".

7. The Pano sell in terms of weights and measures as in the market. For a bottle of *mahuli* liquor, a Pano demands five rupees. But if it is bartered, →

Kuttia Kondh barter are usually cow pea, pigeon pea, mustard and til, in exchange for rice.

The Kuttia Kondh associate the term "economy" with trading for money as opposed to barter. While the bulk of the crops are kept for household consumption, a small part is sold for ready money, either in the market or to traders or their agents. The Kuttia Kondh are aware of the good market value of cow pea, black gram, pigeon pea and castor seeds, produced on their shifting cultivation plots, and mustard and niger seeds, cultivated on plain lands. These are regarded as cash crops although cowpea and pigeon pea are also used for household consumption in addition to little millet, finger millet, bajra, maize, tapioca and tubers. The non-cultivable cash crops sold in the market include the non-timber products gathered from the forests, and bamboo shoots important for consumption during lean periods. *Sal* seeds (*Sargi mara*; *Shorea robusta*), *mahula* flowers and seeds (*Puju mara*; *Madhuka longifolia*), and broom grasses make up the majority of the minor forest produce sold to local traders or the collection centres of the Tribal Development Co-operative Corporation and Agency Marketing Co-operative Society. Game is rarely sold in the market due to the restrictions on hunting imposed by the Forest Department.

By participating in the market economy, the Kuttia Kondh are exposed to increases in the market price of commodities. The cost of goods for daily use purchased in the market, has risen dramatically and to generate cash, the Kuttia Kondh depend on sale of their crops. When the market price for their crops is low, they cannot afford the articles of daily use in the market. They feel that they are unable to generate a sufficient economic income by selling their labour, and dislike the fact that they are becoming landless labourers. However, the present circumstances give them little choice.

→ it is given in exchange of a *mana* (3 kgs) of paddy or little millet or an "*ada*" (250 gms.) of *kandulo (Cajanus cajan)*, or two "*ada*" of mustard grain, etc. The Pano know the cash market rates of such crops very well, but they actually charge a much higher price in kind from the Kuttia Kondh. Accordingly in summer season, Pano sell a bottle of mahuli liquor in exchange of about three to four kilograms of dried *mahula* flowers (*Madhuka longifolia*). Further, for different items being sold by the Pano, different measures for different crops are fixed by them.

The Kuttia Kondh, considered amongst the least developed tribes of Orissa, receive some assistance from the government, namely from the Kuttia Kondh Development Agency (KKDA) and other departments who work in their settlement area. The KKDA has devised developmental programmes such as horticulture, apiculture, seasonal agriculture and cash-crop-cultivation with the objective of up-grading the Kuttia Kondh's standard of living and boosting their economy. However, the Kuttia Kondh attach little value to the hybrid, high yielding varieties of crops, vegetables and fruit trees that they have been provided with. They are reluctant to plant these varieties on the hill slopes, though they have done so in the plains. The KKDA has also endeavoured to educate the Kuttia Kondh in improved land use, and has provided them with irrigation facilities by making drainage canals, culverts, etc. — with little success. The Agricultural Department has attempted to encourage them to cultivate plain lands, but due to the lack of land and irrigation facilities these efforts have largely failed. Furthermore, the tribe continues to cling to its traditional pattern of hill cultivation, despite attempts by the Soil Conservation Department and Podu Prevention Scheme to phase out shifting cultivation.

Inaccessibility of Forests and Deforestation as a Crisis in Resource-Use

The Kuttia Kondh regard forests as their main resource base, however, exploitation of this resource is being discouraged by the forest administration. The compartmentalisation of forests into reserved, protected and village forests by the Forest Department has imposed many rules and regulations on forest dwelling communities who have full rights now over their village forests only. Since much of the forest around Belghar has been declared protected, the access to some parts of the forest is limited and the Kuttia Kondh are prevented from practising shifting cultivation on many hill slopes. The yield from the limited areas of forest that can be used for shifting cultivation is inadequate. This situation is worsened by the fact that the Kuttia Kondh are forced to cultivate the forest patches far more frequently than before; the four to five year fallow period has decreased to one or two years.

Furthermore, the people are restricted in their use of timber, bamboo and fuel wood. Although they are granted some concessions on the grounds that they were the forests' first inhabitants, these particular concessions are limited and insufficient to fulfil their household needs. The Kuttia Kondh believe that these restrictions will eventually also be applied to the collection of mushrooms and spinach in the forests. People are now liable to be prosecuted by the Forest Department and face heavy penalties for clearing patches of forest. The legal fraternity saw this as a chance to make money from the alleged offenders by assuring them that they could be freed from Government cases.[8] The Kuttia Kondh increasingly insist that the forests are their property and accordingly, that they are entitled to clear forest patches for cultivation. The Kuttia Kondh people benefit from a provision that enables them to lease areas of forest from the Forest Department by paying a fixed amount per measure of land.[9]

Deforestation has set in motion the Kuttia Kondh's transition from traditional to new cultural, social, economic and commercial structures. Though the Kuttia Kondh admit that the clearance of bush forest for shifting cultivation contributes to deforestation, they claim that the effect is negligible compared to the Forest Department's felling of large trees for commercial purposes. In contrast, the Kuttia Kondh are reluctant to cut down large trees, believing that the gods or spirits (*penuni* = pl. of penu) are present in all trees, and in the largest, in particular, their gods and goddesses. They are saddened by the fact that they are paid by the Forest Department to cut the large trees and cannot understand why the Forest Department continues to deny them their minor household and subsistence needs. Some of the young

8. One Forest Department official pointed out that women are becoming more involved in clearing the forest in preparation for shifting cultivation. They are unafraid of the forest guards and other officials, having devised a clever tactic that deters them from intervening. The women, who are naked, begin clearing the vegetation early in the morning. Their nudity ensures that the guards leave them alone. The women have warned that they will file a case of misconduct against them if they attempt to prevent the women from felling the trees.

9. These leasehold forests bear an inherent insecurity of tenure because the leaseholders can be expelled from their land at almost any time on some pretext.

Kuttia Kondh are unwilling to continue to live on shifting cultivation, due to the long running disagreements between their community and the Forest Department. Instead, they are now leaving the forests for the cities.

Socio-economic Change and Development in the Kuttia Kondh Area

Rapid changes have taken place in the Kuttia Kondh communities over the recent decades and it is now a society in transition. The development programmes launched by the State Government, Central Government and foreign funding organisations in tribal areas are attempting to make significant contributions towards raising the living standard of the Kuttia Kondh.

There are now remarkable changes in the Kuttia Kondh tradition and culture. Adaptations to market economy, to non-tribal material and religious culture, to a non-tribal health system and a changing environment have transformed their outlook but several factors have prevented them from cultivating the hill lands. Due to the decreasing duration allowed for fallow between two cultivation cycles on a particular patch of land, productivity has declined. The shortened fallow period results from restrictions by the Forest Department on slash-and-burn cultivation. Now restricted to particular patches of lands, the Kuttia Kondh use them for longer periods, so shortening the fallow. The Kuttia Kondh will not give up swiddening as it is their traditional mode of subsistence. Moreover, it facilitates multiple cropping, yields more than paddy in the lowlands, requires no irrigation infrastructure, is safe from grazing cattle when the crop is grown high on the hills, and allows to produce different crops at different times of the year. Programmes launched by the government under the Podu (burning of forests) Prevention Scheme in 1986 tried to wean the people away from shifting cultivation. Furthermore, the Forest Department of Orissa declared a large part of the hills and forests as protected areas, leaving some areas for the tribal people in consideration of their dependence on forests to meet their household needs, fuel wood, etc. The change in the practice of shifting cultivation has led the Kuttia Kondh to search for other modes of income generation, namely, wage labour. This is not something they would have done traditionally, but is now accepted. It has facilitated out-migration of youth, who now seek their fortune outside the settlement areas, working as motor mechanics, motor drivers, as factory workers, etc.

Young women usually do not go to work anywhere else. However, it has been observed that young women living in roadside villages have shown some interest in getting work in the households of the Forest Department and the Kuttia Kondh Development Agency officials. A few young women do not mind working as daily labourers under the Roads and Buildings Department contractors within Belghar. But the migration of the Kuttia Kondh people to the cities is very limited and temporary as the migrants usually leave the cities after some years with funds they can use as start-up capital for a business. They start trading in the villages by procuring crops from their community people to sell to the big traders. They also start small businesses by opening betel and grocery shops etc. Migration has helped the Kuttia Kondh youth to know about the outer world and how to live in the cities. Back home, the young people are sharing their experiences and ideas of city life with the elders and youngsters, thereby motivating the younger generation to migrate to the towns for job opportunities.

In Belghar, the study area, there are several government agencies, a public health centre, a police outpost, an office of the agricultural extension officer, a veterinary hospital, a post office and a weekly market. In Belghar there is also a bank — the Kalahandi Anchalika Gramya Bank — sponsored by the State Bank of India that provides loans to the Kuttia Kondh. There is a Large Size Agriculture Multipurpose Society (LAMPS) that also provides them with short-term agricultural loans.

The Agricultural Extension Office and the Branch Office of Oil Orissa provide the Kuttia Kondh with seeds for different crops throughout the year. Under the agricultural extension programme, paddy, mustard, vegetable seedlings, seeds, etc. are supplied. The field supervisors of Oil Orissa supply mustard, til (sesame), and sunflower seeds to the Kuttia Kondh and in return procure the oilseeds after harvest. The Agricultural Department provides the Kuttia Kondh with seeds, and Oil Orissa also supplies oilseeds, but they have not been supplied with any land. Where should they grow the crops?

The micro-project of the Kuttia Kondh Development Agency has created some awareness among the Kuttia Kondh of the need for sustainable development. This project aims at the overall development of the living standard of the Kuttia Kondh and their quality of life, and the Agency spends a lot of money on providing emergency medicines through primary health centres. It emphasises youth education in various spheres including horticulture, forestry, apiculture and agriculture and provides seeds and seedlings for *kharif* and *rabi* crops[10] on the plains and irrigated lands. In many areas, the Agency has facilitated the irrigation of croplands, provided hand pumps and modern agricultural equipment to people living in a vast stretch of the Kuttia Kondh land. It has supported the development of their health, hygiene, education, occupation, agriculture and economy. But the Agency has not succeeded in educating the Kuttia Kondh for their new vocations.

There is a fair price shop opened by the government under the Tribal Development Cooperative Society (TDCS) from where the Kuttia Kondh may purchase clothes, soaps, cosmetics, rice, oil and many other necessary goods. There is a centre of AMCS (Agency Marketing Co-operative Society) that purchases minor forest products from the Kuttia Kondh. But as AMCS does not have sufficient cash revenue to buy up the larger quantities of goods that the Kuttia Kondh prefer to get from the local traders.

The Government Primary Health centre located at Belghar now provides medical facilities and the Kuttia Kondh are slowly leaving their traditional pattern of curing diseases and have started taking advantage of modern medical facilities. This has also considerably reduced the Kuttia Kondh's use of herbal medicines. The Primary Health Centre renders good services to the Kuttia Kondh of Belghar Gram Panchayat. However, the Kuttia Kondh in Jhiripani Gram Panchayat rarely consult the health centre unless they feel that the disease goes beyond their control. The ANM (Auxiliary Nursing Mother)

10. "*Kharif*" and "*Rabi*" denote summer and winter crops respectively.

centres are functioning properly at the village level and motivate the people to be concerned about better sanitation and personal hygiene. They attend to female patients in their gynaecological problems and in child delivery. Besides, health workers and malaria workers attempt to provide the Kuttia Kondh with their services.

Some Non Government Organisations (NGO) also work in the Kuttia Kondh area. An NGO named AWARE has made significant progress in the field of health by providing deep wells and by conducting health awareness programmes. In addition, Utkal Navajeevan Mandal (headquartered at Angul) with field centres at Burlubaru, Rangaparu and Dupi, cares for women and children. These centres also provide the Kuttia children with a supplementary diet and attempt to educate young girls in the villages. Education in the area is not up to the mark, however. There is a residential high school in Belghar run by the State Government under the Ministry of Tribal affairs where students are mostly from the Pano community. In the primary education classes, some Kuttia Kondh children have been admitted but Kuttia girls rarely go to formal school. Usually, the Kuttia Kondh do not respond well to schools and other formal methods of education. However, in order to boost the literacy level, the micro-project Kuttia Kondh Development Agency has set up non-formal education centres in villages such as Gyana Mandir. But even in such non-formal centres, attendance is poor.

Perspectives on Socio-Cultural Development

The question of social development of India's tribal population has been discussed on and on, and not only after independence. Questions such as whether there are sustainable societies, and what their chances of survival are in a world of rapid socio-economic and political change show that the international community feels concerned about ethnic minorities within complex societies such as India. The role of such minorities is considered to be important for the conservation of biodiversity and the maintenance of cultural identity. Is sustainability possible for a society which, on the one hand, is based on religious world views, mythology and ancestor worship, and on the other hand is confronted by a process of rapid economic growth and modern capitalist achievement, dominated more and more by middle class values? Can it be considered to be particularly sustainable due to the close connection of the large rural section of the society, and in particular, the forest dwellers, with their natural environment?

The existing livelihood patterns, that is, the traditional and the more modern, offer opportunities for multiple options for both resource use and social performance, as a consequence of diversified consumption needs, and the potential for different modes of economic production. Deregulated and largely self-sustaining village and forest dwelling communities on the one hand, urban and sub-urban population with a high degree of dependence on administrative regulation of services, and decentralised food, energy and resource procurement on the other, naturally have diverging interests and goals. When the national economy is allowed to flourish at the expense of local self-sustaining social structures, rather than complementing their strengths and weaknesses, the objective of nationwide socio-economic sustainability is inevitably missed (Fernandes 1992). And to make it very clear, the degree of economic wealth and higher standards of consumption a nation has attained cannot be equated to the degree of socio-cultural development a local society has achieved and is able to maintain at a certain point of its development. While the perspectives and values of the urban and rural population may converge in due course, the overall perspectives for survival in a multi-faceted configuration such as Indian society are still divided into urban or rural for the immediate future. The gap and margin of negotiations possible between the rural population and the Forest Department as the concerned representative of the state administration (and therefore, the mainstream urban population, for example) seems to be getting wider because many environmental activists, the green global community and intellectuals tend to favour a sometimes slightly romanticised rural outlook on how resources are to be managed at a nationwide level.

Within this discourse, forests have borne the negative impact of a rather ruthless and one-sided type of economic development for a long time, irrespective of the future costs of present economic benefits to India or in almost any other country. The tide has not turned, despite much rhetoric, even on the global scale and the global discourse may or may not, in the long run, facilitate the acceptance and the political acknowledgement of rural and green intellectual positions by the urban middle classes and the public administration.

As has been suggested above, various NGOs have entered the political arena as new political institutions, acting as mediators in the national to local interface. Issues pertaining to forests, the scope of their use and management practices, and their overall cultural meaning in the discourse on local knowledge (Seeland 1997) have now paved the way for putting indigenous and local forest knowledge on the international research agenda (Bicker 2004, Silitoe 2004).

5

The Concepts of Space, Environment and Village Settlements

THE Kuttia concept of open space and living space, the path of knowledge from darkness to light, the concept of environment and the appropriateness of an activity, can be summed up in one word — *edu*. *Edu* is also the root of the Kuttia Kondh's understanding of their society, culture, religion and their standard of living and well-being.

Edu itere budhi itere
Inisatisi adine Inisatisi ranjine

Edu literally means "thought" and *budhi* is "knowledge". Translated, the first line states that knowledge is acquired through the thought process; thus, thought is the origin of knowledge. The second line literally means "how it will be right, how it will fit". Thus both lines refer to a process driven by intellect, or in particular to a "resolute intent". *Inisatisi* or "how to" is the question in the mind of a Kuttia Kondh at the beginning of any process. As a result, any activity or process undertaken by the Kuttia Kondh, no matter whether it concerns society or culture, is always a collection of *inisatisi*. The appropriateness of the process is valued using the terms *adine* and *ranjine* meaning "right" and "fit", respectively. The term *inisatisi* may also be used for "what is". Then *inisatisi adine* would mean "what is right", i.e, the course of action to take, that which stems from knowledge derived from thought.

However, *edu* is not simply a thought, but an awareness of what is to be done in the sense of what is desirable and appropriate. *Budhi* and *edu* are verbs concerning the use of the intellect for a particular purpose thus emphasising the appropriateness of things and action, both of thinking and doing. It is best defined by its contribution to the wellbeing of people in the sense of a code of conduct, and provides a society with a value system over a period of time.

Several terms highlight the attributes of value or the appropriateness with regard to time, place and activity. The terms *pune*, *bakaratamu*, *mrangeetae*, *takana*, for example, refer to the activity at that particular moment. *Pune* means "to know", "to understand" and "to remember". *Bakaratamu* means "to lose track/ sight of", "to miss the connecting link". *Mrangeetae* means "to be distracted". *Takana* means "to cover distance", an expression which means, "to retain in one's mind over a period of time". Timely awareness is another definition of *pune,* that is, to know the current activity and task to be accomplished. *Weda silae* denotes "untimely", the expression literally meaning "sun absent" (*weda*-sun, *silae*-absent). This term for the sun's absence describes a condition: the sun is the source of light; when it is absent, there is darkness. The source of light is darkness, both the result and cause of untimely activity. Without awareness and knowledge, there is no light, and vice versa. Therefore, 'to see what is timely' is in the observance of *weda silae*. Those who, according to the Kuttia Kondh, are able to distinguish between *dina mehananga* and *angadina* are well aware of the condition of *weda silae.*[1] People who possess this awareness are described by the terms *satotanja* (*sato*-truth, *tanja*-people) and *nehijella*. *Nehijella* describes a life force or a life free from disability. This particular view of life is reflected in social behaviour. Disability results from the absence of a resolute intent to work; in other words there is an absence of *edu* and the condition known as "*weda silae*". Illness is understood as being the result of inappropriate activity that has provoked the anger of the gods. The person whose life force is *nehijella* is called *satotanja,* a "truthful person".

The Kuttia Kondh's cultural life pertains to beliefs, behaviour, values, knowledge and all other aspects of culture for which they hold traditional feelings. The Kuttia Kondh believe that the

1. Here *dina* means "time" though it literally means "a day". *Meha* means "to see" and *angadina* means not to see what is timely.

environment is both extrinsic and intrinsic. There have been numerous debates concerning the understanding of the outward and inward environment of the Kuttia Kondh, beginning with their understanding of "being" and "Being"; being is a larger whole of which the Kuttia Kondh and other subjects and objects are smaller parts within their surrounding. All the forms of their association with "Being", or the large whole, or the biggest environment are rooted in their knowledge and moral values. The forest habitat has enabled the Kuttia Kondh to understand the significance of different components of the environment. It is this appropriated knowledge that has created their environment.

The Environmental and Spatial Concept of the Kuttia Kondh

The Kuttia Kondh's relationship with nature is manifold, and embraces ecological, organic and spiritual aspects as nature is perceived as a unified whole. This comprehensive understanding of nature makes it easier for them to identify and understand other living beings and these various micro-dimensions of the Kuttia Kondh spiritual association with nature (knowledge, beliefs, moral values, and the principles of living) are those aspects of their culture that contribute to their wellbeing.

An important term that characterizes the environmental concept of the Kuttia Kondh is *basa*, which literally means "environ". Ordinarily, *basa* is the term used for a place, particularly where many people gather for some social reason, such as for instance, a festival or any other cultural event. It can also refer to community feasts in the forest. *Basa* denotes the place and the event and it can also refer to many places or situations surrounding (*gunjare*) one another. Thus, *basa* can be divided into various categories or layers with different names. In terms of a Kuttia Kondh's understanding of the living space, the first *basa* is his or her house (*elu*). The house is located within the borders of the village settlement, known as *naju*, which is the second *basa*. The surroundings of the house are known as *elu gunjare* and the surroundings of the village as *tedi gunjare*. *Elu gunjare* and *tedi gunjare* can be differentiated by the size of the space, and the type of living and non-living things occupying that space.

The names of particular places often end in *basa*, i.e., *madang basa, naju basa, penu basa, maju basa,* etc. The *madang basa* is a place where people sit and converse, gossip, and exchange thoughts and ideas while drinking toddy (palm wine). *Mada* is the Kui name for the sago palm (*Caryota urens*), tapped for toddy. Hence a place is only defined as *madang basa* if it is used for the consumption of toddy. It is an environment shaped by the behaviour and interaction of people and plants. The components of a *madang basa* are a group of people, a sago palm tree, the material items needed for toddy consumption, animals, rocks, etc. *Naju basa* refers to an area of land on which a village settlement (*naju*) stands. Thus *naju basa* refers to all the components that make up a village: human beings, animals, houses, kitchen gardens, and ancestral spirits. The livestock buildings are: *kadi basa* (cattle), *karu basa* (buffalo), and *paji basa* (pigs).

The term *basa* does not always refer to a locally fixed space, but rather describes what a place is used for, so that *kadi basa*, for example, is a place where cattle are kept, and *madang basa* refers to a place where toddy is consumed at social gatherings. Outside the village are the *penu basa,* the abodes of deities (*penu*) and these include all hills, forests, trees, and rocks. The term *penu basa* is particularly applied to hilltops (*soru jaka* or *gati jaka*) because they are said to be the dwelling places and meeting points of the *penus*. The *naju basa* lies at the bottom of a hill whereas the *penu basa* is at the top of the hill. A *madang basa* can be anywhere in between these two *basa*.

A *maju basa* is the name given to an area of forest inhabited or frequented by the sambar (*maju, Cervus unicolor*). The hilltop is the *penu basa*, the hill base is the *basa* of the Kuttia Kondh, and the surrounding forested patches and parts of hills are occupied by the *maju*. Although the *maju basa* is commonly associated with the sambar, it can also be inhabited by many other animals.

Religious Background of the Spatial Concept of the Kuttia Kondh

According to the *Kui Gaani* (see Appendix), all living beings once inhabited the dark underground, until they spotted a ray of light which guided them out of the darkness into a space between the earth and the sky. The space was full of light and shade, and the landscape was covered with trees and forest. Open spaces were living spaces. *Sapangada* is the name for the symbolic centre of this living space, and it is located in Gumma Panchayat of Belghar area, a place surrounded by hills and dense forest. The place is marked by a small hole, which is said to have been much larger a few generations ago. The name Sapangada is symbolic; it refers to open living space as well as to the origin of the Kuttia Kondh and other living beings. In the *Kui Gaani*, Sapangada denotes the Kuttia Kondh's place of origin. The term *sapan* is associated with the word *sate,* meaning birth. However, the Kuttia Kondh have two words for birth-*sate and pdite*. *Sate* means "to emerge from" or "come out", while *pdite* means "to be born". *Sate* refers to the emergence of the Kuttia Kondh from the under-world, a mythological account of the creation of living beings. *Pdite* differs from *sate* in the sense that it relates birth to the physiological aspects of human reproduction. *Sate* occurred only once in Kondh mythology, and from then on *pdite* has been the common form of coming into being. Thus, the Kuttia Kondh have been created in two ways: first, by emerging directly from the Sapangada hole, and secondly, have been born by their mothers. Conception is called "*pao pata aate"* — the swelling of a woman's stomach, and implies that there is life sheltering beneath a protective covering. The development of the embryo in the mother's womb can be compared to the Kuttia Kondh's notion of their mythical existence under the earth, at that point, covered by the earth's crust. In actual usage, the word *jana* can refer to a covering of the stomach or the underground, yet is more commonly used to refer to the covering of a plant seed.

Layout of Village Settlement and Cultivated Land

The following description of the settlement layout begins with the land surrounding the village, which is cultivated by the Kuttia Kondh, and progresses inwards towards the village centre (see *fig.* 1).

The Kuttia Kondh prefer to build a settlement on the slopes at the base of a hill below the lower middle hill slope (*nella),* the one used for shifting cultivation. This physical space is known as the *soru*

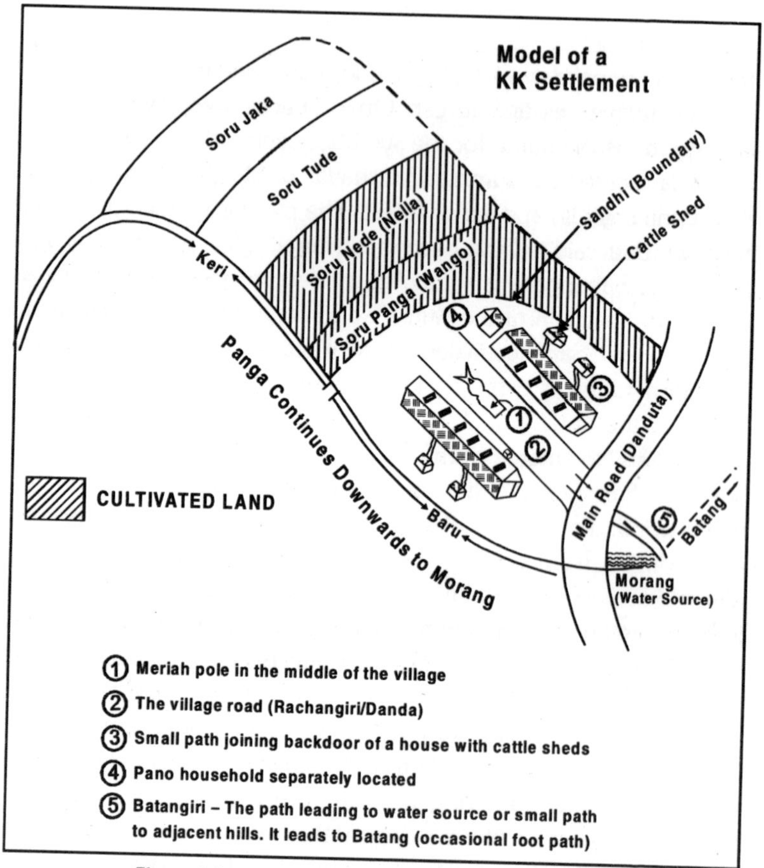

Figure -1: Layout of a village settlement and cultivated land

panga or *wango*, with the exception of the space taken by the village settlement, known as the *baru*. The settlement is built on a slope so that one end of the village is at a higher level than the other. The boundary of the village, known as the *sandhi*, is determined by the village priests rather than according to any official demarcation. There, the Kuttia Kondh set up benevolent deities, believing that these protect the people living within the village perimeter. Thus, the placement of deities around the village represents the boundary (*sandhi*) and the *sandhi* separates the area available for shifting cultivation (*nellang*) from the village settlement (*naju*) itself. Thus, the territories defined as being of Sandhi Penu and Soru Penu alter following the construction of the settlement. In practical terms, the comparatively level ground makes the *sandhi* a suitable area for kitchen gardens. The *sandhi* and the *nellang* are the respective domains of Sandhi Penu and Soru Penu, while Keri Penu is common in both these areas. Sandhi Penu's authority is limited to the area within the boundary, while Soru Penu's authority also covers territory outside the boundary. However, both are claimed to protect the village inhabitants.

Though the Kuttia Kondh build their settlements at the foot of hills, the base of the hill (*soru panga*)[2] is sometimes not included in the village boundary. Thus, a large space exists between the village boundary and the base of the hill.

The upper reaches of the village slope (*baru*) lead to an area known as the *nellang*, while the opposite end of the *baru* descends to the low lands or *morang* where springs and streams can be found. The forest type known as *bati* grows in the *morang* and looks particularly verdant due to the constant availability of water. The *morang* comes under the domination of Eju Penu *or* Gangi Penu, the water god. Eju Penu and Gangi Penu are often used synonymously, although Eju Penu tends to be associated with small, still pools and ditches whereas Gangi Penu is the deity of perennial water sources such as springs and rivers. The area between the *morang* and *naju* is used for rice cultivation because the crop can be easily irrigated. Thus, the village — *naju*, the path — *danda* and water source — *morang* are contained within the perimeter of the *sandhi*. The *baru* is the living space between the hills and water ghats, and separates swidden plots and non-swidden plots in the *nellang*, on the one hand, from rice fields, on the other hand.

The Kuttia Kondh change swidden plots once to twice a year, clearing new patches of hill forest for cultivation. They endeavour to create new swidden plots in the proximity of their settlement thus saving time and making better use of labour. However, if the soil

2. The term *soru panga* is not often used by the Kuttia Kondh to describe the location of the village settlement in relation to the hills; they prefer to use the term *nella* or *nellang* (the cultivated fields in the *soru nede* hill area) as a frame of reference because the village settlement is constructed in the middle of a line extending from *nellang* to *morang*.

fertility of nearby land is exhausted, the tribe is forced to seek land further afield. When cultivating areas at some distance from the village, people live in temporary settlements for the duration of the harvest, returning to their permanent settlements once the harvest is over. The Kuttias purchase any available land suitable for the conversion into rice paddy. Thus, paddy lands never have a specific location in relation to the settlements.

Next to the *morang* is the *batang*, the outermost part of the village settlement. The *batang* does not have an obvious practical or ecological function like *sandhi, nellang and morang.* In its physical aspect, it is sometimes understood to mean the same as *baru*. But *batang* is the space at the hill slope where the settlement is located. The settlement is built on *wango;* thus *batang* is associated with *Wango penu* (otherwise known as Dharani Penu), the earth goddess who is the authority of the land on which the settlement stands. Because *batang* is located at the base of a hill, it is also associated with Soru Penu, a hill deity who safeguards the wellbeing of the villagers.

Most villages plant an auspicious tree such as a jackfruit (*Artocarpus sp.*) or *salap* (*Caryota urens*), at the entrance of the village. Other villages erect a post (*munda*) to signify the presence of Kamatali Penu.

The *badang* is the area at the back of the houses where the livestock sheds are located. Every house and *badang* is watched over by Wanga Penu and the home deity Elu Penu. Since the *badang* comes under the reign of the home deity, it is regarded as part of the house. *Elu* and *badang* are spaces for human beings and domestic animals. A path known as *badagiri* links the house and adjoining sheds (*badang*) of domestic animals, such as pig and goat, with the cattle shed set further apart. Kitchen gardens take up the remaining space behind the houses. The centre of the village, which is composed of these two straight rows of houses, is separated by a path known as *rachangiri*. The houses in each row resemble one long building, due to the fact that they are all attached to each other, and built to a common height. The floor of the houses lies about one foot below street level.

The division of the houses into two rows separates the villagers into two groups: *majhi* and *jani*. The people with the surname *jani* live in one row and people with the surname *majhi* live in the other row. This is the traditional spatial division of Kuttia Kondh village settlements. It appears that the person who first arrives at the settlement site always prefers to construct his house facing east. Thus, the east facing row is taken by his group. If, for example, he has the surname *jani*, then others who may or may not be relatives of the person but who live in the same row will bear the surname *jani*. Should two families of different surnames arrive at the same time, it is the right of the *majhi*, as the political headman in the Kuttia society, to live in the east-facing row. If a *majhi* allows a *jani* to live in the east-facing row, it is because there is a good personal relationship between them. Generally, the east-facing row is open to either of the two sections on the basis of first come, first served. In Burlubaru village both *majhi* and *jani* currently live in their respective rows.

The fact that the houses are attached does not break the rays of the sun (*weda*) and the whole line of houses is either exposed to the sunlight, or sits in shade. Sunlight falls on one row in the morning and the other row in the afternoon. The midday sun is shared by both rows. The Kuttia Kondh believe in the equal distribution of *weda's* favour to all members of the village. Hence, the rows of houses generally face east and west. Other motives associated with sharing the sun's favour derive from the belief that all houses fall equally under its protective, corrective and sustaining gaze. In addition, the sun serves the more practical purpose of providing each house with a warm space where people can sit and work or dry the grain during the harvesting season.

For social reasons, though, the village settlement can sometimes resemble a cluster of houses rather than two rows. For example, if a son gets married and wants to build his own house, he may prefer to build on the space available at any end of his parent's row, immediately behind his parent's house, or failing this, in the other row. When none of these options is possible he may opt to build a separate house in a space behind the houses normally occupied by livestock buildings, which gives a random clustered appearance to the original settlement layout. However, as this practice breaks with the traditional settlement pattern, it is not encouraged by the villagers. The son builds a house behind his parent's home mainly to facilitate a discreet exchange of goods and materials with other members of the household.

In addition to the village houses, two dormitories (*karmbara*) for the younger children are situated at one end of the village: the boy's dormitory is known as a *ladska kuda* and the girl's dormitory is *ladvanga kuda*.

A non-tribal family, usually from the local Pano community, resides in most of the Kuttia Kondh villages. The family members work as cow-herders for the Kuttia Kondh in return for raw or cooked food. Their houses are situated on the upper slopes of the village, while the community recreation house and youth dormitories, if present, are located at the opposite end.

An area at the bottom of the slope outside the village is used for the disposal of rubbish and household waste. The villagers dig compost pits (*kabda*) to deposit the solid and organic waste of the livestock. Wells and tubewells are found at the top of the slope in the upper part of the village settlement.

The *dharani* stones symbolising Dharani Penu, and a *karumunda* pole, used for sacrifices at certain festivals, are set up in the centre of the village on a path separating the two rows of houses known as *rachangiri*. Once placed there, the *karumunda* cannot be moved, with the result that, as new houses are added, the *dharani* stones and *karumunda* seldom remain at the village centre.

If the *rachangiri*, also known as *danda*, that divides the settlement into two halves is narrow, it will join a wider road (*danduta*) at the end of the village. The *rachangiri* is the path that links the upper slope of the *baru* with the lower slopes, sometimes leading from the *nella* through the *sandhi* to the *morang*. Keri Penu is identified as the spiritual "authority" of the path, and thus, the partial authority of the *nellang* and *sandhi*. The term *giri* is used for very narrow paths or passageways, *rachangiri* for the wider path separating two rows of houses, and *danduta* for the road outside the village.[3]

The danduta (also sometimes referred to as *danda*) denotes a wide road. It links two living spaces, such as two village settlements, or a village settlement with forested hills, two areas of forested hills, or a village settlement with the market. *Giri* is a path inside a village settlement, a forest or a narrow path on the hills. The term *rachangiri* literally means "royal path". In the past the path was much wider than it is today. Now, a path must have a width of between 4 to 6 feet to be called a *rachangiri*. If the width is less than 4 feet, it is called *danda*.

Preconditions for a Settlement

The Kuttia Kondh's ecological, social and religious understandings of space influence the criteria that must be taken into consideration when determining the location of a village settlement. Geographical features are assessed as regards their practicality since the area must be able to fulfil the basic needs of the people. The Kuttia Kondh prefer positioning of a settlement at the foot of a hill, so avoiding hilltops as these areas lack a perennial water supply and are situated at too great a distance from the water supply available in the lowlands (*morang*). Dense forest is also considered unsafe as a settlement site due to the threat posed by dangerous animals. Generally, therefore, the slope at the hill base (*baru)* above the *morang* is the preferred location for a settlement. The *baru* must be a reasonably level area with little or no vegetation. Dense vegetation would require greater labour input when clearing the patch to make a village settlement. The proximity of the *soru nede* and the *morang* should be similar and the site large enough for the *rachangiri* and *batangiri.* Thus, the selection of an appropriate site for a village requires the careful consideration of the location of the hills, forests and water sources in relation to the site. Other important factors include the area's potential to provide *sandhi, nellang, danda, rachangiri, morang, batang*

3. In the village there are often several menstrual huts (*jaka kuda*) in the outermost part of the *badang* for common use. Many women enjoy using these despite having one in their own house compound. A vacant *jaka kuda* is sometimes used to house livestock.

and *badang*, and sufficient space to allow a certain amount of expansion.

Parts of the settlement's geography are associated with certain deities. It is evident that certain gods are associated with the environmental landscape, for example, the lowland areas, hill peaks and forests etc., and are also connected with manmade geographical features such as the settlement, i.e. *badang, nellang, morang*. Many of the deities are named after the territory they inhabit, e.g., the deity of the village border *(sandhi)* is called Sandhi Penu. These lesser deities are associated with particular features of settlement geography, but are nevertheless connected with Dharani Penu and Soru Penu, because the settlement is located in their domains. Dharani Penu, goddess of the earth, whose influence is all-embracing, is also associated with this manmade geography that forms part of her territory. When a site is chosen for a settlement, permission is sought from Dharani Penu and Soru Penu, the god of the hill that will become the location of the new settlement, and the god seen as guardian of the village inhabitants. Dharani Penu and Soru Penu influence the Kuttia Kondh's selection or rejection of a new settlement site. A site is abandoned, if the Kuttia believe that the *penuni* are unhappy with their choice.

Religious Sanctioning of a New Settlement Site

When a new settlement site has been selected largely on the basis of practical and physical criteria, ultimately the decision requires religious sanction by the *penuni*. Before settling at the chosen location, the Kuttia Kondh seek the permission of Soru Penu, Wango Penu, Dharani Penu, Keri Penu, Gangi Penu, Satari Penu and Deukuda Penu in order to protect the village from misfortune. Once the settlement site has been decided on, a *kutaka* carries some *kueri* (little millet — *Panicum miliare*) and *pranga* — rice grain, in a *sechi* (winnowing fan) to the base of the hill nearest to the proposed location and prays to the *penuni*, invoking them to the site of worship. When the grains on the *sechi* shake, it is believed that the *penu*ni have arrived. The *penu* enters the body of the *kutaka* who, once possessed, speaks on behalf of the gods. Using the *kutaka* as a medium, the people are able to communicate with the gods and put forward their case for building a settlement on site selected by them. If the god agrees, he allows them to settle there. However, if the *penu* feels that the proposed settlement site has disadvantages, he deters the people from settling there. The disadvantages of a site are likely to be water scarcity, the prevalence of illness, too easy access of carnivorous beasts etc. Thus, the *penuni's* final judgement is intimated to the people via the *kutaka*.

Before building a new settlement, the *penuni* demand the sacrifice of a pig and/or buffalo. Once the gods have given their approval via the *kutaka*, the people arrange a Dharani Penu *puja*. The *jani* (village priest) is responsible for worshipping Dharani Penu. He orders people to search for the *dharani vali* (a line of three stones representing Dharani Penu) that may be on or close to the site, but if there are none nearby, they can be brought from abandoned villages. The *dharani* stones are brought to the proposed settlement site and placed in the middle of the *baru*. The *dharani* stones play an important role in the *Meriah* festival, as the *Meriah puja* is conducted at the location of the *dharani* stones. The stones are placed beneath a hood-like larger stone called *jakel arenja vali*, meaning 'thunder and lightning stone', which is said to protect the *dharani* stones. Once the *dharani* stones have been placed, people go to search a *sal* pole, known as *karumunda* (*karu* meaning "buffalo" and *munda* meaning "pole"), which is placed next to the *dharani vali*. A buffalo is tied to the pole to be sacrificed during the Meriah festival. The pole to be used as *karumunda* is selected in a particular way[4] and engraved and decorated before it is placed next to the *dharani vali*. The *sapangada vali,* which symbolises their place of origin, is another stone used to establish a new site. If it cannot be found close to the site, it is brought from Sapangada. When this has been done, the most important preparations for selecting a settlement site are complete.

Size of Settlement

The size of the settlement depends upon the amount of space available, the potential of that space and the availability of resources. It can

---

4. See the chapter on "Socio-cultural aspects of plants, animals and humans" in this book.

vary from one or two households to as many as eighty or ninety households. After the selection of an appropriate settlement site, one or two families relocate and, over time, if there is sufficient space and it is deemed suitable, people from other villages will follow. In this way, the village settlement continues to expand.

Research work in the Belghar area in 1992-93 showed that villages ranged from about eight to ten households to seventy or eighty. Rangaparu is the largest settlement in the area in terms of the number of households, and is now known by two names, one referring to the original village ("old Rangaparu") and the other, to a more recent settlement nearby ("new Rangaparu"). A population increase in the original village encouraged people to find a new settlement close to the old one. Smaller settlements such as the villages of Guchka and Gulampanga, comprising only eight to ten households, have been established comparatively recently.

Change of Settlement

The Kuttia Kondh may change the location of their settlements for a number of reasons, one of which is overcrowding. Population increase means a directly proportional decrease in living space, a factor that encourages people to look for a new settlement. If the inter-family relationships in the village are very good, the whole village may leave the old settlement for a new one. If some members of the old village are not interested in moving, some families or households may look for a new settlement, preferably near the old one. A change of settlement may also depend upon the availability of area for conversion into swidden plots. As the population increases, the land-man-ratio declines and so does the village's socio-economic status. The search for more cultivable land, therefore, is a significant motive for a change of settlement. The availability of drinking water is also taken into consideration.

The third and most important reason for a change in settlement site is the feeling that the village is linked with inauspicious events such as the outbreak of a serious epidemic. Epidemics and disease in general are attributed to the wrath of gods and goddesses. When such inauspicious events occur that threaten a village, the inhabitants feel that the wrath or "evil eye" of the deities may well be a problem later on.

Home, Habitat and the Placement of Deities

The Kuttia Kondh believe that their environment harbours a host of spiritual beings that have the capacity to be both benevolent and malevolent and while the deities are usually benevolent, if they are ill-treated and neglected, people say that they may suffer misfortune. The Kuttia Kondh feel that the presence of deities in and around their houses, village and beyond, provides them with the physical and psychological qualities needed to live in the settlement. Faith in their gods greatly influences the lives of the Kuttia and is the source of the principles shaping their way of life. The tribe's belief in its religion and in the benevolence and wrath of the deities has ensured the continuation of its traditional lifestyle.

Emotional bonds exist between people and their homes. The home is the centre of family life and it is believed that the home itself is a god or goddess. "*elu*" is the Kui word for house, and "*eja*" for home. The home deity, Elu Penu, is therefore regarded as the family deity who protects family members from disease and danger and wards off evil spirits. There are specific places inside a house meant for gods and goddesses. The Elu Penu is represented either by a single wooden post or by three wooden posts made from *sal,* each simply decorated with carved rings. The post(s) is/are placed in the corner of a room, or in front of the house.

As mentioned earlier, in the middle of the village on the *rachangiri*, stands the wooden post known as *karumunda,* while beneath it are the three stones representing Dharani Penu, the most important of the deities that make up the Kuttia Kondh's religious pantheon. He commands a great deal of respect. The Dharani Penu has the power to counteract misfortunes caused by evil spirits in the village but it is the Goddess who is worshipped at the Meriah festival, the most significant occasion in their festival calendar. It is held every three or four years, depending on the village's level of prosperity and all village rituals are performed at the site of Dharani Penu.

Deu Kuda Penu and Satari Penu are positioned either together or separately in small thatched huts made for them beneath a large tree, such as *baena* (*Terminalia belerica*), *pipada* (*Ficus scandens*), *sal* (*Shorea robusta*), *jambu* (*Syzigium cuminii*), or *maska* (*Mangifera indica*) at the entrance of the village. These deities safeguard the welfare of the villagers and the village settlement by warding off evil spirits and in particular the spirits responsible for epidemics. The deities are represented by two *sal* posts placed together, one of about three feet in height, and the other of a size of two feet. Both have the same design as the post representing Elu Penu.

Sandhi Penu is the deity associated with the village boundary and generally represented by a stone positioned under a large tree, preferably under a *jambu mara* (*Syzigium cuminii*) or a *maska mara* (*Mangifera indica*). However, in Burlubaru village, Sandhi Penu is placed under a *made mara* (*Lannea coromandelica*) as there is no large tree of the preferred species growing on the village border. It is generally considered inauspicious to position the Sandhi Penu beneath the *nelingi mara* (*Tamarindus indica*).

Kamati or Kamatali Penu, Manali Penu, and Mardi Penu are three malevolent sister deities feared by the Kuttia Kondh. They are believed to cause pox, stomach diseases, and blood vomiting. Because the deities are known to dwell in *banyan* trees (*Ficus benghalensis*), the tribe worships beneath a *banyan*, if there is one close to the village settlement. However, the deities are not represented in any material form nor are they established anywhere in the village itself.

The hill above the location of a settlement is particularly revered and the focus of frequent acts of worship. The Kuttia Kondh maintain that the surrounding hills protect them from environmental hazards and dangerous animals, guard their swidden crops and watch over the people guarding these crops. Consequently, they establish the abode of the hill god at the foot of the hill, in the form of a stone or stones.

In addition to the gods worshipped in and around the village, certain iron implements and artefacts, associated with the Dharani Penu, are also worshipped in the priest's house. Such implements and artefacts were used in the past when human sacrifice was practised by the Kuttia Kondh. These objects are also worshipped at the *Meriah* festival. The Kuttia Kondh fear that Dharani Penu will harm the people, if these are not worshipped regularly.

House Patterns

The traditional houses[5] of the Kuttia Kondh are built in two parallel rows and are separated from one another by earthen walls. Generally, a mud wall is built to separate one joint family[6] from another, or houses are separated by partitioning made of bamboo matting known as *tati*. This is more usual when a son separates from his parent's house or constructs another house adjacent to his parents' main house. The youngest son remains with his parents and inherits their house when they die.

The houses are usually divided into three main parts (*fig.* 2a). At the front of the house is the verandah known as the *sui kuda*, which is sometimes divided into a sitting area on one side and a small room on the other. This room, while not universally present, is used by family guests or youth when there is a lack of space in the dormitories, or as a place to keep pigs and goats. The floor of the middle rooms connected to the verandah lies at a lower level and is known as *kutti*. The middle part of the house where most of the household activities take place is known as the *ada eja* (*ada* literally means goat), and is further divided into the *eja kuda* and the *saka kuda*. The *eja kuda,* or interior part of the middle room, has a kitchen area (*vaja naja*) and a hearth. All the members of the household usually sleep in the *saka kuda* with the men on cots and the women on the floor. The *eja kuda* and the *saka kuda* remain in darkness even during the day. The only source of daylight is the front door, and the crack between the wall and the roof, beneath the overhanging leaves.

---

5. Although in some Kuttia Kondh villages people have constructed houses differing from the traditional pattern, the Kuttia Kondh tend to adhere to the traditional design in which the management of space is the same in every house.
6. "Joint family" in this context refers to the nuclear family units of the sons of the same mother.

The main door of the house lies just opposite the entrance to the verandah and leads into the *saka kuda*, which also has a back door. Above the kitchen is the loft (*sicheni*) where the Kuttia Kondh dry grain, pulses and surplus meat, and where foodstuffs and household utensils are stored. The *sicheni* leads to a bigger loft (*papi)* where grain is stored in large bamboo containers (*burlanga*) and all the other agricultural produce of the house is kept. In the middle of the sleeping area (*saka kuda*) is the rice-pounding hole, called *seni,* used to separate rice and other grains from their husks.

House Construction

The ground on which the house is to be built is levelled and a wooden frame constructed by inserting vertical wooden poles (known as *dedhi,* pl. *dedhinga*), (usually made from *sal*) into eight holes in the ground (*fig.* 2b). Horizontal beams *(aru)* are then placed on the vertical poles to form the basic pitch-roof structure. The eight vertical poles *(dedhi)* used to construct the basic framework of the house, are named after the particular horizontal beams that are placed on them, i.e., the vertical poles that support the topmost horizontal roof beam (*nechuri aru*) are known as *nechuri dedhi.* A four-sided house has eight vertical poles that support sixteen horizontal beams. On the four sets of horizontal beams, many slender poles known as *kanda,* are placed at right angles over the horizontal beams, and the roof is then tiled or thatched with straw (*fig.* 2c). The vertical poles that form the doorframe of the house are known as *dara,* while the poles that make the window frames are called *jharaka dara*, even though it is unusual to find windows in Kuttia houses.

The act of placing the poles into the holes is known as *musana* and placing the beams on the poles as *dasana*. Three different methods are used to build the walls of the house:

1. The walls are constructed with wooden stakes (*munda*) and the space between them filled with mud to form a smooth surface. The poles are usually made of *sal* (*sargi mara, Shorea robusta*), of *chara* (*sreka mara, Buchanania lanzan*), or *tangan* (*dengen mara, Xylia xylocarpa*). If these species

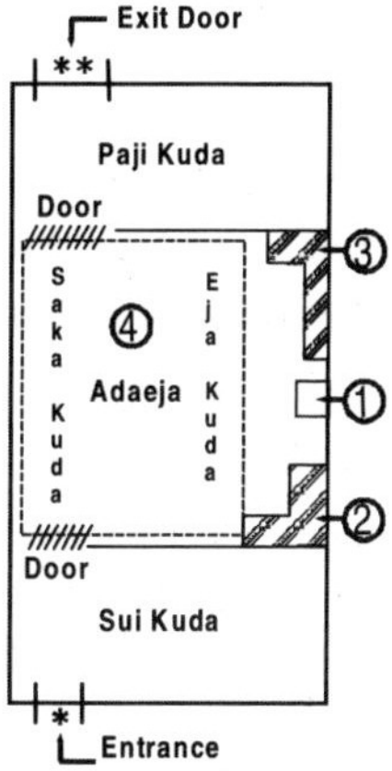

Figure -2(a) : Ground Plan of a Kuttia Kondh house

Vajan Eja:
① Hearth
② Place for eating vessels, utensils, water pots
③ Place for stored food materials

④ Pounding hole

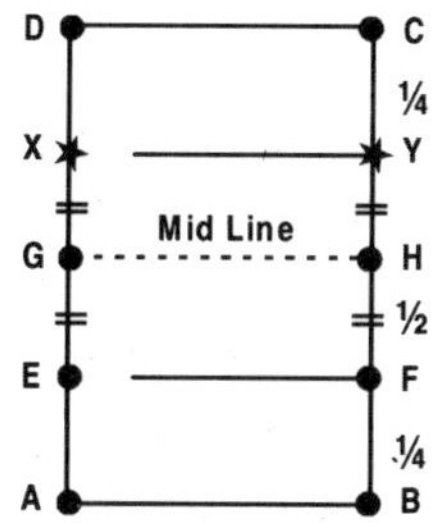

INDEX

●✶ Location of Poles

ABCDEFGHXY : Poles

Figure -2(b) : Location of poles

Poles A & B are of equal size

Poles C & D are of equal size but smaller than A or B

Poles E & F are of equal size but bigger than A or B

Poles G & H are of equal size and bigger than E or F

Poles X & Y are equal in size and correspond to the size of E & F. in some houses poles X & Y are planted

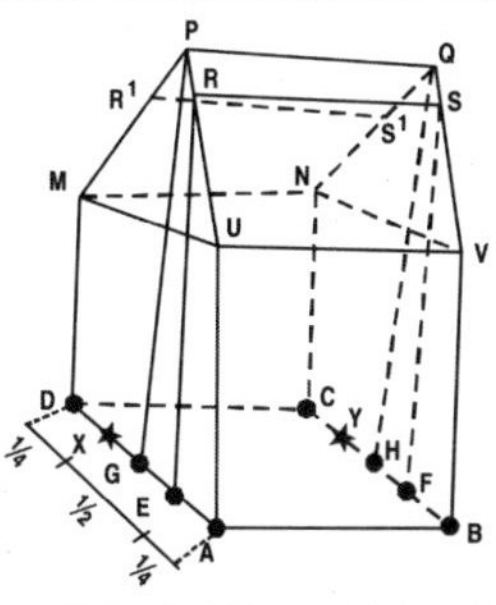

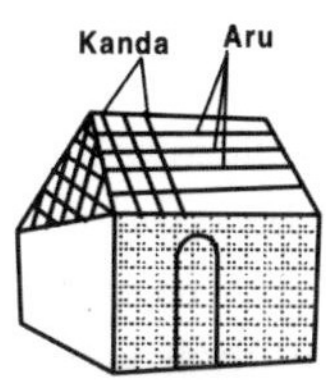

Figure -2(c) : Four sides of a house with roof

Poles G & H are called Nechuri Dedhi (Pole) as they connect P & Q called Nechuri Aru (Beam)

Poles E & F are called Aritachandi Dedhi as they connect R & S called Aritachandi Aru

Poles A & B are called Sui Dedhi as they connect U & V called Sui Aru

Poles C & D are called Saka Dedhi as they connect M & N called Saka Aru

Poles X & Y, if placed are called Aritachandi Dedhi as they connect Aritachandi Aru R^1 & S^1 on the backside of the house. If X & Y are not planted then the beam R^1 & S^1 not used.

The floor plan AE : EX : XD = BF : FY : YC = ¼ : ½ : ¼

Figure - 2: Diagram of a house

are rare or not available in the area, other tree species will be used.

2. Bamboo matting *(tati)* is fastened onto the vertical wooden beams (*dedhis*) and covered with a layer of mud. However, these walls are susceptible to damage and decay and rarely last more than three years.

3. The third method is to build houses of mud. The mud is mixed with water, kneaded and made into small blocks that are placed on top of one another. The blocks are then plastered with mud and smoothened by hand. Further plastering is applied over the cracks that appear in the mud walls when they dry. This is done with a mud and cow-dung mixture that prevents the walls from cracking.

In the past, the roofs of the houses were usually thatched with a forest grass known in *Kui* as *vika* (*sabai ghasa* (*Eulaliopsis binata*) in Oriya). More recently, due to the scarcity of that grass, alternative materials, such as *chhana* (*Themda arundinacea*), a grass also available in the forest, and roofing tiles *(khapari)* have been used. The latter are particularly favoured by the Kuttia Kondh, since a tiled roof is a sign that the occupants are comparatively prosperous. The tiles are made from baked mud and are long-lasting in contrast to *chhana* thatching which only lasts for about one year. In the past, the Kuttia Kondh would purchase the *khapari* from the Panos, but have learnt in the meantime how to make the tiles themselves.[7] Should the Kuttia Kondh change their settlement, these tiles are removed from the houses and reused at the new settlement site.

The houses are kept clean by the female members of the household who regularly smear mud and cowdung on the floor and walls. The houses are decorated with designs drawn on the wet mud and many houses are covered with a black mud (composed largely of

---

7. They take a solid cylindrical shaped piece of wood and cover it by a thin layer of kneaded mud, having first covered the wood with dry ash so that the mud does not actually stick to it. When the wood is removed, a hollow cylinder of mud is formed, which is cut along its length into two equal halves and burnt, producing new tiles.

graphite) called *surma,* up to about one foot above the floor. The rest of the walls are polished with a red coloured mud known as *kambit vira,* and the doorframes are frequently decorated with a variety of designs painted in bright colours.

The Death of a House

A house *(elu)* belonging to a Kuttia Kondh is accorded the same respect as a member of their society. Before settling in a place, various rituals are performed to seek the permission of the gods and goddesses present there, as discussed earlier in relation to the settlement pattern. In the past, when just one or two families were the founders of a new settlement, there was no need to perform an act of worship before building a house. Families abandoned a settlement in search of more land and areas for cultivation, and were, over time, joined by others. But more recently, when a new settlement is established, most of the families of one settlement have migrated there and perform acts of worship requesting the god's permission to settle in a new place.

When a house is destroyed by fire, death rites (*dadi*) similar to those that would be performed for humans are carried out in honour of the house. Whereas the death rites for a human being are performed three days after death, rituals for a house are performed after six days. The seventh day is called the *sata dinata dadi* and is the most important day of the entire death ritual, since, then at least one representative from each family in the village will gather at the 'dead house' to express his/her sympathies to the owner. A discussion takes place headed by the *majhi,* during which people ask the house owner about the cause of the fire. Although the cause is known to all, such a discussion is a formality on the *sata dinata dadi.*

The death rites for a house are performed by all the families in the village. They wash their clothes, smear their own houses with cow dung and mud and burn charcoal and dust resin, the smoke of which fills the houses and drives out the evil spirits. The villagers then help the family whose house has been destroyed to build a new one at the same site or elsewhere while the family's relatives help them with food materials.

6

Sacred Geography of Hills and Forests

THE following chapter describes the Kuttia Kondh living space and how it is shaped by their tribal myths. The hills and forests surrounding their settlement area play a particularly important role in their culture. This chapter will examine village settlements in terms of their location, and the structure of the houses and villages in relation to the landscape.

Mythical Origin of Hills and Forest

According to their cosmological myth, *Kui Gaani,* mankind first appeared on earth from a hole in the ground known as Sapangada or originated from various plants, animals or inanimate objects (see sub-chapter on the origin of clans). The term is an amalgamation of two words: *saponi* meaning "to be given birth" and *gada* meaning "hole", i.e., the hole from which the Kuttia Kondh originated. Following the Kuttia Kondh's arrival on earth, Nerandali, the supreme goddess, thought it necessary to shape the barren and uneven landscape. She asked *Rangan tali* and *Paber tali* (two female mythological figures) to level the earth using a stone. When Nerandali inspected the newly levelled earth, she encountered a white ant or termite hill that inspired her to beautify the earth by creating hills and mountains. The task was completed in two stages: first, through the creation of large hills (*manang)* and then small hillocks (*mooting).*

Manang

Nerandali gave Manang tali (Mother Manang) the responsibility of creating the large hills. To complete the task, Manang tali had to make a *manang* (a bamboo implement used for measuring amounts of grain, etc.). Taking a *manang* full of earth, Manang tali threw it at

Sapangada, so creating the Sapangada hill. Nerandali ordered the Sapangada hill to grow. Manang tali then circled Sapangada, starting at Sapangada east and moving over the earth, so creating the hills known as Ranipalu, Bendipalu, Usarena, Bearena, Tendabedi, Sababedi, Piju Bangeri, Bidi Bangeri, Sunasella, and Rupa Sella among others. When she finally returned to Sapangada, the creation of the large hills was complete.[1]

Mooting

Nerandali was not satisfied with the presence of only large hills around Sapangada. She felt that the earth would be more beautiful if there were some smaller hills, whereupon she began "operation *mooting*". Operation *mooting* followed the same route taken by operation *manang,* moving in a clockwise direction from Sapangada. As Nerandali threw down soil, the entire landscape was transformed into hills. The smaller hills sprang up beside the large hills, around the mountains of Sapangada in the east, Dumbuli in the south, Siram Deu in the west, and Hati Salla in the northern corner of Sapangada.[2]

The Kuttia Kondh consider the mountains and hills referred to in "operations *manang* and *mooting*"[3] to be their territory. These hills lie primarily in the district of Phulbani, while a few can be found in the districts of Koraput and Kalahandi. The Kuttia Kondh believe that after the mythical creation of these hills, their ancestors spread out over the landscape of the territory still inhabited by them today, first forming small groups and then cultivating the land and clearing patches of forest. They claim to have been the first to emerge from the underground darkness and settle close to the Sapangada, while others moved further afield. This myth of origin describes their earliest living space as a flat land circumscribed by forested hills. The Kuttia Kondh settled on the lower slopes between two adjoining hills.

The location referred to as Sapangada has expanded over time to include more of the landscape around the hole. Today, Sapangada

1. See the Appendix for the list of other large hills in the locality said to have been made by the *manang*.
2. See the Appendix for a list of the smaller hills.
3. Only the most significant hills have been mentioned here; the majority are listed in the Appendix.

is a forested and hilly region in the Guma panchayat near the Kuttia Kondh village, Kranja (approx. 8 km from Burlubaru). The site associated with the creation myth is of considerable religious importance to the Kuttia Kondh, whose beliefs ensure that the area remains protected. The hills surrounding Sapangada also possess a spiritual significance as they are deemed to be the domain of the Soru Penuni — the hill gods.

The hills are often named after their physical characteristics and appearance, or after certain dominant tree species found in the area;[4] a name may also refer to a myth or event (often recalled on social occasions) in which the hill played a part, or relate to a description of the first Kuttia Kondh settlement. The Kuttia Kondh link the hills with their social pattern and livelihood and refer to the hills as the mythical centrepoint of their culture. A hill is also appraised on the basis of its more practical assets such as type of vegetation and general productivity, i.e., the collection of minor forest produce and yield from shifting cultivation. In this way, the various hills suggest a variety of associations to the Kuttia Kondh as reflected in their religious, social, aesthetic and ecological views. Furthermore, the people's actions are influenced by their perception of the environment, demonstrated by the fact, for instance, that the Kuttia Kondh only cultivate those hills that they do not hold sacred.

The Kuttia Kondh's Perception of Hills and Forest

The Kuttia Kondh's denomination of hills can help to provide an insight into their understanding of the landscape. They use a variety of terms to distinguish between the different parts of a hill (*fig.* 3).

A hill, *soru* in the Kui language, can be divided into four parts; the topmost level, or peak, is *soru jaka or gati jaka*, depending on the size of the hill; *gati jaka* refers to the peak of large hills, and *soru jaka* to that of smaller ones. The upper middle level is *soru tude*, the lower middle level is *soru nede,* and the base is *soru panga*.

---

4. A list of hills named according to the availability of different flora is contained in the Appendix.

HILLS AND GODS

The type of natural vegetation growing on hilltops has a particular significance to the Kuttia Kondh. They regard their hill god (Soru Penu) as solely responsible for the distribution of such vegetation. They believe that the god of the forest decides on the type of tree species that grows at a locality and claim that he favours growing tall trees on a hilltop. That is his abode because it provides an excellent vantage point for observing the villagers living at the foot of the hill. Furthermore, from there, he can also enjoy the first touch of the

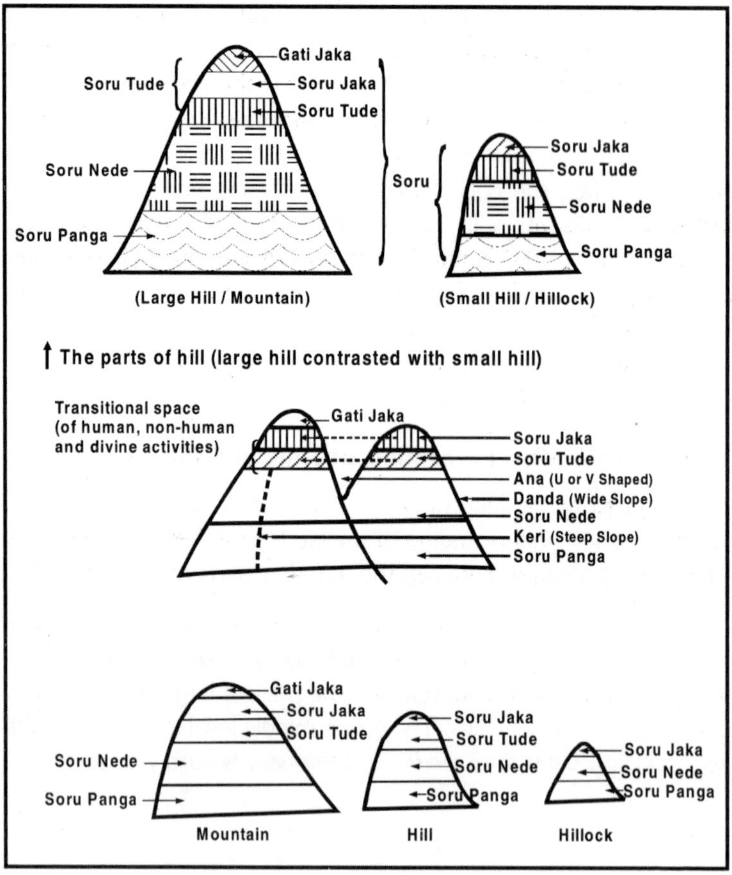

Figure -3 : The various parts of a hill / mountain

virgin rain. He uses a network of tree creepers to move from place to place inside the forest, to meet the other *penus* and discuss the welfare of the tribal people. He also allows the growth of the grass at the base of the trees to make the forest floor softer so that divine beings can roam around freely.

Talabega Penu

Talabega is a small hill whose name literally means "undressed hair". It is worshipped by the Kuttia Kondh for the welfare of human beings, cattle, crops, etc., and when an unkempt, naked man with uncombed hair appears in a dream and demands worship, he is called *Talabega Penu*.

Murlivali Penu

Murlivali is a small hill near Kdukingi, which resembles a pile of small stones. Its *penu* appears in dreams as a man carrying an axe.

Bichabari Penu

Bichabari literally means distribution of crop seed (*bicha* — seeds). It is also the name of a small hill near Sapangada. It is believed that when the Kuttia came out of Sapangada, the Sapangada Penu requested the Bichabari Penu to distribute the seed evenly among the people. The god sat on the Sunasella and seeds were placed on the Bichabari hill for distribution. In dreams, the Bichabari Penu is seen as a woman carrying the different types of seeds in a vessel.

Gunangi Penu

Gunangi is another small hill, whose *penu* is represented by a man with a knot of hair on the back of his head like a woman.

Kitangi Penu

Dera Dueri (large door) is another hill situated near the Hati Salla hill near Golam Panga where there is a large cave. Kitangi is a small hill near Dera Dueri, whose *penu* appears in dreams as a man with a knife enclosed in his hair knot (*kila*).

Dhumamaska and Nisipidi

Dhumamaska and Nisipidi are two small hills lying next to each other. Their *penu* is represented by a man carrying a flute in intertwined hands.

Raji Dandra Penu

Raji Dandra is a large hill with a sharp edged top. The literal meaning of the word is "grand road used by the king". Sometimes the hill is referred to as *penudandra* and there is a large space on this hill where the god sits during a meeting. In dreams, the *penu* takes the shape of a woman wearing a *kagda,* i.e., a ring of silver or aluminium worn around the neck.

Padekanda Penu

Padekanda is a small hill near Ambadola. *Pade* means "small pig" and *kanda* means "sword". There is a story behind this name of the hill. Once, while hunting, the men tried to kill a pig by piercing its stomach with a sword. However, the pig immediately turned into a stone with the sword inside its stomach. Consequently, the pig is found on this hill in the form of a stone and in dreams, this hill god appears in dreams as a man holding a sword with vermillion marks on the tip.

Daramaru, Tundabata & Pusarani Penu

Daramaru, Tundabata and Pusarani are three hills near Bikapanga. Daramaru Penu is represented by a man carrying an open lamp kept on a stand. Tundabata literally means a closed road *(tunda* — close, bata — *road*) and its *penu* appears as a man with a *kapoli* (hair knot) on his head while Pusarani Penu appears in dreams as a red-eyed woman.

Widiokadi Penu

Widiokadi is a part of Dalangbata hill situated near the village Garanga. Literally, the name means expiration of air (*widi*-air; *okadi*-expiration) and the *penu* of this hill is represented by a strong wind.

Bade Gati Penu & Maunli Penu

Bade Gati is a small hill near Garanga. At one time the whole place was covered with *bade* mara (banyan trees) and Maunli Penu resides in one. In dreams, a lady carrying a banyan tree in her hand is a symbol of the Bade Gati Penu.

Sonadueri, Pudrung & Donade Penu

Sonadueri literally means "the golden door" and is near Kotadi in Kalahandi district. Its *penu* is represented by a hen even though the tribe considers the *penu* to be a cock. A hill called Pudrung near Sonadueri is the abode of a *penu* represented by a pigeon. Donade in the same region appears as a cat.

Kamei Penu

Kamei, a small hill near *Batipada*, literally means buffalo horn. A stone in the shape of a buffalo horn is found there and the *penu* of this hill is symbolised in dreams by a man blowing a buffalo horn.

Kandabada & Bakabada Penu

Kandabada-Bakabada is a large hill near Mauna giri. Kandabada literally means both "sharp fence" and "curved fence", and is a bamboo forest. According to the myth, the *penu* here gave shelter to bamboo when it was driven away by Nerandali, and today the bamboo is still abundant. The *penu* is seen to be a man carrying a sword in his hand and since bamboo has an important role in many tribal rituals, Kandabada, the *penu* of the place where the bamboo grows, is highly respected.

Senduroti Penu

Senduroti, meaning "partition of the paddy field", is a small hill near Dumbuli mountain. Its *penu* appears as a man with red, black and white lines on his forehead and people of Sirki worship the hill as the village god. The Kuttia believe that the gods used to cultivate paddy there and its *penu* has the shape of a bird.

Adagadi Penu

Adagadi is a small hill situated near Batipada. The literal meaning of the name is "waterfall" (*ada* — "water", gadi — "fall") and the *penu* is represented by a snake.

Sikadi Bandha Penu

Sikadi Bandha, a hill near Kumudi, derives its name from an iron chain that can still be seen there. It is believed that this *penu* is always present on the hill and their belief is re-inforced by the fact that people find it difficult to sleep soundly there.

Jindangi Penu

Jindangi is a large hill situated near Kumudi. The name literally means "a passage/canal for water" and is associated with a story that with the help of four brothers named Bisa, Kudunga, Sanger and Monger, the gods cut open a large stone (a part of the hill) in order to open up the canal (as proven by an axe mark on the stone.) The water through this canal then drifted into the "Tel" river. The name *jindan* is derived from two words: *jinde anga*, meaning "folded hands" and alludes to the shape of the *jindan* and perhaps as a result, the *penu* is represented in dreams as a woman standing with folded hands.

Sasadanga, Murjikeri and Katamunda Penu

Sasadanga hill is near Rangaparu. The *penu* of this hill is symbolised by a light-coloured man, while the *penu* on Murjikeri hill in the same region appears as a bear. While Katamunda is a straight standing hill at Samboda, in dreams its *penu* appears in the guise of a kutra.

Sechakuriaru Penu

Sechakuriaru hill is situated next to the Madalakura village. The village people worship this hill as the village god and its *penu* is represented in dreams by a deer.

Rupapata Penu

Rupapata hill is regarded as Burlubaru Donger and found adjacent to Siram Deu hill. The *penu* is worshipped as the village god of

Burlubaru. Rupapata is also regarded as the nephew of Siram Deu and its *penu* appears in dreams as a man carrying a brass plate in his hand.

Achanjala and Bamanadeu Penu

Achanjala hill and Bamanadeu hill are the two hills at the far end of Burlubaru village. These two hills are regarded as brothers of Siram Deu. The Achanjala Penu takes the form of a *lambesi* (a large snake-like fish) while Bamanadeu Penu is symbolised in dreams by a man with a very long bunch of hanging hair (*wetinga*).

Soru/Gati Jaka

The *gati jaka* is rarely inhabited by people due to the lack of a perennial water supply and therefore, the tops of hills are generally left to the gods as their dwelling places. The Kuttia Kondh believe that the deities are able to overcome obstacles such as lack of water as this can be brought to the tops of the hills by their servants. Moreover, from their hill top domains, the gods are able to observe the lives of the people in the villages below. As a result of minimal human or animal interference on the *soru jaka* or *gati jaka*, a large number of mature trees, particularly timber species, such as *sal* (*Shorea robusta*) grow there along with other vegetation. The trees, growing to a common height, form a canopy known as *kambani,* or *soru jaka kambani* (hilltop forest).

Other hills of particular religious significance are those with hill top plateaux, generally devoid of vegetation with the occasional exception of a grass species called *chhana* (*Themda arundinacea*) used for thatching.

A barren plateau on the top of a large hill is known as *soru jaka agari*. The term *agari* means "virgin land" while a plateau covered with some vegetation, such as a few groups of trees or bushes, is known as *soru jaka bata*. Both terms can be used to define plateaux covered with varieties of grass.

The Kuttia Kondh claim that these barren hilltops are the preferred domain and meeting place of the gods, who assemble here to discuss the welfare of the tribe. Bamana Deu, Hati Salla, and Dumbuli hills feature plateaux and are therefore important in religious terms. Bamana Deu lies to the west of Sapangada, close to Burlubaru village. Hati Salla lies to the south and Dumbuli to the north of the village. Sapangada as the mythical birthplace is the focal point of the tribe's religious activities.

The *gati jaka,* therefore, is the domain of the gods (*penuni*) irrespective of whether they are forested with *kambani* or topped with exposed, barren plateaux (*agari*). The upper hill, *gati*, is important for religious and social reasons and may also be defined as *jaka,* a place from where water falls or flows downwards.[5] The Kuttia Kondh avoid cultivating these areas for fear that this will disturb the deities who might respond by inflicting illness or attacks by wild animals on the people. Cultivation of these hilltops (*gati*) is therefore taboo.

The Kuttia Kondh combine the term *gati* (upper hills) with the word *ana* to form *anagati,* meaning the place where animals move from one hill to another.[6] The terms, *gati* and *ana* are both important as the animals come down from the hills through the *gati* to drink from the rivers, a tactic that makes hunting easy for groups waiting on the *gati* side.

One group of hunters encircles the animals at the *gati* and drives them towards the *ana* where they are captured by a second group. The *ana* is the preferred environment of many of the animals hunted by the Kuttia Kondh and in fact, some of them inhabit the caves known as *salla* (a general term meaning anything from a small hole to a large cave) that can be found there, usually named after the type of animal inhabiting it. The terms, *ana* and *lada* both refer to the area between two hills, *ana* to the meeting point of two hills with steep sides and *lada* to a wider version of the same juncture.

Soru Tude

Soru Tude is the name given to the part of the landscape below Soru Jaka and above *soru nede*. The bottom of *soru jaka* and the upper

5. Interestingly, the term *jaka* also refers to menstruation; the menstrual flow is called *jaka-wate*. Both uses of the word *jaka* demonstrate a similarity in meaning by referring to the flow of liquids.

6. This is described in detail in *Kui Gaani*.

limit of *soru tude* are characterised by dense vegetation usually comprised of shrubs, bushes, many small trees and a few large. If the hill is cultivated, the swidden plots on the *soru nede* make it easy to distinguish the lower limit of the *soru tude*. The swidden plots are prepared by clearing the area of vegetation whereas the *soru tude* is covered with dense vegetation and therefore, the *soru tude* is home to a rich variety of wildlife, valued for its supply of game. However, the presence of wildlife can be a problem when they graze the crops on swidden plots. The *soru tude* is associated with Gangi Penu.

Soru Nede

Soru nede (lower or middle hill) is the area where the Kuttia Kondh practise shifting cultivation by clearing patches of *bati* forest (bushy vegetation), associated with Dharani Penu, the goddess of the earth.

The belief in the relation between the goddess and shifting cultivation dates back to the time when the Kuttia Kondh, while clearing the vegetation, found some *dharani* stones. These, they believed, were placed there by their ancestors, either because they were living there or because they were farming the land. Since then, people have continued to associate Dharani Penu with *nella* (the name they ascribe to the cultivated fields), and the *soru jaka* and *soru panga* areas. Dharani Penu and *nella* are both associated with agriculture and crop production. Other *gods,* such as Keri Penu and Gangi Penu, are also associated with *nella* and crop production, but are regarded as subservient to Dharani Penu.

Soru Panga (Dharani, Wango)

The land at the hill base has three different names: *panga, dharani and wango.* The general term for the base of the hill is *soru panga.* However, when referring to the area where the village settlements are built, it is known as *wango.* This relates to the fact that *panga* means virgin vegetation at the hill base, whereas *wango* refers to a hill base with very little vegetation, the preferred site for the location of the village settlements. As mentioned above, the cultivated fields on the *soru nede* are known as *nella*. Similarly, parts of the *panga* that are cleared for cultivation are also known as *nella*, and may sometimes be referred to as *soru nede*.

Both *panga* and *wango* are linked with Dharani Penu, though the Kuttia Kondh feel that Dharani Penu is particularly associated with *wango*. When three stones (symbolising Dharani Penu) are found at the base of the forest, the base is known as *dharani;* otherwise, it is known as *wango*.

According to one story, the hill base or *wango* was originally covered by a large number of *bengeri mara* trees (*Pterocarpus marsupium*) until they were exploited by humans and destroyed. The area then gradually became a cultivated field. The term *wango* therefore describes an area where *bengeri mara* trees once stood, whereas *dharani wango* denotes a place that over a long period was a site of the *dharani* stones. The *bengeri mara* oozes a liquid resembling blood and there are cases in the ancient history of the *dharani puja* when the tree was used as a sacrifice for the propitiation of Dharani Penu.

Parts of the hill are named according to their shape and size. There are, for example, two types of hill slope: *keri* and *danda*; *keri* refers to the steep, downward slope of the hill forest, while the area referred to as *danda* is larger than that of *keri* and describes the comparatively wider, more gentle slope of the hill-forest. The term *danda* is used to denote the connecting link between the hilltop, the middle of the hill and the hill base, covered by bushy forest, trees and creepers known as *bati*. The Kuttia Kondh claim that the term *keri* represents the region immediately adjacent to the boundary of an area, normally lying alongside the path that leads out of this area or space. The boundary is known as *sandhi* and the path as *danda*.

Jaka, Jaka Gada and Soru Jaka are also the actual names of three hills in three corners of the Kuttia world. These names are often associated with the early village settlements. It is said that when the Kuttia Kondh emerged from Sapangada, they first created settlements in the southern corner of the world. The Jaka hill is situated in the east, and is associated with Mamali Penu, an unmarried male deity. This god only permits married women to frequent the Jaka hill and trespassers risk angering the god. Jaka Gada hill, on the other hand, lies in the west, is covered by dense forest and associated with Soru Penu and Wanga Penu (thought to be the wife of Soru Penu). As with the Jaka hill, access is restricted to married women only.

In the northern corner stands Soru Jaka hill, a very high mountain with average vegetative cover and associated with Kamatali Penu. According to the Kuttia priests, Kamatali Penu, an unmarried female deity, restricts access to the hill in favour of women, irrespective of their marital status. However, the women take care not to use the vegetation in an attempt to avoid the destructive powers of Kamatali Penu. According to the Kuttia Kondh, there was no hill in the southern corner when they emerged from Sapangada. As a result this location was among the first of their village settlements. Nowadays, village settlements are no longer restricted to a particular area in the southern corner as evident by the scattered nature of Kuttia Kondh settlements.

THE HILLS AS REALMS OF THE GODS

Soru Penu — the Hill God

The Kuttia Kondh greatly revere the surrounding hills and forests and regard them as their benign protectors. There are two principal gods associated with the hills: Soru Penu — the general term for a hill god, of whom there are many, and Dharani Penu — the earth goddess. Dharani Penu is considered the more powerful for she is the ruler of the *panga*, the base of the hill on which Soru Penu stands, although she is considered present only if three stones are found on the hill in a row (*dharani vali*). Furthermore, there are numerous Soru Penuni; every hill is the domain of at least one god (Soru Penu) and generally each god is named after the hill on which it resides.[7] Kamei (buffalo horn) hill, for example, is named after a stone of the same shape that can be found there and is the domain of Kamei Penu. Dharani Penu, however, is a unique goddess known only by one name. While each

---

7. Niggemeyer (1964:148) states that while every bigger hill was believed to be the domain of a god, the smaller hills were only associated with a god if they had specific characteristics.

Soru Penu reigns over his individual hill domain, Dharani Penu reigns supreme over all hills and plains.

Soru Penu's importance is directly proportional to the size of the hill, and his nature can be benevolent or malevolent. When Soru Penu is benevolent, he safeguards the crops against wild animals, yet his curse can ruin the tribe. Unlike Dharani Penu (earth goddess) who is worshipped only on specific occasions, the hill gods are worshipped on many religious occasions and are rarely the focus of a particular event. There are a few exceptions to this rule: when a hill is about to be cultivated, the god of that hill must be informed and appeased with a sacrifice; Niggemeyer claims that the ritual should be repeated before the burning of the felled trees (1964:148). If the sacrifice is not performed properly, divine retribution may be exacted, and people may be harmed by falling trees or attacks from wild animals. When the people of a nearby village feel that they may have angered him and that he is responsible for their misfortune, for example, a village epidemic, this is another occasion warranting the propitiation of a particular hill god. Besides the Soru Penu and Dharani Penu, other *penu's* live in the hills and forests. The presence of a certain *penu* is influenced by the physical features of the landscape. For example, Kidi Penu and Gangi Penu are associated with the water sources on hills; Kama Penu, Mardi Penu and Mauali Penu are known to inhabit large trees and rocks, and Keri Penu and Danda Penu live on the hill slopes. These *penuni* are believed by the Kuttia Kondh to have the ability to punish human beings who break taboos linked to the forest.

THE APPEARANCE OF HILL GODS IN DREAMS

The shamans of the Kuttia Kondh are able to identify the god of a particular hill in their dreams. A god may be envisioned as an old man wearing a short cloth around his waist (*kutaka*) or the appearance of a very old man with white hair (*bhujanga*) indicates the presence of an evil spirit who may harm the tribe. Panga, or Dharani Penu,[8] the god of the base of the hill, is represented in a dream as a man tying a black cloth around his head. The Kuttia Kondh use the word

8. Dharani Penu is called Panga Penu to indicate the presence of Dharani stones at the panga.

penu without referring specifically to the gender of the deity, although the gender of certain gods is sometimes indicated, as in the case of the goddess Dharani Penu. The gods are often represented in dreams as either men or women though this is not necessarily an indication of the gender of the god.

In the dreams of the Kuttia Kondh, certain gods are represented by particular objects, although it is not always possible to see a connection between the two, perhaps because the connection has been lost over time. However, in many cases, the symbolism in the dreams is obvious. Deities are often represented by men or women whose appearance is distinctive or who carry a particular object. The Kamei Penu mentioned earlier, for example, is symbolised by a man carrying a buffalo horn. The objects may relate to a myth associated with the hill or to the physical characteristics of the hill. Bade Gati Penu, for example, resides on a hill known for its many banyan trees (*bade mara*, *Ficus benghalensis*) in earlier times, and the *penu* appears in a dream as a woman carrying a banyan tree.

The following account of hills and their representations as gods provides a general overview of the sacred landscape of the Kuttia Kondh.[9]

Sunasella & Rupasella Penu

Judimuju is a hill near Guma village, believed by the tribe to be a temple. They offer acts of worship to Judimuju Penu when instructed to do so in a dream in which the *penu* appears carrying a bow and arrow. The Kuttia Kondh cannot explain why Sunasella and Rupasella Penu are revered during the ritual for Judimuju Penu, except that Sunasella and Rupasella Penu live near the Sapangada hill and Judimuju hill is also nearby. The tradition is continued even though its origins have been forgotten.

Sunasella and Rupasella are two stones — one gold (*suna*), the other silver (*rupa*), found near Sapangada hill. Sunasella is also considered to be a hill of gold. The symbol appearing in the dream is a woman sitting on a huge stone carrying weapons in her hands.

9. A more comprehensive list is provided in the Appendix.

The Satavali[10] hill near Pedem village got its name because of the presence of a large stone (*vali*) in the shape of an umbrella (*sata*). The stone provides shelter and is worshipped, therefore, as a protector of the people. The god is represented in a dream by a man carrying an umbrella. The deification of this stone is said to originate from the day when the Kuttia Kondh emerged from Sapangada for the first time and took shelter under this stone.

Bangeri Penu

Bangeri is where two hills join near the Sunasella stone. The name has two prefixes: Piju and Bidi. The literal meaning of *piju bangeri* is "the world of rain", while *bidi bangeri* means "the world of breeze". The *penus* of these two hills are perceived as the gods of rain and air, respectively. They are considered to be so powerful that they are normally invoked in all rituals that are performed by the tribe. In the dream, the *penuni* appear in the form of a woman carrying a "*manang*", a bamboo implement used for measuring amounts of grain.

Sandili Penu

Sandili is a small hill near Ambadola. The step-like appearance of the hill resembles three people sitting one behind the other and is said to represent "sisters searching each other's" hair for lice (and this is how they would appear in a dream). The sisters are believed to have been cursed by the hill *penu,* and turned to stone.

Tambadadi & Lakuti Penu

Tambadadi and Lakuti are two hills near Kranjkana. Tamabadi Penu is represented in the dream by a man carrying a *nelingi* (tamarind) tree in his hands while the Lakuti Penu takes the form of a woman carrying a stone in the shape of a trident.

---

10. The hill has a small cave which is considered to be a temple.

Digerisoru Penu

Digeri Soru is a hill near the village near Palki. The *penu* appears as a dog in the dream.

Gadabali Penu

Gada Bali is a small hill near Kumudi. The name originates from a horse-shaped large stone (*gada* — horse, *vali* — stone) and the story is that the *penu* of this hill turned to stone while riding a horse. This is, in fact, how the *penu* is represented in a dream.

Dharani Penu — the Earth Goddess

This female deity appears in a dream carrying a sharp, flat knife (*sechu*) used in *dukeli dakina* (the child-naming ceremony) and *Biakatina* (the Merlah festival). The Dharani Penu resides both in the village and in the hills where she is represented by three stones known collectively as *dharani vali*. When the *penu* feels very hungry she may cause an outbreak of smallpox, chickenpox or measles among the villagers. Dharani Penu is associated with other *penuni* such as Soru Penu, Keri Penu and Sandhi Penu (*sandhi* meaning "boundary") of the hills while Kuti Penu, Gangi Penu, Kidi Penu are water goddesses and Deu Penu is the village goddess.

There is a story about Dharani Penu claiming that she was the first to be born. As there was no one else in existence who could worship her, she gave birth to human beings so that she could be revered. One feature of the worship offered to Dharani Penu, is a chant, part of which is written below:

Sateini wango penu nella penu	Is it true that Wango Penu,[11] Nella Penu
Sateini mala penu deepa penu	Is it true that Mala Penu,[12] Deepa Penu[13]

11. Wango penu (Syn. = Nella penu) is the Earth god.
12. Mala: Iron chain with which the human victim was tied to be sacrificed. Mala penu is the deity of the iron chain.
13. Deepa: Lamp made of brass used in a *puja*.

Sateini sikadi penu kada penu	Is it Sikadi Penu, Kada Penu[14]
Sate dharani atisi	Is it Dharani Penu who has arrived?
Nai paragunda tinum	Please have our rice flour (*paragunda*)

The first part of any chant invokes the most important deity for whom the worship is actually organised. In the next part of the chant, all the hill deities are invoked. In the case of worshipping Dharani Penu, the priest first invokes her and then invokes all other hill gods and goddesses.

This goddess is usually worshipped twice a year at two great festivals, one of which is *puni kalu*, celebrated in January (*Pausha*) and the other, *Asadha*, in June/July. The word *puni* means "night of the full-moon" or "new month" (*puni lanju*), or "new eating" (*puni tinbo*). The *Dharani puja* in *puni kalu* is therefore a *puja* offered to the earth at a festival marking the eve of the New Year, the time that new crops are eaten. The word *kalu* can mean: "festival", "legs" and a fermented rice liquor prepared from a species of *Panicum* (*kueri*). During the *taka kalu* festival, a *Dharani puja* is offered to the earth of the hills, in the hope that this will ensure a good harvest.

Besides the *Puni kalu* and *Taka kalu*, the *Dharani puja* is performed during the Meriah festival (*Biakatina*), celebrated every three to five years, depending on the economic circumstances of the individual village. Two priests are usually present at the *puja*, which consists of seven stages of ritual. In the first step, known as "*jani nuni gata relmu*", the *jani* (priest) draws lines on the earth near the *Dharani vali* using rice and turmeric powder. The second step is "*pranga kitkamu*" which involves placing three pairs of rice grains on the earth; the third is "*penu arpinja*" or the invocation of the deities; the fourth is "*penu wate*" when the *penu* reaches the *puja* site, and the fifth involves the sacrifice of fowl (*kaju dakina*). The sixth stage, known as "*tinje guananga*" is when the *penu* is offered "*prasad*" (fruit and other offerings), and the *prasad* is distributed, and the seventh and final step is "*penu ningite*" when the *penu* is

14. Sikdi and kada: Iron chain and rings used to tie the animal that will be sacrificed.

bidden farewell. People suffering from any illness are not permitted near the *puja* site.

Kama Penu & Mardi Penu

Kama Penu and Mardi Penu are sisters (sometimes referred to as Sima Rani and Maa Rani, respectively) who "were given birth" from a hill called *Simarani Nella*. They are believed to dwell in banyan trees that are abundant in the area. Kama Penu is comparable to Devi Durga (a — goddess who, when invoked, helps human beings in the event of a catastrophe) yet is associated with diseases such as pox and has a propensity to be malevolent. Both *penuni* are worshipped in the village at the *Dassera* festival (normally celebrated in September-October throughout India), during *badbinere* and on *Sravana puni* (the full moon night of Sravana month, i.e., August-September). During the worship of the Mardi Penu the *jani* (priest) chants:

Inu weda mardi, lanju mardi	You are the sun deity, the moon deity.
Inu dina mardi, kasa mardi	You are the Lord of the country, the state.
Anu icheka paragunda, sienja	I am offering you this much rice flour.
Icheka nunigunda[15] *sienja*	Offering you this much *nunigunda*.
Icheka rakatira, sienja	Offering you this much blood.
Icheka juhar pariate	So many greetings to you.

Kidi Penu and Gangi Penu

Kidi Penu and Gangi Penu, thought of as sisters, are worshipped on cropland in the foothills. These gods protect the crops from disease, and the destruction caused by wild animals, particularly elephants. The act of worship is performed in the forest at the base of the hill in a shaded area close to a water source, known to be Gangi Penu's favourite dwelling place. Kidi Penu is found in the same area, nearby a large stone.

15. *Nunigunda*: a mixture of rice flour and turmeric powder. This mixture is placed in a diagrammatic fashion and the resulting diagram regarded as the seat of the god.

When a new area in the foothills is cleared for cultivation, the goddesses are worshipped beneath a very old tree, either a *sargi mara* (*Shorea robusta*), *bengeri mara* (*Pterocarpus marsupium*), or a *laka mara* (*Bombax malabaricum*). The worship is usually conducted twice a year, at the time of sowing and at harvest. The Kuttia Kondh believe that this particular worship protects the crops from a particular disease that is triggered by mud.

Keri Penu

A worship called "*Padaki dakandi*" is organised on a cultivated plot in *Asadh lanju* (July) on the eve of the germination of the crops. The worship is held in honour of Keri Penu — the *penu* of the hill slope (*keri* is the term used for a steep slope of the hill), Soru Penu and Bhujanga, the evil god worshipped along with Soru Penu. The *puja* is usually conducted in the middle of the field where three stones have been placed beneath a *mardi mara* (*Terminalia tomentosa*). The stone to the west represents Keri Penu, the stone to the south, Soru Penu, and the stone to the north — Bhujanga. The eastern side is kept vacant and Weda Penu (Sun god) is said to represent that direction. It is significant that the tree is a *mardi mara*, and that there should be at least one of this species on a hill in an area of land under cultivation. The area is divided into plots and distributed among the families of a village. Ideally each family would prefer to have a *mardi mara* and perform *badaki dakandi* on its own plot, but generally the worship is conducted as a community event under a tree of this particular species in the swidden area. All the cultivators contribute to buying a pig to be offered as a sacrifice (*badaki paji*). After worshipping Keri Penu, and Soru Penu, it is believed that animals will not harm the crops. If Soru Penu feels dissatisfied, he orders the Bhujanga to throw stones (*walinga irkate*) at the cultivators. When this happens, another mid-term *puja* is organised. At the time of the worship, crops should not have exceeded nine inches in height.

Kutti Penu and Sandhi Penu

After a site has been selected for shifting cultivation, *Dharani puja* is performed for Kutti Penu and Sandhi Penu in the hills where the forest has been cleared in preparation for cultivation. The *penuni* are revered and appeased by offerings in fear that there will be a reprisal for the harm that the tribe has inflicted on the abodes of the gods. In addition, Sandhi Penu, the deity associated with the borders of the village, is worshipped for his power to protect the village from wild animals. A translation of the words uttered during the ritual is: "We have now cultivated the hills and in so doing have destroyed your houses. Have pity on us and do not ruin our houses".

Deities Associated with the Sacred Environment of the Kuttia Kondh

The deities referred to above appear to be the most significant in Kuttia Kondh culture, although according to Chandrakant Jani, a priest in Rangaparu village, the Kuttia Kondh acknowledge the existence of 33,000 gods and goddesses, a figure used metaphorically to indicate the inumerable gods and goddesses that make up the Kuttia Kondh pantheon. In fact, all animate and inanimate matter from their surrounding environment is associated with these various deities who are believed to inhabit the Kuttia Kondh's sacred living space.

THE GREAT HILLS OF THE KUTTIA KONDH

Four hills are of particular significance to the Kuttia Kondh: Sapangada and Dimbuli have considerable mythological importance as the focus of worship and location of certain ceremonial occasions, while the hills of Siram Deu and Hatisalla are known for their physical characteristics, of which their caves are the greatest distinguishing feature.

Sapangada

Sapangada plays a central role in the lives of the Kuttia Kondh due to its considerable significance in connection with the tribe's creation myth. Sapangada is also known as Sate Kambani and Pdite Kambani. *Sate* refers to the mythical creation of trees and the emergence of the Kuttia Kondh from a hole in the earth, while *pdite* refers to the birth of trees and people through a biological process of reproduction.[16] The trees then form a *kambani* (forest). *Sate Kambani* is the place where the first tree species were born, the vegetation according to the myth, which is believed to have been created there soon after the birth of the people. The dominant tree species is *sal* (*Shorea robusta*), followed by *asan* (*Terminalia tomentosa*) and *bengeri mara* (*Pterocarpus marsupium*), forming a canopy-like structure. The ground floor of the canopy is dominated by *sindi mara* (*Phoenix acaulis*). The middle floor is dominated by *dengen mara* (*Xylia xylocarpa*) and, to a lesser extent, climbers such as *paeri* (*Bauhinia vahlii*).

The Sapangada *padar* (meaning field or unforested land in Oriya and Kui), lies at some distance from the village of Kranja, to the east of Saperi village. It is encircled by a number of hills, the closest of which are: Bari Soru to the east, Achabandha to the south, Kranja in the west and Masangdia in the north. The hills of Sunasella, Bichabari, Pitrimara and Judimuju are located further to the east. A river, flowing down from Gunjianu-Mahananu lies at one end of the *padar*.

The most commonly accepted version of the creation myth claims that Nerandali, the supreme lady, gave birth to the Kuttia Kondh who later emerged from the earth at Sapangada. However, some of the youth claim that the people were actually born beneath the Dimbuli hill, but failing to find a way out of the earth at that spot, they emerged finally at Sapangada through a tunnel built by Nerandali with the help of a porcupine.

Today, there is a place regarded by the Kuttia Kondh as the original location of the Sapangada hole, although no one can say whether there has ever been a hole at this location. The entire *padar* is named after the hole and may be divided into two parts: Sapangada surrounded by Sati *kambani*, the other, an area called *mardi mara* after the tree (*Terminalia tomentosa*) growing at the edge of the hole. The significance of the *mardi mara* tree, the *Bauhinia vahlii* plant and the white ant or termite hill standing at the edge of the hole

---

16. For a more comprehensive definition of the terms *sate* and *pdite*, refer to the chapter 5 in this book.

is explained in the myth. According to this, a cow followed the people emerging from the hole and using a rope made from the *paeri* plant (*Bauhinia vahlii*), people pulled the cow out and tied it to a pole (*mardi munda*). This turned into a living tree — the *mardi mara*. The *mardi mara* and *paeri tula* are reminders of the fact that the cow was the last animal to emerge from the hole. When the cow attempted to eat the people, Udurengad, a mythical hero of the Kuttia Kondh, came to the rescue and broke the cow's teeth. The blood of the animal then became the abode of the white ants or termites.

This is described by the Kui Gaani :

Kanasai[17] *burasai tiee*	I will eat all the Sahib people.
Udurai[18] *tiee penarui tiee*	I will eat Udurai (= Udurengad) and Panarai (Penerangad)
Timalandu timalakana tiee	I will eat all of the Timaka clan
Palu snichi data snichi sapinjane	Rubbed its teeth
Amigadi Musrangadi paru Sarasema	Sarapusa
Palude datade ketnenje (*Uderengad*)	Broke all its molar and canine teeth.

According to Sapangada's priest, Badupujari,[19] everyone emerging from Sapangada was assigned to one of the following two groups: Rajianga and Kuenga. The two groups descended from two Kondh brothers called Mininguera and Dambinguera, the sons of Raniadu. One day, the brothers challenged each other to jump over an elephant surrounded by a fence of bamboo in order to see who was more powerful. Dambinguera jumped over the fence, and the elephant, in a single leap, but Mininguera failed. Thus, Dambinguera became king. His family became known as Rajianga and included everyone except those Kuttia Kondh people who adopted Mininguera's

17. Kanasai and Bursai are representations of *sahib* people.

18. Urdurai and Penarai refer to the same hero.

19. While the suffixes "*jani*" and "*majhi*" usually follow the names of the priests of the Kuttia Kondh, the term "pujari" is attached to the name of the Sapangada priest.

family name — Kuenga. The Kuenga were then divided into many lineages.

A number of stories are associated with Timaka and Nandruka. The Nandruka, who, it is said, had giant bodies with very long ears and large eyes, were the first to emerge from Sapangada. Their appearance angered Nerandali who swore that she would never provide anything for them and that they would have to survive by eating their own bodies. Furthermore, she was not satisfied with their offerings, so she drove them away from Sapangada.

The next Kuttia Kondh to emerge were the Timaka. However, Nerandali did not want to give birth to the Timaka in the same manner as she had done for the Nandruka so the Timaka went in search of a place to come out, finally reaching Knehelpanga and Damanpanga. There, they were born from bamboo shoots (*terka*). Nerandali felt she could accept offerings from the Timaka, and gave them the status of priests who then worshipped her at Sapangada.

Sapangada is still worshipped today by the Timaka at an interval of five to fifteen years as well as a collective worship, usually performed every seven years. The Timaka were the first to be given crop seeds by Nerandali, and these they distributed among the Kuttia people, first at Sunasella — a hill at the eastern boundary of Sapangada near Pedem village. The paddy was given to the Rajianga people to cultivate, while other crops such as *kueri, mande*, *pokanga*, *kabanga*, *kating,* and *kredanga* were given to the Kuenga people. This influenced the distribution of land to the Rajianga, who had first choice, and were selected to cultivate the plains, land better suited for growing paddy. The Kuenga, on the other hand, were allowed to cultivate the *soru nede* region of the hills, and these hills and slopes were distributed among the heads of different lineages. Mininguera presided over the distribution process, and the people of Damanaka distributed the lands to the Kuttia Kondh.

The Bicha Supinere festival is celebrated in the forest in honour of Dharani Penu and Sunasella Penu. The festival marks the completion of preparations in the field prior to cultivation. The seeds are worshipped and a sacrifice offered to beg the god's forgiveness for cutting down the forest. Otherwise, it is believed that the god may vent his anger on the people by sending a flood to destroy the seeds (*dulu dakina*).

Another place of importance in Sapangada is the *Mila Mitpen Vali*, "the birthstone of children", originally marked by a pile of stones, where, according to the priest, a number of statues were recently discovered and taken to Puri to be conserved there. Today, the *Mila Mitpen Vali* comprises two stones, the larger stone representing a mother as she cradles a smaller stone, the daughter. In the past, it was considered auspicious for a child to bathe here. Afterwards, mother and child would attend the worship of the Sapangada Penu, presided over by the Sapangada *pujari* (priest). Close to the *Mila Mitpen Vali,* a narrow perennial stream, known as Kadakambeli Eju, would flow between two stone walls, believed to have been built by the *penu*. In the past, water from Kadakambeli Eju was prohibited from use as this water was only to be used by the *penu*. Today there is no such taboo and people bathe there freely.

Three *dharani* stones stand within a two-metre radius at the centre of Sati *kambani* and a further fourth stone is used as a seat by the priest (*pujari*). Close to the *Dharani vali* stand two posts used as sacrificial poles. In the days of human sacrifice, the bodies of the sacrificial victims were buried under a nearby *sal* tree. A number of stones still remain at the base of the tree today. According to Badu Pujari, Rungu Majhi was the first priest to perform a human sacrifice there. Although offerings are usually presented at Sapangada, the *penu* remains on the nearby hill known as Masangdia. All village settlements worship the Sapangada Vali, either at the original Sapangada or at substitute sites established close to the settlements.[20]

Dimbuli Soru

Just south of Sapangada, bordering Kalahandi District, lies Dimbuli soru, the biggest hill in the territory of Sapangada Penu, of great

20. A school, under construction close to Sapangada, was never completed. People believe that the *penu*, who was angry that the school was in his territory, destroyed the building and was responsible for the misfortunes that befell the labourers. It is claimed that he instructed a tiger to kill a labourer, and the child of another man was eaten by a python. Moreover, the bricks in the building would not set. The Kondh thus attribute the fate of the school to the anger of the *penu*.

significance to the Kuttia Kondh and topped by a plateau covering an area of several square miles. The nearest Kuttia Kondh settlement, Sirki village, is at the base of Dimbuli and is an excellent source of certain foods, particularly tubers, partially the consequence of an old belief that warned gathering of food from this hill would invite punishment by the *penu*. Today, this belief is not taken very seriously anymore, but the Kuttia are required to perform a ritual in which they seek the god's permission before gathering tubers. There is also a traditional custom in which the gatherer is required to roll down the hill to the tuber before asking the *penu*'s permission to dig it out. Millet (minor & major), and paddy are not collected (as these need to be processed to be edible) whereas tubers can be eaten immediately. Furthermore, collecting millet and paddy on the Dimbuli hill for domestic consumption is prohibited by the *penu*.

One of the hill's significant sites of worship is a place that resembles a nose in its physical appearance and is known as Dimbuli mungeli. Water from a nearby waterfall is used there for the worship. Another part of the hill is considered to be the 'chest' of the Dimbuli mungeli. Here, the Kuttia Kondh plant sweet potatoes, wild varieties of millet and paddy, which is claimed to be of particularly good quality, and tobacco (*dhuan bada*) is also grown at the hill base.

There are a number of myths associated with Dimbuli.[21] Because of its size, Dimbuli hill is believed to be the king of the Soru Penus. The Kuttia Kondh claim that the hill's vast plateau was created following a war between Dimbuli Penu and Sapangada Penu, because Sapangada Penu was hunting in the territory of the Dimbuli Penu without his permission, and the enraged Dimbuli Penu declared war against him. The war was finally won by Sapangada Penu who cut off the head of the Dimbuli Penu, hence the shape of a plateau. A tiger, said to be the vehicle of the *penu*, is believed to inhabit it.

---

21. The hill was once reigned over by a king named Nala raja who was considered to be the king of *penus*. Two sons of the king, Kulisa and Maila, are believed to dwell on the hill to this day and are considered to be the owners of all the crops and tubers growing there. Fields of crops with one-foot-high embankments are considered to have been the paddy fields of the gods.

The religious significance of the hill is also acknowledged in the *Kui Gaani*, which claims that the first people on earth were born inside Dimbuli hill. However, they considered their birth to have been in vain when they were unable to find their way out onto the earth and roamed under the earth and many other hills before finally emerging at Sapangada.

The hill is worshipped once a year on no particular date. Generally the *penu* is invoked on a Monday and worshipped on a Sunday. The *penu* appears in the *kutaka*'s dream demanding worship and a sacrifice, and then worship will take place in a nearby village under a big tree beneath which is a large stone to symbolise the hill. A goat, pig or hen is then sacrificed there.

The Kuttia Kondh begin the *Meriah* festival (*Biakatina*) by performing an act of worship for *Dimbuli soru* in a *puja* performed in a nearby village. The priest presiding over the *puja* faces the hill, and the compulsory sacrifice (which in the past was a human being and now a buffalo) is generally carried out at the ceremonial site as a result of the constraints involved in taking the buffalo high up the hill. For the inhabitants of Sirki village the hill represents the village god and ensures their protection and wellbeing. *Dharani* stones are normally found near the site of the worship, and in this case, a *puja* is also offered to them. The invocation of Dimbuli Penu is common to all occasions of worship by the Kuttia Kondh. Dimbuli hill is also known for its many caves (*sallas*), some of which are inhabited by animals. The Kuttia Kondh believe that any animal killed in that area becomes invisible before the hunter has had time to retrieve the body.

Dera Salla/Siram Deu

Siram Deu is a large hill adjacent to Bamanadeu hill, west of Burlubaru village. This hill is also known as *Dera salla* meaning 'big shed' as it comprises many caves. The forest near these mountains has been subject to little interference from the tribe due to the abundance of sacred tree species, such as *Ficus benghalensis, (bademara), Ficus religiosa (sorupipadi)* and *Ficus scandens (pipadi)*. The Banyan tree (*bademara*), in particular, is regarded as the abode of different gods such as Maunli Penu, Kama Penu, Mardi Penu, Adabai Penu and

Satari Penu. The Kuttia Kondh believe that the presence of the *penuni* allows the trees to grow in such harsh, stony conditions and furthermore, that any harm done to a *Ficus* species will anger the goddess who can potentially threaten the existence of the entire tribe by inflicting an epidemic upon them as punishment. Maunli Penu and Adabai Penu, for example, are malevolent goddesses who cause stomach disorders and other serious diseases. Thus, people's fear of divine retribution ensures that the entire forest is treated with respect. They avoid harming the trees even to the extent that snapping off twigs from the trees is strictly prohibited during religious activities on Siram Deu hill.

Attendance at the worship of Siram Deu Penu, known as *Bangura Dakina*, is restricted to the Bangura community, who were the first to offer homage to the *penu*. The god is worshipped once every fifteen to twenty years and it is believed that the amount of food cooked for the people attending the worship never falls short.

Siram Deu hill lies adjacent to Bamanadeu to the west of Burlubaru village. This god, Siram Deu, is regarded as the headman (*majhi*) of the hill gods because he is the decision-maker among them. He is assisted by Bamanadeu Penu in meetings while Esubali Penu carries water for *Siram Deu* and Eju Penu cooks for him. Siram Deu also has a wife — *Patingi Soru, and a son* — Munde Gati Penu. The *sambar* and bison are believed to be the cattle of Siram Deu Penu.

The Kuttia Kondh believe that the *jani* who presides over the *puja*, dies shortly after the performance, citing as evidence the case of Balu*jani* of Burlubaru who died immediately after finishing the *puja* to Siram Deu Penu. A *jani* of the Bangura caste usually does not conduct the *puja* unless his son or a man from the same caste may become his successor.

The *jani* who performs the *puja* wears garments made of *kejenga* leaves (*Colocasia sp.*) also worn at the *Kdu-pata puja*. Before leaving for Siram Deu, the *jani*, as an act of reverence, is required to throw some rice over the head of an animal to be sacrificed (either a pig, buffalo or a goat). It is then taken to the place of sacrifice on the hill. The people of the Bangura clan go to the *puja* site, actually, a cave situated near a sacred banyan tree (*Ficus benghalensis*). Rice, fried paddy and turmeric are the items usually required for the *puja*.

One large cave comprising five inner chambers, is inhabited by a number of animals, among these, the porcupine (*saju*) is considered the most important. It is Siram Deu's pet, and that is the reason why the cave is known as 'porcupine cave' (*saju salla*). The pink-quilled porcupine (*sonisaju*) and the Indian pangolin (*jerandi*) are said to have shaped the interior of the *salla*. This same cave is also inhabited by tigers (*kdani*), bears (*ali*), and snakes (*srachu* or *masi*).

It is believed that large snakes are used as seats by Siram Deu, while the tortoise (*sambi*) is the money-keeper and the pythons (*boda*) catch fish for him from the nearby streams. The tiger, moreover, is his vehicle of transport, the bear, his porter and the jackal, his bodyguard.

Hati Salla (Katak Donger, Rukuni Katak)

Hatisalla, as it is called in Oriya, is better known to the Kuttia Kondh and local non-tribals as Katak Donger, though their official name found on maps of the area is Rukuni Katak. This hill is surrounded by the villages of Kinadi, Gulam Panga, Pudrungi and Muska Soru and its vast plateau is the focus of all the religious activities and ceremonies associated with the hill. Hatisalla, like Siram Deu, is well known among the Kuttia Kondh for its large caves (*salla*) and its name literally means "elephant caves" because of the large number of elephants (*hati*) that roam the area close to the caves, attracted perhaps by the profusion of banana plants. A small cave on the other side of the mountain is known as *Gada* (horse) *salla,* a place believed to have been inhabited by horses in the past. The vegetation in the foothills consists mainly of a concentration of wild banana, climbers and creepers, interspersed with certain species of timber such as *sal, asan, daman, tangan* (*dengenmara*), *madei* (*manemara*), *chara* (*srekamara*). People from the nearby (undivided) Koraput District graze their cattle on the plateau during summer and winter.

The plateau, known as *"Bata"* in Kui, is believed to be an abandoned paddy field of the *penuni*. The perennial source of water (paddy requires a considerable amount of water) on the plateau helps to foster this belief. In the middle of the plateau lies a huge stone called *"Hati vali"* (elephant stone), which is claimed to be the place where the god tied his elephant.

In the past, a bed-shaped stone, believed to be the bed of the *penu,* could be found on the plateau. Over time, the stone may have eroded, although the Kuttia Kondh claim that the stone is now at Nisipadi hill situated some distance away. The Kuttia Kondh also claim to hear the sound of a flute which they believe is played by the *penu* in summer.

Three huge stones on the top of the hill, close to the water source, are said to be the home of the *penu*. The inauspicious aura surrounding this mountain is perceived by both the Kuttia Kondh and by non-tribals, who avoid visiting this place they associate with death. It is claimed that some years ago a saint, who meditated on this hill, died in a mysterious way. People are reluctant to discuss the incident as they believe this will bring them bad luck. While the non-tribal people living in the area think that he was killed by an elephant, the tribal people believe it was the wrath of the *penu* who may have been angry with the saint for trespassing his domain. The saint's derelict house has remained untouched ever since.

In spite of the many animals — tiger, bear, wild boar and elephant — inhabiting the area, people passing through are generally unharmed, although the Kuttia Kondh maintain that when someone is destined to die for committing an offence, he is brought to the hill by the hill *penu* and killed by elephants. Elephants are considered the vehicles of the *penu* and are thus entrusted with the work of punishing the wrongdoers.

It is claimed that a person searching for medicinal herbs on this hill is always rewarded if he offers prayers to the *penu*. However, particular herbs like *raga mara* and *bichu mara* (their botanical names are unknown) are reputed to save lives and can only be gathered by persons who have received orders from the *Soru penu* in a dream. It is thought that these special herbs will instantly vanish if some unauthorised person attempts to collect them.

Conclusion

An exploration of the Kuttia Kondh's living space demonstrates that the perception of their environment is closely associated with the tribe's religion and its awareness of its mythical origins, as well as with the practical aspects of their daily existence. The tribe's creation myth, *Kui Gaani*, documents the creation of their territory — the people, terrain and its vegetation — and perpetuates the significance of certain characteristics of the landscape, namely, particular hills, forests, and the area known as Sapangada where the Kuttia Kondh first emerged from the underground darkness onto the earth. Their living space has strong affiliations with the past, not only because it is the subject of many myths, but also because certain places are associated with the tribe's ancestors.

The many different physical characteristics of their environment are sharply defined by the Kuttia Kondh. A hill, for example, is divided into four basic areas: the *soru (gati) jaka, soru tude, soru nede* and *soru panga*. When the hill is the location of a settlement, some of these terms change; the *soru nede* is referred to as *nella* once the area has been converted from forest into cultivated plots; the *soru panga* is known as *baru* when it is used as a site for a village. Moreover, all aspects of the physical environment are the domains of numerous gods and goddesses — the most important of these is Dharni Penu — the earth goddess, and, to a lesser degree, Soru Penu — the hill god. While their surrounding environment and its spiritual beings are generally considered to be protectors of the people, there are taboos connected with some places and the people's lack of respect for the gods can transform them into fearsome beings held responsible for death, disease, and other misfortune. For this reason, all deities associated with particular places are worshipped and their permission is sought prior to any significant disturbance of the land.

The spiritual dimensions of the landscape perpetuate many of the Kuttia Kondh's religious beliefs and preserve the authority of those members of society who play a vital role in the many religious occasions associated with the land. Furthermore, the Kuttia Kondh's religious code of conduct, directly or indirectly, demonstrates their respect for their environment and regulates the use of the area's resources. The fact that certain tree species are considered to be the domains of the gods renders them sacred and protects them from being felled; similarly, hills thought to be the domains of malevolent deities are avoided and the harvesting of any forest products in the *tuleni* (burial ground) is taboo due to the Kuttia Kondh's belief that the area is inhabited by ancestral beings.

Finally, it can be said that the Kuttia Kondh shape their immediate living space according to the physical and the spiritual characteristics of the land. They claim to avoid building a settlement on an area believed to be the dwelling place of gods, such as the *soru (gati) jaka* (hill top), although this could also be due to the lack of a perennial water supply. However, by building a settlement at the base of a hill, the Kuttia Kondh believe that the gods inhabiting the hill top are provided with a good view of the village and its inhabitants, an aspect that helps to ensure the latter's protection.

7

Shifting Cultivation

Way of Life and Mode of Production

FORESTS are complex phenomena characterised by locally distinct configurations of vegetation and wildlife that develop under specific climatic conditions and are shaped, to a certain extent, by human interference. The continuous practice of slashing and burning the forests results in changes in the patterns of vegetation and animal population. For example, in the forests around Kusumunda, Belghar, it has been observed that where stocks of timber trees have been burnt, shrub vegetation takes over. Wildlife migrates to a safer region during the period when the forest is being burnt. Hence, the plant and animal interaction in these areas is disturbed.

The Kuttia Kondh, among other tribes of Orissa, depend on forests not only for hunting and gathering forest produce, but also for agricultural production in the form of shifting cultivation, also referred to as "swidden" or "slash and burn" agriculture. Shifting cultivation is a traditional method of agricultural production which involves the clearing and burning of vegetation (mostly dry deciduous tropical forest) in order to cultivate the newly exposed clearings. Crops are usually grown on the land on a rotational basis. These fields are then left fallow for a time, to regenerate for the next cropping cycle, or are abandoned altogether. Shifting cultivation implies the shifting of farm activities to new clearings, but not necessarily the shifting of the settlement of cultivators.

Critics perceive shifting cultivation as an environmentally harmful practice resulting in low yields, giving way to soil erosion and causing environmental degradation. Others argue that shifting cultivation is a farming technology based on a specific adaptation to forests and hill environments.

> In ecological terms, swidden cultivation is characterised by its high degree of integration into the natural tropical forest ecosystem, whose characteristics it conserves to a considerable extent (. . .) it is the only ecologically viable agricultural strategy to have been developed thus far, on a large scale in the tropical rainforests, and attempts to apply intensive agricultural techniques brought from other regions have generally been dismal failures, resulting only in the destruction of the ecological balance of the natural rainforest.
>
> — Seymour-Smith 1986:272

In India, shifting cultivation is generally practised in the interior hill areas inhabited by tribal communities where profit-yielding land suitable for ploughing (usually located in the plains) is scarce and the scope for irrigation and terracing is limited. Mahapatra (1983: vol. 1, p.14ff) proposes a typology of shifting cultivators based on the extent of their dependence on swiddening as a source of livelihood. This typology includes (i) exclusive dependence, (ii) major dependence, (iii) contingent dependence, and (iv) marginal dependence.

The Kuttia Kondh have been shifting cultivators since times immemorial. This method of cultivation is part of their way of life and is recorded in the mythology of the tribe. The Kui terminology for the practice of shifting cultivation is *nella kama, bagada*[1] or *dongar chasa.*[2] The term *nella* is derived from nede ("middle part") that refers to the *soru nede* — the middle part of hills where shifting cultivation is performed. In Oriya, shifting cultivation is known as *podu chasa*, literally meaning "burnt cultivation".

Shifting cultivation among the Kuttia Kondh, as in many other tribal communities practising this type of agriculture, involves both the community and the household: as long as swidden plots are cultivated, they are individually owned by particular household

1. *Bagada* denotes a cleared hill for cultivation.
2. *Donger chasa* means hill cultivation.

members. Lands are primarily owned by the family. When a son moves out of his parents' house, usually after marriage, the landed property is shared among the sons and the father. The Kuttias rarely make any claims over land. While distributing lands among the sons, the father does not forget the welfare of his daughters and retains some land for them. When a daughter marries, her father may give a part of his land to her as dowry. If there are no sons, the land property of the father is divided among the daughters and the ownership goes to their husbands after marriage. Therefore, land passes from family possession to individual possession only after the sons and daughters separate from their parents. In the past, as soon as the land was left fallow, it reverted to the village community only to be redistributed at the time of a new cycle of shifting cultivation. Today, however, all land remains under individual or family possession, whether the land is under cultivation or left fallow.

In recent decades many important species have become rare. A number of plant species of high economic value particularly useful for making household articles, are disappearing in some parts of the forest where the Kuttia claim they once grew in abundance. Today, species such as *Dillenia pentagyna*, *Dalberghia sissoo* and *Gmelina arborea* are rarely found in the Kuttia Kondh settlement area. Other species including *Diospyros melanoxylon*, *Grewia tiliaefolia*, and *Pterocarpus marsupium* are also on the decline. The animals of the area have suffered from a similar fate; the deer, the four horned antelope, the sambar and the wild boar are a rare sight, whereas the Kuttia Kondh maintain that these species once roamed the forest in large numbers.

The rael mara (*Dillenia pentagyna*) has broad leaves that make quite a distinctive sound when they fall.[3] The *sargi* (*Shorea robusta*), *mardi* (*Terminalia tomentosa*) and *sikeri* (*Acacia pinnata*) trees shed their leaves with a characteristic sound. One myth reveals that *Dillenia pentagyna* was the first tree to be born from the sambar, and is thus the precursor of all trees and plants. Its leaves are as

3. The sound of falling leaves in forests is sometimes the theme of songs, e.g., *Rael aku gada gada — Sargi aku pada pada — Mardi aku biri bara — Sikeri aku sar sar.*

broad as the ear of the sambar from which it is said to have evolved. With time, the broad sized leaves of *Dillenia pentagyna* hampered the growth of other trees by blocking out the sunlight. The aged members of the tribe believe that nature created the small leaved trees so that sunlight could fall equally on all plants, and also to enable them to survive on less water. *Ejusilae* (lack of water) and *wedasilae* (lack of light) are perceived as being destructive to the *jella* (life) of trees, due to the fact that with less sun and water the tree species become progressively smaller and give rise to many other plant species. In this indigenous notion of plant succession, *Dillenia pentagyna* is followed by *Shorea robusta* that again is followed by *Terminalia tomentosa, Acacia pinnata, Phoenix sylvestris, Phoenix acaulis, Thysanolaena maxima, Bambusa sps,* and finally *Arundo donax*. This evolution is called "*sal* to *salia*" by the old Kuttia Kondh.

The Kuttia Kondh do not take any measures to prevent soil erosion in the swidden plots that lose topsoil during heavy rains. Many hill swiddens around the Belghar area have been severely affected by soil erosion. Due to continuous slashing and burning, the vegetation is unable to prevent soil erosion because the anchorage of soil by the roots has weakened or is nonexistent. In some areas, soil erosion has been so severe that the surface has been reduced to stones. However, multiple cropping in the swiddens also benefits the soil to a certain extent, particularly the cultivation of different nitrogen-fixing leguminous plants. After harvesting the crops, a certain amount of the plant remains in the ground, so that some seeds of annual plants and perennials remain in the swiddens. In addition, the decomposition of forest leaf litter and post-harvest crop residues make an effective fertiliser.

Site Selection

In spite of the fact that, strictly speaking, any form slash and burn cultivation is forbidden by forest law, in most areas it is tolerated because of the absence of any alternative means of livelihood for the tribe. If a patch of forest has a relatively low vegetation density with few trees or small trees, then it can be brought under community possession, and any fine imposed by the Forest Department is minimal.

However, the community is penalised heavily if they clear a forest that has a good quantity of timber. Usually, they choose a patch of forest less likely to attract the attention of the Forest Department.

A cycle of shifting cultivation begins with the selection of a site and the allocation, by the village chief, of pieces of forest land to be cleared by the cultivators. The political headman, called *majhi*, acts as a decision-maker in accordance with the family heads of the village. After the winter harvest of *rabi* crops, the *majhi* convenes a formal meeting of all heads of households, or their representatives, to discuss the next cultivation cycle. During the meeting, the *majhi* informs them of his selection of a new forest site for shifting cultivation, whereupon the matter is openly discussed by those in attendance. Many factors must be taken into consideration when selecting a piece of land in the forest. The fertility of the soil is particularly crucial; soil fertility can be assessed by the quality of the vegetation cover in the area. If the selected area has been cultivated previously, and then left fallow, the vegetative cover represents a period of natural regeneration.

Another consideration is the distance of the forest from the village. Generally, the Kuttia Kondh try to select land in the proximity of their village settlements, as less labour is involved in transporting the crops to their homes at harvest time. Besides, a perennial source of drinking water near the cultivated fields is desirable for those who work in them.

The possible destruction of crops by cattle and forest herbivores is also taken into account when choosing a patch of land for shifting cultivation. The size of the piece of land being considered for shifting cultivation is also significant, and determined to a certain extent by the availability of the labour necessary for clearing the forest, tending the crops and harvesting. In Kuttia society there is a gender-specific division of labour related to the practice of shifting cultivation: women perform activities like debushing, dibbling, hoeing, weeding, watching the crops, harvesting, winnowing and storing, while men fell and burn the larger trees, plough, watch the crop, and protect it from damage by animals. However, this division of labour is flexible. Men and women support each other and are willing, if necessary, to perform activities usually done by the opposite sex. Importance is given to the per capita share of land available and depends on the size of the selected patch of land, which will be distributed among all households of the village. Land is shared among male persons who are able to work. Hence, human power is regarded as the most important factor as regards the clearing of forests and the tending of the crops.[4]

If an area intended for shifting cultivation has not been in use for some time, additional factors must be taken into consideration, such as, for instance, religious issues or the future plans of the Forest Department. From a religious point of view, a patch of land may be judged auspicious or inauspicious for reasons associated with its previous cultivation, such as severe crop damage by wild animals, a villager being killed by an elephant or tiger, or a case of infant mortality in the place. On the other hand, if the Forest Department has an interest in the selected forest patch and classifies it as Reserved Forest, then slashing and burning is illegal and therefore avoided.

At the close of the village meeting, the *majhi* fixes a day to inspect the field being accompanied by the *jani* and *kutaka* and the senior male villagers. If, after an inspection of the field, all required criteria are judged to have been fulfilled, a follow-up visit is arranged. On this second visit a festival is performed (*wango dropondi*). More than one field is inspected in case the first field is found to be insufficient to provide land for all, or if one piece of land is selected out of two potential sites.

Clearing the Forest

Clearing an area of forest involves slashing trees and bushes in preparation for burning, and takes place in February or March when the Kuttia Kondh are generally free from other demanding tasks. After having selected the areas of land to be cultivated, every household draws up its own schedule for clearing the vegetation.

---

4. Sometimes, bachelors demand a share of their own. Usually, however, it can be observed that in a family, all members contribute to the cultivation as far as labour is concerned. For example, if in a family, 'A' is the family head, "a" being his wife has two sons "X" and "Y". "X" is married and 'Y' is not. "A" has a daughter "Z" who is unmarried. So from a common patch of land "A", "Y" and "Z" share differently.

During the clearing period, people set off for their area of forest each morning; women follow the male members of the family carrying millet or rice gruel for the mid-day meal in the forest. Family labour is the main input to this type of cultivation, and as the slashing of the undergrowth is often arduous work, small families sometimes pool their labour resources on a co-operative basis. A household may also obtain help from neighbours by providing them with a goat for a feast. In return, these villagers will help their host to clear the forest patch allotted to him or his household.

Most of the women take part in clearing the selected forest land alongside the men felling trees. Very large trees that would provide timber are not felled. Creepers are cleared, and smaller trees are cut leaving stumps of about three to four feet height. During the work, women collect the edible seeds of the *Bauhinia vahlii* and *Buchanania lanzan* fruit, and the edible flowers of girili (*Indigofera cassioides*). Children engage themselves in collecting the fruit of *Emblica officinalis* and *Tamarindus indica*, the leaves of *Bauhinia vahlii* and resin from *Shorea robusta*, which they sell. Furthermore, some species of weeds are collected and eaten as vegetables. The grass of *Thysanolaena maxima*, which is used to make brooms, is also collected and largely sold in the market. Larger branches are removed and taken home to be used as firewood. During this process of preparation, land plots allotted to the different households and their members are temporarily demarcated by stones and stumps.

Slashing is followed by burning. The entire forest is set on fire, usually during April or May when the branches, twigs and leaves are reasonably dry. The cleared forest patches can be concentrated in one place or scattered. Tree trunks are usually not set on fire because of their value for household purposes but felled. The research team has observed that not a single branch of *Grewia tiliaefolia* was burnt as the wood of this species can be used for making cot frames and shafts, hoe handles, and other agricultural implements.

The remaining stalks and weeds are burnt, as weeding after the seeds have been sown needs even more time and labour input than the slashing of trees. Weeds are generally annuals that have usually completed their life cycle by May, and are almost dry; thus, they are destroyed, to a certain extent, before sowing. The fire is usually lit at night, at the start of the peak agricultural season, illuminating many parts of the surrounding hill forest. The ash from the patches of burnt forest forms a thin layer on the ground and fertilises the soil, helping the seeds to germinate properly. The ash from twigs and leaves burnt on bonfires is sprinkled over the land. By the end of May, the preparation of the fields is complete, and people wait for the first shower of rain.

As it is rare to find a perennial source of water on the hills where the crops are to be cultivated, the seed germination is dependent on rain. The hard soil of the cleared and burnt forest areas softens after one or two showers of rain and the ash covering the soil blends in. A preliminary hoeing is completed before the seeds are sown. The women are responsible for the dibbling and they decide whether to sow seeds of long or short dormancy. Crop seeds with a long dormancy are put into holes made with dibbling sticks and planted with a regular spacing, whereas seeds with a short dormancy are sown randomly in between. When deciding upon a suitable composition of crops on a common plot, the Kuttia Kondh rely on their indigenous agricultural knowledge and experience. The land on hill slopes (swiddens) is never ploughed, but is simply hoed or dibbled before the broadcasting or planting of crop seeds. Land at the hill base is ploughed[5] to cultivate mustard and niger (*Guizotia abyssinica*).

Weeding takes place early in July when the crops have reached approximately six inches in height. This work is done chiefly by women and girls, though men may also sometimes contribute. Some weeds are used as vegetables and thus contribute to nutrition, while the remainder is gathered, decomposes, and contributes to the fertility of the soil. The Kuttia Kondh take considerable care to safeguard their crops from being eaten by wild animals from the surrounding forest. Lookouts are organized by the households who cultivate the swiddens, rather than at the community level. Young boys stay in watch-huts constructed in the branches of large trees spared from being felled or burned. Keeping watch from a lookout point also

---

5. The Kuttia Kondh use two types of plough, one drawn by oxen and another by buffalo.

favours the hunting of animals that come to feed on the crops. Herds of sambar or bison are driven away by setting fire to dried logs. Porcupines are particularly attracted by the ripening crops, and so the Kuttia Kondh trap these animals near their holes during this period. The young boys, who remain in the watch huts until the harvest is over, occupy themselves by constructing various types of traps for animals and birds during these weeks. Towards the end of the rainy season, most of the inhabitants of a village can be found in their swidden plots (*bagada*) during the day, only returning home during the night.

The various crops reach maturity at different times. The intermittent harvesting of crops such as cowpea or beans is done by women who store the produce in the watch-huts until they accrue to greater quantities. These are then brought to the village. The early maturing legumes such as beans, maize and castor are brought home directly, where they are processed. Millet is brought to the harvest grounds near the settlements, where it is threshed by means of wooden mattocks or trodden by buffaloes to remove the grains,[6] a process which is usually done twice. The bulk of the grain is collected by separating the straw or hay after the first threshing; the remainder is removed by the second threshing. Threshing is done by both men and women and the grain is then carried home by the women where it is stored in large bamboo containers. Cowpea legumes are stored as bundles, while maize grain remains on the cobs that are tied together for storage. Other items are collected in bamboo containers. All grains, with the exception of maize and cowpea, are usually kept in the lofts of people's houses.

Virtually all crops grown by the Kuttia Kondh can be divided into two categories, called in Hindi "*kharif*" and "*rabi*". "*Kharif*" crops are cultivated on swidden plots (*bagad*) at the onset of the summer rain while "*rabi*" crops on the other hand, are cultivated on the fields at the hill base and on homestead lands at the onset of winter. "*Kharif*" crops cultivated in the *bagad* comprise many varieties, whereas there are only a few varieties of "*rabi*". However, rice cannot be cultivated

6. When millet varieties are mature, only the panicles of the plant are reaped with a sickle.

as either crop. Wet rice (paddy) is never grown on swidden land due to the lack of water.

The "*kharif*" crops are a mixture of cereals, pulses, rice, tubers, vegetables and oilseeds. The Kuttia Kondh cultivate millet varieties like *masa* (*Panicum miliare*), *mande* (*Eleusine coracana*) and *kredanga* (Sorghum). *Pokanga* (*Zea mays*) is another important '*kharif*' cereal. Dry land rice (*Oryza sativa*) is also sometimes grown. Pulses include *kanga* (*Cajanus cajan*), *jhudunga* (*Vigna indica*), *arka* (*Pennisetum typhoides*) and *biri* (*Phaseolus mungo*). Tubers and vegetables include *kuna basanga* (*Dioscorea*), *mundranga* (*Cucumis sativa*), *kumuda* (*Cucurbita maxima*), *rani basanga* (*Ipomoea batatas*) and *mara basanga* (*Tapioca Manihot esculenta*). *Kabang* (*Ricinus communis*) is the only oilseed variety.

Of the '*rabi*' crops, *tila* (*Guizotia abyssinica*) and *sorisa* (*Brassica campestris*) are the most common, grown particularly on permanently cultivated lands at the hill base. Apart from these, the winter vegetables, which are grown in their home gardens, also come under this category. Generally, *rabi* crops are grown as monoculture. The Kuttia Kondh practise three methods of sowing: broadcasting, sowing behind a plough, and dibbling.[7]

Crops Grown by the Kuttia Kondh (see Table 1)

Zea mays L. (English: maize; KK: Pokanga)

It is the most important cereal for the Kuttia Kondh, surpassing other cereals in terms of the amount of cultivated area covered and the size of the yield. Maize is cultivated both on swidden land in the hills and in the plains. The time of cropping is June to July. Maize is harvested in October.

Oryza sativa L. (E: rice; KK: Kulinga)

Although rice is a preferred dish among the Kuttia Kondh, its cultivation is not widespread due to the lack of irrigated land. Wetland rice

7. Broadcasting is done on swiddens mixed with other crops. Sowing behind a plough is done in the plains and at the hill base. Planting in dibbled holes is done on homestead land and kitchen gardens.

(paddy) is sometimes grown in the plains and/or on terraces near a perennial water source. Dry land rice cultivation, however, depends on rain and is cultivated in the hills (a variety known as upland rice). It is sown either by broadcasting or dibbling in ploughed furrows and cultivated in the 'kharif' season only. Very little care is given to weeding and other fostering practices.

Panicum miliare (E: little millet; KK: Masa/Kueri)

This is a cheap staple crop, grown on swidden land by the Kuttia Kondh as a "*kharif*" crop on poor soil. It is generally sown in June-July and harvested in January in the second year of a shifting cultivation crop cycle. It is grown together with cereals such as *Pennisetum typhoides* and *Eleusine coracana*, and pulses like *Phaseolus mungo*.

Eleusine coracana (E: ragi or finger millet; KK: Mande)

Finger millet, known in India as *ragi*, also called birds-foot millet, *coracana* millet and African millet. It is one of the principal staple foods of the Kuttia Kondh and grown on swidden land on the upper parts of the middle hills as a kharif crop. Finger millet is sown in June/July and harvested during November/December. The straw is fed to cattle, while the seeds are ground and cooked to make gruel.

Sorghum vulgare (E: millet; KK: Kredanga)

It is one of the most important food and fodder crops and cultivated as a "*kharif*" crop on swidden dry land by many Kuttia people. The seeds are sown in ploughed furrows in June and the crop is harvested in December. Mixed cropping with other cereals, pulses and vegetables is common.

Pennisetum typhoides (E: pearl millet; KK: Arka)

This crop, which yields both food and fodder, is known throughout India as *bajra*. It is grown as a "*kharif*" crop on poor soil. The seeds are broadcast immediately after the onset of the monsoon in June and the crop is harvested in October/November.

Cajanus cajan (E: pigeon pea; KK: Kaanga)

Pigeon pea, or red gram as it is popularly known in India, is an annual shrub cultivated by the Kuttia Kondh on their shifting cultivation plots. It is a "*kharif*" crop that grows well independently as well as in mixed cropping, alongside maize and millet. The best results are obtained by growing it in red soil (Kambit Vira). Seeds are sown by broadcasting and dibbling in June/July and the crop is harvested in January/February. Should harvesting be delayed, the seeds are not lost, as the pods do not scatter them. Fresh seeds are cooked with rice and dried seeds are cooked as a supplementary vegetarian dish. Pigeon pea is grown by the Kuttia Kondh chiefly as a cash crop.

Phaseolus mungo (variety-Radiatus) (E: black gram; KK: Biri)

Black gram is grown with other pulses as a mixed crop. The Kuttia Kondh cultivate it as a kharif crop, sowing the seeds in June/July and harvest it in November/December. After harvesting, black gram is stacked, dried for a week, and then threshed by being beaten with sticks or trodden by bullocks.

Vigna indica (E: cowpea; KK: Jhudunga)

Cowpea, a herbaceous annual creeper, is the most important pulse crop grown by the Kuttia Kondh. The crop, grown both for subsistence and as cash crop, is cultivated on swidden land as a mixed crop with other pulses, and thrives well in fertile soil. The Kuttia Kondh collect seeds from mature legumes, which, in winter, are usually added to rice. The seeds are also added to gruel prepared with ragi and to curry. A major part of the harvest is sold in the market, where there is a high demand for this crop. Sowing is done by broadcasting and dibbling in June/July. Legumes, at an early stage of maturity, are used as vegetables. The crop is harvested in December when the seeds dry in the pod. The kidney-shaped seeds are sold as cash crops whereas the legumes are collected and stored for consumption.

Ricinus communis (E: castor; KK: Kabanga)

Castor is an important commercial crop valued for the oil contained in its seeds. It is a '*kharif*' crop that grows well on swidden land, even in poor soil. It is sown in June/July — earlier than all other crops — by putting seeds in dibbled holes. Harvesting is done in February/ March when the dried fruit is collected by the men, and the seeds extracted by the women. The seeds are usually sold for cash. It is a crop that is sown early and harvested late. Therefore, due to the length of time it remains standing in the field, it is used to mark the borders of the field.

Guizotia abyssinica (E: niger; KK: Tila)

This crop is valued for the oil produced from its seeds. It is used for dyeing, and therefore sold as a cash crop due to its high demand in the market. The oil extracted from the seeds is not edible but of considerable importance in industry. It is grown by the Kuttia Kondh as a "*rabi*" crop on land at the hill base. The crop thrives on light red soil. The seeds are broadcast after ploughing in October and harvested in January/February, when the plants are cut with sickles and stacked in the threshing yard for a week. The crop is then exposed to the sun for two to three days and threshed or winnowed, before taken to market.

Brassica campestris, L.
(E: rapeseed/mustard; KK Sorisa)

This is an annual "*rabi*" crop grown on land at the base of the hill and usually sown as a monoculture in October-November after ploughing. The crop responds well to organic manures and is harvested during January-February by means of hand sickles. The plants are gathered into bundles and stacked in the sun for a couple of days before they are threshed with wooden mallets. It is used by the Kuttia Kondh as a cash crop.

Dioscorea alata, L. (E: greater yam; KK Basanga)

It is the most widely distributed species of yam in the Kuttia Kondh area. The Kuttia Kondh eat yam throughout the year, but particularly in the summer season after the tuber has been harvested in January/ February. It is usually cultivated as a "*kharif*" crop and mostly cultivated as an intercrop in swiddens before, or at the beginning of the rainy season. Large yam is usually dug out by hand but using a digging rod is laborious as care must be taken to avoid damaging the tuber. Porcupines are a particular threat to this crop.

Manihot esculenta, crantz (E: cassava; KK: Mara Basanga)

Cassava is the staple food of the poorer members of the Kuttia Kondh. It is a perennial shrub with enlarged tuberous roots, cultivated on swidden hill land as a "*kharif*" crop, and in home gardens as a "*rabi*" crop. It is propagated by branch cuttings from mother stock plants twice a year, in June and November, and harvested in November and April. A delayed harvest increases the yield but runs the risk that porcupines may damage the produce.

Solanum tuberosum, L. (E:potato; KK : Alu)

Among the Kuttia Kondh, the potato does not have the same level of popularity as the yam. Normally it is cultivated as an annual "*rabi*" crop in the plains, and it requires considerable labour input. As there is a shortage of land in the plains, both of these requirements are disincentives to the Kuttia Kondh. It is also susceptible to frost during its early stages of growth. It is sown in November, and harvested in January/February.

Ipomoea batatas, L. (E: sweet potato; KK: Rani Basanga)

Sweet potato is regarded as the most important starch vegetable crop grown by the Kuttia Kondh. It needs a warm, moist climate and is grown in beds or on ridges. Cropping time is in July/August and it is harvested in December. Its sweet taste compelled the Kuttia Kondh to call it *rani basanga* (Queen tuber).

Curcuma longa, L. (E: turmeric; KK: Meranga)

The Kondh of Orissa are famous for the cultivation of turmeric, yet the Kuttia Kondh cultivate very little. Turmeric is regarded by them as sacred and is predominantly used for religious purpose. If cultivated, the surplus stock is sold. In the past, human sacrifice was offered up in the turmeric fields to ensure that the yield would have a good colour.

Capsicum frutescens, *Cucumis sativa*, *Cucurbita maxima*, *Lagenaria vulgaris* serve as intercrops in the swidden. These crops make up only a small percentage of the total quantity of crops grown. The people never sow seeds of *Capsicum frutescens*. The seeds that are scattered in the field from the mother plant germinate spontaneously in the cropping season. Although these are grown in swiddens, they are not considered to be particularly important. *Zingiber officinalis* is only rarely cultivated on swidden land. However, when it is cropped, it is confined to a very small amount of land. The rhizomes are dibbled in lines during the early rains and it is harvested in late winter.

Layout of Crops in the Bagad

Swiddening is a multiple cropping system and care is exercised as regards the arrangement of crops in the field. Certain species such as castor, maize or sorghum are used, due to their height, to demarcate the boundaries of people's property. However, other crops also grow plants alongside these border. For example, cowpea (*Vigna indica*) is grown between the castor (*Ricinus comunis*) plants, so that the former can use the latter for support. The border of one field planted with the castor seeds of one cultivator follows the plantation of maize and sorghum of the other person whose area begins at the same boundary. The boundary of the second person may be planted with castor seeds. In this way, patterns of crops serve to differentiate patches of individual property. A further reason why castor, pigeon pea and sorghum are planted as boundary species relates to their long dormancy and long life cycle. Maize, which is grown between these crops along the borders, has a relatively short life cycle, an aspect that facilitates an early harvest and does not damage other plants.

The boundary species are sown before all other crops. Yam (*Dioscorea alata*) seed is put along the boundary-fence so that the creepers can be supported by the castor plants. These creeper plants are not sown at the same time as castor, pigeon pea, maize, sorghum, to enable the seeds of the latter to have sufficient space to become established.

Pulses and other vegetables are cultivated at random inside the boundary adjacent to boundary-marking species. Ginger and tumeric, when grown, are planted as an independent crop or only together with species of bird chilli (*Capsicum frutescens*), the only crop to thrive in the company of these spices. Cassava (*Manihot esculenta*) thrives well on soft soil, and therefore is planted at random in the swidden, on land near the houses and in kitchen gardens. It is never planted on land at the base of the hill as this is comparatively hard. Cassava is never grown as a monoculture, but always as an element in mixed cropping. Because both cassava and yam are susceptible to damage from porcupines, the crops need to be guarded. Porcupine traps are also set in the vicinity when the crops attain maturity.

A patch of land is cultivated for two years (or occasionally three years) and then left fallow. When the Kuttia Kondh return to the same field after the fallow period, they cultivate mixed crops in the first year. They believe that the field becomes less fertile in the second year, and for this reason, neither the pulses nor the cereals grow well, with the exception of finger millet, little millet and dry land rice, which are grown on the swiddens in the second year as monoculture crops, but on different patches of the same swidden plot.

If a swidden plot is cultivated in the third year, little millet is the only crop grown in the knowledge that it can produce a good yield where others fail. Sometimes little millet is cultivated in the centre, surrounded by finger millet since the resilience of finger millet stem can protect the former from strong winds during the growth period, a strategy that helps to prevent the grains from scattering. Little millet is harvested earlier than finger millet, and therefore, proper planning and good management of the cultivated species are necessary to assure a good yield.

Productivity in the Swiddens — A Case Study

This case study shows the production potential within an annual cycle of a swidden economy as experienced by Gunugutu *majhi* of Burlubaru, the wealthiest member of the village community. He is one of the political heads of the village and an elected member of the Gram Panchayat. He has three sons and two daughters. One of his sons has passed matriculation and is now a student at the Government College in Angul. There are four working members in the family — Gunugutu *majhi* himself, his wife and two of their sons. He derives income from swiddening, plain land paddy cultivation, and by selling cow and buffalo milk. He possesses about twelve acres of swiddens on three hills and two and half acres of land in the plains. A record of his yield and market value in the swiddens is given in Table 2.

Fallow period

The Kui term for fallow is *nellatu*. During the fallow period, an area of land is left to recover following one or two years of cultivation in favour of better and more fertile areas. Another reason for the abandonment of swiddens is that the fields in the third year of cultivation require a greater input of labour to cope with the tremendous amount of weeds in the plot. The fallow period varies from two to seven years in the Belghar area. In the past, the fallow period was about 10 years, but it has declined to sometimes only two years. As mentioned earlier, the shortening of the fallow period is a result of the population growth and of the demarcation of major parts of forests as Reserved and Protected Forests by the Forest Department in the Belghar area. Bearing in mind that the people almost exclusively depend on shifting cultivation, these two factors have led to a critical exploitation of the remaining land. The short fallow periods are believed to be responsible for the decrease in crop yields reported by the local population. The limited access to forests has impelled the Kuttia Kondh either to return to previously abandoned fields far earlier, or to encroach on reserved and protected forest land. This latter alternative involves trying to avoid the detection by the Forest Department while clearing the forest. For this reason, the Kuttia Kondh sometimes choose to cultivate in the remote pockets of prohibited forests, although under normal circumstances they would prefer to cultivate close by their villages for convenience, and for the additional reason that they are able to guard the crops from damage and loss. If they are caught, they face severe penalties, including, in some cases, prison sentences.

Table 1: Plants Cultivated by the Kuttia Kondh[8]

Cultivated Crops Fodder	Type of Land	Kharif or Rabi	Type and Time	Time of of Cropping	Subsistence Harvest	Used as or Cash Crop
1. *Panicum miliare* KK: Masa/Kueri O: Suan Eng.: Little Millet	dry land	Kharif	Millet, July	Dec-Jan	Subsistence	Yes. The whole plant is used as fodder for cattle & pigs
2. *Eleusine coracana*, KK: Mande, O: Mandia Eng:, Finger Millet	dry land	Kharif	Millet, June-July	Dec.	Subsistence	Husk used for cattle and pigs
3. Sorghum vulgare, KK: Kredanga, O: Jonna, Eng: Sorghum	dry land	Kharif	Millet, June-July	Dec.	Subsistence	Husk used for cattle and pigs
4. *Pennisetum typhoides*, KK: Arka, O: Bajra, Eng: Bajra	dry land	Kharif	Millet, June	Dec.	Subsistence	Husk used for cattle and pigs

5. *Vigna indica*, O/KK: Jhudunga	dry land	Kharif.	Pulses, June	Dec.	Both as subsistence and cash crop	Legume coat used
6. KK: Kaudaka, O: Kating	dry land	Kharif	Pulses, June	Dec.	Both as subsistence and cash crop	Legume coat used; green legume coat for goats, dried coat for cattled
7. *Phaseolus mungo* O/KK: Biri, Eng: Black Gram	dry land	Kharif	Pulses, June	Dec.	cash crop	Legume coat used for goats (green) and for cattle (dry)
8. *Zea mays*, KK: Pokanga, O: Makka, Eng: Maize	dry land	Kharif.	Cereal, June-July	Oct.	Subsistence and cash crop	Pigs eat the residue (cob)
9. *Oryza sativa*, KK: Kulinga, O: Dhan, Eng: Rice	dry land (foothill)	Kharif.	Cereal, June-July	Dec.	Subsistence	Husk and straw for cattle
10. *Ricinus communis*, KK: Kabang, O: Jada, Eng: Castor	dry land	Kharif	Oil seed, June-July	Feb-Mar	Cash crop	Not used

11. *Guizotia abyssinica*, O/KK: Tila, Eng: Niger	dry land (foothil & plain land) winter	Kharif	Oil seed, October	Feb.	cash crop	Not used
12. *Brassica campestris*, O/ KK: Soris, Eng: Mustard	dry land	Rabi	Oil seed, October	Feb.	cash crop	Not used
13. *Cajanus cajan*, KK: Kanga, O: Kandula, Eng: Pigeon pea	dry land	Kharif	Pulses, June-July	January	Subsistence and cash crop	Legume coat
14. *Capsicum frutescens*, KK: Pata Rajeni, O: Dhanua Lanka, Eng: Bird Chilli	dry land	Kharif and Rabi	May and June	Nov.-Dec.	Subsistence and cash crop	No use
15. *Curcuma longa*, KK: Meranga, O: Haldi, Eng: Turmeric	dry land	Kharif	June	Dec.	Subsistence and cash crop	No use

16. *Zingiber officinalis*, O/KK: Ada, Eng: Ginger	foothill, home-stead	Kharif	September	Dec.	Subsistence and cash crop	No use
17. *Cucumis sativa*, KK: Mundranga, O: Kakudi, Eng: Cucumber	dry land	Kharif	Vegetable, June-July	October	Subsistence	No use
18. *Cucurbita maxima*, O/KK: Kumuda, Eng: Pumpkin	dry land	Kharif	Vegetable, June-July	Nov.	Subsistence	No use
19. *Lagenaria vulgaris*, KK: Anka, O: Lau	dry land	Kharif	Vegetable, August-September	December-January	Subsistence	No use
20. *Dioscorea alata*, D. *bulbifera* *D. pentaphyla* *D. glabra* *D. wallichi* (wild)	dry land	All Season	Vegetable (Tuber), June-July	June July	Subsistence	No use

KK: Basanga, O: Matialu, Eng: Yam						
21. *Ipomoea batatas*, KK: Rani Basanga, O: Kandamula, Eng: Sweet Potato	dry land	Rabi	Vegetable, Aug.	Dec.	Subsistence	No use
22. Tapioca, KK: Mara Basanga, O: Gachha Kanda, Eng: Cassava	dry land	Kharif & Rabi	Tuber, June–Nov.	Nov.-April	Subsistence	No use
23. Solanum tuberosum, O/KK: Alu, Eng: Potato	plain land	Rabi	Bulb	Jan.–Feb.	Subsistence	No use

Table 2: Yield and Value of Swidden Crops

Name of the crop	Quantity of seeds sown in kg	Market value in Rs.	Yield of each crop in kg	Market value in Rs.	Market production/ Household consumption
Finger Millet	8	32/-	200	800/-	Consumption
Bajra	2	9/-	30	135/-	do.
Sorghum	2	9/-	25	115/-	do.
Little Millet	4	8/-	65	130/-	do.
Castor	5	30/-	100	600/-	80 kg to market, rest for successive cropping
Pigeon Pea	4	30/-	150	1200/-	120 kg to market
Jhudunga	5	35/-	125	750/-	100 kg to market
Kating	3	15/-	75	300/-	Market
Black gram	3	24/-	45	225/-	Market
Cassava	30 plants	?	-	-	-
Maize	1	6/-	1000 nos	200/-	Consumption
Pumpkin	?	?	80 nos	?	do.

Cucumber	?	?	300 nos	?	do.
Bird Chilli	0.20	10/-	8	400/-	Market 5 kg
Niger	4	30/-	125	1000/-	Market
Mustard	3	30/-	100	700/-	Market
Potato	-	-	-	-	-
Ginger	-	-	-	-	-
Yam	5	25/-	200	1000/-	Consumption
Sweet Potato	3	15/-	50	250/-	do.

David Spurgeon (1982), a critic of the practice of shifting cultivation, expresses a common view when he blames the population pressure for the shortage of fallow periods in shifting cultivation systems and for forest degradation:

> This practice annually destroys ten million hectares of high forest and causes a steady decline in the fertility of the land . . . In the past, the soil's fertility returned to abandoned areas over a period of 25-30 years as a result of natural processes. But as population pressure increased, the cultivators returned to their abandoned sites much sooner, and the period of natural bush fallow was progressively shortened. — 1982: 10f

It is true that the Kuttia Kondh practise shifting cultivation with a reduced fallow period. But the problem of a shortening of the regeneration cycle cannot exclusively be related to the population increase, which is not large enough to justify David Spurgeon's view. Other people in the region, such as the Gonds who are marginally dependent on shifting cultivation, contribute to population pressure, and the policy of creating reserved and protected forests puts additional pressure on forest resources once available to the Kuttia Kondh.

Mythical Background of Shifting Cultivation

References are made to shifting cultivation in the cosmogonic myth of the Kuttia Kondh. This mythological background is an important reason for the Kuttia Kondh to continue with shifting cultivation as a way of maintaining their culturally distinct lifestyle and identity in accordance with the traditions of their ancestors. The *Kui Gaani* describes some mythical views of shifting cultivation, although today, much of this myth can only be recalled by the elderly members of the tribe. They refer to the myth, *Kui Gaani,* as a means to justify their traditional cultivation practices.

---

8. The term "dry land" denotes swidden land that is never irrigated. Homestead land refers to the patches near the settlement. Plain land refers to plain areas below the foothills that can be irrigated.

According to the *Kui Gaani*, the Kui people left the underground world at Sapangada, bringing with them some domestic animals such as bullocks, buffaloes, pigs and goats, together with many household objects. They also carried the "*atpa bicha*", literally meaning "eight types of crop seeds" — which are their staple crops, and samples of different soils on which the different crops were to be cultivated. The *Kui Gaani* mentions how the people brought soil on which pumpkin, tubers and cucumber were grown (see stanza 26 and 27 of the *Kui Gaani*, see Appendix 1). Other types of soil included *kambit vira* (red soil), *garli vira* (fertile soil), *sitka vira* (clay soil), soil from the mouse hole, and soil from the anthill. Their emergence from the underworld at Sapangada is seen as moving house. Although they changed their place of abode, they continued a way of life already extant before their existence on earth. They survived by consuming food that they had brought with them and then by starting to cultivate by sowing the seeds they had brought. Following the female Kuttia, the male camp left the underworld at Sapangada. The men were required to prepare the fields, to clear the forests and to build houses. They were also expected to conduct acts of worship, to share the cultivation activities with the women, and to hunt.

The myth also alludes to the fact that the patches of forest selected for shifting cultivation should contain a *dharani* stone[9] and a bamboo bush. If bamboo bushes are not found, either the field is abandoned or bamboo saplings are planted in the field. The presence of bamboo at the site where worship is offered to Dharani Penu is essential. It is said that bamboo came into existence near Sapangada, from the hair of Nerandali, when she was taking a bath after emerging from Sapangada. The Kuttia Kondh believe that a *dharani* stone, if found in a newly cleared forest patch, must have been left there by the ancestors who had cultivated the area before. As the cultivators require the permission of Dharani Penu before they clear a new patch of forest, she is therefore appeased with an offering of blood from an animal sacrifice. It is believed that without the blood offering, the deity becomes angry and can inflict harm by producing poor yields in

9. *Dharani* Stone: Three stones placed in a line beneath a larger stone are regarded as a representation of Dharani Penu, the earth goddess.

the swidden plots, and inflicting disease and other misfortune on the people.

Neri, Nede and Nella: a Cultural Core Configuration

In the Kui language, *neri* means blood, *nede* means middle, while *nella*, as mentioned earlier, means swidden plot. There is a linguistic correlation and analogy between these three Kui terms. In fact, *nella* is the swidden plot usually located in the middle part of the hills (*nede*). On many religious occasions, a sacrifice is performed in the *nella* area in the hope of obtaining a better yield. The Kuttia Kondh also claim that, generations ago, human beings were sacrificed in the *nella*.

As mentioned earlier, the Kondh (not only the Kuttia Kondh), who are known for cultivating turmeric on hill slopes, believed that they could enhance the colour and yield of the turmeric by sacrificing human beings to Dharani Penu on the fields. The person to be sacrificed was known as *saru.*[10] "*Saru neri*" (the human blood) was offered to Dharani Penu at the "*soru nede*" (the middle part of the hill). This practice, which has long since been abandoned and replaced by animal sacrifice, established a connection between *neri* and *nede*. The Kuttia Kondh claim that prior to the practice of human sacrifice, they appeased Dharani Penu with offerings of tree blood, i.e., the reddish coloured juice that exudes from slits made in the tree bark. Trees such as the *bengeri mara* (*Pterocarpus marsupium*), plant species like *tade mara* (*Musa paradisiaca*), and vegetable species such as *basanga* (*Dioscorea* sp.) and *kumuda* (*Cucurbita maxima*) were favoured as a sacrifice. In short, the sacrifice of tree and plant species was replaced by human sacrifice and this, again, by animal sacrifice. This suggests that the goddess can only be appeased with a 'blood' offering, be it in the form of vegetable, human or animal blood.[11]

The Kuttia Kondh's perception of a similarity between plant and animal blood is illustrated by another myth. According to this myth,

---

10 *Saru* is also the word for salt.

11. Refer to the chapter "Socio-cultural Aspects of Plants, Animals and Humans" for the myth recounting the discovery of Dharani Penu's preference for human blood.

plants were born from the body of a dead sambar (*Cervus unicolor*). When the sambar was cut open, the blood flowing from its body turned into water. Plants depend upon water and thus, *neri* is common to both plants and animals, the implication being perhaps that *neri*, either in the form of blood or water, is the vital element in living beings. *Neri* links the earth, the living beings and the deities in sacrificial cults. The conceptual links between *neri, nede* and *nella* form the basis for plant-animal-human interaction in the process of shifting cultivation.

Nella Dakina

Following the selection of an appropriate site for shifting cultivation, an act of worship, known as *nella dakina*, is performed at the site by the *jani* and *kutaka*, before the land is cleared. The worship is attended only by these religious specialists whom the Kuttia Kondh believe, are the descendents of *damanaka*. He is said to have been the first Kuttia Kondh to have lived in the area, and because he would have been the sole owner of the surrounding forests at one time, *damanaka* is considered to be an ancestral spirit. Before clearing a patch of forest, the Kuttia Kondh ask for *damanaka*'s permission to do so by offering him worship and sacrifice. Because it is believed that the ancestral spirits have considerable influence on the success or failure of a harvest, and must be worshipped for this reason, this ritual is called *nella dakina* and involves the worship of *damanaka*, and of Dharani Penu, the earth goddess as well.

This act of propitiation is performed under a tree at the site of a *dharani* stone. The preferred tree species for the ritual include the *sargi mara (Shorea robusta), bengeri mara* (*Pterocarpus marsupium*), *mardi mara* (*Terminalia tomentosa*), *jambu mara* (*Syzygium cuminii*) and *laka mara* (*Bombax malabaricum*). Dharani Penu is invoked and asked for permission to cultivate the land in a ceremony called *dedhi useni*. A hen or a pig is the blood sacrifice offered as

* *Soru dharani* refers to the *dharani* stones found on a hill. The KKK chose that particular place for any worship or offering to the hill god there. In that way, the Soru Penu and Dharani Penu are both placated. It is believed that somewhere on each hill there is a *dharani* stone — noticed or unnoticed.

part of her propitiation. *Damanaka* is also invoked and offered a cock sacrifice. He is requested to safeguard the welfare of the people and to provide them with a plentiful harvest.

Wango Dropondi

In contrast to the *nella dakina* worship attended by the religious heads, *wango dropondi* is a ceremonial occasion in which the entire village participates. This ceremony is organised only if permission to cultivate a particular site has been granted by the respective deity at the *nella dakina* worship. If permission has not been given, the area remains untouched.

The ceremony is performed in honour of Dharani Penu and Soru Penu during *Chaita lanju* (March-April), shortly after the *nella dakina* worship, when the land is prepared for cultivation. On the appropriate day (which is fixed by the *kutaka* in consultation with the *jani* and *majhi*) a group of about ten senior members of the village accompany the *jani* and *kutaka* to the first swidden plot (*bagad*) to be cleared. They construct a small house for the *Dharani* and return to the village, leaving the *jani* and *kutaka*, together with two of their associates, to conduct further religious performances. The *jani* leaves seven pairs of rice grains in the field, and returns to the village along with his helpers. They do not eat in anybody's house for seven days and seven nights. Then, they return to the field to examine the position of the rice grains. If two pairs are missing, it is considered a good sign and after a collective ceremony in the fields on a Wednesday or Sunday, the *bagad* is cleared and left to dry. A hen or goat is sacrificed in honour of the hill god, Soru Penu.

Any sounds made by wild animals during the ceremony are considered to be inauspicious and a sign that the *penu* is angry. People fear that they may be attacked by wild animals, so they abandon the field and search for another site.

Bicha Supandi Dakina

The next ritual is the *bicha supandi dakina* or the *bicha supinere* festival, organised in the forest when the field preparations are complete, shortly before the first rain. In this ritual, the seeds previously stored for sowing are worshipped in the centre of the field, together with Dharani Penu and Suna Sella Penu, a hill god. Suna Sella Penu is worshipped because he is believed to have been the first to distribute crop seeds amongst the Kuttia Kondh after they emerged from Sapangada. Furthermore, they need his forgiveness for cutting down the forest to plant the seeds; otherwise, he may destroy the seeds by sending too much rain during the rainy season (June - September/ October). Afterwards, a hen or cock is sacrificed and the priest distributes some seeds and asks the deities to protect them and ensure their quick germination.

Burlanga Kalu

It is organised, after an interval of every 4 to 5 years in *Baisakh lanju* (April-May) or *Kuda lanju* (May-June) following *bicha supandi dakina*. On this occasion a crop liquor called *kalu* (prepared out of little millet (*kueri/masa*) is prepared in each and every household of the village. Kalu has three literal meanings "festival", "crop liquor", and "legs". In this context, kalu means crop liquor. *Burlanga* is the term for a bamboo container used for storing grain such as millet, rice etc.

Burlanga kalu is a festival in which old burlanga are ceremonially burnt and new burlanga are bought and taken home. It's an occasion of merry making and getting drunk, involving two major steps of religious performance, one for ceremonial burning of burlanga and one for taking home a new burlanga filled in with little millet. On this occasion, the goddess of property, the home deity, along with other important gods and goddesses, are offered worship and sacrifice. Here prayer is offered in gratitude with a wish for an abundant crop. Hence, the goddess of property is perceived to be more important than all the other gods and goddesses in this festival.

On the scheduled day, one old *burlanga* from each household is taken to the site of worship. The priest, after invoking the appropriate gods and goddesses, sacrifices a cock or pig, though occasionally the penuni request a goat. The blood of the sacrificed animal is smeared on the containers and the priest chants. By that time people have sown the seeds that were stored in the *burlanga*. The surplus millets or grains are removed from the *burlanga* and kept separately in other containers, new or old, to empty the *burlanga*. Some time after the sacrifice, the empty containers are burnt ceremonially. Following that, every household offer *kalu* to those who attended the ceremony, be they people from the same village or outsiders. The *kalu* is served by the female folk, often assisted by the males and it is customary that the first measure of *kalu* from each household is offered to *jani* and *kutaka*. After drinking the *kalu*, sometimes a feast is organised with buffalo meat or meat of another sacrificed animal. Along with burning of the *burlanga*, bones of previously hunted animals (*kutra, sambar*) that have been preserved in Kuttia houses are also burnt on that day.

On the occasion of *burlanga puja*, the *bichavali* stone is also worshipped by the *jani* or *kutaka* in the house of the person where the stone is found. In every village, the *bichavali* stone is set up in the house of the last householder of the *majhi* line (*rout majhi*) when they begin to build a new settlement. The *bichavali puja* begins from the *rout majhi*'s house and it is believed that the stone changes its place on its own from one house to another.

In the beginning of *bichavali puja*, a chicken selected for sacrifice is taken to every house and in each, is fed with *kueri* (Panicum miliare). It is then sacrificed in the *rout majhi*'s house. In the *puja*, the home deity is also worshipped along with the *Bichavali* stone.

After the sacrifice of the chicken, the new *burlanga* filled in with *kueri* is taken home. It is believed that, after a certain interval, the old containers must be replaced with new ones so as to placate the goddess of property, the *bichavali* (seed-stone) god and the home deity. Furthermore, the new containers should not be taken home empty, for then the goddess of property would feel insulted. Hence, the new ones are first filled with little millet outside the home (near the place of worship) and then taken home. For this reason, the festival is organised after a bumper harvest.

Whoever does not fill the *burlanga* with little millet before taking the containers home loses the chance of procuring blessings of the goddess of property and the Bichavali Penu. Once they are upset, the *burlanga* will always remain empty. So everybody tries to fill the new *burlanga* with his own surplus stocks of *kueri* or some, borrowed or purchased from others. A legend provides the basis for this tradition as it tells how a poor man who had no surplus stock or money to buy a sufficiently large quantity of *kueri* to fill the container, in fact, managed to show the goddess a "full" *burlanga*. The emphasis on *kueri* in this festival points to the fact that it is the primary crop of Kuttia Kondh as well as the principal source of nourishment.

Taka Kalu

In the month of *Asad lanju* (June-July) or *Sravan lanju* (July-August) the *taka kalu*, a fertility rite, is performed in the recently cultivated fields. It is an occasion when sacrifices are offered to *soru dharani* in the swidden plots for all the crops grown in this god's name (and these include *kueri, mande, pokanga, kabanga*, etc.). The rite is performed to seek the blessing of the hill god, the earth goddess, and other deities associated with the hill god who, in turn, should ensure a good yield.

The ritual involves the sacrifice of a bullock and a buffalo. However, when the sacrifice of a bullock and a buffalo is considered to be too costly, the less valuable of the two animals is sacrificed, usually a buffalo. If a buffalo is not available, a pig takes its place. On the day of *taka kalu*, some mango (*Mangifera indica*) kernels (*taka*) are taken to the field, washed with water and, during the ceremony, the mango endocarp is removed and cut in a symbolic act that represents the germinating seeds piercing the earth. The *taka kalu* ceremony is celebrated when the majority of the crops in the swiddens have attained a height of about six inches, or, depending on the monsoon rain, a height of one foot, if it is performed later. The blood of the sacrificed animals is then smeared on all the crops, the mango endocarp is then powdered and a *samba*, a gruel is cooked that is first offered to the penu and later on, eaten by everyone.

Dulu Dakina

In October, which is the month when the crops have almost reached maturity and the time of harvest is near, *dulu dakina* is held. If the harvest is poor, the *jani* consults *dulu*, the goddess of wealth, to establish the cause of her unhappiness and asks whether the people are to blame. If the goddess is discontent, she sends the rain god and wind god (who create storms) to destroy the crops. The *dulu dakina* is, therefore, a form of worship to appease the goddess with sacrifices in order to ensure that the following year's harvest will be a success. In case the right amount of rainfall produces a bountiful harvest, the Kuttia Kondh also give thanks to the rain god during *dulu dakina*.

The *dulu dakina* is performed in the threshing grounds near the village where particularly millet and peas are threshed. It's a small *puja* done by the *jani* accompanied by a chicken sacrifice, with a prayer for a bumper crop in the next agricultural season and gratitude to the goddess for whatever the yield may be in the current harvest. The *jani* may offer cooked and sweetened rice along with this sacrifice to the goddess, according to his wish.

Policy Measures to Control Shifting Cultivation

In an effort to curb slash and burn cultivation, the Podu Prevention Scheme, launched by the Government of Orissa in 1987-88, continued for a period of five years until 1991-92. During that time, the Integrated Tribal Development Agency (ITDA) managed the scheme involving 58 villages in the Belghar area of Phulbani District.[12]

The Podu Prevention Scheme aimed to contribute to the tribe's economic development by prohibiting cultivation in the swiddens and replacing it by other methods of production on permanently cultivated land. Though it has not been possible to end the slash and burn practice completely, the scheme has managed to control it to some extent. As there seems to be no immediate alternative to shifting cultivation, measures to confine the practice to a smaller area were called for, as well as ways to improve the techniques of shifting cultivation, to diversify the cropping patterns and to increase the

12. The total project outlay was Rs. 377.70 lakhs, of which Rs. 145.90 lakhs were allocated till the end of March 1991. Progressive utilization of funds till the end of March 1991 was Rs. 116.06 lakh and the balance of funds available till the end of March 1991 was Rs. 29.84 lakh. The funds available during 1991-92 were Rs. 231.80 lakh. Ultimately, the approximate average allocation of funds per village was Rs. 6.52 lakh.

productivity of the land under shifting cultivation.[13] The Government took steps to provide the Kuttia Kondh with alternative, and therefore largely unfamiliar, means of cultivation, mostly of paddy. The horticultural plantation programme, for instance, was introduced by the Government of Orissa to encourage tribals to change their cultivation practices.

Although the Kuttia Kondh are aware of the crisis, they are reluctant to forsake old traditions. They argue that they have left certain flora on the hilltops that they worship as gods and goddesses. The Kuttia Kondh claim that it is their birthright to live in the forest and that they are aware of the need to utilise its resources in an appropriate way. They have detailed knowledge of the whereabouts of plant and animal species in the forest and maintain that they are the protectors of these species. If they ruthlessly destroyed the forest, they argue, how would they be able to continue to live there?

In the years following Indian independence in 1947, the Orissan Government demonstrated its awareness of the need to preserve the forest wealth of the state, including both flora and fauna by declaring areas of forest as "Reserved Forest". Substantial parts of it were protected and declared as natural sanctuaries. However, the Kuttia Kondh who continue to live close by and in the forest still enter these reserved forests, believing it to be their property and prepare land for cultivation.

---

13. Shifting cultivation, though it is one of the causes of deforestation and environmental crisis, has been defended for various reasons. In the opinion of Shri M. S. Sivaraman, a former member of the planning commission (1953): "It is a mistake to assume that shifting cultivation in itself is unscientific land use. Actually it is a practical approach to certain inherent difficulties in preparing a proper seed bed in steep slopes where any disturbance of the surface by hoeing or ploughing will result in washing away of the fertile top soil. The tribal people therefore, take care not to plough or disturb the soil before sowing. The destruction of weeds and the improved tilth necessary for proper seedbeds are achieved with the help of fire. In most of the interior areas where communication is not developed and sufficient land suitable for terracing is not available. Jhuming alone can be done for thoe present and as such every effort should be made to improve the fertility of jhummed land". (Patnaik 1993:54).

There are two reasons why they prefer to cultivate forested areas: firstly, they regard forestlands as being more productive for the subsistence of self-contained communities than any other type of land; and secondly, because forestlands are in the vicinity of their habitat. They associate the forest not only with their economic survival, but also with their emotional needs. The clearing of forests for shifting cultivation is a community effort and largely carried out by co-operative forms of labour. Thus, shifting cultivation is strongly associated with the collective identity of the Kuttia Kondh.

The legislation on forests contains new provisions and regulations that concern the forest dwellers. In the tribe's locality, increasing amounts of forest have been categorised as Reserved or Protected Forest and as a result the tribal people have had only limited access to the forests, particularly for the purpose of shifting cultivation. The Forest Department has accused the tribal people of destroying the forest with their shifting cultivation practices and although the Kuttia Kondh are clearly aware of the problems associated with trying to maintain a traditional way of life in the face of so much opposition, the Kuttia Kondh attribute their crisis to the presence of development programmes in their area. They feel that these programmes, which aim to improve living standards and boost the economy, have attempted to change their notion of well-being as well as their attiude towards preservation and conservation, in order to make them adopt different values and become integrated into the social mainstream of the Indian society. The Kuttia Kondh, however, are unwilling to see anything wrong with their own traditional way of life.

8

Socio-cultural Aspects of Plants, Animals and Humans

THE Kuttia Kondh live in remote pockets of a district characterised by densely forested hills, obtaining their food, much of their medicine and shelter from their natural surroundings. Their traditional social and cultural activities are the result of this close relationship with the forest environment. Due to the association of the Kuttia Kondh with the forest, plant and animal world, they are considered as people living within a particular eco-system by non-tribal communities of the region, in the main, by the Hindu farmers of the plains (who are not forest dwellers) as they have only indirect access to its products.

The forest has formed the basis of the Kuttia Kondh culture. They perceive plants and trees as creatures akin to animals and human beings, the former contributing significantly to the belief system of their material and religious culture. The relationship between the Kuttia Kondh and the plant world can be traced back to many myths and beliefs (Kui Gaani and Kapaka Gaani).

The life of a plant, its pattern of growth, germination and association with other plant species, suggest to the Kuttia Kondh that the plants socialise with one another, communicate and interact with other plant species. This is the most likely explanation of why the Kuttia Kondh attribute gender characteristics to plants, implying that plants and trees reproduce through sexual union. The attribution of sex to plants and trees is a common phenomenon among tribal societies (Parkin 1997). The Kuttia Kondh not only believe in the presence of gender in plants and in the concept of tree birth, but also that two different plant species acting as the parent generation may generate a completely new species which does not resemble either of the parents. From an evolutionary point of view, the interspecific and intraspecific hybridisation process in natural vegetation is responsible for the diversity in plants.

The Kuttia Kondh regard seeds (*penka*) as the sexual organ (*linga*) of plants and trees. *Jana* is the term given to the outer covering or seed coat. Trees, like any other plants, marry to produce a new species, so that the types of trees can be both the product of evolution or of the union of different species. In terms of a taxonomic classification, this plant/tree marriage system and the subsequent birth of plant species different from parental types, represents a type of classification of plants and trees by the Kuttia Kondh.[1]

An example of how the Kuttia Kondh view familial relations between plants and trees is given below. Two tree species of particular religious significance are the *sargi mara (Shorea robusta)* and the *mardi mara (Terminalia tomentosa)*. These are considered to be the first pair from which other tree species evolved.

In Table 1, which shows a part of the folk taxonomy of the Kuttia Kondh, twenty-two trees are mentioned. *Shorea robusta* and *Terminalia tomentosa* are species of religious significance, described in the oral tradition of the Kuttia Kondh. The two species are somewhat similar in appearance and hence are regarded as a standard pair that has given birth to other plants and trees. *Shorea robusta*, because of its huge size, is regarded as the male, while the smaller *Terminalia tomentosa* is considered to be the female. The offspring of the first two species are *sale mara* and *palche mara*, whose respective partners are of opposite gender — *karla mara* and *pade mara* are foreign species. The Kuttia Kondh claim that the marriages between plants and trees result in the evolution of new species as a consequence of the mixing of the parents' blood. In some cases, when the Kuttia Kondh observe that one tree species grows over another species, or if one tree appears to be clinging to another tree, they consider

1. For tree marriage practices among several Indian tribes see Parkin, R., Tree Marriage in India. In: Seeland, K. (ed.), Nature is Culture – Indigenous knowledge and socio-cultural aspects of trees and forests in non-European cultures. London 1997, p. 51-56.

these trees to be linked by marriage. In such cases, the more dominant tree is considered to be male and the other female.

Table 1: Folk Taxonomy of Significant Trees in Kuttia Kondh Lore

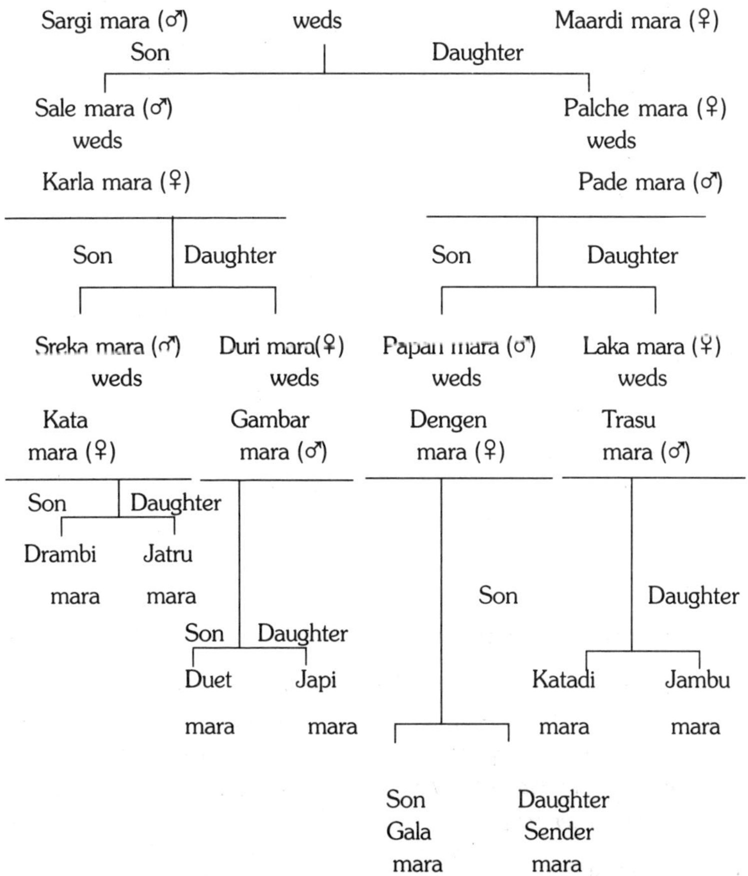

♂ = Male ♀ = Female

Kui terms of trees and their botanical names

Sale mara	:	*Lagerstroemia parviflora*
Palche mara	:	*Calophyllum inophyllum*
Karla mara	:	*Strychnos nux-vomica*

Pade mara	:	*Butea monosperma*
Sreka mara	:	*Buchanania lanzan*
Duri mara	:	*Anogeissus latifolia*
Papan Mara	:	*Ficus* sps.
Laka mara	:	*Bombax malabaricum*
Kata mara	:	*Schleichera oleosa*
Gambar mara	:	*Gmelina arborea*
Dengen mara	:	*Xylia xylocarpa*
Trasu mara	:	?
Drombi mara	:	*Sterculia urens*
Jatru mara	:	*Artocarpus lakoocha*
Katadi mara	:	*Bauhinia* sps.
Jambu mara	:	*Syzigium cumini*
Duet mara	:	*Ficus glomerata*
Japi mara	:	*Michelia champaca*
Gala mara	:	*Caesalpinia digyna*
Sendur mara	:	*Mallotus philippinensis*

Kuttia Kondh familial relations with trees and other plants

An example of how the Kuttia Kondh view familial relations between plants and trees is given below. Two tree species of particular religious significance are the *sargi mara* (*Shorea robusta*) and the *mardi mara* (*Terminalia tomentosa*). These are considered to be the first pair from which other tree species evolved.

For the Kuttia Kondh, trees are symbolic representations of their gods and an important part of worship, ritual and ceremony. Generally, it is sufficient to use parts of a particular tree, such as tree stumps, as substitutes for trees in a religious function or the image of a god may also be carved in the form of a wooden pillar, and this becomes an icon of the tree god. The prayer offered to them is a kind of fellowship and communication with the deities, for trees are both a token of the deity's presence and a magnet to attract their supernatural powers.

Trees and plants, or parts of them, used for worship, thus constitute the link connecting human beings with the deities or supernatural powers. Any attempt to understand the role of plants and trees in the socio-cultural life of the tribe must take many different factors into consideration. The tribal people's knowledge of the plant world, if judged by botanical standards, may appear very poor, and their use of plants in every day life is limited to certain species. However, the Kuttia Kondh's view of the plant world as well as their ability to exploit its resources shows their skill in making use of the vegetation around them. The knowledge of the average Kuttia Kondh person, as regards the practical uses of plants, is species-oriented: i.e., each person exploits a certain species for a particular purpose. If a certain plant cannot be found, a substitute is often selected which requires the individual's knowledge and experience.

An enquiry into the tribe's social and cultural life with regard to plants, trees and animals reveals the role that these play in social customs (particularly with respect to actions that are taboo) and also in rituals and ceremonies. A greater understanding of this role can be achieved by examining the tribe's oral lore and myths. Their religion is based on myths, and in order to justify and perpetuate the myths, they use plants, trees and animals in religious ceremonies in the same way they believe that their mythical ancestors did. Plants are denominated according to their different dimensions; a tree is known as *mara,* and large trees of timber species are known as *dera mara*; smaller trees and large shrubs are called *lika mara*; grass is *randa*, bushes are *bati* and creepers *tula*.

The Kuttia Kondh myth of origin, *Kui Gaani* (see Appendix), describes the evolution of plants and trees. According to the myth, vegetation evolved from two different sources. The first occurred when plants and trees were born from the body of a sambar deer (*Cervus unicolor*) and the second, when the first crop planted by the Kuttia Kondh grew from the seeds they carried with them on emerging from the mythical Sapangada hole. Whether the seeds came first, or the plants and trees, the myth does not specify. The plants that evolved from a sambar's body include timber species, shrubs, herbs, creepers and grasses. One exception specified in the myth is bamboo, said to have developed from coarse turmeric powder and the hair of Nerandali, the supreme earth goddess. From their early history, the Kuttia Kondh have categorised plant groups by distinguishing between domesticated plants and wild plants.

Jella and Palla: a Universal View of Forest Life

The Kuttia Kondh are aware of the life cycle of a tree having observed the different changes that occur during its growth, something that they describe as a sequential process. At the time of birth, in contrast to human beings and animals, plants do not possess a distinct shape and are virtually indistinguishable from one another. However, during the later stages of growth, new structures ("organs") of plants/trees evolve, whereas animals and human beings are limited in their structural evolution (namely, their organs), and over time, these organs age but do not change. In short, at birth, plants are all alike, but at later stages of growth, they develop different characteristics and become distinctly different plants. The phenomenon of the birth of plants is known as *sate* (Kui: "emerging from the earth") and the birth of animals and human beings is *pdite* (Kui: "emerging or coming out from genital organs").

The changes observed in the life span of plants are described in Kui language: i.e., the planting or dibbling of a seed in the earth is known as *penka mete*; when the germinating seed breaks through the upper soil layers, it is known as *tana genjite*, and when it emerges from the soil, it is known as *kana aate*; the stage when foliar leaves appear is termed *aaku gate*, the growth of shoots *peda late,* and the emergence of inflorescence[2] *tula parite*. The flowering stage is called "*punga pute*" and the shedding of petals, *punge dumbite*. *Padasi kadgai ate* means "the early fruiting stage", *padasi juri ate*, "the fruit maturing stage". Finally, the fruit drying stage is known as *padasi bachite* and the bursting of fruit to scatter seeds is known as *penka ate*.

The Kuttia Kondh claim that the different stages from *penka mete* to *penka ate* describe the life cycle of a plant/tree from the post germination phase of the seed to the pre-germination phase. Trees are bound to a certain locality and therefore, appear to be constant. However, the Kuttia Kondh believe that trees are formed more than once during their life cycle. Consequently, what distinguishes plants from animals/humans in a specific locality is that the former are believed to go through a sequence of lives, whereas the latter live only once from birth to death.

The life cycle of a plant/tree is dependent upon water and according to the Kuttia Kondh, water is the most fundamental element of a plant's survival. In a plant/tree, the bark (*palla*) represents the skin that keeps the water in the plant. The Kuttia Kondh maintain that *lenja* is the plant's internal water transportation system, although water absorption is not possible without *palla*. If *lenja* is absent, *palla* can still absorb water, but if *palla* is absent, water absorbed by *lenja* evaporates. Naturally, without its *palla*, a tree would perish just as animals would, if they had no skin. The Kuttia Kondh believe that any abnormality occurring in the plant is due to a failure of the water transport system. For example: the drying up of a tree, or the branches of a tree, is due to inadequate water absorption. *Paskadi*, for example, is a disease caused by the irregular swelling of parts of a plant as a result of a blockage in the water supply to the affected areas, and *bachine* refers to the drying up of a plant due to the lack of water supplied from the roots. *Kita bachine* is the drying of one part of the plant/tree and "*pakodake bachine pakodake silali*" refers to the drying of one lateral half of the tree/plant while the other part remains alive.

Their understanding of the relationship between water and *palla* is demonstrated by the technique known as "girdling", used by the tribe to kill a tree. The Kuttia do not fell large trees. Instead, they use a labour-saving technique that involves the removal of a ring of bark at the base of the tree. The tree dies a few days later. This type of death of trees and plants (following the removal of the *palla)* is known as "*mara grudu sate*", literally meaning, "tree full dead". In their terminology, "*eju*", i.e., water, "*daki*", i.e., the root base, and *palla* give plants and trees, *jella*, the life force. *Eju* is a metaphor to describe the *jella* that moves up and down in the infant stage of plants and

2. Inflorescence — a tree's floral axis.

trees while *eju* becomes stationary at *daki* when the plants and trees attain maturity. It is conceived that *palla* and *jella* are therefore mutually supportive. One cannot survive without the other and the tree/plant survives or perishes according to the relationship between *jella* and *palla*.

Mythical Evolution of Plants and Trees

The cosmogonic myth, *Kui Gaani*, gives an account of the creation of the Kuttia Kondh's world. According to this myth the Kuttia Kondh emerged from Sapangada, the cosmic hole to find a completely barren landscape, devoid of plants, trees and animals. Nerandali, the earth goddess, felt that there should be plants and trees to make the land more beautiful, provide shelter for animals and people who were to be created later on, and to enable the people to build houses.

Bamboo was the first plant to grow from turmeric paste and Nerandali's hair when she was taking a bath in turmeric paste. Nerandali then asked Betamangera (who was born after Nerandali and is believed to be her husband) to grow plants on earth. Betamangera went hunting. He was followed by a mass of people who were the relatives of the Kuttia Kondh. He explored a large part of the earth passing through mountains, hills and plains in search of an animal to hunt, searching all caves, hill slopes and those riverbanks often frequented by animals. Finally, he was successful in killing a sambar. During the ceremony of worship, he asked the earth goddess, Dharani Penu, to provide them with more animals for their nourishment. After worshipping Dharani Penu, he cut up the sambar. The blood flowing from the animal's body turned into water and the pieces of flesh turned into plants, e.g., the ear (*kirusiri*) of the animal became *rael mara* (*Dillenia pentagyna*); the intestines (*wahinga*) turned into creepers; the body hair (*burka*) and moustache (*sadonga*) became grasses and herbs; the skull (*kapda*), limbs (*kalka*) and teeth (*paika*) of the animal were transformed into large hills, small hills, and stones, respectively. These metamorphoses are however not universally accepted by the Kuttia Kondh.

The people of Rangaparu village, near Belghar believe that the parts of the sambar turned into different types of land rather than plant species. They claim that the limbs of the animal metamorphosed into fertile plain lands, the bones to stony lands, and the stomach and intestines to waterside paddy lands. The backbone of the animal gave shape to the ridges of the hills, the head turned into large stones and the testes were converted to a large stone called Bichabali, a hill. From the lungs of the sambar came *urla bada* (*Barleria cristata*) belonging to the family "acanthaceae"; the liver became *dhuan bada* (*Nicotiana sp.*) and the skin (*panda*) of the animal developed into other trees, climbers and grasses.

Although the origin of plants and trees is recorded in the *Kui Gaani*, contradictory versions of the story are told by inhabitants of different villages. What seems to be common to all accounts is that plants and trees originated from the body of a sambar. Among the different tree species that evolved from the flesh of the sambar, the *kara mara* (?), *asa mara* (medicinal plants — not identified) *rael mara* (*Dillenia pentagyna*), *mnia mara, maku mara, bade mara* (*Ficus benghalensis*), etc., are trees described in the myth. The further tree/plant species originating from this animal are as follows:

Table 2: The Names of Trees Relevant to the Kuttia Kondh

Botanical name	Kui	Oriya	English	Family
Shorea robusta, Gaertn. F	Sargi Mara	*Sal*	*Sal*	Dipterocarpa-cae
Bombax malabaricum DC	Laka Mara	Simili	Semul	Bombacaceae
Pterocarpus marsupium Roxb.	Bengeri Mara	Piasal Bija	Indian Kino Tree	Fabaceae
Terminalia tomentosa (D.C.) WA	Mardi Mara	Asan	Sain	Combretaceae
Syzygium cuminii Skeels (L)	Jambu Mara	Jamu	Blackberry	Myrtaceae
Emblica officinalis Gaertn.	Surga Mara	Amla	Indian Gooseberry	Euphor-biaceae

Mangifera indica L.	Maska Mara	Amba	Mango	Anacardiaceae
Xylia xylocarpa (Roxb) Jaub	Dengen Mara	Tangan	Ironwood	Leguminosae
Terminalia bellirica (Gaertn) Roxb	Baena Mara	Bahada	Myrobalan	Combretaceae
Woodfordia fruticosa Kurz	Jatru Mara	Dhakuti	not identi-fied	Lythraceae
Gmelina arborea Roxb.	Gambar Mara	Gambhari	Coomb tree	Verbenaceae
Grewia tiliaefolia Vahlii	Daman Mara	Dhaman	?	Tiliaceae
Linnea coro-mandelica	Mane Mara	Mahi	?	Caprifoliaceae
Ficus scandens	Pipada Mara	Jari	?	Moraceae

The sequence of the trees is told in the *Kui Gaani*, although the story can differ, depending on the singer. In an effort to avoid contradictions of other versions, one person in each village is recognised as the legitimate lead singer who, during a recitation, is joined by other villagers. Sometimes, casual singers or those who are not recognised singers of Kuttia society will recite the name of any plant/tree not found in their immediate surroundings. In other instances the plants and trees, more commonly used in their everday life, will replace the traditional ones mentioned in the *Kui Gaani*.

Stanza No. 250 of the *Kui Gaani* (see Appendix) refers to the creation of landscape and trees. Then, the hills and holes were silent and barren. There was nothing to see but barren fields. Then, Nerandali thought (*edu itere*) and attained wisdom (*budhi itere*). She decided what to do (*inisatisi adine*) so that it would fit (*inisatisi ranjine*): in order to make the hills and valleys look more populated (*soru usumgaisi gada usumgaisi*), trees and leaves were created (*mara linganjane dadi linganjane*).

Then the myth goes on to describe the sequence of origin of different trees and plants from the body of the sambar. It is remarkable that the creation of trees and forests ends the cosmogonic myth of a forest dwelling tribe. In their myths, the Kuttia Kondh distinguish between three sets of plants. The first set comprises plants and trees that yield edible crops, particularly subsistence crops, grown from the seeds the Kuttia Kondh carried with them from the underground when they first populated the earth. The second set of plants contains the species originating from the sambar, namely, primarily tree species. Included in the same set are grasses, herbs, shrubs and creepers. The third category of plants resulted from plant "marriages". The plants described in this third set are not completely different from those of the second set. In this set, however, if two plants represent the evolutionary parents, then other trees are produced through genetic variation and mutation of the parent species, and this process continues again and again to produce more varieties.

Bamboo

According to the myth of the Kuttia Kondh, bamboo was created from coarse turmeric powder that Nerandali rubbed on her body when she took a bath. The bamboo was born while everyone who had joined Nerandali on the earth slept soundly. It was midnight (*tudeka*), and the air filled with the sounds of a hornpipe, the roar of carnivorous beasts, the calls of elephants and horses, and the collective mourning for the dead. Nerandali and the people awoke and saw that bamboo was growing from the pond (*ejumundi*) where Nerandali had bathed. The bamboo bushes coming up were being chained (*sikulibandha, kada bandha*) on earth and a bad odour emanated from them. Nerandali was angered by the hoarse "*dre dre gedra gedre*" sound of the bamboo which had disturbed her sleep, and because the bushes occupied such a large space close to her home. So she decided to uproot the bamboo in the area and drive the bamboo away to Kandabada and Bakabada hills.

These events are chanted in the *Kui Gaani* (stanzas 50-53, see Appendix). According to the Kuttia Kondh myth, bamboo was significant in shaping the landscape. It is believed that soil was placed in a *sareni* (a bamboo vessel with holes in it, used today to separate husks from the rice grains) and dusted over the earth to level it while soil was thrown from a bamboo *manang* (a measure) to make the hills. Bamboo also plays a significant social role in the livelihood and the religious practices of the Kuttia Kondh, as it is required for Dharani *puja* (worship of the earth goddess) during *masa juda gasnali* (or harvest) in Diwali lanju (November), and the practical uses of bamboo in the every day lives of the tribe are manifold.

Animals and Hunting Practices in Forests

Although the Kuttia Kondh are predominantly shifting cultivators, hunting and gathering are important secondary pursuits. When it is available, people prefer meat to vegetables. Hunting has enhanced people's knowledge of certain hills and their significance as habitats of certain animals, namely, *pidipada*, *bazargada*, *akadanja*, *pidipadanja* and *deusana*, even though they are areas difficult to penetrate. The Kuttia Kondh believe that the gods of these areas, appeased by offerings and worship, will send the animals to forests which are more accessible. The tribe also worships *Gopal* and *Nirdar* — two deities who guard the animals grazing in the forest — in the belief that they might otherwise be reluctant to let the animals be approached by hunters.

The Kuttia Kondh use various hunting techniques. The mouse deer (*Tragulus sp.*), rafous tailed hare (*Mnalu, Lepus nigricollis ruficandatus*), red jungle fowl (*Katani kaju*, *Gallus gallus grey-Gallus sonmaratii*), and peacock (*melu, Pavo cristatus*) are caught using traps. The traps set for these species are usually kept under particular species of trees, the most common being *surga* (*Emblica officinalis*), *baera* (*Terminalia bellirica*), *katadi mara, baela mara* (*Aegle marmelos*), *denga mara* (*Schleichera oleosa*). These trees usually bear fruit from December until May.

It is claimed that forests rich in the species *gambar mara* (*Gmelina arborea*) attract *kateri* (barking deer), and forests where phoenix species predominate, attract wild boar *(braha, Sus scrofa cristatus)*. barking deer (*kateri, Muntiacus muntijack*), bison (*gayal, Sama, Bibos gaurus*) and sambar (*Cervus unicolor*) are among the animals hunted by group hunters in the jungle. The deer and wild boar prefer the fruit of *gambar mara* (*Gmelina arborea*), *puju mara* (*Madhuka longifolia*), *surga* (*Phyllanthus emblica*) *katadi, baena, denga* (*Schleichera oleosa*).

References to the food habits of animals are made in the *Kui Gaani*. In particular, the *saju* (porcupine, *Hystrix indica*) and *jerandi* (pangolin, *Manis crassicaudata*), whose preferred food was determined by Nerandali, are believed to have been responsible for digging the mythical hole, Sapangada, through which the tribe was able to come out onto the earth's surface. The pangolin helped the porcupine in levelling. After finishing the channel, the porcupine and pangolin demanded their wages from Nerandali who, in return, allowed them to eat the tubers in the Jendabedi hills. According to the myth, the musa-squirrel (*Funumbulus pennanti*) was also involved in the creation of the landscape; the squirrel cut the *sarena* (tips of the large trees) to prevent them from touching the sky. As a reward, Nerandali gave mango (*Mangifera indica*) trees to the squirrel. Besides mango, it was also permitted to eat any other fruit it pleased. Trees hung with creepers provided the squirrel with a safe habitat.

This tale alludes to the dietary needs of different animals, thus enabling people to gauge the whereabouts of certain animals. However, only a few hunters actually use this knowledge when hunting.

Kdu Pata Worship

Immediately following the *Puni kalu* festival [see also Niggemeyer, 1964:114ff.] in the village Burlubaru, the villagers prepare for hunting. First of all, they are obliged to worship *kdu pata* (*kdu pata dakina*), a huge stone (*pata*) found in the direction of Jhiripani, immediately after the village Kusumunda. The *kdu pata puja* is organised at an interval of two, three or four years and the form of worship is a request to the *penu* to supply a plentiful number of animals for the hunt. Each village has a different site for the worship. While the people of Germel village worship *tiba vali*, the inhabitants of Saperi village worship *kanda vali* (a sword shaped stone), and the people of Pukuri village worship *sareni vali* (a porous stone). All the males attend the *puja*, which involves the sacrifice of a goat or hen, and is later followed by a feast. The females in the villages do not work on this particular day as it is considered taboo. Some men are excluded from the hunting group, such as those whose wives are menstruating, or who have newborn children of less than twenty-one days old. The hunt is moreover only open to members of the Kuttia Kondh.

After the *jani* has declared the end of the worship, the men from all the villages form a group and enter the forest (usually a *bati* forest) for the hunt, armed with bows, arrows, and occasionally guns. The *jani* remains at the *kdu pata* to cook the sacrificed animal for the hunters. A number of armed people gather at one end of the forest to kill the beast, which, by that time, has been encircled and driven towards them by the other villagers. When the hunt is successful, the meat is distributed among all members of the village.

Hunting the Sambar

With reference to *Kui Gaani*, the Kuttia Kondh's cosmogonic myth, a god has two names viz; *penu* and *maju*. The *maju* (sambar, Cervus unicolor) is venerated as it is thought that the plants and trees first grew from the body of a sambar even though the same animal is also killed for meat. The preferred habitat of the sambar is a kambani forest, as it is restricted by its size from entering the denser forest (*bati*). Kambani is considered to be the abode of *penu*, so the sambar is accorded as much honour as a god. It is thought that the animal is guided by the *penu*, and coming across the animal when hunting is sheer chance. It is estimated that the village is successful in bringing down a sambar only every four to five years. If an animal is located every year, it is regarded as an indication of the *penu*'s satisfaction with the villagers.

When a sambar is killed during a hunt, some soil from beneath the head of the animal is collected and worshipped. The animal is then worshipped by the *kutaka* before being cut into pieces. The *kutaka* chants while touching a panicle of saparaka (*Thysanolaena maxima*) and a twig of surga (*Emblica officinalis*), a hen's egg is usually put in one of the animal's ears and a chick is encouraged to eat the rice placed over the animal's head and neck. Then, the *kutaka* cuts off a piece of skin (*panda*) and takes it away; the egg inside the ear is taken out and it is kept with the soil collected earlier, to be preserved by the man who killed the animal along with the jaws of the sambar. After some days, a *gauda dakina* (worship of the divine herders) is celebrated in the village, an occasion in which the people request the deities, *Gopal* and *Nirdar*, to bring them more animals to hunt. The first phase of *gauda dakina* is organised at the *dharani vali* in the village, a goat is sacrificed along with the jaws of the animal, and this is followed by a second worship which is offered somewhere near a hill. In the second phase, an umbrella made of bamboo leaves, a pair of slippers made from the bark of *mane mara* (*Lannea coromandelica*) and some brush sticks of *sargi mara* (*Shorea robusta*), a walking stick and a shoulder rod are given to the herder (*gaudu*). The jaws are also taken to the site of the worship and a chicken and a pig are sacrificed to the *gauda*. The jaws are then safeguarded until the next sambar hunt and then they are burnt.

The horns of a male sambar are sold for approximately fifty rupees. The horns (*kamanga*) and jaws of a *kateri* are also stored in the belief that this helps to ensure successful hunting of this species. The horn is then burnt at *burlanga dakina* (the crop worship) celebrated in *Chaita lanju* (March-April) every five years. As mentioned earlier, the *burlunga kalu* is celebrated to ensure bountiful harvests and continuously good propagation of the animals whose jaws and horns are buried. At this time, old bones, except those originating from the current year's hunting, are also burnt.

Animals in Dreams and Religious Belief

Wild and domestic animals that appear in dreams are said to be either auspicious or inauspicious signs of impending social events. Similarly, the appearance of certain types of people in dreams are said to determine the success or failure of a hunting expedition: dreaming of a maid, for example, indicates the availability of at least one beast during the hunt, while dreaming of a pregnant woman indicates that the hunt will be a failure. It is also claimed that if the hunter trips over a stone as he sets out for the hunt, the availability of an animal is guaranteed.

The appearance of a tiger (*kdani*) in a dream is usually auspicious for the family of the dreamer, but it can also indicate hunger. Dreaming of a bear (*ali*) is a sign of crop damage by grasses and weeds (*priba*) that compete with the crops for nourishment and result in a poor harvest. In contrast, a horse (*ghoda*) is a sign of good millet production in the same year. Dreaming of an elephant (*hati)* is a good sign of prosperity and is an indicator of *Bidi penu*, the goddess of crops, assuring a good crop harvest, particularly paddy. A cow, which is a symbol of the goddess Laxmi, is also indicative of a good harvest. A hare (*mnalu*) in a dream is an omen signifying an inauspicious event in the family. If the animal is seen as trapped or "being killed", it signifies the likelihood of a family member being struck down by an incurable disease. Deer (*jada*) with whitish patches seen in a dream indicate leprosy. Dreaming of a jackal (*kulia*) is very inauspicious, and if seen while hunting, indicates a scarcity of game, while to catch sight of the animal when going for important work indicates failure. Porcupine (*saju*) and pangolin (*jerandi*) are always thought to be auspicious, while the peacock (*melu*) and peahen are deemed inauspicious. A peahen standing in front of a house in the dream signifies that someone in the family will suffer an attack of epilepsy (*doali*). The sight of a peacock on the way to any work indicates some failure. The buffalo (*poda*) in a dream indicates a never-ending conflict between husband and wife. Dreaming of a pig (*paji*) indicates the demand for an offering to Gangi Penu and Kidi Penu. The appearance of a black goat in a dream indicates a bad "*graha*" or unlucky phase of life resulting from the bad influence of any of the planets (*graha* means planet), and the sight of a cock (*todara kaju*) when men set out to hunt is also thought to be an auspicious sign.

Cutting up a cow, bullock, buffalo or sambar in a dream represents the death of a person in the family, and the cutting up of one's own pet goat or pig in the dream indicates the death of somebody. Dreaming of a feast also indicates the death of a family member. Certain animals in dreams are believed to be incarnations of gods. A list of these relations is given in Table 3. It is remarkable that the sambar is not mentioned here.

Table 3: Animals and Related Deities

WILD ANIMALS	*GODS*
Deta (rabbit),	Kraha Penu
Khebda (mouse deer)	not identified
Mnalu (hare)	Rasi Penu
Lakda (monkey)	Maunti Penu
Sitadi (deer)	Sechkuriaru Penu
Kateri (kutra)	Katamunda Penu
Ali (bear)	Murjikeri Penu
Melu (peacock)	Dimbuli Soru Penu
Masi (python)	Adagadi Penu
DOMESTIC ANIMALS	*GODS*
Kaju (hen)	Kandi Penu
Ada (goat)	Kuti Penu
Parang (pigeon)	Judangi Penu
Meskari (cat)	Dandadi Penu
Tadra kaju (cock)	Pdiudupa Penu
Poda kama (buffalo)	Kamei Penu
Mera kaju (yellow hen)	Sanadueri Penu
Mendha (sheep)	Eju Penu
Paji (pig)	Gangi Penu
Nakudi (dog)	Digeri Penu
Goda (horse)	Gada Vali Penu
AQUATIC ANIMALS/ AMPHIBIANS	*GODS*
Sembi (tortoise)	Banda Penu
Panan (frog)	(snake god) Masi Penu
Minu (fish)	Kidi Penu
Ejuminduli (otter)	(fish god) Minu Penu
OTHERS	*GODS*
Pata (birds)	Runengi Penu
Mera gadri (stork)	Kiuti Penu
Srachu (small snake)	Esu Penu

Lambesi (big fish)	Achanjala Penu
Dani (chameleon)	Pod Penu
Kikla (grasshopper)	Wali Penu

Animals constitute the other important element in the forest besides trees and other plants. Wild animals in forests are recognised as having had particular functions during the creation of the universe, while domesticated animals are not considered to have any purpose other than their practical benefits as providers of food and money. Domesticated animals such as dogs, pigs, and cattle including buffaloes and goats, are important for religious performances. A brief account of these animals as providers of food and other materials, and/or their roles in rituals demonstrates their significance for the tribe.

PAJI (PIG)

Pig is the most common domestic species found in the villages of the Kuttia Kondh. It is regarded as one of the ritually cleaner species, even though it is dirty itself. Pigs are kept by the tribe because they are cheap to maintain and have high reproductive capabilities: one litter, for example, can contain between 6-10 or more piglets. They consume vegetative waste from seasonal crops and vegetables, such as the seeds and solid waste of maize, the pods of leguminous crops, waste parts of tubers and the mango endocarp. The faeces of children are also removed by pigs. However, they can be destructive as they damage the roots of the banana trees and tubers grown in the kitchen garden. The faeces of these animals are used as manure.

The animal is also ritually important for sacrifice and exchanged as a gift in different festivals. As part of a death ritual, the meat of a pig is shared between the related families. The pig, rendered as a gift, is cut into two pieces in a symmetrical manner, one half kept with the villagers and the other half returned to the donor. The pig sacrifice is said to satisfy Gangi Penu who is represented in a dream as a pig. An important medicine is prepared from pig fat (*Paji knahanga*) prescribed for coughs and asthma. To prepare the medicine, the fat of the pig is first boiled and then mixed with different types of honey wax.

KADI AND KADINGA (CATTLE)

Kadi literally means bullock and *kadinga* means cattle. Cattle are the second most common animals after the pig and are important to the Kuttia Kondh for religious and economic reasons. The animal is auspicious as it is considered to be an incarnation of the goddess Laxmi (the Hindu goddess of wealth) and it forms an important part of their cultivation practices as a draught animal, used primarily to plough the fields. The cattle dung and urine is also used as fertiliser. The Kuttia Kondh do not consume much milk and although milk is sometimes collected from cows, it is never used to make dairy products such as curd or butter. It is evident therefore that cattle are kept mainly for ploughing. Separate *kadi sala* (cowsheds) are erected behind houses with a wooden floor at some height above the earth level.

PODA (BUFFALO)

The animal is very important for it is considered to be a suitable substitute for the human sacrifice, performed at one time in the *Meriah* festival *(bia katina)*. Buffaloes are also sacrificed at the naming ceremony (*dukeli dakina*) and on other occasions of worship, if deemed necessary. A feast that includes buffalo meat, moreover, is an essential part of a marriage ceremony if good relations between the two fathers-in-law are to be established. It is common practice for the bride's family to send a buffalo when the bride leaves her house for the groom's house, and vice versa when the bride returns to her father's house. However, a buffalo is never presented as a gift in death rituals.

The Kamei Penu appears in a *kutaka*'s dream, carrying a *poda kama* (buffalo horn). Moreover, horns, as musical instruments, are made out of buffalo horn. The animal needs little maintenance. Domestication has resulted in the Kuttia Kondh ascribing primary importance to its meat and secondary importance to its milk and its use in ploughing.

NAKUDI (DOG)

The dog is particularly useful as a hunter due to its tracking ability and as a guardian, warning villagers and livestock against possible danger from other people and animals. It is a friend of the *soru* (hills) and *saru* (salt), an expression that implies that the animal is associated with the human beings in the house as well as those in the forest. Certain dogs are also trained to chase or to point at game in the forest. While the tribe keeps dogs primarily for their use during hunting, they are also regarded as one of the village "cleaning agents" as they consume the remains of slaughtered animals and also human faeces. The animal symbolises the Digery Penu deity (Digery is also the name of a hill).

ADA (GOAT) AND SHEEP

The goat is considered important as a sacrifice in different festivals as in some instances, a pig is sacrificed in place of a goat. (The appearance of a goat in the dream represents Kuti Penu.) Goats need little maintenance and fodder is available in nearby forests. The skin is consumed with its meat. Sheep, on the other hand, are rarely domesticated but are required by the sorcerer to be sacrificed for curing *doali* (epilepsy).

KAJU (FOWL)

Fowl are kept in most households in order to have eggs and meat, and also to have an economical sacrifice at hand. A hen represents Sana Dueri Penu and a cock represents Pdiudupa Penu, i.e., a hill named after a centipede that climbed to its top. The sight of a cock immediately prior to going for hunting is a good omen for the success of the hunt. It is useful in farming as it feeds on small worms and insects, and is also exchanged as a gift between formal groups.

Sacrifices to Satisfy the Penuni

The sacrifice of animals and plants to their gods is an important aspect of the culture of the Kuttia Kondh. They claim that plants were used in sacrificial ritual before the advent of human sacrifice due to the similarity of a plant to that of a human — its component elements: root (*siru*), leaves (*aaku)*, branches (*kena*), root base (*daki*), and bark (*palla)* — representing legs, body hair, hands, waist, and the skin of human beings respectively. Although the *Meriah* festival (*bia katina*) has, in the past, been of particular interest to anthropologists because of human sacrifice, the Kuttia Kondh claim that in the early history of the festival, there was no human sacrifice; rather, plants were used to represent the blood needed to appease the *penu*. Such plant species included pumpkin (*kumda* — *Cucurbita maxima*), yam (*Nangal kanda* — *Dioscorea sp.*), banana plant (*tade mara* — *Musa paradisiaca*) and pia *sal* (*bengeri mara* — *Pterocarpus marsupium*). These plants were sacrificed as an offering of blood to the penu. Furthermore, the exudation of *Pterocarpus marsupium* looks like blood and is known as *neri* (blood).

Later on, when it was felt that the god was no longer satisfied with this offering, the Kuttia Kondh began sacrificing human beings, though the idea of human sacrifice as a means of satisfying the penu had accidental origins. The god's preference for human blood is recounted in a tale. In the *Meriah* festival, performed by the Kuttia Kondh, maternal nephews had traditionally played an important role in their uncles' festival. Once upon a time, a maternal nephew was making a bamboo fence around the *Meriah* pole. While working with bamboo slices and blades, the nephew cut his finger and blood fell drop by drop on the *dharani vali* (the three stones representing Dharani Penu placed under the Meriah pole). The boy died immediately, something that the priest (*jani*) and the sorcerer (*kutaka*) interpreted as a sign that the *penu* wanted human blood[3].

At the time of the boy's death, his mother had been sent to bring water from a *jholla* (stream) in a porous pitcher (the pitcher had seven holes). When she returned, she could not find her son. She asked everyone she met, but could not find her son anywhere. Nearly mad with grief, she collected corn (*bicha*) from the villagers and set out on a never-ending search for her son. She is known as *kamati penu*, the goddess who, for her own sustenance, causes small pox, chicken pox, measles and other similar diseases.

The Kuttia Kondh believe that the Kamati Penu took food (*bicha*) from the villagers when she set out in the never-ending search for her

3. Niggemeyer (1964:223f.) reports a slightly different tale about the origin of the *Meriah* festival in which human blood was asked by the goddess Nerandali instead of the sap of *Pterocarpus marsupium*.

son. But when her food (*bicha)* supply was exhausted, she looked upon the pox (*bicha*) she causes in human beings as a food. Hence *bicha* has a dual meaning: first, crop seed, and secondly, the pox itself.

Gochchi — A Plant Disease

The term *gochchi* has several meanings. As a general term, it means diseases of plants and trees. More specifically, it refers to orchids, epiphytic and parasitic plants that grow on various tree species. It also means leprosy, i.e., white or reddish patches on the body of a plant or a human being. *Gochchi* assimilates its food from the host plant by affecting the bark. The Kuttia Kondh believe that any white patches found on parts of a tree affected by *gochchi* constitute its "mouth" (*guti*) and from these, it absorbs food from its host. *Gochchi* orchids are believed never to grow on a healthy tree, but on weak trees and plants. The trees affected by *gochchi* are never useful for medicinal purposes though the *gochchi* orchid is used in medicine. *Gochchi* therefore refers primarily to plant diseases, and secondly, to the disease caused by epiphytic and parasitic plants.

Daka-Daki-Dakina

Daka-daki-dakina describes the Kuttia Kondh's view of the spiritual nature of plants and trees. *Daka, daki* and *dakina* are interrelated terms emanating from the root, *daka*. Daka means "sleep", *daki*: "root base" (the root-stem transition point) and *dakina*, worship. The interrelation between the three terms is explained as follows: *daki* is a very stable part of the plant body as it is responsible for the flow of water through the plant. It is always dormant or "asleep", but remains conscious of the flow of water through the plant body. *Daki* is, therefore, understood to be "stability" and to sustain the *jella* or life force of plants and trees. *Jella,* in the form of water, always moves up and down in young plants only and not in old plants and trees. Therefore, *daki* stabilises the *jella* after a certain stage of growth, but maintains the physiological process of growth in plants.

When a *kutaka* (astrologer, sorcerer) is possessed by a deity (as he is at the time of performing an act of worship (*dakina*), he enters a state of trance. During a *dakina*, the *kutaka* concentrates on the process and loses himself as if in deep sleep. As a result of concentrating, he is able to see the deity in a vision akin to a dream-like state or that experienced in deep sleep. In that way, *daka* (sleep) is related to *dakina* (worship): the mind remains conscious while the body is in a dormant state.

One aspect of the supernatural power possessed by the *kutaka* is that he is believed by the Kuttia Kondh to be able to transform himself into a tiger. This phenomenon is known as "*mniba kdani*" and occurs during deep sleep, when the *jella* of the *kutaka* is confronted by an accident with the *jella* of some other being (either plant, animal or human). The *jella* of the human then leaves the body and joins the *jella* of the animal. After the merger of the two, the *jella* of the human, during his sleep, forgets that he is a human being and turns into an animal. If the man opts to turn into a tiger, the *jella* of that man roams around in search of the *jella* of the tiger and when the two meet, the conversion of shape takes place. The Kui word for this shape conversion or transmutation is *mniba*. After the complete metamorphosis, half of the life-force of the man remains in his host body (this remains in deep sleep) and the other half of his life-force departs for the metamorphosed form. If the plant or the animal with which the man's *jella* has merged is killed during the process of the metamorphosis, then the man also dies.

The term *daki* is also compared to *kamba*, a word meaning a human navel. The Kuttia Kondh claim that the *daki* in plants and trees is functionally similar to the *kamba* of human beings since it is believed that the abode of *jella* is the *daki* in plant beings and *kamba* in humans. Both *daki* and *kamba* are similar in terms of their placement in the plant body and human body, respectively. If *daki* is regarded as the centre of plants, and *kamba* as the centre of human beings, then the lower and upper part of plants and human beings can also be compared to each other. The roots of trees correspond to the legs of human beings and the branches to human hands.

One aspect of the tribe's understanding of *jella* is that human tendencies are found in animals, and animal tendencies are found in human beings. This idea is reflected in the Kuttia Kondh's belief in "shape-shifting" or transmutation (*mniba kdani*) something they relate to human beings' desires as expressed in dreams. In a dream, a person may wish to become an animal or something other than a human being — dreams, provoked perhaps by thoughts incurred prior to going to sleep. Thoughtful people often reflect about the nature of a plant or animal around them. For example, if somebody feels a strong desire to eat meat, like a tiger might feel in the jungle, then the same desire may be activated in a dream. The sleeping human being runs to satisfy his desire for the meat of jungle beasts, and at that moment, his human nature is transformed into a tiger's nature. If meat is not available, he may kill domestic animals like cattle, goats, pigs, etc. It should be said, however, that not all Kuttia consider themselves capable of such metamorphoses. These persons are exceptional and able to muster a high degree of concentration.

Saru-Siru-Soru-Linkages Between Human Beings, Animals and Plants

Saru, siru, and *soru* are the basic components of nature. The three terms refer to the existing forms of life and landscape within the tribe's life-world. *Saru* refers to a man or woman offered by the Kuttia Kondh as a blood sacrifice to dharani penu, even though, in general, the Kui word for human being is *maane*. *Maane* refers to any human being in their society while *saru* refers to human sacrifice. The Kuttia Kondh myth of origin claims that human beings were the first living beings on earth, before trees, animals and hills existed. Following their arrival on earth, according to the myth, the Kuttia Kondh planted vegetation. But it is also claimed that plants (with the exception of food crops) originated in the body of a sambar. In the myth there is no description of the birth of animals.

The term, *siru* (roots) refers to the anchoring of the plants in the soil. Hence, in the *dharani* (earth), the *siru* acquired space and developed after plants came into being as a component of nature. *Dharani* (earth) made a division of space for *saru* and *siru* in the way that human beings collect food from the vegetation covering the earth while roots derive nourishment from the earth's crust.

Soru refers to the hills in the Kuttia Kondh area. According to the myth, Nerandali created the hills to beautify nature. *Soru* also provides a habitat for the plants and the Kuttia Kondh. Ultimately, the Kuttia Kondh world started with these three main components: human beings, plants and hills. Dharani Penu (the earth goddess), who brought the above components together, receives her nourishment directly from human blood. Human beings survive on vegetation and animals. Thus, vegetation, wildlife and human beings share a common abode on the hills, the dwelling places of the deities (see chap. 6). These interconnected notions of fertility, habitat and cultural identity, linked through phonetically similar terms — *saru, siru* and *soru* — emphasise the degree to which the Kuttia Kondh view the landscape as a mythic template.

Material Culture

MARA AND MRAKA

Earlier in this book, the term, *mara* was defined as tree. The word, *mraka* is derived from the term *mara* and refers to the utilisation value of plants and trees, i.e., to the materials made from wood, used by the Kuttia Kondh. Furniture and implements such as poles and beams designed for house building, cot frames, combs and brooms, etc., are first identified as *mraka* before specific names are given to these items. The economic value of plants and trees is described by the term *mraka*.

Mara also has a social meaning in the culture of the Kuttia Kondh. If used as a suffix, *mara* refers to some kind of courtesy. For example, when the Kuttia Kondh sit together to drink toddy or fermented liquor made from crops or liquor prepared from flowers of *madhuka longifolia*, liquor is equally distributed among all participants. But on special occasions, an extra cup or glass is offered to newcomers or guests who do not regularly sit with the Kuttias. This extra cup or glass of liquor offered to guests or newcomers as a sign of courtesy and hospitality is called *sira mara*.

INTOXICANTS AND STIMULANTS

In all tribal societies, it is common to drink liquor. There are no social restrictions as to sex or age. Imbibing liquor is approved of by the society and forms a major part of ceremonial and religious functions.

The Kuttia Kondh are addicted to two types of drinking, daily drinking and festive or occasional drinking. Men and sometimes also women drink *mada* or toddy from the *mada mara* (*salap*) or sago palm, also known as the kittul palm. The *salap* tree gives juice from early winter till late summer, but does not produce toddy during the rainy season. Toddy drinking is not as common among women as men because women rarely frequent the *madang basa,* i.e., the toddy drinking place. They do drink toddy, however, if it is brought to them by men, or if they are invited to *madang basa* where they are served separately. Toddy is considered to be food.

Salap juice is collected in an earthen pot and mixed with many types of roots or bark to make it more intoxicating. The owner of the tree then calls his peer group and others to drink together. The earthen pot is kept on the floor and its contents divided equally between everyone present in the *madang basa*. It is believed that this type of community drinking has been learnt from the stars in the sky. There is a group of stars called "*kukurpunganga*" which have the shape of a tree with people sitting around it. When toddy is fresh juice taken from a tree, it is considered to have a positive effect on health.

A *salap* tree in the forest is an important plant in the Kuttia Kondh culture as it is the focus of get-togethers in the forest. It is the property of a particular individual and only that person has the right to harvest the juice. The tree can change ownership if in agreement with the person who planted it. If the owner is still alive but old (*dera*) and no longer physically able to harvest the tree, he can choose a successor and allow him to collect the inflorescence known as *kama* to obtain the juice ("*kama*" is likened to a mother's breast). When the owner of a tree dies, it is inherited to his relatives or, indeed, to anyone chosen by the person who planted the tree. Occasionally, the owner allows others to collect juice from the tree, but it is rare for an individual to climb it without the permission of the owner. If this should happen, this transgression may lead to murder, since it will provoke the owner to great rage.

Certain rituals are normally performed before the first juice from the tree is collected. The owner invites the *jani* — village priest, the *kutaka* — the sorcerer/astrologer, the *majhi* — village headman, and other people for the first drink. The *jani* worships the tree and offers a *puja* to the *dukeli* (ghost/spirit) of the dead person who planted it. If however, the person responsible for the planting is alive, the *puja* is given for his ancestors. *Pranga* (rice) and *paeriaku* (leaves of *Bauhinia vahlii*) are used for the *puja*.

The *jani* addresses the ghost thus:

> We are cutting your tree for toddy. You could also share it with us if you were here. But you are away. May your goodwill be with us. May your tree secrete plenty of sweet, tasty juice for your "*mila dali*" (offspring).

This occasion is a social event in which village guests sit together and drink. They sit beneath a tree in the circular arrangement representing the cluster of stars called "*kukurpunganga*". The person distributes the toddy equally, serving himself last, so that all "*jella*" (life) may be satisfied. The first "*dumuni*" (a gourd measure) is generally given to an elderly man before being passed on to other age groups.

When the drinking party ends, as so many people are gathered together in one place, the occasion is recognised as a good opportunity to hold a meeting to discuss problems or forthcoming events likely to involve most of the villagers, e.g., attending a court case or the clearing of forest for shifting cultivation. Topics not deemed relevant to the welfare of the village people are avoided. Everybody at this stage is in a good mood and takes an interest in the matters discussed.

When the juice of the tree has been tapped, the good or bad qualities of the man who planted the tree are sometimes assessed according to the quantity of juice produced. If the tree's yield is weak, this is believed to represent the dissatisfaction of either the *dukeli* or someone's *jella*. When this is the case, the *kutaka* investigates the reasons for the poor harvest by throwing some unhusked rice grains at the tree. By appealing to the gods, the *kutaka* may identify the spirit to ensure a better yield in the future. In case the juice has been stolen from the pitcher, the *kutaka* must decide whether or not the culprit deserves to be punished.

Mada (toddy) is important for gift exchange, normally a feature of a number of social occasions such as marriages or funerals. When a person visits a friend's house, he takes some toddy with him, preferably of the *salap* tree. The *jani* and *kutaka* are sometimes served with this juice during festivals (*kalu*). During the festival known as "*badbinere dakina*" — the "farewell *puja*" offered to "Kamati Penu" — the *jani* and *kutaka* live on the fermented or non-fermented juice of *salap* or on the distilled liquor of *mahula* (*Madhuka longifolia*). On other ceremonial occasions, villagers drink the juice that is available and the *jani* and *kutaka* have the lion's share.

The *salap* tree or "*mada mara*" generates certain feelings in the Kuttia Kondh, and is subject of a number of folk songs. In one song about *mada mara*, the effects of drinking toddy juice are recounted as follows:

> There was a "*mada mara*". It developed my appetite. I drink it to quench my thirst and "*nisa*" (addiction) developed and my hunger demanded meat. I found some and ate it. Then I slept soundly.

Due to its high sugar and starch content, the juice of the tree has a high nutritional value. The fermented juice is easily digested and also is a welcome source of energy. In winter the juice acts as an "internal blanket", and in summer as a "cooling agent". In summer, the substantial yield of sap from the tree sustains the tribe over the lean periods. Besides the sap, the central part of the young tree called "*jendi*" is collected and ground after drying for use as flour for *chapatti* (bread) and cakes. *Jendi,* more widely known as sago, is an edible starch. "*Ganju padasi*", the fruits of the tree *Semecarpus anacardium*, are made into a garland and tied to the "*kama*" as protection against the evil eye, (e.g., if there is no secretion of the inflorescence). From time to time, magic is performed for the same reason.

The cutting of the "*kama*" needs constant attention as it has to be cut two or three times a day in order to obtain a good yield of juice. A filtering net, a pitcher and a knife are usually kept beside every tree. If juice is collected from more than one tree in the same place, people usually sit under the youngest tree to drink together.

In fact, it is claimed that the affinity between the Kuttia Kondh and *mada mara* is so powerful that they experience "illness when it is ill, and wellbeing when it is well", and furthermore, that an outsider who plants a *salap* tree will always be remembered by them.

The second type of drink consumed by the Kuttia Kondh is *"irpi kalu"*, i.e., *adkinga* or *mahula* liquor prepared from the flowers of *Madhuka latifolia*, and mainly prepared by the Pano all year round. Nowadays, the Kuttia Kondh sometimes make their own liquor during the flowering season of the *mahula* tree (*puju mara*). This is an innovation, however, as it was previously regarded as a trade commodity of the Pano only. One bottle of pure *mahula* liquor costs about twelve rupees; mixed with water, it costs five or six rupees. Basically, the Pano community purchases the *mahula* flowers from the Kuttia and sells it back to them in the form of liquor. *Mahula* liquor is indispensable in their ceremonies and rituals as it is used by the sorcerer, to appease malevolent or benevolent deities. He himself is offered *mahula* liquor before he starts a "*dakina*". This liquor also plays an important role in marriage ceremonies as it forms a part of the bride price.

Apart from the *mahula* liquor, the Kuttia also prepare beverages from crops and these are used like liquor, for example, *katul* or *kalu* from little millet called *kueri* (*Panicum miliare*). *Kueri* is pounded in small quantities and after some water is added, a paste is produced. This is stored on *siali* leaves near the fireplace or hung from the loft over the hearth. The *kueri* paste is then left for fifteen days to one month and, during this time turns red. A fine powder produced from it afterwards is called *kena*.

Sometimes the grains are cooked with a little water to soften them, then they are kneaded to form balls they call *richkinamu*. These are placed in earthen pots called *guna*. Water and one handful of *kena* are added to the balls. The mouth of this pot is then stuffed with *siali* leaves. After three days, there is further kneading of the balls and *kena* by hand to blend them. Water is then added and the resulting liquor acquires a pinkish-red hue and is ready for drinking.

There are many restrictions as regards the preparation of *kena*. Only after a *puja* is offered by the *jani*, new *kueri* can be used to prepare *kena*. This worship is called "*kena dakina*". *Kena* is prepared only on Tuesdays and Fridays, as other days are considered inauspicious for its preparation.

Another beverage, *katul,* is usually prepared during festivals and ceremonies and is the easiest to prepare. *Katul* is prepared in everybody's house for the festival called *puni kalu*, a celebration of the new or full moon (*puni*) and organised in January. (Kalu stands for "liquor, legs and pestle"). Before the *puni kalu* festival, the preparation and drinking of *katul* are restricted to religious occasions. It is also very cheap compared to *mahula* liquor. *Salap* toddy is available in small quantities only but large quantities are required during festivals and ceremonies. *Mahula* liquor is a token to be offered to the deities and used as a customary gift in many social events. If *salap* toddy is available for a ceremony, only the important guests, i.e., the *kunia*, are given one glass each, whereas *mahula* is served to all guests. *Katul*, on the other hand, may be consumed at any time of the day since the alcoholic content is very low by comparison to the distilled *mahula* liquor. To drink *katul*, men and women sit separately. It is served with the long-handled gourd called *kreti*, and drunk from an aluminium pot.

In the past the Kuttia claim to have produced liquor from the fruit of *maska mara* (*mango, Mangifera indica*), *puju mara* (*Mowra butter tree, Madhuka longifolia*), *pansi mara* (*Jackfruit, Artocarpus heterophyllus*), *tade mara* (the banana plant) (*Musa sapientum*) and molasses. Today, they largely consume toddy from the sago palm and date palm, distilled *mahula* liquor and crop beverages. Liquor derived from molasses is also prepared by the pano and sold to the Kuttia Kondh. Toddy from the sago palm tree is locally considered to be the best of all liquors.

The Kuttia Kondh also use tobacco as a stimulant in addition to liquor. Dry tobacco leaves (*dhuan bada*) are mixed with lime and ground to a powder known as *dua* or *nasa*. *Dua* or *nasa* are important gifts that are offered to people as a token of hospitality. Dry tobacco powder rolled into a *siali* or *sal* leaf is smoked as a *kali* (cigar). Another type of stimulant is *gudakhu,* a substance kept under the tongue or lips, or used to brush the teeth, and is usually purchased from the Pano or local shops.

HOUSEHOLD ARTICLES

Over recent decades, modernization has increasingly created an impact on the material culture of the Kuttia Kondh. The use of radio, electronic devices, and vehicles has become part of Kuttia Kondh's material culture. Moreover, there have been other changes in the social life of the Kuttia Kondh, such as housing structures and architecture. Economically disadvantaged families still stick to the old traditions, but wealthier families have begun to adopt modern items in their material culture. Most of the Kuttia Kondh families keep guns (*banang*) for example, some are licenced, and some not. The use of bows and arrows, once the traditional weapon, is waning and the skills required to use them are declining. The material culture of the Kuttia Kondh is described below with particular emphasis on those household articles in every-day use, made from materials derived from the forest.

KITCHEN EQUIPMENT

The Kuttia Kondh cook their food in earthen pots (*bandi*) purchased from *kumbhar* (potters) and often marketed by local Pano traders. Although they sometimes use aluminium pots and kitchen utensils, they prefer to cook in the earthen pots even though they are far less durable. Aluminium utensils are more often used to carry food to their work sites.

An earthen pot is known as "*verga bandi*" and its lid as "*situ*". The aluminium pot is called "*javi*". A long handled spoon with a cup-like scoop at the end is referred to as "*kreti*". The hat-shaped spoon is called "*sata*" made from wood of *gambar mara* (*Gmelina arborea*). Other species like *dengen mara* (*Xylia xylocarpa*), *sal* (*Shorea robusta*) and *Grewia tiliaefolia* may be used for the purpose. Besides these cooking items "*ketali*", mostly made from gourds, are used to carry food over long distances.

A working instrument is the *kalu*, i.e., the pestle used to pound paddy and other grains. The *kalu* is a wooden club with an iron or brass ring at the base, made from *sal* wood, *piasal* (called *bengeri mara-Pterocarpus marsupium*) and *sissoo* tree (*muje mara-Dalbergia sissoo*). *Piasal* wood is often used for *kalu* while *sissoo* wood is preferred for its considerable durability and rigidity. The *seni*, i.e., the rice pounding mortar moulded into the earth is mostly made from the wood of *sal*, *piasal* or *sissoo*. For grinding spices, chilly etc., two smooth stones called '*manda vali*' are generally used.

WATER STORING ARTICLES AND EATING VESSELS

Water is usually carried in aluminium or brass pots (*gara*) to the house from streams, wells or tube wells. The *kreti* (or long handled gourd) is used to take water from the pots. The Kuttia Kondh usually eat from a *batki* which is a bowl with a flat base, rounded body, preferably made of brass, though steel and aluminium are also used. Besides this, they have *gina* made of aluminium or brass and *thali,* i.e., plates called *jadai*. They do not usually use glasses, but drink water directly from the *kreti*.

ARTICLES TO KEEP CLOTHES

In the past, clothes were kept in boxes made from bamboo (called *suka* or *kappa*). Nowadays, these have been replaced by tin and zinc boxes, used to store women's clothes — men have fewer clothes than women — and ornaments of value. Clothing, frequently worn, is hung inside the house on a rope line made from woven *siali* (*Bauhinia vahlii*) bark. Often the rope is replaced by bamboo (called *mani*). The Kuttia Kondh collect forked tree branches, bent bamboo roots and pieces of bamboo with short branches (*mani gadi*) to fix them as hangers on the walls of their homes. For decoration, people hang up horns of *kateri* (barking deer) on the walls.

SLEEPING FURNITURE

The Kuttia Kondh usually sleep on cots known as *kadeli* with wooden legs and ropes. The ropes are made from *bobe randa* (sabai grass-

Eulaliopsis binata), or from *siali* bark. There are four types of cot design and materials, namely, *barpo kadeli, bana kadeli, kandra kadeli and tati kadeli.*

For *bana kadeli, nana* (rope) of *kahanria* (jute fibre: bark of *Corchorus capsularis* or *Corchorus aestuans-bya: C. acutangulus*), *nana* of *babe* (*sabai grass; Eulaliopsis binata*), *nana of kapeli* (*Malvaceae*), and *nana of paeri* (*Bauhinia vahlii*) are used. The legs (*khuranga*) and frames (*sandanga*) of this type of cot are made from *daman mara* (*Grewia tiliaefolia*), because it is a light but hard and durable wood. The cots are woven (*sachina)* by the Kuttia Kondh.

For *barpo kadeli,* the same type of ropes is used as for *bana kadeli*, but the weaving design is different. The wood used for frames and legs is *Grewia tiliaefolia*.

For *Kandra kadeli*, the rope of *kahanria* and blades of cane called *veta* (*Calamus tenuis / C. guruba / C. latifolius*) are generally used. The weaving pattern is different from the others.

Of all cot types, *kandra kadeli* is a status symbol for the Kuttia Kondh, while *barpo* and *bana kadeli* are standard, and *tati kadeli* is the most common, made of siali rope and damoa wood. Some of the cots are also made using the wood of other species like *gambar mara* (*Gmelina arborea*), *muje mara* (*Dalbergia sissoo*) and *bengeri mara* (*Pterocarpus marsupium*).

The production of cots relates to the availability of grass species. *Siali* is commonly available in the forest. *Babe* is sometimes cultivated and also found in forests. *Babe* grows on stony and dry places where it does particularly well if it rains in winter. The grass is cut twice a year, (i.e., at the onset of the rainy season and at the onset of the winter season) and it regenerates with new young shoots (*kanang sapine*). The regeneration of grass species is called *kadgali sapine* and the tuff of the *babe* grass is called *brejene*. *Kahanria* is cultivated, but wild species are also available. The Kuttia Kondh do not cultivate *kahanria*, as the *kapeli* plant is widely available in the forest.

Cots are usually made shorter than the normal height of a man since they believe the life span of a man sleeping in a bed bigger than himself will be reduced, a decline referred to as *ainsi katelane* in their language. The Kuttia Kondh also sleep on a bamboo mat (called *tati*) with some clothing on top, mainly women and children do so.

STORING ARTICLES

The Kuttia Kondh generally do not buy containers to store their food grains, but make their own out of bamboo. Sometimes, they purchase bamboo containers of various types from the Pano and from the market. The biggest container is called *gaddi*, a medium-size one called *burla* or *burlanga*, and the smaller type to store grains for immediate use, *kacha*.

For measuring grain, the Kuttia use containers called *mana* and *ada*. *Mana* is a bamboo container or a container made out of *veta* (*Calamus sp.*), which weighs about three kilos. *Ada* is a similar container but, weighs only half a kilo. Besides *mana* and *ada*, other bamboo containers like *kacha* are used for borrowing and exchange of goods, as the barter system is practiced.

MUSICAL INSTRUMENTS

The Kuttia Kondh communal ceremonies are made much more lively and interesting by the performance of songs, accompanied by musical instruments made from raw materials of plants, trees or animals, or sometimes goods from the market. One of their musical instruments, for example, is a drum called *tapka*. The body of the drum is made from the root base of young *mada mara* (*Caryota urens*). The rough outer surface is removed and perfectly polished until it looks like a big bowl. The inner hollow space is then filed down so that the thickness of the bowl is about one to two inches thick. The open end is then covered with leather (*panda*). The leather (usually goat or cow) is tied tightly over the face of the bowl and often stuck on using glue from a plant called *jrikeni dakinga*. The leather is first completely dried and then tied to the rim of the drum, and then, to tighten it further, a cane or bamboo stick called *sira* is fixed around it. The base of the drum is bound to the rim by tight ropes made of *siali* bark. The same stick used to pound the leather is used to create the sound and this *tapka* drum is generally beaten ceremonial events on to accompany group dances and in the *Meriah* festival.

Dapkari is a tambourine made from a flat wooden ring of *daman* (*Grewia tiliaefolia*) wood (called *Lada*) covered by a piece of leather, usually goatskin. On the under side of the ring, small holes are drilled and ropes made from *siali* are inserted through them. The ropes on the edge of the ring are then tied to a central ring, also made of rope, and in this way, the ropes radiate out from the wooden ring to the rope and the wooden ring is held tightly in place by this ring. The radial ropes are called *satpinere* while the central rope ring is *sambari*. This instrument produces a different sound from that of the *tapka*.

Kama and *singa* are windblown "horn" pipes (*kama* literally means horn) blown to indicate the beginning of an event. *Kama* is usually blown at marriages, the *Meriah* festival, and the *puni kalu* festival and is made from wild bison horn (*Sama*) just like *Singa*.

Bansi or *bains* is a flute made from bamboo by the Kuttia Kondh to accompany their songs, while a *laudi* is an extraordinary instrument consisting of two sticks, the longer, *muans laudi* and the shorter, *gani pakanga*.

When the Kuttia Kondh dance in groups, they play the *laudi*. The longer stick (sometimes replaced by an iron rod with two or three iron balls attached by fine wire at one end) is held in the left hand with one end perched on the shoulder, while the smaller stick is held in the right hand, and beaten with the longer one in a rhythmic manner producing a jingling sound.

MISCELLANEOUS ARTEFACTS AND HOUSEHOLD EQUIPMENT

Kumang katna mraka is an instrument used to squeeze the testes of young male calves to castrate them, consisting of two wooden cylinders usually made *of daman mara* (*Grewia tiliaefolia*). These are tied to each other at one end by a rope. The testes of the calf are held in between the two rods. Two pieces of bamboo can also serve the purpose, if necessary. Before the process the testes of the calf are massaged with oil, and afterwards, turmeric paste is applied.

Combs (*sireni*) are highly esteemed by the Kuttia Kondh. Kuttia women, and also men with long hair wind their hair in knots to which they attach a comb. *Sireni* are usually made from the stem of *satranga* (i.e. broom grass; *Thysanolaena maxima*). Fine pieces of the stem are tied together with bark fibre from the *salap* tree (*Caryota urens*). The Kuttia Kondh also fashion combs from the wood of the *gambar mara* (*Gmelina arborea*) tree by carving out pointed teeth in a piece and shaping it like a comb. Very small combs are made of *satranga* while slightly bigger ones from *gambar mara* wood.

A *dua duna* is a container in which tobacco is kept. There are two types of containers: one is made by the Kuttia Kondh and pipe-shaped while the other is a tiny box purchased from the market. The locally made version is made from hollow bamboo (or from a grass species similar to bamboo that could not be identified botanically) by cutting the cylinder from the plant in such a manner that one end of the pipe is sealed by the node of the plant, while the other remains open. The outer surface is then engraved using a sharp knife. Kuttia women generally use this type of *duna* and tend to fix it to their waistbands or under a lining of cloth on the waist.

The Kuttia Kondh have modest material needs. Almost all families share a common set of materials. Some household equipment possessed by various families do vary according to their status in the village, and some items are specifically used by men while some are specific to women. For example, the materials possessed by a religious headman differ from those owned by a political headman in the village.

The Use of Prominent Tree and Plant Species

This chapter is dedicated to the use of trees and other plant species that play an important role in Kuttia Kondh culture. Of particular interest are the plants that are highly esteemed or venerated and have a special socio-economic or spiritual significance. It is, by far, not an exhaustive compilation (see also Satapathy 1981).

ACHYRANTHES ASPERA, L

Family : Amaranthaceae
Oriya : Apamaranga/Apmarg

Kui : Nakudipalu
Eng. : Prickly chaff/ Rough Chaff flower

This entire plant is used in rituals for the protection of crops from theft. It is worshipped in a ritual involving the teeth of the *kutra (kateri*/barking deer/*Muntiacus muntijack*) and the twigs of the date palm (*Phoenix sylvestris*); it is then tied to a bamboo stick and placed at the centre of the kitchen garden. It is believed that if crops or vegetables are stolen, the culprit's cheeks will swell up. Usually, the fear of discovery deters most people from stealing food from kitchen gardens. Pieces of the root of the plant are given to the poultry to cure severe cases of diarrhoea. Local Oriya people also use the plant in various rituals.

ARUNDO DONAX, L./BAMBUSA SP.

Family : Poaceae/Gramineae
Kui : Mani
Oriya : Baunsa
Eng. : Giant reed, Spanish cane/bamboo

Giant reed, cane and bamboo species are perennial grasses that grow wild throughout the area, particularly in the hill forest and along ditches, streams (*jadi*), and on barren land (*agari*). Although botanically distinct, the Kuttia Kondh use the same term for all three as they play a significant social role in their livelihood and religious practices. For example, they are required for *dharani puja* (worship of the earth goddess) during *masa juda gasnali* (harvesting) in *Diwali lanju* (November). In addition, their utilization value is immense: they are used in house construction and woven to form walls between the main poles (called *sella* or *tati*). Mats laid on the ground are also made from it and used to sleep on. Storage baskets (*kacha*), boxes (*kapa*) for storing womens' clothes and valuables as well as large reservoirs for storing corn (*burda*) are usually made by the Kuttia Kondh themselves and sometimes purchased from the Pano. Bamboo is also used to make containers for measuring grain, namely, *mana* and *ada*. Bent bamboo shoots are used as hooks (*mani gadi*), and flattened bamboo is used to make shelves. It is also used for making flutes, bows and arrows, bed frames and posts. A bamboo pipe can also serve as a type of oven for cooking meat: meat is put inside the bamboo pipe, the ends are sealed with earth or leaves and the pipe is burnt, so imparting a good flavour to the meat.

During the lean periods, from April/May until July/August, the Kuttia Kondh eat bamboo shoots to supplement their diet. The tribe collects young bamboo shoots (*terka*) and ground them into a paste. This is pressed to remove the water and the residual bamboo (which now is solid) is ground again and the flour is boiled in hot water to which rice is added. If the water is removed from the cooked rice, it is known as "*terka bidi*" (meaning *terka* rice); otherwise, it is called "*terka jada*". "*Kanji*" is another delicious food prepared from bamboo shoots: the shoots are cut into thin chips that are dried in the sun and added to *dhal* (lentils) or curry. The chips can also be preserved for the lean period.

BAUHINIA VAHLII, WT. & ARN.

Family	:	Caesalpiniaceae
Oriya	:	Siali
Kui	:	Paeri

The leaves of this plant are flattened and used for plates and packages, while corn is stored in vessels made of *siali* leaves. The Kuttia Kondh also fashion pumpkin-shaped vessels from these, putting mustard seeds (*Brassica campestris* of the dichotoma variety) inside, and hanging them on pumpkin creepers in the belief that this will increase the pumpkin yield.

The seeds of the plant are eaten raw or fried like cashew nuts and the plant plays an important role in the tribe's culture and religion, e.g. in acts of worship, in festivals and in ceremonies. *Siali* leaves are used in the preparation of a drink known as *katual*, liquor derived from *kueri* (*Panicum miliare*, little millet) and an important ingredient in the celebrations of the *puni kalu* festival in January. The *kueri* seeds are ground, wrapped in *siali* leaves and hung over the fire for about 15 days. This preparation method is called "*kena*". When the rice powder in the leaves has turned blood red, it is mixed with fresh rice powder and water to prepare *katual*. The bark of the plant is also used to make ropes, such as those used to make a drum.

BOMBAX MALABARICUM, DC. (= BOMBAX CEIBA)

Family	:	Bombacaceae
Kui	:	Laka mara
Hindi	:	Simul
Oriya	:	Simuli
Eng.	:	Silk cotton tree

The simul tree, known by the Kuttia Kondh as *laka mara*, is widely used for cultural and practical purposes. Although the tree grows on many different types of land, it grows best in cool valleys and is easy to grow either from seed or by transplanting. The sap tapped from the trunk is often used by local people to treat diarrhoea while the seeds are boiled and eaten during the lean period (summer). The "silk cotton" is used for stuffing pillows.

A branch of the simul tree is worshipped at the child-naming ceremony, known as *dukeli dakina* ("worship of the ghost"). A simul pole (*laka munda*) is erected facing east, towards Sapangada, the mythical birthplace of the Kuttia Kondh in front of the house of the family concerned. A child is usually named at around three years of age, and is given the name of the paternal grandfather. He is invited to *dukeli dakina* and a hen or pig sacrifice is offered to the *dukeli* (ghost/spirit) of the child's grandfather.

The *jani* (priest) and *kutaka* (*gunia* — astrologer/sorcerer) preside over the *puja*, and the *jani* addresses the penu and the *dukeli* of their ancestors. The words chanted by the *jani* can be translated as: "our fathers' grandfathers used to offer *laka munda* (the simul pole), in the same way we are making the offering." The *jani* never uses the name of the *dukeli* as it is taboo to use the name of the dead. Rather, the worship is offered to the "Elu Penu" or home deity. For *laka munda,* the main trunk of the tree is not cut but instead the side branches. The *jani* chants:

sarikena sarimoru bamu	Come (deities) from four corners
lakamunda simda munda sina	We will offer you *laka munda* (simul pole)

la adedhi la apati bamu	Come *la adedhi* and *la apati**
karamara bidimara bamu	Come *kara* (?) tree and *bidi* (?) tree.**
nachadanga, ta adanga bamu	Come Nachadanga, *ta adanga*
lakamunda simuda munda gaisi	For *Laka Munda.*
daru padasi inji arapimaja	We offer it to you.

Simul wood materials are also a feature of the *dasera kandanga dakina* festival, celebrated during Durga puja in October (the month known as *Dasehra lanju*), and also at the "*badbinere*" ("farewell") festival, celebrated during March-April (*Chaita lanju*). These are the only occasions when a *puja* is offered to *Kama Penu/Kamati Penu, the malevolent goddess who causes small pox, chicken pox, measles and other bodily manifestations collectively known as "*bicha*", literally meaning "seeds". *Laka munda* is collected from the trunk of a virgin (before flowering) simul tree and is formed in the shape of a horse. The legs of the horse called '*kalka*' are made of bamboo. Three pieces of simul wood are needed to make the three swords (*kanda*) kept on the back of the wooden horse. This horse is then worshipped as it is the sacred *bahana* (vehicle) of the *Kama* goddess.

At the *badbinere* festival, the goddess is invoked (*basni*) on a Monday, and on a Wednesday, she is bid farewell (*badbinere*). Immediately afterwards, the villagers fetch some castor oil in a *sal* leaf pot (*dana*) with some *kueri* (*Panicum sp.*), rice and the plucked feathers of a chicken. The feathers are dipped in the oil and all *kutakas*, including those from the surrounding villages, are given one feather. Then the villagers offer *mahula* (distilled liquor of *Madhuka longifolia*) to the *jani* and the *kutaka* who attend the ceremony and escort them to their houses. The leaves of the tree are worn by the *jani* during the worship.

Besides the simul pole, other plant species and plant parts (e.g. coconut, plantain, rice, ganjei leaves (*Cannabis sativa*), *afu* (Opium;

(* *La adedhi* and *la apati* are parts of a wooden structure regarded as "*elu penu*" — the home deity.** These trees are only known to the *kutaka* or *jani*.)

Papaver somniferum), the flowers of *Hibiscus rosasinensis* and *Holarrhena antidysenterica*, and the leaves of *Azadirachta indica* and *Shorea robusta* are also used in the *puja*.

Moreover, simul wood is occasionally used in the forest to make fire. A hole is bored into a small piece of wood. Another piece is then inserted into the hole and rolled back and forth in a drilling action. The heat produced by the movement of wood against wood ignites the dry leaves kept beside it.

CASSIA FISTULA, L.

Family	:	Cae Salpiniaceae
Kui	:	Pundeni mara
Oriya	:	sunari
Eng.	:	Indian laburnum

It is believed that the home deity will leave the house, if the wood of this particular species is used as fuel. Moreover, it is claimed that the wood produces a smoke that attracts insects into the house, and if this wood is burnt inside the nephews of the house owner will fall ill. Consequently, using the wood of this tree as firewood is taboo.

The root bark of the tree is a good fermenting agent and the partially burnt bark is used for the fermentation of toddy. Toddy treated with this bark is taken to prevent diarrhoea.

CARYOTA URENS, L.

Family	:	Arecaceae
Kui	:	Mada mara
Oriya	:	*Salap*
Eng.	:	Indian Sago palm

The *salap* tree is reasonably common in some parts of the Kondhmals of Orissa and moreover it is sometimes planted. The tree has numerous practical uses, the most significant of which is the manufacture of toddy from *salap* sap produced by the tree from early winter until late summer. The *salap* tree, known to the Kuttia Kondh as "*mada mara*", is regarded as one of the most important plant species and in terms of forest conservation it is a tree that every member of the tribe would like to own. The sap derived from a 15-20 year old tree, regarded by the tribe as its "elixir of life", is said to be delicious and endowed with a high starch content.

CISSAMPELOS PAREIRA, L. VAR. HIRUSTA (DC) FORMAN

Family : Menispermaceae
Kui : Dindidipa tulla
Oriya : Akanbindhi
Eng. : False pareira brava

The Kuttia Kondh wear the roots of this plant on their person in the belief that it cures fever which may come periodically. Children are made to wear the splinters of this plant on their arms to prevent fever and ward off the evil eye. The root of the plant is also a very good fermenting agent in preparing *salap* toddy and when treated with it, it is good for children. The roots of the plant are pounded in a pestle, and taken against diarrhoea.

EMBLICA OFFICINALIS, GAERTN.

Family : Euphorbiaceae
Kui : Surga
Oriya : Amla
Eng. : Indian gooseberry

A twig of the tree is used in specific ceremonies, for example, when a sambar is killed, the *kutaka* will worship the dead sambar using a twig from this tree. Its fruits are collected, dried and sold in the market. The Kuttia Kondh also eat the fruits as a side dish with rice. Normally, this tree would not be used as firewood in houses. If it is burnt as firewood, it is believed that no chicks will hatch from hens' eggs.

FICUS SCANDENS ROXB.

Family : Moraceae
Kui : Pipada
Oriya : Jari

The leaf of the *pipada* shrub is a necessity in almost all magic rituals, festivals and religious ceremonies. Before offering a *puja* to the *kama* penu, a garland is made with *pipada* leaves to be worn by the *kutaka* and *jani*. It is said that penu has directed the *kutaka* to wear a garland of *pipada* leaves before offering *puja*. The leaves in the garland are tied into bunches with *paeri nanka* (the bark or fibre of *Bauhinia vahlii*). A tree in nearby settlements is selected for worship three times a year, namely, in Kama Penu (Durga) *puja*, in *puni kalu* and in *badbinere*.

Sometimes the leaves of *bel mara* (bael tree/*Aegle marmelos*) and of *maska mara* (mango tree/*Mangifera indica*) are also added to the garland of *pipada* leaves. Furthermore, a twig of the tree is used in a ritual to cure people from illnesses such as fever. This twig is placed on the thatch of the house of the sick person and joined by a thread to a leaf, suspended above the patient's head. It is believed that life comes to the patient through the *pipada* leaf.

People do not cut this tree or its branches as the tree is regarded the abode of goddesses. Moreover, the hill forests where many trees of this species are found are regarded as very sacred places, such as Siram Deu hill, for example.

GREWIA TILIAEFOLIA

Family : Tiliaceae
Kui : Daman
Oriya : Dhaman

Though generally occuring throughout the state in the forest area, this tree particularly thrives in valleys and on the lower slopes of the southern exposed hills. *Daman mara* is known to every Kuttia Kondh as a very valuable source of wood used in the construction of agricultural and household equipment. The distribution of the species is adequate in and around their locality. Axes are the most common weapon used by the tribals to protect themselves from dangerous animals. Axe handles and handles of other agricultural implements such as hand hoes are made out of the branches of this tree. "Every tribal knows the plant like his axe" is their saying about the use of the plant. The wood is also used for making a *juadi* (yoke) and *data* (harrow).

A tool used to castrate male calves is made from *daman mara*. A percussion instrument resembling the tambourine, known as a *dapkari*, is also made from the wood of the *daman mara*. The Kuttia Kondh prefer to use *daman mara* above any other for the making of cot frames (*sandanga*) because the wood is strong and light. The wood is sometimes used to make *kreti*, the long handled ladle/spoon from which the Kuttia Kondh drink water or serve toddy.

HOLARRHENA ANTIDYSENTERICA (Roth) wall, ex Dc

Family : *Apocyanaceae*
Kui : Kude mara
Oriya : Kuduchi

This small tree is distributed throughout the state and its roots are used to ferment *salap* juice. The roots, when kept in the pitcher used for collecting *salap* sap, give the juice a bitter taste, and the bark is ground raw and taken against diarrhoea. Other parts of the tree are said to be effective in curing epilepsy, indigestion and worms while the flowers of the plant are used in *puja*s and worn by Kuttia girls in group dances.

LAGENARIA VULGARIS (Seringe, *Cucurbita Lagenaria*)

Family : *Cucurbitaceae*
Kui : Anka, Pita
Oriya : Lau
Eng. : Bottle Gourd

This plant is sacrificed in the *puni kalu* (Full Moon) festival celebrated in *Pusa lanju* (January). Before *puni kalu*, it is forbidden to eat the fruit.

MADHUKA LONGIFOLIA (KOENIG) MACH.
= (BASSIA LATIFOLIA. ROXB.)

Family : *Sapotaceae*
Kui : Puju mara
Oriya : *Mahula*
Eng. : Mowra Butter tree

The sweet pulp of the ripe fruit is edible and is an important drink of the Kuttia Kondh and other forest dwellers. The liquor is prepared from its flowers called *adkinga*. The Kuttia Kondh have traditionally regarded the production of this liquor as a trade privilege of the Pano. They were providing them with the mahuli flowers and after processing they bought the liquor from them. Recently, though, the Kuttia Kondh have also developed an interest in this trade.

The *puja penka,* or seeds of the tree, are fried and put into a large wooden pot, are then pulverised and pressed. Filtered it is used as hair massage oil for children. The bark of the tree is also ground up and taken to cure epilepsy.

This tree has a religious significance, in particular, when the wooden images of Dharani Penu are to be worshipped and set up on land that has been slashed and burned. The Kuttia sometimes put their clan deities under large *mahula* trees if neither a large *sal* nor a mango is available in the area, since a huge tree is believed to be auspicious for the placement of Dharani Penu.

MANGIFERA INDICA

Family	:	Anacardiaceae
Kui	:	Maska mara
Oriya	:	Amba
Eng.	:	Mango

In Kuttia culture, the mango fruit is associated with a festival called *taka kalu,* celebrated in the month of July (*Asad lanju*). The endocarp of the mango is worshipped in the *podu* fields (slash-and-burn sites) called "*bagada*" at a *puja* usually organised when crops are one foot heigh. The mango seed is cut and the endosperm (*taka*) offered to the Dharani Penu, so that the penu will not be angry when the crops germinate and break the soil layer. A pig or hen sacrifice is also offered to the penu and the blood of this sacrifice is spread on the crops in the fields. Meanwhile, the people pray to the penu for a good harvest.

The endocarp is dried and powdered to make gruel, preserved and later eaten by the Kuttia during the lean months, or to feed the pigs. The endosperm can also be pestled and the paste be applied to deep cuts, for instance, by an axe. The bark of the tree is ground, mixed with water and given to patients against diarrhoea. Both unripe and ripe mangos are preserved by indigenous means as a dish served with rice and the Kuttia Kondh make garlands with mango leaves to decorate their house premises on festive occasions. The bark of the tree is also used successfully to induce fermentation in *salap* and date palm toddy. In the past, the Kuttia Kondh obtained toddy from the mango tree, but now they replace it with toddy from the *mada mara (Caryota urens)* and *puja mara (Madhuka longifolia).*

MUSA PARADISIACA, L.

Family	:	Musaceae
Kui	:	Tade mara
Oriya	:	Kadali
Eng.	:	Banana

In the Kuttia world of religion and medicine, the banana plant is significant. According to the legends and tales of the Kuttia Kondh, this plant was once used as a sacrifice in the *Meriah* festival and its juice, considered to be a blood offering to the deity. Nowadays, the plant is used in magic rituals to cure illness. The *kutaka* will be instructed by the god in a dream to sacrifice a plant on behalf of the sick person, it is believed, and when the *yama penu*, i.e. the demon god, has been appeased with a plant sacrifice, the patient will begin to recover.

The Kuttia Kondh also maintain that evil may befall a house nearby a banana tree if it flowers in the direction of the house. The juice of the plant is used to treat burns and the fresh juice is used to treat the bleeding from cuts and wounds. In addition, the flowers, fruit, and pith of the plant are eaten and it is also used as a detergent.

OCIMUM BASILICUM

Family	:	Lamiaceae
Kui	:	Jaranga
Oriya	:	Bana landa baguli
Eng.	:	Sweet basil

This annual is moderately distributed throughout the state. Burning the seeds of this plant produces a smoke that rids poultry sheds of lice, while the raw leaves, when scattered on beds, are said to repel bed bugs. The juice of the leaves is applied to cuts and wounds to stop the bleeding.

SHOREA ROBUSTA GAERTN. F.

Family : Dipterocarpaceae
Kui : Sargi mara
Oriya : *Sal*
Eng. : Sal tree

This tree is particularly valued for its timber and is found throughout the state. *Sal* timber has an important role in the *meriah* festival, known as *biakatina* — the greatest festival of the Kuttia Kondh. The *meriah* pole (*karumunda-karu* means buffalo) is made from *sal* and is cut down about fifteen days before the festival. This festival is celebrated at an interval of five to seven years in January or February (*Magha lanju*) when the village economy, which is dependent on the annual crop yield, is reasonably healthy. The *kutaka*, who maintains total abstinence (*upavas*) on the day the *karumunda* is collected, enters the forest accompanied by two or three people who are also fasting. He selects a *sal* tree, chants a *mantra* and throws rice at the tree. When he has received the necessary auspicious signs, he orders his followers to cut down the tree. If, during the cutting, a cat, jackal, dead snake, monkey or empty pitcher is seen, or the sound of a monkey, woodpecker or peacock is heard, this is interpreted as an evil sign and the tree is rejected. The tree for the *karumunda* should be straight and devoid of bigger branches, have no traces of resin or broken branches, be not affected by "*gochchi*" (plant parasites or epiphytes, mostly orchids), and have emerged from the earth as a single, independent tree.

The Elu Penu or home deity (established in front of or inside every house) is made of *sal* wood and is represented by a stand comprised of a base pole "*dedhi*" and another piece of *sal* placed on top called "*pata*". The *sal* base pole is constructed differently according to the particular deity it is to represent. Sacrificial posts and posts for worship and rituals are also made of *sal* and in addition, *sal* leaves are required for *puja* activities and for making pots (*dana*) in which all things used in a *puja* are kept. Powdered resin is used in all types of worships and rituals.

In house construction, the Kuttia Kondh use *sal* poles to construct the structure (*dedhi* are vertical poles while *aru* are the horizontal). The spaces between the poles are filled in with branches of the *sal* tree, or with sheets of woven bamboo, as mentioned earlier. It is believed that poles cut from mature *sal* trees are rarely damaged by insects, while the smoke from burning *sal* resin in houses also helps to drive away mosquitoes.

Sal is one of the preferred woods used to make agricultural implements such as ploughs (*nangeli*) and harrows (*data*). Two varieties of plough of different design are used — the *sechipala* drawn by a bullock on hard, stony land, and the *kasnapala* drawn by a buffalo over softer ground.

Sal is sometimes used to make the *kreti*, the long handled ladle/spoon from which the Kuttia Kondh drink water or serve toddy. *Sal* is one of the woods used for making domestic pestles (wooden clubs with a brass ring at the base, usually decorated) to be used for pounding paddy and other grains (*kalu*). The *seni*, the mortar or hollowed-out object in which the grain is pounded is also made from *sal*. The fruit of the *sal* is eaten during the lean season and oil is extracted from the seeds by boiling. This is used for cooking and burning. Moreover, *sal* leaves are wrapped around dry tobacco leaves to be smoked as cigars (*kali*).

TERMINALIA TOMENTOSA (DC) W & A

Family	:	Combretaceae
Kui	:	Mardi Mara
Oriya	:	Asan
Eng.	:	Sain

In Kuttia Kondh myth, it is said that long ago, a pole cut from this tree was used as sacrificial post when humans were sacrificed. A mythical "sacrifical post" made from this tree can be seen in

Sapangada, the mythical birthplace of the Kuttia Kondh. In oral myths it is often described that the Kuttia Kondh came out of the earth with the help of a creeper (*Bauhinia vahlii*), one end of it being tied to the post. Thus, it is a tree with immense religious significance.

The smooth bark is added to the *mahula* flower mixture when brewing *mahula* liquor, and this is said to minimise its toxicity. Moreover, the raw leaves are crushed to a paste and used as a hair shampoo.

THYSANOLAENA MAXIMA, O. KTZE.
= (T, AGROSTIS, NEES)

Family	:	Poaceae
Kui	:	Satranga
Oriya	:	Phool Jhadu
Eng.	:	Ravine broom

Satranga is a tall grass that grows on moist and shady slopes in the forest, especially on steep banks along ravines and water sources. Elderly people with long hair make a knot in their hair and fix it with a comb made from the soft stems of this plant. This comb looks like a brush since the thin stems of the plant are tied together with fibre extracted from the leaf sheaths of *Caryota urens*. This comb is not especially good for combing the hair, but regarded as a traditional ornament. A piece of *satranga* worn or kept on the body is said to keep the ghosts away while the panicles are used in many rituals. In addition, panicles of the plant are made into brooms that are widely sold.

XYLIA XYLOCARPA (ROXB.) JAUB

Family	:	Leguminosae
Kui	:	Dengen Mara
Oriya	:	Tangan

The wood of *dengen mara* is used in the construction of ploughs and its branches are preferred for construction of walls between the poles of the house structure.

THEMDA ARUNDINACEA

Family : Gramineae
Kui : Chhana
Oriya : *Chhapar ghas*

Chhana is a forest grass traditionally used in thatching the roofs of houses, but since the thatch needs replacing after little more than a year, it is more and more replaced by tiles.

PTEROCARPUS MARSUPIUM (ROXB.)

Family : Fabaceae
Kui : Bengeri Mara
Oriya : Piasal Bija
Eng. : Indian Kino Tree

Bengeri mara wood is used for making both bed frames and the pestles (*kalu*) used for pounding grain.

DALBERGIA SISSOO

Family : Leguminosae
Kui : Muje Mara
Oriya : Sisso, Shisham
Eng. : Sisso

The wood of *muje mara* is used for making bed frames and the *seni*, a wooden mortar used for pounding grain. It is also preferred for making ploughs. As *muje mara* has become rare in the forest, alternative species are often used.

EULALIOPSIS BINATA

Family : Gramineae
Kui : Babe randa
Oriya : Sabai grass
Eng. : Bharbur grass

Babe is a grass species that is cultivated, but also often found growing wild in the *kambani* forest. This grass is used to make ropes from which the latticework forming the bed and strung between the two bed ends is woven.

MICHAELIA CHAMPACA L.

Family : Magnoliaceae
Kui : Japi Mara
Oriya : Champa

Japi mara is among the woods used by the Kuttia Kondh to make harrows and to level the field after ploughing.

DIOSPYROS MELANOXYLON ROXB.

Family : Ebenaceae
Kui : Kendu Mara
Oriya : Kendu

A small to moderately sized tree, used to construct the wooden sections of the yokes worn by draught animals.

9

Religion, Magic and Disease

THE Kuttia Kondh myths, rituals and customs have developed from their natural environment, while the worship of animate and inanimate elements indicates their love and fear of nature. The folklore symbolising this relationship, including their primordial song *Kui Gaani* (see Appendix), and the concept of the environment derived from *Kapaka Gaani* (see Appendix), indicate that the Kuttia Kondh's interaction with the forest world is represented in their world-view. Their songs and tales document social processes, and play an important role in the religion of the tribe. The Kuttia Kondh, in fact, consider them to be a record of their religious customs and the *jani* will often refer to these tales at rituals. The folklore portrays the tribe as traditional forest dwellers and at the same time, it can be said that nature has played a significant role in creating the religious framework of Kuttia Kondh society.

In the lore of the Kuttia Kondh, the performance of acts of worship (*dakina*) is given highest precedence, the task allotted only to the religious headman or priest (*majhi*), who is thought to have been chosen by a god to serve society. The priest is the only person powerful enough to deal with the disasters caused by the wrath of those malevolent supernatural powers that inhabit large trees, stones, mountains, hills and other particular landscapes. The religious practitioners (*jani* and *kutaka*) who perform magic and witchcraft are said to possess superhuman powers, but powers inferior to those of gods and goddesses. The Kuttia Kondh ascribe the term "supernatural powers" to deities, goddesses and other unseen powers who create spontaneous and miraculous phenomena which can influence or cause environmental or physical change, or who can influence the lives of human beings and their work. The ordinary tribal layman is unable to see these powers but worships them nevertheless. The *kutaka*, however, has the ability to see and recognise the supernatural powers, and these often appear in the form of a particular plant or animal during dreams. As we have seen, the Kuttia Kondh name them after the places in which they are believed to reside, such as the names of particular tree species, hills or characteristics of the landscape.

Animism is an important facet of the tribe's religious culture. Objects from nature such as large stones, wooden posts and tree stumps, symbolic of gods and goddesses, are set up or placed under a tree in the village and at other places of worship. Wooden posts are designed to represent particular deities. In the context of the village, for example, the *karumunda* or Meriah pole represents Dharani Penu, while in the forest, wooden posts are erected to represent other *penuni*. Supernatural powers may also be represented by the bones of particular animals, such as the jaws of the sambar (*maju*, *Cervus unicolor*), and these are worshipped in people's houses.

The tribe also practises ancestor worship (*dukeli dakina*), for it is believed that unless they are obedient to the ancestral spirits and give offerings, including sacrifice, to show their respect, they risk being punished by those spirits who are able to inflict fatal diseases. An outbreak of fever is thought to represent the wrath of an ancestral spirit. On these occasions, *dukeli dakina* is organised immediately, as otherwise the victim's fever could prove fatal. The tribe's respect for the ancestral spirits ensures its protection from their potentially evil nature and is reflected in many of its social customs.

The Kuttia Kondh maintain that the ancestral spirits generally dwell in the graveyard forests (*tuleni*) and people are not allowed to visit there unless for the purpose of performing death rituals. Again, it is believed that continual disturbance of these forests angers the peace-loving spirits who may harm the individual concerned. Ancestral spirits believed to dwell on the roadside or in big trees must also be respected. It is customary to offer the first crop (after the harvest yet before it is consumed) to these ancestral spirits in gratitude for their beneficence.

The Kuttia Kondh believe that the forest that surrounds them is inhabited by an ancestor known as "*damanaka*" (a name is associated with a species of tree used extensively by the tribe for making material objects (*daman; Grewia tilaefolia*) while *aka* means "grandfather" in Kui). He is regarded as the owner of the forests and his permission is needed before a forest can be exploited. Fear of retribution deters the Kuttia Kondh from randomly exploiting the forest, with the notable exception of forest clearance as part of the preparation for shifting cultivation. On these occasions, some tribes believe that *damanaka* must be worshipped before a patch of forest may be cleared, a claim reiterated in their song, *Kui Gaani*.

As mentioned earlier, the Kuttia Kondh also revere and worship certain tree species directly, namely, *bade mara* (*Ficus benghalensis*), *pipada mara* (*Ficus scandens*), and *eju pipada mara* (*Ficus religiosa*) out of the conviction that these trees are the preferred abodes of the deities. Indirectly, they also worship *jambu mara* (*Syzygium cumini*), *maska mara* (*Mangifera indica*), *mardi mara* (*Terminalia tomentosa*), *baena mara* (*Terminalia bellirica*) and *sargi mara* (*Shorea robusta*), by placing stones, symbolic of the gods, under these trees. Children are also named after the auspicious tree species mentioned above. Patches of forests are as well named after certain plants. The nomenclature of these areas depends upon the abundance of a particular plant or tree growing there.

The *Kui Gaani* also refers to the birth of the vegetative world from the body of a sambar, suggestive of a belief that plants, or at least certain plant species, evolved from animals. For this reason, the sambar is worshipped when one is killed by Kuttia hunters. Many clans in Kuttia society, moreover, are considered to have descended from different types of plants and animals. According to the myth, the Timaka clan, for example, originated from bamboo shoots (cf. chapter 3). They also believe in the transmigration of souls and the ability of a human soul to enter any living creature (although the *kutaka* is thought to be the only person capable of this miraculous act).

It is clear that the phenomena of "nature", the elements and their mysterious forces, form the basis of the Kuttia Kondh religious faith. Moreover, the Kuttia Kondh worship different aspects of nature on specific occasions during the year for they feel that maintaining a reciprocal relationship with nature is essential in order to be protected. Examples of such reciprocal relationships are given below:

1. *Ficus scandens:* its twigs have the power to drive out witches and ghosts. The tree is therefore worshipped, its branches are never cut and efforts are made to ensure that at least one tree of this species grows within the proximity of every village.

2. The hills or forests with a relatively large population of *Ficus scandens* are especially deified, thereby ensuring a minimal exploitation of natural resources in these areas, e.g. the *Siram Deu* hill near Burlubaru.

3. Land ascribed particular religious or mythological significance is rarely exploited by the Kuttia Kondh.

4. The various deities and spiritual beings, which generally inhabit hills and forests or trees, are offered sacrifices in recognition of their benevolence as the force behind a good harvest and the availability of plentiful minor forest produce.

5. Before collecting medicinal plants, the hill deity is worshipped to seek permission to gather the plants. This may also involve a sacrifice depending on a decision by the *kutaka* or *jani*, collector of the medicines. When this is granted, the collector gathers only the quantity that is actually required at the time, rather than storing some up for future use.

6. Similarly, before hunting on a patch of land of particular religious significance, the *kutaka* or *jani* performs a worship to seek the deity's permission to hunt. During the act of worship, they assure the deity that they will only hunt game sufficient to meet their minimum requirements.

In the past, the sacrifice of human beings and offerings of blood to the penu were commonplace amongst the Kuttia Kondh. However, before human sacrifice, people offered the sap of the *bengeri mara* (*Pterocarpus marsupium*) that resembles blood in the belief that it was "tree-blood". Since the late nineteenth century, human sacrifice has been replaced by animal sacrifice.

Sacrifice, taboos and beliefs, music and dance — all have their origins in the Kuttia Kondh's interaction with nature, and are performed by the tribe either as a token of its gratitude or for fear of angering supernatural powers. The conservation and preservation of religious structures, images and symbols, therefore, is either a lesson they have learnt from nature, or an offshoot of their understanding of nature.

Important Religious Events

Festivals are scheduled in the yearly calendar of religious events, and organised on particular days or months of the year. These are events that involve the whole community and culminate in meals attended by everyone. An act of worship, on the other hand, is organised several times a year on different occasions, and involves certain individuals and kin of a family, rather than the community as a whole.

PUNI KALU

Puni kalu, which is the largest regular festival of the year, is celebrated in *Pusa lanju* (December/January) for the worship of Dharani Penu, Deu Kuda Penu and Satari Penu. *Puni* refers to "full moon" and "new moon", and *kalu* to "pestle", "crop liquor" "festival", and "legs". Accordingly, *puni kalu* is organised on a bright moonlit fortnight to mark the beginning of consumption of the yield (mainly millet) from the winter harvest. Particular ceremonial importance is accredited to *kueri* (little millet, *Panicum miliare*) during the festival, and it is first consumed in the form of fermented liquor (*katul*).

The *puja* is performed by two *jani*, one of whom performs obeisance to Dharani Penu and Satari Penu, the village deity, with offerings of pigs, cocks, *kueri, katul*, turmeric and *mahuli* liquor, while the other continues with worship of the Deu Kuda Penu. The Deu Kuda Penu, who represents the god of the nearest hill, is not given a sacrifice other than an offering of eggs. Other *penuni* such as *elu penu, adabai penu* (he who protects the home from fire) and *weda* (sun) *penu* are also worshipped. During the invocation, the priest also invites different hill deities to the site of worship.

During this *puja*, freshly harvested *jata* (*simba, Lablab purpurens*) and *anka* (*Lagenaria piceraria*) are eaten by the villagers, either at a community gathering or by families in their own homes. The new *kueri* offered to the *penuni*, is later used to make *katul*.

MERIAH FESTIVAL (BIA KATINA DAKINA)

The festival is generally celebrated every three years, in the wake of a good harvest, though the gap between festivals may be four or five years, depending upon the economic circumstances of a village. It is always held during full moon in *Chaita lanju* and a *puja* is performed to thank the deity for its goodwill and to ensure that the wellbeing of the village and high yields from agriculture will continue. The identity of the deity to be worshipped, and the place of worship are believed to be revealed to the *kutaka* in a dream.

Nowadays, the main sacrificial offering is a buffalo, though the festival is known for its past tradition of sacrificing human beings. The name of the festival literally means "buffalo-slaughter"; the buffalo to be sacrificed is called *bia*, while the term "*katina*" means slaughter. First of all, the hill where the sacrifice is to take place (of particular significance to the village) is given an offering of cocks and goats. Pigs and cocks are offered when the *karumunda* pole is set up at the *dharani* (the altar of Dharani Penu), site of the *dharani vali* (dharani stones). The *karumunda* is erected beside the stones and there, the worship (*dakina*) is performed. On this occasion, *katul* is prepared several times over, depending on the size of the village population and taking into consideration the population of the host village and those invited from the neighbouring villages. Larger villages, that have good communication links with other villages, usually act as hosts to many guests.

BADBINERE

Badbinere is celebrated annually in *Dasehra lanju* and *Chaita lanju*. In this, two malevolent deities, *kamatali penu* (also known as *kama* penu) and *mardi penu* are invoked, worshipped and bidden farewell (*badbinere*) during this important *puja*.[1] This festival is intended to encourage the departure of malevolent deities.

Some of these evil ones are believed to cause the spots or wounds (*saju*[2]) associated with smallpox, chickenpox and measles, called by the Kuttia Kondh: *bicha* and *sengu* (eczema). *Bicha* is the Kui term for seeds, and it is said that the deity shows her dissatisfaction with the people by sowing her seeds (*bicha*), so causing poxes to form, and then collecting her "food" when the *bicha* develop on the human body. The tribe particularly fears the wrath of these deities, but because they are said to be the carriers of every seed type, their veneration is also associated with obtaining a good crop yield.[3]

The *puja* lasts for three days: the Monday performance is called *Basani*, when the deities are invoked, Tuesday is the main *puja* and Wednesday is the day of *badbinere*. It is preferred that three *kutakas* and *jani* preside over the worship; however, if necessary, one will suffice. The priest fasts throughout the three-day period, drinking only *salap* toddy and *mahuli* liquor.

On the first day, the *jani* or *kutaka* performs the *basani*, with an invocation done by the priest who chants:

inu kamapenu atisi	:	You, *Kamapenu*, come
inu tatibui, bitulbui	:	You *Tatibui Bitulbui* [ie synonyms of the name of the deity above]
kuna maga, dadi maga	:	You *Kuna* (Yam) beggar, death ritual beggar
tipang deu tarang deu	:	*Tipang deu, Tarang deu*
inu sate atisi	:	You really coming
kandabana, japina tatisi	:	Sword, Gun, Weapon to sit upon.
nai lia pitha japinati	:	I *Lia*, cake prepared

1. These malevolent deities are thought to be sisters who live in banyan trees at a place called sima rani.
2. The term *saju* also means porcupine.
3. Refer to the myth of the origin of Kamatali Penu, in "Sacrifice — the Means to satisfy *penuni*" (See chapter 8).

anu icheka bagu sienja	:	These many offerings I am giving
inu imba simarani[4]	:	To you there, *Simarani-Maarani* from *maarani kata*
inu imba linga janani atati	:	Your birth took place
deupuru, nandan puru	:	*Deupuru, Nandan paru* [ie. placenames]
kasigada, rendagada inu manati	:	*Kasigada, Rendagada,* you are present
usugada, belagada manati	:	*Usugada, Belagada* [are] present
teligada, maligada manati	:	*Teligada, Maligada* [are] present
atisi inge sindur sienja	:	Come — for you vermillion giving.
*tipang deu**	:	The deity who smears [the] *Tipa* of vermillion on the forehead".

The priest requests the deity to come and sit upon their weapons, viz : *kanda* (sword) *bana* (gun) and *japina* (hand weapons), and to accept the offerings painted with vermillion. This chant is also used to bid the deity farewell, the only difference being that the term *atisi* (come) is replaced by the word *guamu*, meaning "go".

On Tuesday, the *kutaka* conducts the *puja* in honour of the *penuni* responsible for the welfare of the village. *Penu aramu* means "the presenting of seats" inviting the *penuni* invoked (*dakibamu*) to the site of the worship. The *penuni* are then offered a cock sacrifice (*kaju crana*). Traditionally, other offerings included rice, fried paddy (*lia*), vermillion, molasses, cannabis, opium (*afu*), sarees and bangles (*paja*), but now, coconut, bael leaves and china rose (*Hibiscus rosa sinensis*, *mandara puju* in Kui) are recent additions. A cock, goat and pig are sacrificed on the same occasion. Three swords (*kanda*) made from semul wood (*Bombax malabaricum*) are offered to the three gods, *Kama Penu, Mardi Penu* and *Durga Penu*, as they are believed to favour swords. These particular swords are believed to

4. Simarani-maarani is the abode of the deity who is requested to come to the seat of *puja*.

* Tipang deu is the deity who smears vermillion on the forehead of the goddess.

have the power to destroy the evil that threatens the village inhabitants.[5]

On the third day, other animals are sacrificed. Castor oil and *kueri* are placed in a pot made of *siali* (*Bauhinia vahlii*) leaves. After the *penu* has been bidden farewell, the senior villagers use a cock's feather to smear oil onto the forehead of the *kutaka*. The *puja* ends and the people escort the *kutaka* home (*kutakai tukana*).

DASEHRA KANDANGA DAKINA

Until recently, this festival, which is celebrated in *Dasehra lanju* (September/October), marked the Kuttia Kondh's worship of *Thakurani penu* exclusively. Now, however, as a result of a gradual process of "Hinduisation", the tribe has also started to worship *Durga penu*. While *Dusehra* is a Hindu festival, the *Dasehra Kandanga Dakina* of the Kuttia Kondh is an amalgam of Hindu and Kuttia Kondh traditions, designed to appease the deities, prevent or mitigate epidemics and ensure people's social and physical wellbeing.

Thakurani penu and *Kamati penu* are offered a *puja* in the village and stress is given to worship of the *semul* wood swords (*kanda*). Every household is expected to contribute a chicken and the whole village shares the costs of purchasing a goat.

On the day of the festival, the Pano arrive in the Kuttia villages selling *mahuli* liquor. This is purchased by the Kuttia Kondh and shared with the Pano. In fact, both communities have an interest in this transaction: the Pano, selling knowing that they will receive a share from the Kuttia Kondh, and the latter believing that unless they share some of their liquor with the Pano, the Pano's desire will remain unsatisfied and their souls will be malcontent. The Kuttia Kondh believe that the unhappy souls of the Pano might cause them stomach problems.

BASA DAKINA

Basa dakina is celebrated in winter on occasions when climate and rainfall have been particularly propitious to cultivation, and the *jani*

5. See the chapter on Socio-cultural Aspects of Plants, Animals and Humans in this book.

or *kutaka* have been instructed in a dream to appease the sun god (*Weda penu*) and god of the place (*Basa penu*). It is therefore not a regular festival. On this occasion, a goat, a cock, and *katul* liquor are offered to the *penu* and if during this period, visitors from other villages arrive, they are met with silence. The villagers do not speak for about one hour, though this custom varies from village to village. But when the singing and dancing is over, the girls present a pig to the boys as a token of their appreciation. In return, they are given a buffalo. On this occasion the *Basa Gaani* is exclusively sung, though each village has its own improvised version (in Kui).[6]

Magic and Magician

The word magic is derived from the word "magician", a term first used for priests of the Zoroastrian religion (Kachroo & Kachroo, 1990) who could use their spiritual powers to great effect. The magician, by using his art and manipulative abilities, and due to his seemingly superhuman powers, was sometimes accorded religious status. M.F. Koesing, quoted in Kachroo & Kachroo (*ibid.*) defines magic as follows:

> in its technical sense, magic is a term which summarises a variety of methods by which man supports to influence automatically the course of events by that touch of the supernatural. A magical act is a rite carried out to twist nature in a specific way to satisfy human desires. It is thus regarded as religious and holy.

According to Max Weber, magic is "religious action believed to be automatically effective, whether the goal be empirical or non-empirical". Malinowski, in his functionalist approach to magic, defined it as the use of supernatural means to try to obtain empirical ends (Kachroo & Kachroo, *ibid.*).

The Kuttia Kondh believe in the abilities of magicians and witches, their female counterparts, to concoct powerful magic remedies which will overcome the evil aspects of supernatural forces. Their acceptance

6. Sometimes conversations using riddles or metaphors will take place between the boys and the girls. Questions in the form of riddles will be asked by the boys, which will be answered by the girls using a standard riddle or an improvised song. The composers of these songs pay particular attention to the rhythmic pronunciation.

of these powers may be attributed either to the successes they achieve, to fear of the supernatural and external and/or unseen forces, or to a need for security against these elements.

The Kuttia people have considerable faith in the spells performed by magicians, but to undertake a study of the procedures performed by the magicians, and their consequences is a difficult task. Those who are able to use magic for good (white) or evil (black), perform their spells in secret. When an individual suddenly vomits blood or falls ill, and does not respond to treatment with medicines, it is believed that he or she is the victim of black magic.

In the socio-political organisation of the Kuttia society, as we have learned, the *kutaka* is regarded as a superhuman being, and the village authority insofar as the performance of rituals, magic, worship and sacrifice is concerned. He is also renowned for his competence as an astrologer and healer. The *kutaka*, therefore, is highly respected for his skill in applying his many talents towards maintenance of the social order and well-being of the village. Of the three main spiritual practitioners in Kuttia society, viz. *majhi*, *jani* and *kutaka*, the *kutaka* is awarded the highest status. Though the *jani* sometimes performs independently of the *kutaka* during rituals and worship, he will generally work under the direction of the *kutaka*.

RESPONSIBILITIES OF THE KUTAKA

Religious leadership is almost exclusively the privilege of males, and the domain of the *kutaka*'s activities is limited to his society. The term '*kutaka*' can be broken down into two parts. Men's names in Kuttia society carry the suffix "*ka*"[7] while the term "*kuta*" refers to engagement with the supernatural in acts such as magic, witchcraft, and the ability to effect a transformation into another person's image.

His profession can be put to both good and evil uses, and an individual may be the beneficiary or victim of these powers. In the event of disputes, rituals and astrological matters, the *kutaka* begins with an invocation to a god. As the *kutaka* is particularly respected for his ability to perform witchcraft to protect people from the ill-will

7. Womens' names are followed by the suffix "adu".

of malevolent deities and spirits, he may then be required to take decisions relating to worship or offerings, or to diagnose a disease and administer the appropriate remedy, the latter being the application of witchcraft or herbal medicines. Witchcraft is applied to cure those particular diseases believed to have been caused by witches and supernatural powers. His performance involves a number of important steps that many occasions of ritualistic worship and sacrifice have in common. In special cases, (such as acts of worship to cure someone of a disease) the *kutaka* must preside over each stage of the worship but normally, the daily worship is begun by the *kutaka* and continued by the *jani*. Although the order of events in an act of worship is composed spontaneously, care is taken to avoid mistakes. Before beginning to worship a god in the event of disease, the *kutaka* convinces himself of the need for the worship, and by using his supernatural powers, attempts to identify the malevolent god or evil spirit who is responsible for the disease and any other misfortunes affecting people.

Worship involving magic is performed when evil spirits are considered responsible for something unusual that has occurred to an individual or to the society as a whole. The *kutaka* is required to make a connection between the cause of the disease and the actions required for its cure, and so uses one of two methods to do so. One method involves his sitting in a particular position chanting a few hymns, animatedly moving his hands, legs and body and rubbing rice into a winnowing fan, while at the same time, invoking various gods to the site. He questions the deities, thereby detecting the perpetrator and determining the appropriate remedy. The second entails the *kutaka* listening to an account of the misfortune, but rather than initiating a worship immediately, the matter is left undecided for one night. Before going to sleep, he requests the supernatural powers to appear in his dreams and to reveal the cause of the problem, and the necessary remedy. In this instance, he focuses on the performance of an act of worship, when it should take place, and the nature of the god's preferred sacrifice or offering.

More rarely, a third method is used to identify the cause of a problem and the action to be taken. Occasionally, when the *kutaka* presides over a ceremonial worship, he can fall into a trance-like state. During this, he is questioned about people's misfortunes, and to establish the cause of these, the *kutaka* takes grass (*Themda arundinacea*), which he breaks into small pieces, selects a piece of about ten centimetres in length and begins to chant. The piece of grass may either lengthen or shorten. From this, he is able to assess the event, identify the deity or other agent that is responsible for the illness and determine how to placate or overcome it.

In some cases, he may place the blame on certain people, particularly on women who are said to possess an inherent ability to cause illness by inflicting the evil eye on a victim. Individuals suffering from the evil eye become anaemic, their health deteriorates and they eventually die and witchcraft is sometimes thought to be the cause of this disease.

The chanting of hymns is a common feature of the acts of worship. The *kutaka* begins the worship with the words "*Jo-on*" — a request to the deities to listen to him. He then invokes the deities by saying "*Inu nehi baamu*", meaning "Come, after listening to my words", and continues by chanting the names of different gods and goddesses in sequence, inviting them from the four corners of the world to attend the worship and accept the offerings. The duration of the chanting varies, depending on whether or not the *kutaka* has identified the god responsible for the misfortune. If he has, then he just invokes this particular god; otherwise, he goes on summoning the deities at random until all are present at the site of worship. After being satisfied with offerings, they reveal the cause of the illness. There is no regular sequence of worship after an invocation of a *penu*; rather, every worship is specific to a particular problem and its individual solution.

In addition to its use for diagnosing and curing illness, magic is also a feature of the Kuttia Kondh lifecycle rituals. The rituals of birth, marriage and death involve the use of magic, as do a number of other ceremonial occasions, e.g. the selection of a suitable site for shifting cultivation or to erect the *karumunda* pole (used in the *Meriah* Festival) or even to establish the cause of any abnormality in the toddy sap produced by the *sago* palm (*Caryota urens*).

Certain individuals may also use magic as an instrument of destruction, and this malevolent application of witchcraft can be fatal, if the victim is not cured immediately by another witchcraft practitioner. The *kutaka*'s ability to turn himself into a dangerous animal (a process whereby the human soul enters the soul of an animal and human behaviour becomes animal behaviour) is one of magic's evil uses. The case studies below elaborate on this, and on other ways in which magic is used as either a benevolent or a pernicious tool.

EXAMPLES OF THE KUTAKA'S POWER AND INFLUENCE

Lochan *jani*, the *kutaka* of Burlubaru village, for example, is feared by local people for his ability to transform himself into a tiger. Evidence of this transformation has been asserted by many people who were told by this *kutaka* to go to a certain place and when they arrived in this place, they saw tigers, bears, etc.

"Mniba" meaning "converted", is a prefix attached to the different types of animal species, such as *kdani* (tiger), *ali* (bear), *srachu* (snake), depending upon the animal the *kutaka* has converted himself into. Lochan *jani* claims that this skill is limited to the very experienced *kutakas*. After entering the body of an animal or plant, half of his being remains his own while the other half is inhabited by the animal or plant.

The transformation occurs when the *kutaka* is in deep sleep. If the animal is killed, the *kutaka* will also die. A *kutaka* who has transformed himself into a tiger, can be identified only by another *kutaka* who has a similar ability. If, for example, a *kutaka* turns himself into a tiger and kills a cow, the owner of the dead cow may ask another *kutaka* to find out if his cow has been killed by a 'real' tiger or a "converted" tiger. Should the latter be the case, the second *kutaka* would identify the individual responsible.

The following examples show how magic affects the social life of the Kuttia Kondh.

FEAR OF REVENGE DUE TO MARRIAGE DISPUTES

Kumudini *jani* of Burlubaru village did not want to marry Lokanath of Germel village. However, as her father had accepted a cock and two bottles of *adkinga* (liquor of *Madhuka longifolia*) from Lokanath's father, the marriage was considered fixed. Kumudini wished to marry another young man, but was afraid that if she married anyone other than Lokanath, the villagers of Germel would use witchcraft to kill the husband of her choice, and that the people of her own village might be attacked by evil witchcraft inflicted by the Germel villagers. Consequently, Kumudini reluctantly married Lokanath.

IDENTIFYING A THIEF

Badu *jani*, of Burlubaru village, owns a *salap* tree (*Caryota urens*). On one occasion the tree stopped providing toddy, so Budu *jani* attempted unsuccessfully to use magic to solve the problem. He then requested Lochan *jani*, the *kutaka* of the village, to find out what had happened. Lochan *jani* went to the tree, threw some rice on it, and discovered that toddy from the tree was regularly being stolen. He identified a man from Madalakuna village as the thief, who confessed his deed. An act of worship was then organised under the tree to satisfy the ancestral spirits who had halted the secretion of toddy sap because of the theft. Two or three days later, toddy could again be collected.

DIRECTING ANIMALS

The late Balu *jani* of Burlubaru was a regular priest of Siram Deu hill. Descendents of the Saraka lineage regard Siram Deu hill as their most important god. At a place called *dera balla* (big cave), Balu *jani* organises an important worship for Siram Deu, which involves the sacrifice of a buffalo, at an interval of nine to fifteen years according to the date fixed by the priest, Balu *jani*.

The rarity of the occasion increases its significance and the act of worship is performed to ensure the well-being and prosperity of the Saraka lineage. When the buffalo has been worshipped in the village, it is set free and instructed to go to the place of the sacrifice, which it does entirely of its own accord. As part of the buffalo worship, the priest chants and throws some rice grains onto it, and smears some vermilion on its head. It is believed that this causes the animal to go to the place of sacrifice. The Kuttia Kondh claim that it is a worship involving magic since, they argue, how otherwise could the animal find the site of sacrifice of its own accord?

Certain plant species (namely, *chhana* (*Themda arundinacea*) *surga* (*Thysanolaena maxima* and *Phyllanthus emblica*) and *babe* (*Eulaliopsis binata*)) are essential for this type of worship, without which the spells and procedures cannot be carried out. Using plants and plant parts is a common ingredient in magic, although the exact benefits of these species, and the reasons for using them, are not explained.

The Concept of Disease

This sub-chapter has been divided into subheadings, based on the research team's categorisation of the Kuttia Kondh's concept of disease. According to the beliefs of the Kuttia Kondh people, disease is influenced by their relationship with the environment and their belief in the supernatural powers, rather than on the basis of physiological evidence. The approach taken here attempts to give an accurate overview of the health of the Kuttia Kondh.

The Kuttia Kondh believe that health is a state of well-being on which the supernatural powers have considerable influence. In virtually all cases, a god or spirit is thought to be responsible for a health problem, and at the first sign of illness, the troubled individual visits a priest in the belief that a religious performance is the necessary cure. According to the Kuttia Kondh informants, "disease is something that affects body and soul"; it manifests itself as a physical problem in a part of the body, while the sensation of pain weakens the victim psychologically. They believe that their life force or soul known as *jella* has been disturbed by some unseen power (god, goddess or spirit), which, in turn, causes problems throughout the body.

The Kuttia Kondh distinguish between physical and psychological diseases. The physical diseases include dermatitis, accidental injuries, pathogenic illnesses, fever, diarrhoea, leprosy and other physical ailments that result from food and exposure to the environment. The psychological illnesses include fear, anxiety, epilepsy, hysteria, said to be caused chiefly by evil spirits, supernatural powers, and witchcraft and cannot be cured. Different deities and spirits are believed to be identified with different types of disease.

The Kuttia Kondh believe that the cause of a disease can be due to a single reason or a combination of reasons. The search for a cure involves concepts and practices that form part of indigenous culture. Disease is a manifestation of people's interaction with their environment. The causes which may be of spiritual, natural and/or of social origin are discussed in greater detail below.

FOLK MEDICINE

The concepts and practices in folk medicine are based upon numerous theories, cosmological speculations, the use of magic in scholarly and oral medicine, and on religion (Reddy 1986). It is popular among the Kuttia Kondh who have had considerable success with remedies using herbal medicine and other natural products freely available in their immediate environment. Folk medicine can involve the simultaneous application of magic and herbal remedies. The process may remain the same, but the prescriptions of therapeutic agents vary. If the disease is cured, it is said to have been the wish of the gods, imparted through the healer and religious practitioner (*kutaka*). The death of a patient is also said to be god's will, although this can also cause people to lose faith in the effectiveness of the practitioner.

The Kuttia Kondh regard their medical practitioner as an influential spiritual leader who attends to the spiritual practices and medical problems of the society. In the use of folk medicine, the practitioner refers to magic and religion to conceptualise the ultimate reality of their culture and activities.

Accordingly, three types of medical practitioners exist in Kuttia society: herbalists, divine healers and witch doctors. Both *jani* and *kutaka* practise medicine, though the *kutaka* possesses greater spiritual powers than the *jani*. A *jani* can be a herbalist and act in some way as a 'divine' healer, but can never be a sorcerer. The *kutaka* is able to act as herbalist, divine healer and sorcerer.

A sorcerer has traditionally been respected for his ability to intercept or exorcise the evil spirits that possess the patient, and tends to use plants as part of the treatment. Divine healers are those who depend upon their supernatural powers to make a diagnosis, and who administer medicinal plants thought to hold spiritual powers, while herbalists, who are generally the elderly, enjoy the prestige and reputation ascribed to genuine practitioners of traditional medicine as they have considerable local knowledge of the plants that can be used to treat illness. In most cases, before administering the herbal medicine, a religious performance is conducted as a necessary part of the treatment, from which it would appear that the profession of herbalist is closely linked to that of the witch doctor and divine healer. Folk medicine for the Kuttia Kondh, therefore, can be said to incorporate methods of treatment involving magic, religion, the use of supernatural powers in diagnosis, as well as the use of herbs, plants and animals.

Two methods of treatment that come under the category of folk medicine are *dakandi pdukandi* and *wechinja* (see p. 262f.), the first tools the practitioner uses. These are sometimes performed after an offering or sacrifice has been made to the deities. Medicinal plants are also administered during these treatments.

SPIRITUAL DISEASES

Spiritual diseases are inflicted by the evil influence of certain unseen supernatural powers. This belief is not confined to the Kuttia Kondh; it is also a belief in Hinduism and is referred to in the earliest Hindu literature, the "*Rig Veda*". Disease was ever since believed to be largely due to the anger of gods and the effects of evil spirits, while the art of healing consisted of prayers, hymns, and often, the application of herbal remedies (Reddy 1986). The Kuttia Kondh have a deep faith in both the benevolent and the malevolent powers of the deities, whom they appease and venerate through worship. It is believed that if this is neglected, they risk the wrath of the gods who may cause illness in human beings and domestic animals. Disease is, therefore, seen as a consequence of the actions of supernatural agents.

When two or three people die from a disease, other villagers fear that this "epidemic" has been caused by witchcraft. The nature of the treatment in such cases varies accordingly (Choudhury &

Choudhury 1986). The Kuttia Kondh believe that diseases such as smallpox, chickenpox and measles are caused by *kamati penu*. Other conditions believed to be the result of divine retribution include blindness, other physical handicaps, and miscarriage. In these cases, people seek the advice of the *kutaka*.

NATURAL DISEASES

Every Kuttia Kondh village has at least one compost pit on its periphery. The village girls, when they are not doing agricultural work, (generally in summer) are instructed by the *majhi* to collect household waste for depositing in the pits (*kabda*). However, during the rainy or winter seasons, when people are needed to work in the fields, the cleanliness of the village premises is neglected. Hence, in most of the villages, the compost pits remain unused. Among the more common diseases caused by the insanitary conditions of the village, and therefore believed to occur "naturally", are: scabies (*sengu*), eczema and ringworm (*dadu*), and vomiting (*sechkanti*). Contaminated water causes diarrhoea (*patadae*), blood dysentery (*neripata*), ascariasis (*danginpdika*) and amoebic dysentery (*pataklipangane*). Malaria (*brapa nemberi*), fever (*nemberi*) and rhinitis (*mungei giri eju*) are also prevalent.

Some very common ailments such as cold, headache and stomach ache are believed to be caused by prolonged exposure to the environment (*aku saritei*), particularly to woods, air, sun and water. Nutritional deficiency diseases also come under this category. The Kuttia Kondh subsist chiefly on a daily diet of carbohydrate and protein based foods such as two species of tubers — yams and taro — and potato with rice, finger millet, little millet and maize. Nutritional deficiency diseases are more apparent in children, who particularly suffer from protein energy malnutrition, but also from night blindness. The research team classified diseases caused due to malnutrition as poverty diseases.[8] The Kuttia Kondh consider their low economic status to be responsible for the poor health of their children.

---

8. Ali (1983) points out that "the less recognised, but nevertheless more important health problems lie in the vulnerable areas of malnutrition,

→

Examining the prevalent diseases on a seasonal basis it can be shown that the Kuttia Kondh suffer a great deal from water-borne diseases and many other common illnesses during the rainy season, when disease levels are highest. The summer is second to the rainy season in the frequency of diseases; in terms of food availability it is regarded by the Kuttia Kondh as the lean period. The winter season is a time when disease is at its lowest level.

DISEASES RELATED TO SOCIO-ECONOMIC RELATIONS

For the Kuttia Kondh, illness and death are disruptive events that can inflict considerable economic, social and psychological costs. The

---

particularly among women and children and a wide range of communicable and other diseases that result from an insanitary environment and poor drinking water facilities. This combination of health problems of the primitive tribes would definitely point to the inadequacy of a purely curative approach of health care and increases the importance of community education for health care. The most significant causes of illness like malnutrition, poor water supply and environmental insanitation were not perceived by the people and hence totally ignored. In the constant struggle for daily survival, health was a low priority. Their chief concern was the problems of acute illness, childbirth and trauma that interfered with their work. Even major chronic illnesses like tuberculosis were ignored till they reached a stage of gross debility. Many enteric ailments can be eliminated by drinking water from protected sources". Ali (1979) reported that "the most common disease is malaria. Other types of diseases are water borne and due to unhygienic conditions of the surroundings in which they live and malnutrition and low intake of food. The source of drinking water is the hill stream which is not only polluted but also has high content of graphite causing irritation in the gastrointestinal tract resulting in gastric discomfort, abdominal pain, hyperacidity and constipation. Further, in Ali's investigation, it was found that the incidence of some viral diseases is common, particularly that of the upper respiratory tract with symptoms of rhinitis (running nose) pharyngitis, bronchitis, cold, cough and fever. Among skin diseases, which are very common, scabies tops others. Dental disease is very common". In his medical survey in Burlubaru village among Kuttia Kondh, Ali (1979) reported some incidences of tuberculosis. According to him, "the incidence of T.B. is also high, the most common form of it being pulmonary tuberculosis. Semi starvation, inferior diet and unhygienic living conditions, attribute to the prevalence of T.B. Their houses are rectangular in ground plan with some having two rooms while most of them have only one room each. The walls are made of planks of sal wood in most cases and of bamboo wattle plastered with mud in a few cases. In all cases the room is grass thatched. There are no windows. Hardly any light gets into the hut. Poor ventilation and close contact with infected members of the family are largely responsible for widespread contagion".

prevalence and distribution of disease are influenced by socio-economic factors, in particular, by economic status. Children are particularly affected because parents tend to neglect the hygiene of their children, and rarely consult local health centres when their children are not well, preferring to seek the advice of the village healer.

The social organisation of the Kuttia Kondh stipulates that, in the case of illness, an individual consults a healer (either the *jani*, or the *kutaka*) before going to any practitioner of Western medicine. Failure to do so is regarded by these authorities as disrespectful and may result in his refusing co-operation in future cases. In general, it is observed that a healer is consulted for children's and women's diseases and that people are unwilling to spend money, of which they have very little, on expensive medicines, in spite of the fact that if a child dies, the parents may spend far more on the customary death rituals.

A Local Additional Primary Health Center (LAPHC) at Belghar provides medicines free of charge under the provision of the State Government. The Kuttia Kondh Development Agency also has provisions for providing people with free medicines. However, this medication is for treating common minor ailments and injuries. More serious illnesses require the expensive medicines available in the market. The expenses deter the Kuttia Kondh from buying the medicines, regardless of the seriousness of the patient's condition.

Omens and Beliefs Associated with Diseases

The Kuttia Kondh have a strong belief in the significance of dreams, claiming that they can sometimes forecast disease. The presence of certain animals and plants in dreams are omens of particular diseases. For example, dreaming of a cucumber (*mundranga*, *Cucumis sativa*) signifies an immediate attack of fever, an elephant in a dream indicates malarial fever, a buffalo is also a bad omen, and a pig forecasts death. A mango (*Mangifera indica*) or jackfruit (*Artocarpus heterophyllus*) is a sign that the patient should eat meat, while the poisonous plant *kantakari* (*Solanum xanthocarpum*) indicates an early cure from a serious disease. It is considered a bad omen for a man to sit underneath an eucalyptus tree for any length of time as he may contract *gochchi* (leprosy) from the white patches on the tree.

DAKANDI PDUKANDI

This is an invocation to the gods, a common method of treatment involving intervention of the gods or divine healing. Although generally used on children, it is also beneficial to adults, particularly as a cure for women's diseases. It is considered an effective treatment for the exorcism of evil spirits from body and mind, snakebite, early fever and injuries due to accidents and *dakandi pdukandi* is used to treat prolonged crying, vomiting, trembling, pallor in the eyes, and anaemia in children. Generally, the sacrifice of a small chicken is required. *Dakandi pdukandi* is considered to be the basic tool for healing and is usually performed by the *kutaka* and, occasionally, by his students.

First of all, the practitioner (*kutaka* or *jani*) chants in Kui to invoke the deities from all corners of the world. Their permission is needed before he can begin the healing process. He invokes the deities in the *kara* and *bidi* trees (species of these trees believed are to be visible only to the healer during times of need), and calls those connected with the administering of herbal medicines. He then informs the gods of the patient's sufferings and attempts to establish the cause of the illness in the belief that the *kutaka* and *jani* can converse with them. The cause of the disease is said to be either that the patient has ignored the deities while he/she was in the forest, or because the patient has neglected to pray to them. Finally, the deities present decide whether the patient should be forgiven — in which case the *kutaka* enquires into the nature of the remedies that will cure the patient; or punished — whereupon the *kutaka* must continue to pray for the patient's recovery. Accordingly, the *kutaka* tries to appease the deities by arranging an appropriate worship and sacrifice.

WECHINJA

Wechinja is a method of treatment that includes various rites described below. It does not include the collection of herbal medicines. It is claimed that only the *kutaka* with his supernatural powers can perform these difficult rites with any success, although others have attempted to replicate them and failed. *Wechinja* is commonly used to cure aches and pains affecting the head, stomach and chest, in particular. The *kutaka* first identifies the painful area, and places his thumb on it while chanting; he then puts an arrow, with the arrowhead pointing away from the body, on the affected area. The *kutaka* chews on the shaft of the arrow until he draws out blood and insects. By identifying the type of insect, he can establish the nature of the illness and the identity of the god responsible for causing the pain. If the patient suffers from a headache for example, an insect resembling the honeybee, called *boirbisa* (unidentified zoologically), is extracted, while the appearance of a long tailed insect signifies stomach troubles. The extraction of a *boirbisa* proves that *mara penu* (the tree god) is responsible for the pain as the violation caused by any tree growing near, or over, the trees known as *bade mara* (*Ficus benghalensis*) or *pipada mara* (*Ficus scandens*), is said to cause headaches.

DOALI

Doali is a disease that afflicts both sexes. Its symptoms include frothing at the mouth, unconsciousness and immobility. Since it is believed that the individual may have been attacked by a malevolent spirit called *khati*, this condition is commonly known as '*khati* disease'. The treatment involves the *kutaka* placing his thumb on the left nipple of the man's chest (or between the breasts if the patient is female) and chanting. When the chant is over, the magic healer extracts some sap from the roots of *khati asa* (*Vanda roxburghii*), especially if the plant is found growing on certain tree species such as the *madei mara* (*Lannea coromandelica*), which is particularly favoured, the *mardi mara* (*Terminalia tomentosa*), or the *bela mara* (*Aegle marmelos*). The sap from this plant is then dropped into the patient's nostrils.

The whole process normally culminates in the identification of the responsible agent (the god, goddess or spirit), and a prescribed mode of treatment though the duration of the process can vary, depending on the nature of the illness. Headaches, or aches and pains in the body that involve the extraction of insects, can be cured quickly, while the treatment of *doali* is more complicated and requires the performance of a number of *wechinja*. In complicated cases like *doali*, it is necessary to rub rice on a winnowing fan while simultaneously invoking the gods, goddesses and spirits. The late Lochan Jani, *kutaka* of Burlubaru, claimed that if gods and goddesses were invoked by rubbing rice on a winnow, they believed they were being invoked for an important reason: from these deities, the *kutaka* is able to learn the cause of the illness and the necessary prescription. During the treatment, all gods and goddesses are invoked and the identity of the evil perpetrator of the illness is established, either by a confession from the perpetrator, or because his identity is revealed by another god. The *kutaka* then asks for the reason why the illness has been inflicted. The god or agent responsible for the affliction then generally demands a sacrifice, which is provided by the *kutaka*.

JAKA DAKANDI (TOP-WORSHIP)

In *jaka dakandi*, there are two sites of offering worship to *yam penu* (the demon god): one, outside the patient's house and the other, inside the house where the patient is sleeping. The materials used for the act of worship remain outdoors and only a thread is extended from the arrow (placed outside), through the roof, down to the patient. On the end of the thread that is dropped down to the patient, a leaf from a *Ficus scandens* is tied. This leaf must remain suspended over the head of the patient but should not touch him/her. Inside the house, near the patient, the healer chants.

If the *yam penu* feels happy with the invocation and prayer of the healer, or the *yam penu* feels that the patient has some more life to live, he then asks for a sacrifice. To give the patient "life", another "life" has to be sacrificed. At that point, the *yam penu* requests the *linga penu* (god of creation) to "give life to" or cure the patient. The *linga penu* then gives "life" to the patient by passing it through the thread (like current in an electric wire) from the place the arrow is kept, (the "electricity pole" outside the patient's house) down to the leaf, and to the patient's body.

If a patient is suffering from a serious illness that is difficult to diagnose, the magic healer orders "*jaka dakandi*", an act of worship in honour of *yam penu*, performed on the roof of the patient's house. Following the sacrifice of a black hen, a fistful of earth is placed on a bamboo mat made of fourteen interwoven bamboo strips. A line of turmeric powder is then drawn around this clump of earth, and some rice grains placed at its centre. The four edges of the mat are smeared with ash from the hearth and an arrow is placed vertically above the ash, on one end of which is tied a branch of *pipada* (*Ficus scandens*) that is suspended over the patient's head. It is believed that this will satisfy the *yam penu,* as he will then order the *linga penu* (birth god) to restore life (*jella*) to the patient by means of the leaves of the *Ficus scandens*. The exact prescription for *yam penu* worship depends upon the symptoms of the patient: if the patient is extremely weak and feverish and refuses food, magic healers will need to be consulted.

EJU PENU DAKINA

Eju Penu *dakina* (the worship of the water god) is another ritual performed to cure diseases caused by evil spirits. If a husband or a wife is sick for a long time, then his/her partner arranges an act of worship and presents an offering to the water god in return for the life of the patient. This ritual is organised on a Saturday at places where water can be found, as it is believed that the water god "washes away" the patient's suffering. The thorns of the *bael* tree (*Aegle marmelos*), twigs of *tuturi mara* (*Solanum xanthocarpum*), and a *tade mara* (*Musa sapientum*) plant are the usual requirements for the ritual. Sometimes non-tribals are requested to perform it.

If the *jani* or *kutaka* in the Belghar area is unable to perform the worship, the Kuttia Kondh request a priest and known herbalist — Mahadev Patra of the Shiva Temple — to conduct the worship. Because the Kuttia regard Lord Shiva as Shiva Penu, and know of Mahadev's reputation as a herbalist, they feel that Mahadev can perform the same duties as their *kutaka*. Furthermore, the Kuttia Kondh believe that anybody who worships in Lord Shiva's temple can perform the ritual. Whether or not the priest has any knowledge of the Kuttia Kondh's religious pantheon is unimportant. However, the act of calling on a non-tribal to conduct such a ritual has taken place only recently and is evidence of the urgency of the situation and an ongoing process of Sanskritization, in Hindu manners, customs and beliefs taken over by the tribal population.

OTHER DISEASES AND TREATMENTS

Women suffering from water retention like dropsy are instructed to worship *gangi penu* at a site where water is found. The worship involves the sacrifice of a piglet and a twig of *Ficus scandens*, believed to drive away evil spirits, placed at the worship site. The prescribed medicine is a root known as *kranjiasa* (*Rauwolfia serpentina*).

The worship of *gangi penu* is also necessary in the treatment of leprosy. Following the worship, the bark of *raga mara* (a species visible only to the *kutaka* at the time of need) is prescribed. Leprosy is regarded as a form of punishment by a village god (*deukuda*), and he may show his unwillingness to cure the patient by making *raga mara* unavailable to the witch doctor.

On the occasion when a child is named, the ancestral spirits are invoked, and both a *semul* pole (*Bombax malabaricum)* and bamboo twig are used for the ritual. The child is given the name of one ancestral spirit and the accompanying worship of these spirits assures the well-being of the child.

In conclusion, therefore, the Kuttia Kondh believe that most diseases are caused by evil spirits who enter the body through the medium of air, water or plants (by the anger of ancestral spirits (*dukeli*), and healers and witch doctors have the capacity to identify those powerful forces thought to influence and control these afflictions.

HERBAL MEDICINE

The herbal medicines administered by the Kuttia Kondh fall into the category of 'great traditional' medicine practised in Hinduism. While the range of herbal medicines is vast there, the use of herbs in Kuttia society, usually by the *jani* and *kutaka*, is minimal. A few individuals are aware of some of the herbal remedies for minor ailments, and it seems that the knowledge of herbal medicine has been transmitted orally from generation to generation, even though the Kuttia Kondh claim that an individual receives the knowledge of herbal medicine from the gods in his dreams.

A respected member of Kuttia Kondh society achieves the status of healer when this person is chosen by the gods to ensure the welfare of the society. Those healers with insufficient knowledge of plants receive instructions from the gods concerning the type of plant to use, and how it is to be administered. Furthermore, it is claimed that the knowledge of these medicines is confined to the healer alone. The healer does not disclose his knowledge for fear that by doing so, he may lose his powers of healing. Certain plant species that can be used as medicine (and in rituals as described above) can only be found under the guidance of the gods, including the species *kara mara, bidi mara, raga mara* and *bichu mara*. The *kutaka*'s divine powers enable the healer to locate these species, but should he attempt to use them as medicines without the god's instruction, the plants will lose their efficacy.

In recent years, the use of herbal medicines has been adopted by non-tribal cultures. The local non-tribals administer herbal medicine using the knowledge collected from ancient manuscripts and other literature. It is difficult to trace to what extent the Kuttia Kondh's knowledge of herbal medicine is imparted to local non-tribals and vice-versa, but it appears that the Kuttia Kondh have adopted some non-tribal knowledge of medicine, and for this reason, it can be said that the knowledge, practice and the limited use of herbal medicine by the Kuttia Kondh is dynamic rather than static.

Health Care and Traditional Medicine

There is no satisfactory and comprehensive definition of the term traditional medicine that is able to cover all aspects of the subject. Briefly though, it can be said that traditional medicine centres around two long-established systems of medicine: the little traditional folk system of medicine that exists among the Kuttia Kondh and many other tribal societies, and great traditional medicine which includes all developed types such as ayurveda, allopathy and homeopathy, including herbal application.

The WHO (1978) defines traditional medicine as "the sum total of all the knowledge and practices whether applicable or not, used in diagnosis, prevention and elimination of physical, mental and social imbalances and relying exclusively on practical experiences and observations handed down from generation to generation, whether verbally or in writing".

This definition however, is not very appropriate or comprehensive as it does not include the "sub-systems[9] of medical theory and practice" (Reddy, 1986). Reddy's definition considers all aspects of traditional medicine when he claims:

> it is that part of the whole, which includes holistic knowledge and practices, oral and written functions in diagnosis, prevention and curative aspects of illness and disease, to promote total well-being, to confide explicitly or implicitly on practical experiences and observations or know-how techniques with or without local/regional cultures having an overtone of religion or not.

Dunn (1977) defines a medical system as the patterns of social institutions and cultural traditions that evolve from deliberate behaviour to enhance health. With regard to this definition, a traditional medical system is a collection of experiences and knowledge relating to the diagnosis of an illness, and its cure, that has been passed on from generation to generation. The Kuttia Kondh depend on their immediate environment, more specifically on the distribution and availability of its plants, animals and other naturally occurring substances, for remedies that will cure common ailments. The treatment is often assisted by magic and mysticism. Traditional medicine systems founded on religion, magic, and the use of folk and herbal medicines still prevail in Kuttia society in spite of the fact that modern medicine is now available free of charge.[10]

---

9. The "sub-systems" of medicine's theory refer to local concepts of disease, how disease attacks the body, its cause, and the treatment and healing processes involved.

10. Ali (1983) commented that ". . . the Kuttia Kondh believe in their traditional medicinal system because it fits in with their way of thinking. If they believe in wrath of gods, evil spirits and magic, it must be remembered that it pervades their whole life and does not apply to their view of medicines only. These tribals are mostly not exposed to new ideas and techniques that evolved among civilizations over the centuries and continue living in an insular present. Nor have they changed their beliefs and customs. Thus the belief in their taboos, totems and superstitions and these beliefs shape their thoughts, ideas and practices in their daily activities. Moreover the study of tribal culture indicates that public health

→

Ali (1983) claimed: "it is very difficult to accord appreciation and acceptance by the Kuttia Kondh to the modern health and hygiene measures". In response to this statement it can be said that over the span of a decade, many changes have taken place among the Kuttia Kondh. With the proper functioning of the Additional Primary Health Center (APHC) at Belghar and with the provision of free medicine by the Kuttia Kondh Development Agency, the Kuttia Kondh take interest in modern Western medicine, especially when it is available free of charge.

Vidyarthi and Rai's (1977) categorisation of four types of spirits in which tribal people believe, proves true for the Kuttia Kondh. They distinguish between four types of spirits: those protective deities or spirits believed to safeguard the welfare of the village including ancestral spirits (*dukeli*), village goddesses (*deukuda penu* and *satari penu*), *linga penu*, the birth god, and *soru penu*, the hill god. Benevolent spirits such as *dharani penu* (the earth god), *wanga penu* (the wind god) and *panga penu* are regularly worshipped by the community and the family as otherwise, they may cause disease, death and other misfortune. Evil or malevolent spirits and deities controlling smallpox, chickenpox, measles, and miscarriage include *mounli penu, mardi penu* and *kamati penu*, which all are living on the *Ficus beghalensis* tree. They also inflict diseases on anyone violating taboos. Ancestral spirits are known to protect family members, but can become malevolent if they are forgotten or neglected. Sorcerers and witches can also inflict diseases, either working for their own interests, or on someone's behalf, by spirit possession or the evil eye.

The Kuttia Kondh concept of diseases, and their cure is therefore based on an interaction of man and spirit. It is recognised that

---

→ is an integral part of social process in which wants, beings and functions, his body and mind, activity, emotions and social relations are interwined into an organic whole. Therefore any imbalance in the unity of functions of this whole or any part thereof may result in illness in any of the parts of the configuration. Against a background of such beliefs in supernaturalism as one of the strong causes of illness, it is very difficult to accord appreciation and acceptance by the Kuttia Kondh of the modern health and hygienic measures."

supernatural beings can play a benevolent role in their daily lives, but human suffering at the individual or societal level is attributed to the malevolent powers of the supernatural. Even accidental injuries such as falling from trees are attributed to spirits, ghosts and deities, thought to be more powerful than human beings. It is believed that supernatural powers dominate human beings, but also that a witch doctor's skill is able to counteract or defeat these malevolent powers. Within the Kuttia Kondh's concept of disease and cure, the supernatural undoubtedly occupies a significant place.

10

Life in the Forest

THE Kuttia Kondh's love for nature and forests is reflected in their cultural traditions, religion, and social organisation, which still function as a legacy of the past. The forest as a phenomenon of nature has shaped Kuttia Kondh's religious ideas and moral values, expressed in their myths and sentiments, and has inspired and influenced their patterns of habitation in concentric areas of forest, hills and mountains.

Now, the Kuttia Kondh who use their forests according to their traditional life style are regarded as outsiders by the non-tribals. The commercial exploitation of forests has widely destroyed the interest of the tribals in conservation and preservation, and under the pretext of serving "the development of the tribe", measures are being taken which are likely to expose the Kuttia Kondh livelihood system to a crisis.

The Kuttia Kondh collectively claim that they should not be deprived of their rights and demands on the forests. They argue that they are the first inhabitants of the forests, that they have been brought up there and that they have developed their culture in a symbiotic relation with their environment since time immemorial. They regard the forest as their main resource and perceive it as their world. They live in a caste-free society that gives each person the freedom to experience, touch, smell, see and to hear all aspects of the forest and its products. By contrast, the non-tribal dwellers of the plains know the forest as a reservoir of natural, renewable resources and not as a home. They live in a caste society that restricts individuals' freedom to know the forest in any way other than as an exploitable resource.

The socialisation of the Kuttia Kondh in the modern world, however, has now begun through contact with traders and government officers who are compelling them to live in areas where forest productivity (forest products and products from shifting cultivation) is substantially reduced, or where there is a restricted supply of forest produce available in daily life. In areas where the Kuttia Kondh's traditional ways of food collection, shifting cultivation, and horticulture are alive and well, based on minimum requirements of time, space, materials, work relations and knowledge, they are not subject to any crisis. Their social life in relation to the forests remains intact as long as they experience a relation with the forest through work and living. Their concept of well-being in a forest habitation remains wedded to their desire to remain in a state of symbiotic equilibrium with the forest.

As a result, the Kuttia Kondh are continuing to live in a way which is familiar to them, and that they believe to be the most appropriate, favouring the well-being of both the people and nature. They are reluctant to live their life in the manner of the outsiders and non-tribals. The Kuttia Kondh are aware of the changes the government is attempting to bring about, and that may mean that the forests will no longer be available to them for earning their livelihood. Time and again, the Kuttia Kondh have reiterated their desire to continue their practice of living in the forest. They have made clear that they do not wish to abandon the place of their dwellings or to give up their way of life since this is the basis of their well-being. This reflects not merely the sentimental attachment of the Kuttia Kondh to their place of origin, but also their view that one must continue to do what one knows best.

The Kuttia Kondh's life in the forest has however caused an increasing number of problems. The Kuttia want to be regarded as a forest-dwelling community and the following statement by Dati *majhi*, an old man living in the Muskasouru village, may serve to show how strongly the Kuttia people feel towards the forests surrounding them:

> What I get from here is not known to me exactly. But this place means more to me than anything else in my known world. From my boyhood onwards, I came to sit on this particular place,

> watching the forests, the cattle, the streams flowing down from the rock. But at present, I feel as if the place is calling for me all the time. I have reached the age to leave my friends and relatives. There is not much time left to watch the forests, this enchanting landscape, and to feel this pleasure. Therefore, I spend most of my time here for when my lifetime runs out, it will mean leaving the forests as well.

The Kuttia people want to live in a part of the forest, and are willing to act in a way that ensures its preservation and conservation. Their perception of their life in the forest is reflected in the statement: "We want to live, not just exist".

Life in the Forest: the Tribals Non-Tribals's interface

"We are Adivasi. The Pano are not Adivasi. We live in the deep forest — they live in the plains. We are the first inhabitants — they followed us. We emerged from Sapangada — they came afterwards. We love the forest — they fear the forest. The forest is our dwelling place. The Kuttia is king, the Pano, his minister. We live for the forests — they live for us. We produce what we can grow on the fields and what we can get from the forests — they take the products to the market. Yet the Pano are our immediate, non-tribal neighbours, with whom we deal a lot. We are different in many respects, yet we are friends. They provide us with salt, dry fish, *mahula* liquor and buffalo when we need it".

This is what Kapera *majhi* of Saperivatta village once said about the Kuttia Kondh's relationship with the forest and the Pano people. What Kapera *majhi* says, accurately expresses the Kuttia Kondh's attitude and the difference in status as regards the two communities. Although both communities are often regarded as forest dwelling communities, the Pano cannot be considered a tribal community as they are migrants to the abode of the Kuttia. Still, both the Pano and the Kuttia depend on the forest, the Kuttia in a more direct way, the Pano, less so. The Pano depend upon the forest in that they depend on the Kuttia Kondh and the products they get from the forests. A Pano seldom gets into direct contact with the forest. The Pano require firewood and forest products for their households, but only rarely collect wood themselves and only in areas with light vegetation. They lack the experience of the Kuttia people as to where to find specific materials and presumably feel much more afraid of the forests' dangers. Furthermore, the Pano do not practice shifting cultivation. They cultivate the plains.

The Kuttia Kondh used to regard the Pano as the communicating agents between the hills and the plains, and even more so between a forest-based subsistence and the market economy. From the plains, the Pano would bring salt, matches, dry fish and many articles of daily use to the Kuttia Kondh. The Kuttia Kondh received the commodities from the Pano by paying in kind. For a measure of salt, a measure of *mahula* flowers, of paddy, of cowpea, or of pigeon pea, the price was fixed. The quantities of crops that the Pano obtained in exchange exceeded many times over the value of the commodities they sold. Still, the Kuttia Kondh feel that the Pano are inferior to them. Though both communities have depended on a similar type of livelihood and food habits, they are culturally different. The Kuttia are quite egocentric about their origin and emphasise their pedigree as the 'first' inhabitants. The Pano are considered as outsiders and viewed as the servants who carry the goods to the Kuttia Kondh. As superior beings, the Kuttia Kondh did not and still they are reluctant to allow the Pano to live with them in their villages. Thus, the Pano live on the outskirts of Kuttia Kondh villages. They selected their settlement sites mainly on the basis of easy access to the market and the Kuttia Kondh. Whenever the Kuttia took an interest in the market, the Pano dissuaded them from going, and provided the items that the Kuttia Kondh required.

Gradually, services by the Pano community to the Kuttia have now become more intermittent and over time, the Pano and the Kuttia Kondh have begun to compete for space. In Kuttia Kondh areas, governmental development programmes have started up, enabling the Kuttia to sell their products at a good price. These developmental programmes have motivated the Kuttia people to try out new working methods in order that they can earn more with fewer inputs. They have also introduced cash crops and were thus persuaded to take more interest in markets.

With the launching of development programmes in Kuttia Kondh areas, the migration of non-tribals into these areas has increased considerably. People needing to settle there temporarily to perform tasks within the scope of development programmes have accounted for a small share of non-tribal migrants only. A much larger proportion of migrants is comprised by business people who have settled there permanently, with the result that the market for goods has expanded and become more competitive.

Recently, forest legislation has been extended by the addition of new provisions and regulations affecting the livelihoods of forest-dwelling people. A growing number of forest areas have become protected and certain uses of forest restricted. The tribals have been given limited access to the forests, and traditional cultivation by means of shifting cultivation is now not allowed.

The Kuttia people blame the Government development programmes for threatening their livelihood although their crises have been caused by different factors. They feel forced to change their notions of well-being and attitudes to preservation and conservation and in contrast with their traditional lifestyle, there is pressure on them to look towards the so-called "civilised world", associated with an improvement of the standard of living and a boost to their economy, and away from their own culture.

In order to evaluate the Kuttia Kondh understanding of the present crisis affecting them, informal group discussions were organised at different places as part of this study. It seems that the Kuttia people are still confused as to the reasons for and extent of the crises affecting them. The feelings of the Kuttia towards these government programmes can be understood from the following statements:

> Our happy life in the forests is in danger. We feel that the forest legislation is formulated in a way which makes it impossible for us to stay in the forests. Because we are deprived of our right to cultivate the forests, we are forced to give up shifting cultivation, our only form of subsistence. The motivation and awareness generation programmes under the Podu Prevention Scheme, and the increase in forest areas designated as protected and prohibited

for cultivation are both meant to stop shifting cultivation. All that is left for us are the nearby areas, which will not provide a good yield when cultivated continuously because cultivation without a prolonged fallow period of at least two years will adversely affect soil fertility. Thus, the production will not meet our household consumption. Then, what shall we sell in the market for cash?

We do not think that our practice of shifting cultivation has converted any patch of forest into barren land. Forest regeneration is ensured by leaving the fields fallow for a reasonable period of time. From our experience and observation, we believe that after a fallow period of two years, the fields have regenerated sufficiently since within that time, low-level bush forest has already grown up there. But a fallow period of two years is necessary. We feel that we cannot do shifting cultivation any more as the penalty charged by the Forest Department for cutting a new patch is beyond our capacity to pay. If we do it, we will be put in jail for violating forest rules and regulations. Who will look after our children when we are in jail?

Our practice does not hamper the soil at all. We do not plough the forest soil deeply. We only slash and burn the vegetation and then wait for rain showers, after which we sow seeds on the forest ground or insert seeds into dibbled holes, so there is no possibility that the soil could be washed away by the rain. Could you show us a patch where soil has been washed away and the forest ground has become rocky?

We are hardly interested in gathering minor forest produce because we do not have enough time for that. By the time the minor forest produce in the forest is at its peak (which is in summer) we are preoccupied with other work. We do not even have time to collect tamarind. We do not collect *sal* resin but rather, *sal* seeds. We collect *mahula* flowers and broom grass when we see them growing. We do not search for them. We collect thatch grass. All we get from the forest is used as food or for household maintenance. We do not want to live on the sale of minor forest produce. We want to live on crop resources. Why, then, would we destroy large trees and what business would we have with such trees?

We depend on forest materials to maintain our households, the poles for constructing the houses, the fodder for our cattle, and the roots that we consume. We do extract poles to construct our houses. However, we do not construct houses every year. Once a house is constructed, it lasts for a number of years, let's say about ten years. Hence, we require building material from the forests at a time interval of roughly every ten years. Of course, within these ten years, some ten more houses are added to the village. Does the forest get exhausted or denuded if, within one year, poles are collected to build one house?

We are cautioned not to continue with shifting cultivation. It has been suggested that we cultivate the plains and we have been provided with seeds and irrigation facilities where possible. We have been provided with seeds to grow cash crops which other people are interested in and in which we do not have any interest. Those crops cannot satisfy our consumption needs. We have been provided with seeds, but where shall we sow them? Should we clear patches of forests in the foothills in order to acquire more land on the plains? Has the government made any provisions for land on the plains?

We are being motivated to develop fruit tree cultivation and saplings have been provided. We will have to plant these on the plains in our possession where we now cultivate cash crops like mustard and niger. But whatever fruits we like, we have grown them already. Our jackfruit production is sufficient to satisfy our needs. Papaya is not a very important component of our nutrition. One guava tree per family can cover the needs of a family. So what shall we do with this huge quantity of fruit? If we cultivate such crops in our kitchen gardens or on the plains, where can we grow chilly, mustard, niger and paddy? Can we get enough money to purchase rice and other goods that we need from the market by selling this fruit crop?

We could earn money from transferring our labour into fruit tree plantations and we are told that such crops could be beneficial to us. However, our demand for such crops is very small. A "jungle" to us is a collection of many types of trees, bushes and creepers. Such plantations are not the forest. They are like our

> gardens where the papaya trees grow. Growing such trees is economically beneficial to those who take an interest in planting them. We, however, would only grow them in order to get wages and earn income. We do not have any interest in such trees. Can a *sal* tree be compared to an oak tree? Can a *mahula* tree be compared to a *champak* tree?
>
> We are recommended to sell our minor forest produce to government collection centres like TDCC and AMCS. But do they always have ready money to purchase minor forest produce? And do such agencies give us rice in advance during our lean periods?
>
> We are given temporary employment in developmental work. We, the Kuttia Kondh people, do not like to work as daily wage labourers. But to cover our cash needs, we build roads and buildings. Does the government want us to become landless labourers and lose our indigenous culture forever?
>
> We are faced with a crisis and we are told to participate more in the market economy. What is left to us to sell in the market in order to get enough cash to cover our needs?
>
> We are provided with loans to purchase ploughs, bullocks etc. However, we do not have enough land in the plains. We do not use ox-drawn ploughs for shifting cultivation. As we are not provided with any land in the plains, what are we supposed to do with ox-drawn ploughs and loans?
>
> Many outsiders point out that our lifestyle is of a poor standard and based on an irrational adherence to superstition. Those who regard it as such do not know our culture and tradition. What may be superstition to others is not irrational to us but part of our culture and thus, a source of our happiness and pleasure. Our culture is just as important to us as your culture is to you. If our culture has no value, then why has the KKDA taken an interest in taking us to the Adivasi Exhibition ground at Bhubaneswar every year in January?

These are some of the questions and anxieties the Kuttia feel and are expressing today. The development programmes are seen as a cause of their crises rather than solutions to their problems. The programmes have brought about many changes and the Kuttia people feel that their traditions are threatened by them. They do not know whether they can maintain their well-being in a society where the market, rather than the forest, is dominant. They have difficulties in giving up their close relation with the forest and are afraid of the cultural transition that is going on. The polarity between a dominance of the forest and a dominance of the market is reflected by introduction of a new language system. Whereas the language of the Kuttia Kondh (Kui) reflects their traditional lifestyle closely connected to the forests, the Oriya language, recently introduced, is part of a new, so-called "modern" lifestyle putting the market at its centre. The Kui and the Oriya language reflect different world-views. To get a chance to continue to live in the forests in the face of technological changes, the Kuttia Kondh are required to learn Oriya, a language spoken outside their territory. This has become clear in the course of the last few years when the Kuttia people have been confronted with modern technology and development programmes. Only few of the people who have contacted the Kuttia Kondh in this aim have attempted to learn Kui. In order to benefit from the process of technological changes, the Kuttia Kondh are however making efforts to learn Oriya.

Generally, in the context of bilingualism, the language of the stronger culture will replace the language of the weaker culture, thereby dominating the process of cultural exchange. In Kui, the Kuttia Kondh can describe the forest as their living space. Oriya, in contrast, is a language of people living outside the forest. The differences between the communities, speaking in either of the two languages are reflected in the languages themselves.

Oriya may be considered as a means to integrate the Kuttia Kondh into development programmes and consequently, into the unfamiliar, living world of the market and the people living outside the forest. Oriya has begun to infiltrate into Kui and the influence of Oriya on Kui is an indication of the change in the lifestyle of the Kuttia Kondh. The Kuttia people are aware of the importance of Oriya and of its influence on their language. However, the objective may best be not to preserve the purity of Kui by all means, but rather to preserve the tradition of songs and folklore that may help the Kuttia Kondh to live under new circumstances.

Irrespective of any criticism from the developed world outside, the Kuttia Kondh are continuing to lead their lives in the manner they are familiar with, as they believe it to be the most reasonable response to the crisis affecting them. At the same time they are aware that the changes the government wishes to bring about may jeopardise their traditional way of life. They may lose the forests as the basis of their livelihood. The Kuttia Kondh continue to express their view that they do not wish to abandon the place of their dwelling and their practice of shifting cultivation. The crisis has generated an awareness amongst the Kuttia people that they are as much part of the forests as the forests are a part of them. According to the Kuttia people, as both these systems tend to feed into each other, it is necessary to maintain a boundary between human beings and nature. From this, it follows that to the Kuttia Kondh, self-preservation also means the preservation of the forests. The Kuttia believe in the ability of forests to regenerate. Forests are viewed as living organisms, just like human beings and consequently, the preservation and conservation of forests depends on both organisms involved in this symbiotic relationship between human beings and the natural world.

Judged from the outside, there are no visible steps taken by the Kuttia Kondh aimed at the preservation and the conservation of forests. Everything they do is embedded in religious ritual and other cultural traditions that depend upon the forest world. The Kuttia Kondh's work pattern may be described as being both conservationist and conserving, as well as constructive and destructive. All in all, it is their cultural tradition that ensures an ethical relation between themselves and forests.

The protection accorded to many plants by this tribe, (viz. bamboo (*Bambusa sp.*), *siali* (*Bauhinia vahlii*), *semul* (*Bombax Malabaricum*), *sunari* (*Cassia fistula*), *salap* (*Caryota urens*), *amla* (*Emblica officinalis*), *akanbindi* (*Cissampelos pereira*), *daman* (*Grewia tiliaefolia*), *mahula* (*Madhuka longifolia*), *sal* (*Shorea robusta*), and *asan* (*Terminalia tomentosa*) is well known. There are also instances of entire biological communities, such as aquatic communities, which receive protection because of their association with a deity. The tribe venerates plants and trees, regarded as symbols of deities, abodes of deities, or as representations of deities. The tradition of maintaining sacred groves as part of their villages is one of the most valuable legacies of the forest dwellers' attitude towards nature. The sacred groves contain plant species considered as climax type vegetation. Apart from the preservation of rare and endemic species, the sacred groves also contribute in general to the preservation of biological diversity (Godbole/Sarnaik 2004).

The life of the Kuttia Kondh in the forests is now confronted with a great number of problems. These have thrown the tribe into a crisis and initiated a process of transition. The tribe, though regarded as a forest dwelling community, will not be able to continue to regard the forest as its property any more, and may be prevented from using its resources, or at least part of them. Yet the tribe does not want to abandon its practice of shifting cultivation, although it is conscious of the crisis severely affecting and probably changing its traditional way of life. There is a stanza in the *Kui Gaani* that says:

edu itere budhi itere
inisatisi adine inisatisi ranjine.

And life does not cease.
It goes on.

Conclusion

THE results of the research venture into the forest life of the Kuttia Kondh of Phulbani district in central Orissa, described in detail in this book, was, though not purposively, but *de facto,* a re-study of this ethnic group after forty years. In the time since the German *Frobenius Expedition to India,* a small team under the leadership of Hermann Niggemeyer, did research in the villages of Burlabaru and Belghar in 1955/56, various social changes in these villages and in other parts of the district have altered living conditions for many sectors in the Indian society, tribal and non-tribal. Life in modern Indian mainstream society and particularly, the lifestyles of those regarded as the "lower social strata" (Scheduled Castes and Scheduled Tribes) living in the many rural and remote parts of the country have undergone tremendous transformations. Despite this, most of the forest dwelling tribes, including the Kuttia Kondh, show remarkable persistence in pursuing their patterns of livelihood being almost self-substained communities. They still depend on the forest and its various products to a large extent (Samal 1997). Their material culture can still be called forest-based and their lore and legends, their religious practices and economic rationale are core elements of their self-consciousness and cultural identity. The Pano community, which has lived amongst the Kuttia Kondh since time immemorial, has exposed them to influences outside their tribal world and constituted their link to Orissan mainstream society. Kuttia Kondh cultural values were, and still are, contested by those of the Pano community who were exploiting them as intermediaries and who are much more economically oriented than the their host community. Kuttia social values, having their origin in the cycles of forest life, under threat of scarcity of food supply, uncertainty and the prospect of danger in so many aspects of daily life developed in conditions of poverty, but in an atmosphere of common sense. These still prevail in modern times just as the state is providing services to the Scheduled Castes and Tribes that were hitherto unknown to them.

For centuries, forests used to be domains of common property, but also of "common poverty" (Singh 2000). Since forests were appropriated by British colonial rule and nationalised almost all over India in the nineteenth century, poverty has increased and the livelihoods of those who previously depended on them for sustenance have eroded. The decades following Indian independence have brought about improvements for the forest dwelling tribal population, but economical entitlements and political rights to forest land and forest produce were never re-transferred to those groups. (Fernandes 1988, 1992a&b&c, 1996a, 1996b). Many socio-economic aid programmes and so-called micro-projects aimed at improving the tribals' living conditions did not improve their low living standards either. Despite all the shortcomings of their meagre living conditions, it can be said that they have not become "clients of the state", destined to be looked after, and cared for, through state revenues. Self-determination in many social and economic spheres of life is actually more the rule than the exception, if not denied to tribal communities or NGOs for political reasons. The tribes' traditional lifestyle and knowledge may have lost much of its significance in everyday life within one or two generations, but their socio-economic and political relevance has not faded away. Nationwide environmentalist movements all over India, urging people taking a vivid interest in their fate and that of the countries' forests for ecological reasons, has sparked interest in their plight. The question of how great a share of the forest and forest products should be allocated to those forest-dwelling tribes with rights to the forests is a cultural and political one. For the Indian state, forests are a source of revenue to be appropriated and redistributed for the benefit of the entire nation. For the tribal communities, it is a life world.

Forest as World of Representations

The cultural and political challenge for a modern nation state and a fast growing economy such as India is to mediate between this dual, and often conflicting, outlook on forests: their use and management relating to lifestyles of different groups of people, and how these natural resources embody forms of social and cultural representations. What do forests represent for a tribal community such as the Kuttia Kondh?

Forests are a living cosmos where economy, society, culture and spirituality meet at the crossroads of tradition and an emerging understanding that a new era is dawning, one in which traditional or indigenous knowledge is becoming socially and strategically important to a wider community with a relevant international concern than that of forest dwellers only (Posey 1999). As one of the last realms where archaic lifestyles are practised, these are small communities that share a common outlook on life and only occasionally encounter modernity. Forests are examples of an undifferentiated and uncompartmentalised world, where plants, animals and human beings interact in a unique blend of material and spiritual forest culture. Kinship relations between plants, animals and humans, or beliefs of "shape shifting", for instance, join together parts of their particular life-world in a way that would appear to an outside observer as seemingly separate phenomena. Where nature and culture merge together to form an indivisible amalgam, lifestyles cannot fall apart. They become, to a certain extent, resistant to forces that intrude from outside this world. For those dwelling inside this nature-culture continuum, forest lifestyles such as practised by the Kuttia Kondh, encompass spheres of reality. The landscape that surrounds them and the hills with their distinct features, in particular, constitutes a sacred realm, in the Kuttia Kondh perception, the abode of gods and ancestor spirits.

Challenges for a Modern Forest Policy in a Traditional Cultural Setting

A modern forest policy in developing societies such as those in Orissa is forced to confront various difficulties: on the one hand, forest-based industries like the politically influential "*kendu leaf bidi*" (simple country cigarettes) manufacturing enterprises, mining companies, timber contractors and paper mills with enormous economic importance for the state (there is a wide range of non-wood forest products in Orissa (Patnaik 2003) highly relevant to its economy) and on the other hand, 63 tribes living predominantly inside, or close to, the forest who have to eke out their living from its rich variety of products in daily life. The conflict between these two overlapping worlds revolves around the rationale of forest use and styles of management as defined by indigenous people, and that defined by modern "conceptual approaches".

Modern forestry developed in Europe during the nineteenth century where only a very few people, if any, were living in the forests who were entirely economically dependent on its products. Furthermore, the forest as a spiritual world did not matter much when forestry scientists took over forests in overseas colonies. The idea of maximum economic return slowly transformed those jungles (inhabited and extensively used by indigenous populations up to that point) into resources to be exploited for their valuable commodities, be it timber or non-timber produce. Thus, over the past 150 years, the predominant goal has been to make significant economic profits from forestry.

Forestry legislation in India, from the first forest law issued in 1865 until the late twentieth century in independent India, has so far never succeeded in overcoming this fundamental conflict of ownership und usufructory rights between the tribes of India and the government. Only recently, the draft of the, as it is provisionally called, "Scheduled Tribes (Recognition of Forest Rights) Bill 2005" (Government of India 2005), however, foresees a radical change by granting almost exclusive rights to the Scheduled tribes. Ownership rights of up to 2.5 ha shall go to the nuclear family and basic political rights of identifying the beneficiaries are to be given to the village council (*gram sabha*). For this inheritable but unalienable and not transferable right the tribal communities have the responsibility to care for the protection, conservation and regeneration of the forest areas that have been allotted to them.

Major changes in the hitherto prevailing forest management and administrational practices at the State and Union level are likely to be inevitable in the near future and are long since overdue (Praharaj 1988, Areeparampil 1992). This is not only indicated by the strong national and international green movements that are challenging the perpetuating post-colonial state forest policies all over the world, but as thousands of grassroots movements and local Non-Governmental Organisations become more and more conscious of their bargaining power and are backed by strong political trends, they are increasingly influential at the national level as well as world-wide. Changes in some sectors of a post-colonial society such as India are long since overdue. The forest administration has continued to be one among the last internal colonies in the partly post-colonial and partly modern nation state, and as a result of its discrepancies, is becoming more and more an anachronism in a rapidly modernising country. The shift from a post-colonial towards a modern civil society with greater citizen involvement in political decisions began in India only a few decades ago and tends ultimately to lead, not only to the quest for a new forest policy, but for a new social policy, lest society becomes polarised and split between local cultures and global players in one and the same country. An integrative social policy that unites social demands and a natural resource use policy for all concerned sections of the population is therefore inevitable.

To Whom Do Nature and Natural Resources Belong?

As amply discussed above, Kuttia Kondh culture and their surrounding environment are inseparable. This is reflected throughout their world-view and cosmology. And although changes have been taking place in all aspects of life with modernization spreading everywhere, the Kuttia Kondh have been able to retain their ethnic and cultural identity. Strong social and spiritual ties with forests, plants and animals have contributed to the continuous co-existence of the tribe and the natural environment with direct and indirect give-and-take relationship. Forests, trees, sacred groves and certain landscapes are held with kinship relations as brothers and sisters of the Kuttia Kondh and these relationships with nature or parts and elements of nature matter a lot to many members of the tribe. They see their notion of a good life as living within a harmonious relationship with nature. Natural landscapes, forests, earth, sun, water, sky, rain make their life enjoyable and worth living. The vision and philosophy of the Kuttia Kondh is reflected in their relationship with the divine powers as gods, goddesses and spirits and nature is the collective whole of these divine powers. In their world-view, man and nature are interchangeable, but within certain limits. Supernatural spirits are manifest in the form of trees, animals, birds, hills, mountains, landscapes and anthropomorphic forms. In their dreams, they identify certain gods and goddesses with a particular tree, animal, bird, reptile, hill, mountain, water, rock, landscape, anthropomorphic forms and human work processes.

This relationship of Kuttia Kondh with nature is, however, not free from critique. The swiddening practice of the tribe ignites arguments in which they are accused of being destroyers of nature and environment. But the tribe gives special value to this traditional form of dependence on shifting cultivation. It is culturally valued and could even from Western scientific perspective be argued as topographically appropriate. For the tribe, swiddening is a sound subsistence practice as there is no risk of total crop failure, even if drought or excessive rainfall occurs, because the crops ripen at various intervals of time, not all at once. Furthermore, they calculate their labour input and productivity according to this system. When productivity decreases in relation to the labour input, they shift to another plot, thus ensuring a period of fallow till the fertility of the soil is regained. Swiddening produces both cash and subsistence crops and provides them with a minimum security.

While thinking about conservation of forests and biodiversity, care must also be taken to conserve their cultural diversity (Posey 1999). Development programmes and forest policies are to give due importance to people's culture to help them to avail an optimum, positive outcome as a result of increased labour participation. It does not seem to be realistic, looking at the present circumstances, to stop the swiddening practices of the tribe by imposing restrictions and regulations through policies on the tribal people. One important step in this regard could be the classification of all forests into different human use intensities, so that areas critical for conservation, e.g., swidden lands can be well conserved. A strategy to conserve the locally managed forests with indigenous local knowledge is required since conservation and local sustenance emerge as twin priorities out of forest and biodiversity conservation. To a member of the Kuttia

Kondh, abandoning shifting cultivation is like losing his or her culture, or an element of it.

More and more forestlands are being brought under the "reserved" and "protected" categories by the Forest Department. Some of the fallow swiddens where good undergrowth is visible, have even been brought under the category of protected forest. Through regulations and restrictions of forest law and policies, the government has been to some extent successful in directing the Kuttia Kondh to certain patches of degraded swiddens that barely needed fallowing. With no alternative immediately available or accessible, the tribe is continuing to practise swiddening on limited patches of land, hardly able to leave land fallow after an interval of three or more years. As a result, the older generation has reacted negatively and has criticised the government measures as detrimental to their life and culture. The random multiple cropping system has been reduced to selected crops in certain areas, and this, the result of a decrease in fertility, has affected their livelihood earnings. Older tribal people argue that when there was a multiple cropping system with about thirty to thirty-five crops in the swiddens, there was less pest infestation. When under the compulsion of policy regulations, they were forced to come back to a swidden after a short fallow of about three to five years, they could, at best, cultivate about twenty varieties. This has further reduced the number of crops to a maximum of five to six under these same forced conditions, and in some cases, compelled people to cultivate the same patch of land continuously, on the one hand, as a result of abject poverty, and on the other, as a result of new regulations regarding convertion of new forest patches into swiddens. These changes from multiple crops to selected crops, coupled with the decrease in productivity, and increase in pest infestation, are the reasons why the younger generation wishes to climb down the hills and move towards alternatives. It seems as if government regulations have been a deliberate attempt to change the Kuttia Kondh's exclusive dependence on forests to a marginal dependence on the same.

As an alternative to swiddening, agriculture in the plains is not rewarding as far as the subsistence requirement for the whole year is concerned. There is very little land available to the Kuttia Kondh in the plains as most of the available land is in non-tribal possession. The tribe, therefore, restricts itself to rain-fed paddy cultivation in the low lands once in a year. Lowland paddy cultivation is perceived as a non-viable livelihood option, as the traditional crop varieties cannot be grown there. This means a risk to their livelihood earnings. The per capita low land holding is so small that they cannot countenance maintaining a family on the basis of the small yield from the low lands.

Modernisation has significantly influenced Kuttia Kondh life and culture. It has brought tangible and intangible change to their lifestyles, attitudes, perceptions and worldview. On the one hand, these changes may be seen as a trend towards a development; on the other, such changes pose a threat to their traditional patterns and paradigms. Over the last couple of years, the Kuttia Kondh have been brought under the ambit of development through holistic and sector approaches. While such development initiatives primarily address their economic development, their cultural development is ignored entirely or dealt with very superficially.

Development initiatives also influence the knowledge, attitude and perception of the community. This has created a communication gap between elder and younger generation in the Kuttia community. The elder generation argues that the development programs are addressed with a bias towards the market economy, ignoring their culture and traditional life style. The younger generation finds itself easily influenced by these models and in their rush towards an easy cash-based economy, young people fall prey to development programs, gradually losing their traditional culture and traits. The younger generation, argues more in favour of the world-view of a developed society, one which would be possible, if better income opportunities existed.

This primitive-modern continuum has sparked dialogue on value differences within the community. Keeping the resource base the same, the elder generation strongly advocates continuation of traditional practices while the younger generation is adamant that adopting newer technologies for more positive outputs from the same base would be better. Adoption to newer technologies is perceived as a threat to traditional technologies by the elder generation. They believe that the traditional technologies and techno-economic pursuits are outcomes of decades of innovation and are appropriate to the environmental condition of which they are a part and thus, very valuable.

Development as modernisation has set in motion the occupational mobility of the Kuttia Kondh. This occupational mobility may be seen as a move from forest to market, from tradition to modernity, from exclusive subsistence earning to marginal cash income. The younger generation has been showing greater interest in prioritising alternative sources of income, considered better than swiddening and gathering forest produce, in one way or other. Wage earning is one of the occupations Kuttia youths are inclined towards, although traditionally, they have spurned it. But under conditions of relative marginalisation and the need to practise swiddening in accordance with government rules and regulations, they are submitting to wage labour. The younger generation, in particular, has taken up jobs in road and building construction, mining, bridge construction, earthworks, the digging of rrigation channels, nurseries, *agave* harvesting and fibre production, vhenever an opportunity is available in their area. Their participation n wage earning tends to lead to many attitudinal changes and also changes in their lifestyle.

Wage earning is sometimes seen as an employment opportunity, nd sometimes as a crisis management endeavour. At the end of the ay, the few wages earned by the youth are spent in the local market n sweet meat, small stationeries and video shows. The girls have lso started working as wage earners and even though they are paid ss than boys, they try to make best use of their wages by spending ne money on essential commodities for the family. While wage earning as not affected the girls much, it has has a tremendous impact on e boys, such that they are content to work at the houses or farms of etty traders. These traders employ the tribal boys in the processing agricultural or forest produce, weighing and measuring, packaging nd transportation works. The driving factor behind the employment these tribal boys is the desire to motivate their community members sell their collected produce to the concerned trader. This strategy of the traders yields fruit in that they profit accordingly. Through the go-between of their tribal workers, the traders are able to contact needy tribal families in the lean periods, or time of need, and arrange with them to sell off their future agricultural harvests by paying a very small amount in advance.

Poor tribals consider this assistance from a wellwisher. But by posing as people easily approached for financial help, these traders are able to exploit the tribal population by buying their produce at a lower price. Thus, the tribal groups fail to make a sound earning from either their harvests or their produce. For the sake of maintaining a good relationship with the traders and moneylenders who stand beside them during their need, the tribal people agree to such exploitation.

What the women lament most is the breakdown in the traditional system of co-operative labour that used to perform various labour-intensive activities for the society, mainly in agriculture. They view it as an impact of modernisation as well as a matter of individuals' quest for earning options, and more direct participation in the market. Previously, the co-operative labour use was very well organised and the tribe received many benefits as a result. With the change in perception and emergence of alternative modes of livelihood, the co-operative labour system has dwindled. Basically, the participation of male members in the co-operative labour system is declining and there are now few instances where tribal families employ their own community members to work in the forest, as a result of the decline

Modernisation, moreover, has significantly influenced their traditional knowledge system and traditional knowledge, skill and technology are gradually losing their importance in the community. In their traditional lifestyle, direct and positive links between the traditional knowledge system and resource use were obvious. The knowledge system pertaining to agriculture, forestry, healthcare and other fields was a valuable asset for the survival of the tribe, and was part of their tradition that passed down from generation to generation through work processes and lore. But this system is becoming more and more ignored by the younger generation.

It is generally believed that the knowledge system of the Kuttia Kondh was holistic in nature. Centuries of association with a certain environment has produced a deep understanding of interrelationship among the different elements of a landscape or a habitat and their survival needs and because fluctuation in an environment requires adaptive responses, the Kuttia Kondh have developed diversified survival strategies at intra- and inter-household level as well as community level. However, this traditional knowledge system, generally holistic, does contain some reductionist elements. In order to cope up with the complexity of ecological change, some people are trying to specialise now by knowing more and more about less and less. This is going to reduce the diverse survival strategies to a more monotonous style of living.

The Kuttia Kondh knowledge of work traditions, environmental perceptions, technology involved in various kinds of work processes in the field of natural resource utilization and management are scientific in their own accord. Forms of knowledge, technology and skills are very specific and to a certain extent scientific in their environmental set-up and operate very much within their territory or landscape. Erosion of these traditional knowledge systems would no doubt affect their livelihood systems absolutely. Effective natural resource utilisation undertaken to the exclusion of traditional knowledge systems would be detrimental to the tribe as it may cause almost a depletion of the resource base. The older generation of the Kuttia Kondh believes that their livelihood practices, for example swiddening, is a rational form of cultivation to the kind of environmental set-up and involves time-tested, useful traditional knowledge. They are sure that no alternative system of livelihood would match swiddening and thus, advise the younger generation to equip themselves well with the traditional knowledge and skill, which, they think, would help them to survive.

The tribe is definitely in a transition between tradition and modernity. External programs or policies intending to increase the efficiency of resource use so as to cope with increasing population pressure, scarcity, fluctuations in the environment or other contingencies, will require a blending of relevant formal and informal knowledge and institutions.

Social equity is an indispensable requirement for socially just and politically legitimate access to the use and management of natural resources. Throughout their recorded history, the Kuttia Kondh have been oriented towards an egalitarian command over the natural and labour resources within their reach. Inside the boundaries of their customary law, they have managed to make use of, and distribute, the natural wealth within their settlement area among themselves, allowing the Pano community to participate as an inherent element of their larger social set-up.

Historically, foreign rulers or superior political powers have occupied their territories from time to time, but a formal administration found its way into the Kondhmals by the middle of the nineteenth century only. Their beliefs in their rights to property in land and natural resources, denied to them under the British colonial administration, were disputed from time to time and were mostly uncertain. In this process, not only did customary rights and economic wealth vanish, but the forest and the natural wealth of their homelands as well. Expropriation and pauperisation of the Kuttia Kondh led them into a state of alienation and a desire to withdraw from outsiders and the paramount powers of the British administrators and their Indian successors after Indian independence. What remains today is the conviction that they are the users of the territory they are inhabiting, yet not the masters over it. What happened to the Kuttia Kondh over the past 150 years was a history of deprivation. However, they have managed to survive as tribe without rights, solely dependent on the forests and their local knowledge of how to make a living from it, with the Pano community as mediators.

Yet, there is a paradox in this history of dispossession, as they have ceased to be the owners of their homeland, though it is legally forbidden to buy or sell it to anybody. Tribal land is, and was always meant to be, state property. Thus, the Kuttia Kondh have been made guests on their own territory, required to ask for what, in their perception, belongs to them. What they get in return from the state are welfare amenities such as schools, for instance, dispensaries and a certain degree of security, aimed at uplifting their living standard. Yet, the Kuttia Kondh have neither asked to be dispossessed nor to be socially uplifted. The overriding rationale of being integrated into a nation state, a larger political unit unbeknownst to them, and what this means to their way of life, has left them with no alternative than to cling to their traditional lifestyle and indigenous local knowledge. With the survival of their local knowledge, their mode of appropriating the local environment has survived. They continue to appropriate their culture through a process of transforming nature into culture — that is, they appropriate without becoming proprietor. The Kuttia Kondh have so far survived the deterioration of their forest surroundings although this process has not yet come to a halt and it is not clear if this ability to survive will continue, should the environmental and political situation worsen. The Kuttia Kondh's cultural identity, however, will be always linked to a feeling of belonging to their landscape and cosmos in central Orissa, even if their faint hopes to own land or to gain material wealth from the land, may fade away with every passing decade.

Glossary

Important Cultural Terms of the Kuttia Kondh

Aaku	:	Leaves
Aba	:	Sister-in-law (brother's wife) elder brother's wife
Achisata	:	Marriage by elopement
Adkinga	:	Liquor made of *Madhuka longifolia*
Adu	:	Women
Agakata/Agat latha	:	Ancient tales, songs and stories that are associated with the Kuttia Kondh's perception of nature and culture
Agari	:	Barren land, referring to forest which changed into barren land
Aji	:	Maternal grand mother
Aku gate	:	The stage in plant life when foliar leaves come out
Aku saritei	:	Excessive exposure to the outward environment
Ana	:	Hill slopes
Anga-dina	:	Inability to see the timely
Angakatu	:	Nature regarded as the precursor of all resources in Kuttia Kondh understanding
Areaja	:	Thunder
Argada Majhi	:	A person took birth when an earthen pot burst without visible reason
Asad lanju	:	June/July
Atarnaka	:	Maize
Atpta bicha	:	Mixture of eight varieties of crop seeds
Bachine	:	Drying up due to lack of water supply in the root
Badang	:	Area adjacent to the back of a house

Badbinere	:	Farewell
Bagada	:	A cleaned hill land for or under cultivation
Bahana	:	Vehicle
Bahe	:	Useless, unnecessary
Bahe gaani	:	Folk songs, dance songs, etc
Bakaratamu	:	To loose tract of, to loose sight of, to miss the connecting link
Baki mudadu	:	A goldsmith woman with finger rings of brass
Bana gabuli	:	Long haired woman
Bana jeting	:	A woman having a long chained hair knot
Baru	:	Slope
Basa	:	Place, tubers (becomes specific with a prefix)
Basa gaani	:	Environmental song (social environment)
Basiliadu	:	Rice frying woman
Basing pirida	:	The flute player
Basni	:	Invocation
Batang	:	Outermost part of the settlement
Bati	:	Bushy forest
Began mara	:	Leaves of a tree that repel insects (*Vitex nigundo*)
Besthamu	:	Tell me
Beta	:	Hunting
Beta mangera	:	The real king or lord on earth
Bhetti	:	Gift from a guest
Bia Katina	:	Meriah festival
Bicha	:	Seeds, pox disease, conceptually refers to regeneration and reproduction capacity of resources
Bicha supandi	:	Sowing
Bidi	:	Wind
Bidi bangeri	:	The hill named after wind
Brapanemberi	:	Malaria fever
Budhi	:	Knowledge, often equivalent to personal intelligence
Budhi itere	:	Wisdom, thoughtfulness
Burda	:	Big reservoirs for keeping grains

Burka	:	Body hair
Burlanga	:	Stored seeds in a bamboo container
Capta	:	Upper cloth of a woman's dress
Dadi	:	Death rites of a man or a house
Dadu	:	Eczema and ring worm
Daka	:	Sleep
Daki	:	Root base of plants and trees
Dakina	:	Worship
Dakina gaani	:	Worship songs, religious songs
Damanaka	:	The owner of the forest
Dana	:	*Sal* leaf pot
Danduta/Danda	:	Village main road leading up the hill slope (syn : wide)
Dangin pdika	:	*Ascariasis*
Dankandi pdukandi	:	A process of curing diseases like snake bite, intensive crying of children, vomiting, trembling, paleness of eyes, bloodlessness etc through religious sacrifices
Dapa dedhi	:	Vertical poles on either sides of a window
Dashera lanju	:	September-October
Data	:	The seeds that are used for raising seedlings
Data puri	:	A woman having big front teeth
Date	:	Harrow
Dedhi	:	Pole with a base from *sal* wood
Deheradu	:	The wizard women (syn : *Pejeradu*)
Dera	:	Old
Dera mara	:	Smaller trees
Deranja	:	An expert singer of a group, preferably an old man
Deranja	:	Old man
Deukuda Penu	:	Village goddess
Dharani Penu	:	Earth Goddess
Dharani vali	:	Three stones are worshipped as Dharani Penu placed under the *Meriah* Pole
Dia	:	Young *Lagenaria* (bottle gourd)

Dimbuli Soru	:	It is the base of a hill where *penu* (God) cultivated all varieties of food
Dina	:	Day
Dombuli mila	:	Children of the *dom* scheduled caste
Dua	:	Powdered tobacco leaves
Dukelanja	:	Ancestor of the Kuttia Kondh
Dukeli	:	Ancestral spirits (ghosts)
Dukeli dakina	:	Worshipping the ancestors
Dulu	:	Wealth goddess
Dulu dakina	:	Worship of wealth deities or goddesses
Dumuni	:	A gourd measure
Diwali lanju	:	October-November
Edu	:	Thought
Edu itere	:	Thinking
Eia	:	Mother (child calls his/her mother)
Eja	:	Home
Eju	:	Water
Eju mundi	:	Small pond
Eju penka dakina	:	Worshipping the water god
Eju silae	:	Drought
Ekkagandadu	:	The woman who steals young children to sacrifice them in a certain ritual
Elu gunjare	:	Surrounding of the house
Elu Penu	:	Home deity
Elu	:	House
Enda	:	Dance
Enda gaani	:	Dance song
Engari aba	:	Sister-in-law; separating a mixture of solid things by filtering them through a bamboo strainer
Gaani	:	Song
Gada	:	Hole
Gaptamu	:	Teaching

Garli vira	:	Fertile soil
Gati	:	Hill tops
Giri	:	Path
Gochchi	:	Parasite plants (orchids also considered parasite plants); also clan
Grudu	:	The whole or collective body
Guisata	:	Marriage by elopement
Gunjare	:	Environment around the Kuttia Kondh settlement
Guti	:	Whitish patch on a tree
Ichek wedate	:	Position of the sun
Ilu	:	House
Inisatisi	:	How
Ispajagela	:	Man who distributes seeds equally among people
Ita utimena	:	Maintenance
Jaana	:	Covering or the mask
Jadi	:	Stream
Jaka	:	Top, menstruation, a hill standing in the east
Jaka dakandi	:	A worship on the roof of the patient's house
Jaka kuda	:	Menstruation huts
Jana	:	Seed coat
janiadu	:	Female shaman
Jella	:	Life force
Jendawenja	:	Referring to ancestors
Jendi	:	Pith of sago palm
Jendi	:	The central strand of younger trees
Jholla	:	Stream
Jokal	:	Lightning
Jrikeni	:	Gum which is used for paste
Juadi	:	Yoke
Jupina	:	Hand weapons
Kaatha	:	Tales
Kabadmai	:	The man who makes the compost pits

Kabda kada	:	Compost pits
Kabda/Kada	:	Hole (man made)
Kada bandha	:	Iron ring that is worn on the wrist
Kadi	:	Cattle
Kadibasa	:	Cattle shed
Kahagandadu	:	Woman who steals
Kaju gnepata	:	Cock crowing time
Kalka	:	The leg of the horse
Kalu	:	Pestle; legs
Kama-ate	:	The utilitarian character of a thing
Kamba	:	Navel of human body
Kambani	:	Canopy forest; forests
Kambit vira	:	Red soil
Kana aate	:	The stage when a seedling comes out
Kanda	:	Sword
Kandrubadi	:	The bamboo slashing man
Kanji	:	A delicious food preparation with bamboo shoots
Kapaka gaani	:	Song about a mythical hero
Karu grasnali	:	Buffalo teasing during the *Meriah* sacrifice
Karumunda	:	*Sal* pole established as sacrificial post
Katul	:	A beverage, which is prepared with millet flour in the leaves after developing a blood red colour is mixed with fresh millet flour and water
Kena	:	Branches
Kerandi	:	Oral tales
Kereena	:	Very short proverbial tales having an ambiguous meaning
Keri	:	Hill slope (narrow)
Khati	:	An evil spirit causing disease
Kikla	:	Grasshopper
Kreti	:	A gourd with a long handle is used as mug
Kuenja	:	Kuttia Kondh males

Kui Gaani	:	The Kuttia Kondh's mythical song
Kui/Kuvi	:	Language spoken by the Kuttia Kondh
Kuianka	:	Kuttia Kondh are known as Kuianka
Kuiladu	:	Kuttia Kondh females
Kumber badi	:	The potter man
Kuta	:	Miraculous performance like magic, witchcraft, sorcery
Kuta kadu	:	Female astrologer
Kutaka	:	Medicine man, astrologer or wizard
Kutani	:	A hole made in a piece of wood
Kuttimai	:	Traditional house building specialist
Kutunaik	:	Astrologers
Kutuni	:	Wooden hammer
La-angi	:	Night
Ladska kuda	:	Young boys' dormitory
Ladvanga kuda	:	Young girls' dormitory
Laesi	:	Early morning
Laudi	:	Two sticks, one long and the other short used as musical instrument
Lenja	:	Conducting vessels of plants for water transport
Leptimai & Kumbarmai	:	Potter women who are specialised in making decorative earthen pots
Lika mara	:	Large shrubs
Linga	:	Male penis
Linga nainjane-Jananainjane	:	Taking birth, getting covered
Linga Penu	:	Birth God
Lohru badi	:	Blacksmith
Loo-angi	:	Night
Maane	:	Manpower
Mada	:	Palm wine (toddy)
Madang basa	:	A place where people sit and drink toddy

Madeni	:	Mid day
Mahananga	:	To be able to identify auspicious moments like an astrologer
Majhi	:	The political headman of the Kuttia Kondh society
Maju	:	Mythical sambar (*Cervus unicolor*) out of whom the vegetable world has evolved
Maju basa	:	Abode of the sambar
Maka puju	:	Maize flower
Manang	:	A measure made out of a hollow bamboo vessel
Mani godi	:	Hangers made of bamboo
Mara	:	Tree
Mara gunda	:	Turmeric powder
Mara penu	:	Tree God
Masajuda gasnali	:	Harvesting
Maska mara	:	Mango tree
Michu	:	Friend, beloved person, wife, husband
Michulani-tatanja	:	Sororate and levirate
Mila	:	Children
Mileni	:	Evening
Milla dali	:	Offsprings
Mniba	:	Metamorphosis
Mniba kdani	:	Ritual specialists practicing shape shifting (preferably into tigers)
Morang	:	Lowlands
Mraka	:	Things made out of wood
Mraka kama	:	Woodworking
Mrangee tae	:	To be distracted
Mranjali	:	Woman showing her chest with pride
Musana	:	Placing of poles in holes
Naju	:	Village
Nani mai	:	Lady-in-charge of fire
Nede	:	Middle part

Nehi sapa itina	:	Proper preservation
Nehi-jella	:	Well-being
Nella	:	Swidden plots
Nella kama	:	Shifting cultivation work
Nellatu	:	The fallow period between two successive clearings of forest followed by cultivation
Nemberi	:	Fever
Ne-ri	:	Blood
Nerputa	:	Blood dysentry
Ninipani-nipandi	:	Conservative upkeep of tradition
Nisa	:	Addiction
Noa bachra kata	:	Since many years
Paberi tali	:	Mythical mother who levelled the earth with a stone
Padani	:	Heaven
Padasi bachite	:	Fruit drying stage
Padasi kadgali ate	:	Fruit ripening stage
Pajibandi	:	Name of a man who was born from an earthen pot
Palupuri	:	Woman having only molar teeth
Panga	:	Foot hill
Pangaliadu	:	Women specialised in tattooing
Panjin gaani	:	Addiction song
Pareni	:	Guests
Pata dae	:	Water contamination causing diarrhoea
Pdite	:	To take birth — birth of animals and human beings
Peda late	:	Growth of shoots
Penka	:	Fruits
Penka ate	:	Bursting of fruit to scatter seeds
Penka ganjite	:	Bursting of seed coats under earth
Penka mete	:	Putting or dibbling a seed into the earth
Penu basa	:	Abode of godly beings
Penuni	:	Plural of Penu (gods)
Pijubangeri	:	Hill named after rain

Pranga	:	Rice
Pujumara	:	*Mahua tree*
Pune	:	To know, to understand and to remember
Punga pute	:	Flowering stage
Punge dumbite	:	Shedding of petals
Punikalu	:	New liquor/full moon festival
Rachangiri	:	Path separating the two rows of houses in a Kuttia Kondh village
Randa	:	Grass
Rangantali	:	Mythical woman who is levelling the land with a stone
Rani	:	Queen
Raniadu	:	Queen
Ranjine	:	Fit
Ra-tudeka	:	Midnight
Sachkanti	:	Vomiting
Sadonga	:	Moustache
Salla	:	Cave/shed
Sana mudada	:	Woman wearing finger rings of gold being regarded as goldsmith
Sandhi	:	Border
Sandra liadu	:	Rice frying women
Sapangada	:	The mythical place where the Kuttia Kondh came to the earth
Sapina	:	Clearings for cultivation
Saponi	:	Take birth (like the germination of a seed)
Sarenitali	:	Elderly woman separating a mixture by using a large porous bamboo vessel
Sareni	:	Porous bamboo basket
Saru	:	Victim to be sacrificed/salt
Saru neri	:	Human blood
Sate	:	To come out
Satotanja	:	A truthful person

Sechkuri aba	:	A woman who separates things by winnowing
Sedi	:	Marriage by negotiation
Sedi daani	:	Marriage song
Sengu	:	Scabies
Seni	:	Pounding hole
Si-eete	:	Production and reproduction
Sira mara	:	One extra measure of toddy offered to a newcomer at the *madang basa*
Sitki vira	:	Clay soil
Soru	:	Hills
Soru jaka/Gati jaka	:	Hill top
Soru Penu	:	Hill God
Sungi butni	:	Country cigar smoking man
Taka	:	Endocarp
Takakalu	:	Mango kernel festival
Takana	:	To cover distance — a corollary that is kept in mind over a period of time
Tala gabuli	:	Woman having few hairs on her head
Tala jeting	:	Woman with short chained hair-knot
Tali	:	Mother (with a name as prefix)
Tana	:	Earth
Tana ganjite	:	Germination of seeds
Tapka	:	Root base
Tedi Gunjare	:	Surroundings of a village
Tendali	:	A woman having a hunchback
Tikanga	:	Tattoo marks on the face
Timaka	:	A clan that originated from bamboo shoots
Titikirini	:	Woodpecker
Treyena	:	Cyclic movement
Treyenja	:	Nomads
Tudeka	:	Midnight
Tudekena	:	Midnight

Tula	:	Creeper
Tuleni	:	Graveyard forest
Tunda pirida	:	Players of organ pipes
Upavas	:	Fasting
Urmali	:	Waist wrap of women
Wango	:	Earth
Wango Penu	:	God associated with shifting cultivation
Wechinja	:	A process of curing diseases like headache, stomach pain, chest pain, etc.
Weda dueri	:	Door located towards the sun
Weda Penu	:	Sun god
Weda sile	:	Sunless/lightless
Wika juda	:	Thatching grass
Wisang gurad	:	Man who was born with a small axe on his shoulders
Worpu aba	:	Bamboo artisan women
Yam Penu	:	Demon god

Appendix - 1
Kui Gaani

Linganainjane jananainjane
Taking Birth, getting covered

Daen wanga dae, daen nella daeti
Under the Earth, under the Nella

Nerandali toduta, kapandali toduta
Following Nerandali, following Kapandali

Sengelaji judeka, brabelaji judeka
Sengel and Brabel grand-mothers joining

Sringulaji judeka, gundelaji judeka
Sringuli and Gundeli grand-mothers joining

Palupuri datapuri judeka
Palupuri & Datapuri grand-mothers joining

Tendaliaji judeka mranjalaji judeka
Tendali and Mranjali grand-mothers joining

Nerandalit toduta, kapandalit toduta
Following Nerandali, following Kapandali

Katimai judeka, Kabadmai judeka
Katimai and Kabadmai joined

(1) *Nanamai judeka, Kabamai judeka*
Naramai and Kabamai joined

Daen sapangadata daen sarchangadata
Under Sapangada, under Sarchangada

Atpa bichalega atpa jaralega
Like a mixture of seeds

Saradlinga manjane baradlinga manjane
Like a flow of water

Sarenitali judeka banjuritali judeka
Sareni and Banjuri mothers joined

Linganainjane jananainjane
Taking birth, getting covered

Rangantali, pabertali judeka
Rangani and paberi mothers joined

Kandra aba judeka warpu aba judeka
Kandra's wife, warpu's wife joined

Enguri aba judeka sekuri aba judeka
Enguri and sekuri sisters-in-law joined

Gachi ganata binagana ta
Of all vamsas, all types mixing

(2) *Linganainjane jananainjane*
Taking birth, getting covered

Kudaganata parjaganata
All castes, all citizens mixing

Lemburasi lega tukurasi lega
Like ants and termites

Kadirasilega karurasi lega
Like bullocks, like buffaloes

Daen wangarete daen nellarete
Under the earth, the fields

Sanamuded judeka bakimudad judeka
Sunamuded, Bakimuded mixing

Deheradu judeka pejenadu judeka
Witch and barren woman mixing

Kutakadu judeka lambikadu judeka
*kutaka*du and Lambikadu mixing

jani adu judeka sisa adu judeka
jani adu, Sisa adu mixing

Eder adu judeka pejen adu judeka
Eder adu and Pejen adu mixing

(3) *Kudaganata parjaganata*
All castes and all citizens mixing

Judekainjane alekainjane
All are mixing

Daen sapangada daen sarchangada
Under Sapangada, under Sarchangada

Daen ranipalu daen bendipalu
Under Ranipalu, under Bendipalu

Daen usarana daen bearana
Under Usarana, under Bearana

Anasila daen ujadsila daen
Under there is no light, no sparkle

Malasila daen dupasila daen
Neither light nor lamp is under

Sikadisila daen kadasila daen
Chains and rings are not inside

Ate judekajan ate alekajan
Again all are gathering

Dia trelu duditrelu judeka
Dia Trelu and Duditrelu mixing

(4) *Sanamudadu judeka bakimudadu judeka*
Women wearing gold ring-silver ring mixing

Pangaliadu radaliadu judeka
Pangaliadu-Radaliadu mixing*

Sandraliadu basiliadu judeka
Puffed-rice making women mixing

Pangaliadu Radaliagu judeka?
Pangaliadu radaliadu mixing.

Titikumbari matikumbari judeka
Potter woman, earthen pot making women mixing

Nerandali toduta kapandali toduta
After Nerandali, after Kapandali

Ra linga padeta ra janan padeta
From one source taking birth, getting covered

Linga pdie mangana jana pdie mangana
Taking birth, getting covered

Damu mila judeka gasimila judeka
Dom children, Gasi children mixing

---

* Konds living on plains are called Panga Kondh. Pangaliadu is a Panga woman whose face is tatooed.

Hadimila judeka chandal mila judeka
Hadi children, Chandal children mixing

(5) *Nulugunu judeka putugunu judeka*
Nulugunu, Putugunu are mixing

Leptimai, kumbarmai judeka
Leptimai, Kumbarmai mixing

Gurasaibi judeka batulisaibi judeka
Gora sahib, collector sahib mixing

Ekkagandadu kahagandadu judeka
Ekkagandadu kahagandadu are mixing*

Kudaganata parjaganata
Many castes, many citizens

Judekai Alekai Manjana
Again gathering mixing

Gachiganata binaganata
Of many Vansas, many types

Seing sapa tuking sapa nangani
All are of equal size (height)

Tanu Nerandali tanu kapandali
She is Nerandali, she is Kapandali

Icheklinga itede ichekjane itede
Gave birth to this much

(6) *Sapangada daeti sarchangada daeti*
Under Sapangada, under Sarchangada

Kuelinga bihite achalinga bihite
Kui woman took birth

Iribati adite iribati ranjite
How it would hold good, how would it fit

Tanu nerandali tanu kapandali
She is Nerandali, she is Kapandali

Sapangada daeti sarchangada daeti
Under Sapangada, under Sarchangada

Linga kangra manjana janakangra manjana
Observing people, who have taken birth

---

* Who steals children for sacrifice

Wari achaliadenjali wari kuel denjali
(It's) looking only women-women

Iriba adate iriba ranjate
How'd it hold good, how'd it fit

Wari achaliajate wari kueladu ajate
Only women have come into being

Irid dina ade irid kasa ade
How can the world be made (with only women)

(7) *Na wanga dinawa na nella dinawa*
If some day (we) move towards earth, fields

Na darni dinawa na jaker dinawa
If some day (we) move to Dharani stone, Jaker stone

Kuenwanga dinawa ruen nella dinawa
At the time of going onto the earth

Ina itke jiane ina daek jiane
Who will worship

Iriba Adate Iriba Ranjate
How'd it hold good, how'd it fit

Linganmane sa-apa janan mane sa-apa
Still, it is to take birth

Ade lingan manenje ade janani manenje
Again giving birth

Betamanger judeka prambumanger judeka
Betamanger mixing, Prambumanger mixing

Kandragurad judeka nipingurad judeka
Kandragurad, Nipingurad mixing

Sapangada daeti sarchangada daeti
Under Sapangada, under Sarchangada

(8) *Nerandalan toduta kapandalan toduta*
Following Nerandali, Kapandali

Linganai manere, jana naimanere
Taking birth, getting covered

Anamanger judeka prambumanger judeka
Anamanger mixing, Prambumanger mixing

Gachigana tara bina gana tara
People of many castes, many types

Tada gata tara kakugata tara
All are (like) brothers and uncles

Palupuri judeka datapuri judeka
Palupuri and Datapuri mixing

Tala gabuli judeka banagabuli judeka
Short haired women mixing

Tala jeting bana jeting judeka
Long haired woman with chained hair mixing

Gachigana tara binagana tara
Like of many castes, many types

Atpabichalega atpa jara lega
Like a mixture of seeds*

(9) *Wasinga pirad judeka, tunda pirad judeka*
Flute blowing man mixing

Kutanaik judeka lambinaik judeka
Sorcerer mixing

Sanamuden judeka baki muden judeka
A man wearing finger ring of gold/silver mixing

Dia majhi judeka purbu majhi judeka
Rice hawling man mixing

Rake majhi judeka gurpa majhi judeka?
Rake majhi Gurpa Majhi (leaderly men) mixing

Paji bandi judeka argada majhi judeka
People from Paji bandi clan mixing

Wisangurad judeka, sungi butni judeka
Axe man, tobacco smoking man mixing

Taka puju judeka, atra naka judeka
Taka *puju*, Atra naka mixing

Sui dedhi judeka dapa dedhi judeka
Who makes Sui dedhi, Dupa dedhi mixing

Margunda judeka bandan majhi judeka
Man pasted with turmeric powder mixing

(10) *Wikajuda judeka ka jagela judeka*
Wika juda and Bandan majhi mixing

---

* Atpabicha-literally eight seed varieties

Judekaimanere alekai manere
Mixing up and gathering at one place

Gachiganatara binaganatara
Of many castes, many types

Lembu rasi lega tuku rasi lega
Like ants, like termites

Sara sambu judeka sara basa judeka
Yam haunters mixing

Mnia meru judeka mnia gati judeka
Mnia meru from Mnia gati mixing

Dia Trelu Judeka, Dudi Trelu Dudeka
Dia Trelu and Dudi Trelu mixing

Itrikang judeka itri data judeka
Itrikang and Itridata mixing

Mnia meru judeka, mnia gati judeka
Mnia meru from Mnia gati mixing

(11) *Todu paeri, judeka todu pungera judeka*
Todu paeri and Todu pungera mixing

Lohru badi judeka binjar badi judeka
Blacksmith and his type mixing

Dedhi mulenga pati mulenga judeka
Dedhi and Pati carrying people mixing

Kandra wadi judeka warpu wadi judeka
Bamboo slashing and bamboo weaving people mixing

Kumberaladu, kumberadudu judeka
Potter woman and her types mixing

Gachiganatara binaganatara
Of many castes, many types

Daen sapangadata daen sarchangadata
Under Sapangada, under Sarchangada

Linga pdie manere janan pdie manere
More and more people are taking birth, coming out

Atpa bichalega atpa jaralega
Like a mixture of different seeds

Kanga bichalega berenga bichalega
Like Kangu seeds, bean seeds

(12) *Eka gane judeka ka-aa gane judeka*
Oriya people and Paika People mixing

Sethimila judeka sanimila judeka
Pano children mixing

Salasethi judeka gapla sethi judeka
Sala Sethi and Gapla sethi mixing

Sander lienja judeka basar lienja judeka
People of Sander lineage, Basar lineage mixing

Radamlienja judeka pangalienja judeka
People of Radam lineage mixing

Urla lienja judeka sirdi lienja judeka
People of Urla lineage mixing

Iribati adite iribati ranjite
How'd it hold good, how'd it fit

Linganeta atena jananeta atena
So much people took birth

Bae linganite bae jananite
Unnecessarily took birth

Wanga sila dinata nella sila dinata
(At a time) when land is not there

(13) *Sapandi sila dinata pdibandi sila dinata*
No land is available on the earth and down the earth

Bae kdaye lajate bae nnaye lajate
It was unnecessary to give birth to a lot

Wendaa gena-a narabi wenda gena-a durabi
Should they go underworld again !

Inisatisi adine inisatisi ranjine
How should it be done, how will it fit

Ate akad mangane ate gangad mangane
Thinking again

Tanu Nerandali tanu Kapandali
She is Nerandali, she is Kapandali

Bae linganiteye bae jananiteye
Unnecessarily gave birth

Isi akad machisi isi gangad machisi
Thinking only can't solve

Irad dina adeye irad kasa adeye
It can't form a world

Wanga wide meka-a nellawide meka-a
(She) set out to inspect the earth

(14) *Tanu Nerandali tanu Kapandali*
She is Nerandali, she is Kapandali

Wanga widgai nella widgai
To roam about the earth

Anasila daeti ujad sila daeti
No light was there under the earth

Mala nani aisi dupanani aisi
(She) carried lamp and fire with her

Wae malandali wae dupandali
She called for Malandali and Dupandali

Sikadi nani atati kada nani atati
Carrying fire with them

Tide pendi atati sakrapendi atati
Fire with dried sesame plants

Wanga wide mekana nella wide mekana
Going to inspect the earth

Tanu Nerandali tanu Kapandali
She is Nerandali, she is Kapandali

Tide nani aisi sakra nani aisi
Carrying burning sesame sticks

(15) *Wanga widi mangane nellawidi mangane*
To see and inspect the earth

Sapandi basagai pdibandi basagai
For how to come to earth, where to emerge?

Kata munda gena-a beimunda gena-a
Could it be near hedges, near bamboo mats

Sati kambani gina-a pditi kambani gina-a
Could it be near Sati Kambani, Pditi Kambani

Pena kambani gina-a maja kambani gina-a
Could it be at Pena Kambani (God-forest), Maja kambani (Sambar-forest)

Ragamara gina-a bichumara gina-a
Could it be near Ragamara, Bichumara (trees)

Amba sapandi adeye amba pdio adeye
Here (We) can't take birth

Like mulu injina like data injina
Is it a matter of few people !

Sitka mati gina-a katpa mati gina-a
Could (we) take birth near clay soil

Pidel nella gina-a kadel nella gina-a
Could it be at Pidel nella, Kadel nella

(16) *Masangdia gina-a kadangdia gina-a*
Could it be in millet fields,

Achekawidi tede acheka preji tede
This much is already covered

Basa panpi silene gari panpi silene
No place, to take birth is available,

Bahe linganiteye bahe jananiteye
Unnecessarily gave birth

Basa sila dinata gari sila dinata
In a world where no earth is available,

Ele sapa panene ele dia panene
(Perhaps) we can't come out anymore

Embe nanga saina embenanga poiena
Where (then) shall we take birth,

Kude panga gina-a tendi panga gina-a
Could we take birth near Kude panga, Tendi panga

Kakibaki gina-a barabaki gina-a
Could it be at Kakibaki, Barabaki fields,

Siende asuri gina-a mada asuri gina-a
Could it be at Siende fields, mada fields?

(17) *Susabata gena-a pagarpadi gena-a*
Could it be at Susabata, Pagarpadi,

Salapadi gena-a krichitula gena-a
Could it be at Salapadi, Krichitula

Munda vali seka vali gina-a
Could it be at Munda vali, Seka vali,

Adavali gena knahavali gena-a
Could it be at Adavali, Knahavali

Maavali gena-a partivali gena-a
Could it be at Maavali, Partivali,

Siramar gena-a baimbar gena-a
Could it be at Siramar, Baimbar

Siradandangi gena-a sirawokadi gena-a
Could it be at Siradandangi, Sirawokadi,

Elede sapandi panene elede pdibandi panene
(harassed) Can't take birth any where

Ichek wanga, nella widitede
So much of the world has been already covered,

Wenda gena narabi wenda gena durabi
Not a single place is found suitable

(18) *Bae linganiteye bae jananiteye*
Unnecessarily gave birth,

Sapandi sila dinata pdibandi sila dinata
No place is there to step on after emerging out

Ichek bide mitede ichek preje mitede
This much of the places I have seen,

Embenanga sai embenanga pdie
Where to take birth, where to emerge out

Muchdi kala gena-a muchdikala gena-a
Could (I take birth) at Muchdikala hill,

Laka jada gena braba jada gena
Could it be at Laka jada, Braba jada

Kranja nella gena bari nella gena
Could it be at Kranja nella, Bari nella,

Utisira gena tangisira gena
Could it be at Utisira-Tangisira

Kutududi gena bananjala gena
Could it be at Kutududi, Bananjala

Nuamunda gena purnamunda gena
Could it be at Nuamunda-Purnamunda,

(19) *Pijubangeri gena bidibangeri gena*
Could it be at Pijubangeri, Bidibangeri hills,

Pedem nella, dasri nella gena
Could it be at Pedem nella, Dasri nella

Sikeri kalangi gena atadi kalangi gena
Could it be at Sikeri kalangi-Atadi kalangi hills,

Jendabedi gena sababedi gena
Could it be at Jendabedi, Sababedi hills

Bari gati, pati gati gena
Could it be at Bari gati or Pati gati,

Jatrikupda gena banakupda gena
Could it be at Jatrikupda, Banakupda hills

Sarenvali gena jagervali gena
Could it be at Sarenvali, Jagervali,

Irapukri, balipukri gena
Could it be at Irapukur, Balipukur

Pringeli nella, gapas nella gena-a
Could it be at Pringeli nella, Gapas nella,

Embe sachanjie embe pdianjie
Where to take birth, where to come out

Elede sapandi panene elede pdibandi panene
(It seems) No place is available where we can take birth,

Wanga sila dinata nella sila dinata
In this world there is no plains to take birth , to come out

Bae linganiteye bae janani teye
Unnecessarily gave birth,

Solubiri gena bandi biri gena
Could (they emerge out) at Solubiri, Bandibiri

Gunjinanu gena mahananu gena
Could it be at Gunjinanu, Mahananu

Gunjervali gena pudgavali gena
Could it be at Gunjervali, Pudgavali

Sandi maska gena deda maska gena
Could it be near mango trees,

Kalangura gena endangura gena
Could it be at Kalangura, Endangura

Majimunda moelmunda gena-a
Could it be at Majimunda, Moelmunda,

Kanga soru bereng soru gena-a
Could it be at Kanga Soru, Bereng Soru

(21) *Vira panga, vali panga gena*
Could it be at plain areas,

Indiramundi kadakmundi gina-a
Could it be near a small water pool

Jujabata gena, kelabata gena
Could it be at playgrounds,

Widi-okadi gena, dalang bata gena
Could it be near Widi-Okadi-Dalang bata

Guma gada gena seda gada gena
Could it be at Guma gada, Seda gada,

Jenanguda gena nisanaguda gena
Could it be at Jenanguda, Nisanaguda

Tikipadari gena bandi padari gena
Could it be at Tikipadari, Bandipadari,

Ranipalu gena bendipalu gena
Could it be at Ranipalu, Bendipalu

Sapangada gena sarchangada gena
Could it be at Sapangada, Sarchangada,

Sapangada daeti sarchangada daeti
Under Sapangada, under Sarchangada

(22) *Ranipalu daeti bendipalu daeti*
Under Ranipalu, under Bendipalu,

Tanu Nerandali tanu Kapandali
She is Nerandali, she is Kapandali

Ichek wanga itede ichek nella itede
After covering so much of the earth,

Wanga panate nella panate
No earth, no field is found

Nae linge itali nae jananitali
My birth became meaningless,

Wenda nar wajane wendadur wajane
Unnecessarily gave birth to so much people

Asi akad mangane asi gangad mangane
(She) is thinking deeply,

Kapda udi akadi manju udi akadi
Thinking with her hand on head

Genda udi akadi kani udi akadi
Knee down, elbow on knee (She is thinking),

Kandar meste akadi muchi meste akadi
Tears rolling down, water coming out of the nose

(23) *Asi akad machawa asi gangad machawa*
(She is) thinking like that,

Daen sapangada daeti daen sarchangada daeti
Under Sapangada under Sarchangada

Lembu uler ati tuku uler ati
Living like white ants and ants under the earth

Anajana katkane, ujadjana katkane
Suddenly light came,

Banbijada katkane biadijada katkane
Light fell on earthen pots

Rasijana katkane bakari jana katkane
Light flashed the cattle and calves,

Muluni jana katkane batani jana katkane
It lighted all people living inside

Tanu Nerandali tanu Kapandali
She is Nerandali, she is Kapandali

Iba inati wedanga imba inati lanjuwa
It may be the light of sun or moon

Nai akad manawa nai gangad manawa
She started thinking again deeply,

(24) *Weda sila daeti lanju sila daeti*
There was no sun, no moon inside,

Anajana katkane ujad jana katkane
Again light came and cut the darkness

Wae aji tendali wae aji mranjali
Hey, Tendali-Mranjali grandmother

Kangaria mebamu sinadia mebamu
Come to see, to observe

Tani tendalaji tani mranjalaji
She is Tendali grandmother-Mranjali grandmother,

Tende tende sane mranje mranje sane
Bent she walked with palm on eyebrows

Tanu sacha merane tanu pdia mekane
She came out from others and saw,

Tani kangarinawa tani sinadinawa
She looked around

Kuen weda denjali kuen lanju denjali
Above sun seen, above moon seen,

Tani kangarina tani sina dinawa
She saw, she observed

(25) *Wani recha manjane padani recha manjane*
Heaven (has) came down, sky (has) came down,

Dedhi rechanjane pati rechanjane
Pole came down, beam came down

Aru rechanjane danda rechanjane
Aru came down, Danda came down,

Kanda rechanjane baeni rechanjane
Kanda came down, Baeni came down

Kangarianganga sinadiananga
(After) seeing, observing

Nerandalan weskane kapandalan weskane
Going to report Nerandali-Kapandali

Tanu tendalaji tanu mranjal aji
She is Tendali grandmother, she is Mranjali grandmother,

Eledela nerandi eledela kapandi
Hello Nerandi, Hello Kapandi

Ari kuen weda ari kuen lanju
Above, sun and moon (are present),

Ni sani nechu ni pdeni nechu
At the time when you will come out

(26) *Bakarajanjia pida dajanjia*
(Should) come out remembering everything,

Wani rechanjane padani rechanjane
Heaven has come down, sky has come down

Aru rechanjane danda rechanjane
Aru has come down, Danda has come down,

Tide dedhi aisi sakra dedhi aisi
Tila pole and Sakra pole have come

Punden dedhi aisi punden pati aisi
Pundeni pole, Pundeni beam have come

Wani kiri lesisi padani kiri lesisi
To push the heaven and sky up

Dedhi udi samu pati udi samu
Get Dedhi and pati

Wani lesi samu padani lesi samu
To push the heaven and sky up

Asik wespingane asik grapingane
Ordering this much, instructing this much

Tanu tendalaji tanu mranjalaji
She is Tendali grandmother-Mranjali grandmother

(27) *Nerandalani weskane Kapandalin weskane*
Going to report Nerandali-Kapandali

Tanu Nerandali tanu Kapandali
She is Nerandali, she is Kapandali

Asi besnigai asi grapni gai
To tell like that

Ate akad mangane ate gangad mangane
Thinking again deeply

Ina itenjei ina dungenjai
What shall I carry

Asi edu mangane asi budhi mangane
Thinking for knowledge, for wisdom

Ete sapa gaisi dunge sapa gaisi
To carry children

Bicha dapingane jara dapingane
To carry seeds

Rasivira takane bakarvira takane
To carry soil from cattle sheds

Bara bicha gai bara jara gai
For all types of seeds

(28) *Kadi grihun karu grihun takane*
To take cattle and buffalloes

Paji dudi takane ada dudi takane
To carry soil from pigstys and goatpens

Kali saler takane daru saler takane
Black soil to get, red soil to get,

Kumda vira takane mundra vira takane
Pumpkin soil to get, cucumber soil to get

Jana tad takane minu tad takane
Crab soil to get, fish soil to get,

Taratad takane minu tad takane
Red ant soil to get, black ant soil to get

Garli vira takane sitka vira takane
Fertile soil to get, clay soil to get,

Ari tad takane pake tad takane
Mouse soil to get, small mouse soil to get

Bara bichagai bara jara gaisi
For all types of seeds

Etenje inji dungenja inji
(I shall come out) Carrying (soil and seeds) in a cradle

(29) *Bara bicha takane bara jara takane*
To get all types of seeds

Tani dangani eluta tani dangani kudeta
She swept her house

Runda biengane guta biengane
Getting things gathered

Runda biananga guta biananga
Gathering all things

Bicha pakatane jara pakatena
Finding all seeds

Tani bara bicha tani bara jara
Her seeds of all types

Etenje sapingane dunge sapingane
Carrying them on her waist coming out

Tibe dedhi aisi sakra dedhi aisi
Carrying dry twigs of Tila plant, Sakra plant

Tdasu dedhi aisi katadi dedhi aisi
Carrying poles of Tdasu and Katadi tree

Punden dedhi aisi punden pati aisi
Carrying Pundeni pole and beam

(30) *Kuen wanga kueti kuen nella kueti*
Above the earth above, the fields

Wani kiri lesisi padani kiri lesisi
To push heaven up, to push the sky up

Deye wani nachisi tinitana nachisi
One hand pressing the earth, the other hand pushing heaven,

Dedhi lespingane pati lespingane
Fixing Dedhi and Pati and in between

Wani dalam lesisi padani dalam lesisi
Pushing heaven up, pushing the sky up

Wani pata ijisi padani pata ijisi
Pushed heaven and sky completely

Kuen wanga kueti, kuen nella kueti
Came up to the earth above

Tanu Nerandali tanu Kapandali
She is Nerandali, she is Kapandali

Ate tibamanjane ate dai manjane
Giving oath again

Ala tila dedhi ala sakra dedhi
Hey Tila dedhi, hey Sakra dedhi

(31) *Nai sanijai nai pdinijai*
Till I come out,

Suku Diasa Guni Diasa
Don't allow insects to eat you

Ala punden dedhi ala punden pati
Hey Punden Dedhi, Punden Pati

Nai tiba toduta nai bai toduta
Act according to my oath

Sata dina jai sata bara jai
Till seven days,

Dedhi gdujalaya pati gdujalaya
Never break down, hey dedhi and pati

Ganek saisa ganek pdiesaa
Till we all come out,

Dedhi utinanja pati utinanja
Till the dedhi and pati are (permanently) made

Lingana ajanenje janana ajanenje
There are people to come out

Suku diasa guna diasa
Don't allow insects to eat you

(32) *Asi tibaine asi daine*
Dictating the oath

Iiba iananga dai iananga
(She) made them to take oath

Sachanjie mana pdianjie mana
People coming out,

Nerandalan toduta kapandalan toduta
Following Nerandali-Kapandali

Kuen wanga kueti kuen nella kueti
On the earth above,

Palupuri sakane datapuri sakane
Big tooth women coming out

Kanu teri sakane muku teri sakane
Sqint eyed women coming out

Tala dareng sakane bana dareng sakane
Long haired women coming out

Talakambi sakane banakambi sakane
White long haired woman coming out

Tendal aji sakane mranjalaji sakane
Bent waist hunch-back women coming out

(33) *Kukud aji sakane bumbudaji sakane*
Ash polished women coming out,

Sengelaji sakane brabelaji sakane
Woman carrying walking stick came out

Gachi gana ta bina gana ta
People of all types

Atpa bichalega atpa jara lega
Like a mixture of many seeds

Kuen wanga kueti kuen nella kueti
On the earth above

Wanga retinanga nella retinanga
To fill the earth

Sarad japingana barad japingana
Coming out one after another in a line

Kuen Sapangadata kuen Sarchangadata
Above Sapangada, above Sarchangada

Kuen ranipalu kuen bendipalu
Above Ranipalu, above Bendipalu

Deyeradu sakane tejenadu sakane
Wizard women came out

(34) *Kutakadu sakane lambikadu sakane*
Sorcer women came out

jani adu sakane sisadu sakane
Priest women came out

Guru aba sakane sisa aba sakane
Potter women came out

Kuen Sapangada kuen Sarchangada
On the Sapangada, Sarchangada

Kuen usarena kuen bearena
Came out on a plain area,

Dia chelar sakane dudi treladu sakane
Beautiful girls came out

Sanamudadu sakane bakimudadu sakane
Finger ring wearing girls came out,

Lamuraba sakane binjaraba sakane
Blacksmith women came out

Dedhi mulengi sakane pati mulengi sakane
Dedhi and Pati making people came out,

Kandraba sakane warpu aba sakane
Bamboo slashing women came out

35) *Lenguraba sakane pakaraba sakane*
Bamboo mat weaving women came out

Titi kumbar sakane mati kumbar sakane
Earthen pot making women came out

Gachiganata binaganata
Of many castes, many types

Kukudaji sakane bumbudaji sakane
Ash smeared women, dirty women came out

Enguri aba sakane sekuri aba sakane
Winnow carrying women came out,

Mutindali sakane gralindali sakane
Women with seeds in their fist came out

Ejandali sakane manandali sakane
Counting women, measuring women came out

Ranganaji sakane paweraji sakane
Earth levelling women come out

Muti barad ignali grali barad ignali
Came to sow seeds

Kuda gana ta parjaganata
Of all kinds, all varieties

(36) *Kuen Sapangadata kuen Sarchangadata*
On Sapangada on Sarchangada,

Gachi Ganata Bina Gana Ta
Of many castes many types

Sarenitali sakane banjuri tali sakane
Sieving women came out,

Katimai sakane kabadmai sakane
Measuring women came out

Udandali sakane tadandali sakane
Earth digging women came out,

Nanamai sakane kabamai sakane
Singing women came out

Ekka gandadu sakane ka gandadu sakane
Oriya girls came out,

Damu mila sakane gasi mila sakane
Domo children, Gasi children came out

Hadi mila sakane chandal mila sakane
Hadi children, Chandal children came out,

Gasi mila sakane duba mila sakane
Gasi children, washer children came out

(37) *Iribati adite iribati ranjite*
How would it be alright, fit

Bara sapan bihate bara pdiban bihate
Now coming-out-to earth finished

Nerangsapa bihate kapan sapa bihate
Women coming out finished

Tanu Nerandali tanu Kapandali
She is Nerandali, she is Kapandali

Ejaia mekane ganaia mekane
To count the number of people

Tani kangarina tani sinadinawa
She saw, she observed

Tani ejainawa tani gana inawa
Thinking to start counting

Wari achal denjali wari kuel denjali
Everywhere only women and women were seen

Iriba adate iriba ranjate
How would it be alright, fit?

Wari achal ajate wari kuel ajate
Only women have come out

(38) *Irad dina ade irad kasa ade*
How the world can be made

Wari Nerandi adeye wari kapandi adeye
Only of Nerandali, Kapandali

Lingamana saapa janani mane saapa
Still are to take birth

Na wanga dinawa na nella dinawa
Who will roam about earth and fields?

Na darni dinawa na jakeri dinawa
Who will roam about Darni Jakeri?

Inali dakenjiate inali itkenjiane
Who will organise the worship?

Na wisang dinawa na kaning dinawa
Who will move carrying axe?

Na ana sisnaba na gati sisnaba
Who will roam around Ana and Gati?

Inal ana wangine inal gati wangine
Who will climb hills?

Inal keri dine inal danda dine
Who will roam around Keri and Danda?

(39) *Inal puki anasane inal kriya ana sane*
Who will collect honey?

Inal maju ana dineye, braha ana dineye
Who will kill sambar and wild boar?

Iriba adate iriba ranjate
It's not ok, does not fit

Na paren dinawa na sawden banawa
Who will talk to in-laws?

Inal kadel siane inal tati siane
Who will give cots, beds?

Na raji banawa na penu banawa
Who will be the king, who will be the god?

Inal jariane inal pari ane
Who will salute, who will welcome?

Sapandi nane saapa pdiwandi nane saapa
Are to take birth

Betamanger sanenje prambumanger sanenje
Betamanger came out Prambumanger came out

Anamanger sanenje, gatimanger sanenje
Anamanger came out, Gatimanger came out

(40) *Kandangurad sanenje nipingurad sanenje*
Kandangurad came out Nipingurad came out

Nerandalan toduta kapandalan toduta
Following Nerandali, following Kapandali

Pusarani Batarani Toduta
Following Pusarani - Batarani

Jendeng sapinere kadeng sapinere
Elders and youngsters coming out

Palupuri sanenje datapuri sanenje
Big tooth men came out

Taladare sanenje banadare sanenje
Long haired men came out

Kanuteri mukuteri sanenje
Small eyed, squint eyed men came out

Sapimanere pdiemanere
Taking birth, coming out

Nerandali kapandali toduti
Following Nerandali - Kapandali

Basing pirada paing pirada sanenje
Flute playing men came out

(41) *Kutanaik lambinaik sanenje*
Sorcerers came out

Pejer naik deyer naik sanenje
Wizard men came out

Dia trelu dudi trelu sanenje
Male folk came out

Ispa jagei ka ajagel sanenje
Workers came out

Sara sambu sanenje sara basa sanenje
Sara sambu, sara basa came out

Itir kango sanenje itir dana sanenje
Came out from here, from this place

Mnia meru sanenje mnia gati sanenje
Mnia meru, Mnia gati came out

Todu paera sanenje todu kaera sanenje
Todu paera, Tadu kaera came out

Todu pungera todu satara sanenje
Todu pungera, Todu satara came out

Taka puju sanenje atar naka sanenje
Taka puju and Atar Naka came out

Paji bandi sanenje argad majhi sanenje
Paji bandi and Argad majhi came out

(42) *Suidedhi sanenje dapadedhi sanenje*
Suidedhi and Dapadedhi came out

Eran pinate eran dasate sanenje
One after another

Kuen wanga kueti kuen nella kueti
Came out on the earth

Wangarete sanenje nellarete sanenje
Filled in the earth, the fields

Wisangurada sanenje, sungibutni sanenje
Long shaft axe carrying men, short shaft axe carrying men came out

Mara gunda sanenje badal majhi sanenje
Mara gunda came out, Badal majhi came out

Wikapendi sanenje banjan majhi sanenje
Straw-carrying men came out

Weda dara sanenje lanju dara sanenje
Sun door came out, moon door came out

Gachigana tara binagana tara
Of many lineages, many clans

Atpa bichalega atpajara lega
Like mixture of many seeds

(43) *Lemburasi lega tukurasi lega*
Like ants and white ants

Kulunjapinere busunjapi nere
Clinging to each other, bundled together

Sanamuden sanenje bakimuden sanenje
Finger-ring-wearing-men came out

Pangalian sanenje rodalian sanenje
Tattooed men came out

Nandarulienja sanenje timalienja sanenje
Nandruka and timaka lineage people came out

Sanderi lienja sanenje baseri lienja sanenje
People of Sanderi lineage, Baseri lineage came out

Urla lienja sanenje siedi lienja sanenje
Urla lineage, Siedi lineage came out

Laurwadi sanenje binjarwadi sanenje
Blacksmith came out

Dedhimulen patimuleni sanenje
Dedhi - pati making people came out

Kandrawadi warpuwadi sanenje
Bamboo mat makers came out

(44) *Awan sani bekati awan pdini bekati*
After birth of all these

Ate sapinere ate pdienere
Again coming out

Titi kumbar sanenje mati kumbar sanenje
Potter people came out

Kumralaku sanenje kumradudu sanenje
Big-earthen-pot-making-men came out

Ekkagandenja sanenje kaa gandeja sanenje
Oriya speaking people came out

Kira gandenja sanenje kira pakinja sanenje
Oriya people came out

Hadimila sanenje chandal mila sanenje
Hadi children-chandal children came out

Sethimila sanenje sanimila sanenje
Sethi children - Pano children came out

Sala sethi sanenje gopla sethi sanenje
Sala sethi and Gopla sethi came out

Awani sani deasi awani pdini deasi
One after another coming out

(45) *Sabimala sanenje butudku mila sanenje*
Sahib children coming out

Gurasaibi sanenje batlisaibi sanenje
Gora sahib came out, collector sahib came out

Bara sapa bihate bara pdiba bihate
The emerging out finished

Iribati adite iribati ranjite
How would it be ok, how'd it fit?

Sapanbati bihate pdio bati bihate
Taking birth, coming out finished

Tanu Nerandali tanu Kapandali
She is Nerandali, she is Kapandali

Sapangada wanga sarchangada wangadta
At Sapangada earth Sarchangada earth

Kangaria mekane sinadia mekane
To see, to observe

Tani kangarina tani sinadinawa
She is seeing, she is observing

Sapangada wanga sarchangada wangadta
Sapangada earth, Sarchangada earth

(46) *Mulu sachanjane data sachanjane*
People have come out

Tanu Nerandali tanu Kapandali
She is Nerandali, she is Kapandali

Ade ade betaka ade ade prambuka
Hey haunter-men (Betaka-Prambuka)

Isi akad manjina isi gangad manjina
Why are you sitting thoughtful

Isi guma manjina isi seda manjina
Why your face pale, unhappy

Memu piju tektane memu bidi tektane
Rain coming, storm coming

Dendru repinjanede kudu repinjanede
Rain is approaching

Ja anasa gasmu ja atunga gasmu
(Go and) make houses for people

Ja elu kepamu ja kanda kepamu
Go, make houses

Kadigasanjimu guad gasanjimu
Make houses for cattles, goats

(47) *Asi bespinjane asi grapinjane*
Said like that, instructed

Asi wesnigai asi grapni gai
Telling like that

Tanu Betamangera tanu prambumangera
He is Betamangera, he is Prambumangera

Sapangada wanga sarchangada wangaoja
At Sapangada earth, Sarchangada earth

Ranipalu wangaota bendipalu wangaota
At Ranipalu earth, Bendipalu earth

Kadigaspinenje gahadi gaspinenje
Constructing cattle sheds

Elu kepinenge kanda kepinenge
Constructing house for his own

Elu kepenenja kanda kepenenja
To stay in house

Elu bati adate kandabati adate
House making is good

Iribati adite iribati ranjite
How'd it be ok, fit?

(48) *Tanu Nerandali tanu kapandali*
She is Nerandali, she is Kapandali

Sapangada wanga sarchangada wangaota
At Sapangada earth, Sarchangada earth

Eju mikainji kudu makainji
To take water bath

Tedi gura aisi renigura aisi
Took earthen pot (pitcher) on her waist

Tanu Sajinenje Tanu Repinenje
She is going

Eju mikagai kudu mikagai
To take water bath

Mera panda achisi sringapanda achisi
Taking turmeric paste

Ine vira achisi gadi vira achisi
Taking hair cleaning soil

Tanu sajine tanu repine
She went

Tani eju mundita tani kudumundita
To her small water pool

(49) *Eju miengane kudu miengane*
Taking water bath

Eju miananga kudu miananga
Continuing water bathing

Kine muchine gadi muchine
Applying hair cleaning soil on head

Kine muchenanga gadi muchenanga
After applying soil on hair

Mera miene, sringa miene
Smearing turmeric paste on body

Mera miananga sringa miananga
After smearing turmeric paste

Eju miananga kudu miananga
Bathing in water

Eju tapimane kudu tapimane
Filling water (in pitcher)

Eju tachananga kudu tachananga
Came carrying water

Tanu bidiwajimane paga wajimane
She is cooking rice

(50) *Bidi bajenanga paga bajenanga*
Cooking rice

Bidi bihangai paga bihangai
Rice preparation finished

Jau wajimangana jakan waji mangan
Started cooking curry/dal

Jau benigai jakan benigai
For cooking curry

Tanu barandali tanu pagandali
She is the distributing woman

Bari imangane paga imangane
Going to distribute

Bari iananga paga iananga
Finished distributing

Alin arpine najani arpine
Called (her) brothers-in-law

Tinja wihainji goanjinainji
To have food and drink

Serunai arne patlenai arne
Called brother-in-law and father-in-law

(51) *Tau tinjina tau gapina*
They are eating, drinking

Tinja muchananga gapa muchananga
(they) finished eating

Milenai aniga laanga anigai
By the approach of evening, darkness

Tanu kadel gaspine tanu tati gaspine
She is making the bed

Dachanjio gai kurenjio gai
To sleep on, to relax on

Idangio gai susungiba gai
For sound sleep

Tau idamangana tau susumangana
They all have gone asleep

Tami idanga manawa tami susung manawa
When all were deep asleep

Ra kaju gnepata ra melu gnapata
Till the time the cock called

Ra mila idata ra dali idata
Kids were fast asleep

(52) *Ra tude kena ra neke rena*
In the midnight

Linganainjane jananainjane
Taking birth, getting covered

Tane ejumundi tani kudu mundita
At her small water pool

Sikdibandha ajane kada bandha ajane
Chained bundles coming up

Mani linga manjana dambilinga manjan
Bamboo taking birth

Mera pala ditali sringa pala ditali
Coarse turmeric pieces had fallen there

Tala puju ditali bana puju ditali
Long hair had fallen there

Ra tudekena ra nekerena
In the midnight

Kama lega ajane tutu lega ajane
Like sounds of horn pipes, trumpets

Sawandi lega, nawandi lega ajane
Like a mourning

(53) *Reda lega ajane jugalega ajane*
Like tiger's roar, like beast's howl

Tani idanga manawa tani susunga manawa
When she was deep asleep

Dre dre injane gedre gedre injane
Dre, Gedre sound heard

Hati lega ajane gada lega ajane
Like elephant's voice, horse's voice

Tanu idangnali manjana susungnali manjan
Her sleep was broken

Idang nandinawa susung nandinawa
By the time she woke up

Sawandi lega ajane, nawandi lega ajane
Heard noise like mass mourning

Wanga gena doali nella gena doali
Thought something inausipicious on earth happening

Darni gena doali jakergena doali
Whether the earth is good or bad

Sapan gena adate pdibang gena adate
(Perhaps) Taking birth here was not good

(54) *Erek sawand ajate erek nawand ajate*
Why such sounds came

Tanu Nerandali tanu Kapandali
She is Nerandali, she is Kapandali

Wae aji tendali wae aji mranjali
Calling for Tendali and Mranjali grandmothers

Bamu kangari bamu bamu sinadibamu
Come to see, come to observe

Sani lega ajane nani lega ajane
From where noise like mass mourning coming

Reda lega ajane juga lega ajane
Like tiger's roar, beast's cry

Asi arpi mangane asi kelpi mangane
Telling like that

Asi argangai asi kergan gai
To come (and) see, observe

Tanu Tendel aji tanu Mranjel aji
She is Tendel aji, Mranjel aji

Tende tende mekane mranje mranje mekane
Walking with bent body and watching

(55) *Tani kangarinawa tani sinadinawa*
She saw, she observed

Tani eju mundita tani kudu mundita
At her small water pool

Dre nijanjane gedre nijanjane
Upright bamboos sound like dre-gedre

Sikdi Bandha Ajane Kadabandha Ajane
Chained bundles coming up

Manibandha ajane drambibandha ajane
Small and big bamboos coming up

Tani Tendelaji tani Mranjelaji
She is Tendel aji, Mranjel aji

Ate nerandalani weskane kapandalin weskane
Going again to report Nerandali

Eledela Nerandi eledela Kapandi
Hey, Nerandali listen

Ni eju mundita ni kudu mundita
At your small water pool

Linganainjane jananainjane
Taking birth, getting covered

(56) *Wangamete dasa nella mete dasa*
Don't hate the earth, the fields

Wanga doalinawa nella doalinawa
Not the earth is bad, not the fields are bad

Ni eju mitali ni kudu mitali
At your water bathing place

Mera panda ditali singapanda ditali
Turmeric had fallen

Tala puju ditali banapuju ditali
Hair had fallen

Sikdibandha ajate kada bandha ajate
Chained bundles came up (from those)

Ara achakinjina ara durinjina
Are you afraid, are you scared

Eledela tendali eledela mranjali
Hey Tendali Mranjali listen

Bae linganite bae jananite
Unnecessarily it has taken birth

Wanga nade siasa nella nade siasa
Don't give it earth or field

(57) Sapangada Penu *sarchangada penu*
Sapangada deity, Sarchangada deity

Ganda saelaege baeni saelaege
Can't tolerate its bad smell

Bae linganite bae jananite
Unnecessarily has taken birth

Wanga prejasa nella prejasaa
No earth will be available (for it)

Ala sikdibandha ala kadabandha
Hey, chained bundles, coiled bundles

Imba ada mua imba ranjamua
(you) can't stay here

Na parenbani nechu samandbani nechu
When relatives will come, in-laws will come

Pareni kata benene samdani kata benene
Relatives', in-laws' words can't be heard

Dre dre injandi gedre injandi
With dre dre-gedre-gedre sound

Na tiki dinawa na bandi dinawa
Meriah festival can't be organised

(58) *Tikikata benene bandikata benene*
Nobody can hear about Meriah

Babi bani nechu turkubani nechu
When Sahib people will come

Sabikata benene tudkukata benene
Sahib's words can't be heard

Sawandani nechu nawandani nechu
When guests would come

Sawandi kata benene, nawandi kata benene
Talks about deads can't be heard

Imba adamua imba ranjamua
Where would you stay

Sapangada Penu sarchangada penu
Sapangada deity, Sarchangada deity

Ganda sae laeke baeni sae laeke
Can't tolerate bad smell, harsh sound

Imba ada muade imba ranja muade
Here you can't stay

Pinga pinga sarandi murka murka sarandi
Smelling like stool and urine

(59) *Kesa kesad sarandi mara marad sarandi*
Smelling like rotten mouse

Nanek adamua nanek ranjamua
You can't stay with me

Bae linganati bae jananati
Unnecessarily (you've) taken birth

Nanek linganati nanek jananati
Took birth with me

Soru prejasa gada prejasa
No hill, hole will be given to you

Dina preja sa kasa preja sa
There is no world (place) for you

Sapangada Penu sarchangada penu
Sapangada deity, Sarchangada deity

Ranipalu penu bendipalu penu
Ranipalu deity, Bendipalu deity

Siru depkingane dalu depkingane
Would uproot you and throw away

Imba adamua imba ranjamua
Here you can't stay

(60) *Nanek adaa nanek ranjaa*
No place for you to fit in

Ela manibunja ela dambi bunja
Hey, Bamboo bush

Saendi dina guamu saendi kasa guamu
Go away to low lands, low countries

Guamu mani guamu dambi
Go away Bamboo

Kanagana guamu mujugana guamu
Go here and there

Sae pujumara mesa erpimara mesa
Stay with Mahula trees

Aligasi mangamu tanegasi mangamu
Stay together, as friends

Bandagasi mangamu drahagasi mangamu
Stay as bushes, stay in bundles

Wari kenangakamu wari atangakamu
Stay there with your branches

Saer punel danari nella guamu
Go out to Punel Nella

(61) *Sreka rapeli guamu ganju rapeli guamu*
To guard Chara and Bhalia trees

Bitirieni guamu banarieni guamu
Go away to Bitirieni, Banarieni fields

Naringnella guamu deringnella guamu
Go away to Naringnella - Deringnella

Guamu mani guamu dambi
Go bamboo, go

Sikdi bandha akamu kadabandha akamu
Stay together with your bushes

Paji bdesu akamu pada bdesu akamu
Stay with small bamboos and large bamboos

Pidelibandha akamu jadelibandha akamu
Stay with bow making bamboos

Pujuguda guamu erpigada guamu
Go away to Pujugada-Erpigada

Srekamara mesa ganjumara mesa
To stay with Chara tree, Bhalia tree

Aligasi mangamu tanegasi mangamu
Stay together

(62) *Nanek adamua nanek ranjamua*
you can't stay with me anymore

Atugada guamu bdinjagada guamu
Go away to Aluguda, Bdinjagada

Kejelgada guamu rachelgada guamu
Go away to Kejelgada - Rachelgada

Nejurgada guamu palurgada guamu
Go away to Nejurgada, Palurgada

Atubata guamu bdinjabata guamu
Go away to Atubata, Bdinjabata

Saendi dina guamu saendi kasa guamu
Go away to low lands

Wanga rete guamu nellarete guamu
Get scattered all over the earth and fields

Sae kirakeli guamu sae balekelu guamu
Go there to Kirakeli and Balekalu

Asnagada guamu parangada guamu
Go away to Asangada, Parangada

Kasigada guamu karanigada guamu
Go away to Kasigada, Karanigada

(63) *Wanga risida guamu nella risida guamu*
Go away to Wanga risida, Nella risida

Valigada guamu tulagada guamu
Go away to Valigada - Tulagada

Kanagena salmu mujugena salmu
Go away elsewhere

Ate bendek salmu ate junek salmu
Go back again where you came from

Vanipatna guamu senapatna guamu
Go away to Vanipatna (Bhavanipatna), Senapatna

Asangsoru guamu parangsoru guamu
Go away to Asangsoru, Parangsoru

Rengani soru guamu rengani gati guamu
Go away to Rengani hill, Rengani ghats

Nangel wadi guamu juadiwadi guamu
Go away to Nangee wadi, Juadi wadi

Nanek adamua nanek ranjamua
(You) Can't stay here, don't fit here

Kanagana guamu mujugana guamu
Go away to four corners

(64) *Daikal guamu mungada guamu*
Go away to Daikal - Muniguda

Wanga sirchudi guamu nella sirchudi guamu
Go away to Wango Sirchudi - Nella sirchudi

Tatikana guamu kasaladi guamu
Go away to Tatikana - Kasaladi

Ramaniguda guamu bamaniguda guamu
Go away to Ramaniguda - Bamaniguda

Ate bendek guamu ate junek guamu
Go back again where you came from

Weda dueri guamu lanjudueri guamu
Go away to sun door - moon door

Sarukuda guamu nunukada guamu
Go away to Sarukuda - Nunukuda

Ejukumbeli guamu kudukumbeli guamu
Go away to Ejukumbeli-Kudakumbeli

Minumrengi guamu janamrengi guamu
Go away to fish house, crab house

Wariserangakam wari atangakam
Get spread elsewhere

(65) *Ate bendek salmu ate junek salmu*
Go back again

Karenagada salmu bakerigada salmu
Go away to Karenagada-Bakerigada

Kejarapeli salmu jenarapeli salmu
Go away to Kejarapeli - Senarapeli

Asa brumbur salmu para brumbur salmu
Go away to Asa brumbur - Parabrumbur

Kasi kdanda salmu karen kdanda salmu
Go away to Kasi Kdanda, Karen Kdanda

Iribati adite iribati ranjite
How would it fit?

Sirubati bdakteye dalubati bdakteye
Rooted it out completely

Tanu Nerandali tanu Kapandali
She is Nerandali, she is Kapandali

Ate uhingane ate machingane
Again transplanting

Nehi gaba mehisi nehi dani mehisi
Looking for fertile lands

(66) *Basa kada mehisi kunakada mehisi*
Looking in tuber holes (for planting)

Usejiengane matejiengane
Planting transplanting

Sae kandabada sae bakabada
There in Kandabada - Bakabada

Kandabada gabata bakabada gabata
In moist plains at Kandabada, Bakabada

Use jiengane mate jiengane
Planting and transplanting

Tanu Nerandali tanu Kapandali
She is Nerandali, she is Kapandali

Tute li ene bange li ene
Warning, cautioning

Ala kandabada ala bakabada
Hey Kandabada, hey Bakabada

Pdiudupasia paradupasia
Don't allow insects to eat it

Kira kadisia bale kadisia
Don't allow birds to eat it

(67) *Kanja depkisia musu depkisia*
Don't allow monkeys to touch it

Darupanginbali pada panginbali
Keep the name of Bamboo

Jenda lajanbali kada lajanbali
Keep it thick and bushy

Liwi nijanbali baka nijanbali
Keep it tall

Etede manmu dungede manmu
Keep it in your cradles

Na sananja wanenje na pdinanja wanenje
More people are to come out, they will come

Bae manisia bae dambisia
Unnecessarily these bamboos

Para kandinmu gunda kandinmu
Demand rice flour from them

Sanda kandinmu dana kandinmu
Demand offerings from

Palu taspinu data taspinu
Rubbing teeth with anger

(68) *Nache peinmu toe peinmu*
Drive them out, push them out

Ni eta baka dunga baka
Your share

Ninge parabane ninge gundabane
You'll get rice flour

Ni eta baka dunge baka
For your share

Ninge sandabane ninge danabane
You will be paid with rice

Asi tutelina asi bangelina
She (Made kandabada) to promise

Tute liananga bange liananga
Promising again

Tanu Nerandali tanu kapandali
She is Nerandali, she is Kapandali

Ate edu mangane ate budhi mangane
Thinking again deeply

Ate uhingane ate machingane
Again planting and transplanting

(69) *Mio udurgai mio penargai*
In the name of Udurengad - Penarengad

Mio rakegai mio gurpagai
For her Rake - Gurpa

Mio diagai mio purbugai
For her Dia - Purbu

Na sanangai na pdinan gai
For other people (who are) to take birth

Kena sirigai maka sirigai
For stitching leaves

Kali sirigai dana sirigai
For stitching leaf plates, leaf cups

Ate use jiengane mache jiengane
Again planting, transplanting

Mio jendawedi mio sababedi
Near Jendawedi - Sabawedi

Use jiananga mate jiananga
After transplanting

Tanu raniadu tanu bendiadu
She is Raniadu, she is Bendiadu

(70) *Tani sapangada tani sarchangadata*
She is Sapangada, she is Sarchangada

Tanu wanga bidingane nella bidingane
She is roaming around earth

Wanga bidineba nella bidineba
Roamed around earth and fields

Dene dene ajane denge denge ajane
Saw mud everywhere

Jaba meralega jaba keta lega
Like muddy lands, swampy lands

Tanu bidimekane tanu prejemekane
She is inspecting

Tanu Nerandali tanu Kapandali
She is Nerandali, she is Kapandali

Sareni sajanjilepa banjuri sajanjilepa
The earth is not levelled

Dina prejenjilepa kasa prejenjilepa
The world is not levelled

Anang wanga silepa gating wanga silepa
Ana and Gati are not levelled

(71) *Inisatisi adine inisatisi ranjine*
How to do, how it will fit?

Manisila Dinata Dambisila Dinata
In the country there was no bamboo

Inis sareni ee inis banjuri ee
How can seive be made?

Tanu Nerandali tanu Kapandali
She is Nerandali, she is Kapandali

Eledede betaka eledede prambuka
Why do you think Beta Prambu?

Sareni saja sile banjuri saja sile
Sieve is not there

Inisatisi axdine inisatisi ranjine
How to do, how it will fit?

Tanu Betamanger tanu prambumanger
He is Betamanger, he is Prambumanger

Ali ali Nerandi ali ali kapandi
Hey Nerandi, hey Kapandi

Ni kucha karata ni dadi karata
Had you been to get spinach?

(72) *Nı kundu karata ni teru karata*
Had you been for mushroom?

Mani Muni Meanjina Dambi Meanjina
Did you come across bamboos?

Eledede betaka eledede prambuka
Where is Beta - Prambu?

Kucha karatba dadikaratba
At time of plucking spinach

Teru karatba kundu karatba
At time of picking mushrooms

Mani mea silene dambi mea silene
No where (we saw) bamboos

Sinjel silene barel silene
No where in the plains

Asanatisi nerandi asanatisi kapandi
You might not have seen Nerandi

Sinjel sia silena barel sia silena
Have not seen bamboo

Eledela nerandi eledela kapandali
Why do you think Nerandi - Kapandi?

(73) *Nai rapamandata nai kapamandata*
Where I was keeping guard during haunting?

Ana ditabena gati ditabena
I'd been to guard Ana and Gati

Mani mea mache dambi mea mache
Had seen bamboo there

Mio jendawedi mio sabawedi
At Jendawedi, Sabawedi

Era mea mekana era parja meka
I shall go there where I saw it

Like dipanjina like seka injina
That place is not closer by

Tanu betamanger tanu prambumanger
He is Betamanger, he is Prambumanger

Kajasajinenje mada sajinenje
Going to locate bamboos

Sinjel mekainji barel mekainji
To find bamboo

Mio Jendawedi Mio Sabawedi
At Jendawedi-Sabawedi

(74) *Tanu sajinenje tanu repinenje*
He is going

Jendawedi nenenje sabawedi nenenje
Reached at Jendawedi, Sabawedi

Jendawedi mecha sabawedi mecha
On reaching Jendawedi, Sabawedi

Jendawedi penu sabawedi penu
Jendawedi deity, Sabawedi deity

Ini nati tati ini puti tati
(Asked) Whose grandson are you?

Imba kaja dianbandi mada dianbandi
Why are you here?

Dua mestanbandi mada mestanbandi
Why you shaded over me?

Nachè peinjane toe peinjane
Driving him out

Jendawedi penu sabawedi penu
Jendawedi deity, Sabawedi deity

Abare jendawedi abare sabawedi
Dear Jendawedi, dear Sabawedi

(75) *Inak siru datandi inak dalu datandi*
why do you ask about Vansa?

Ala jendawedi ala sabawedi
Hey, Jendawedi - hey, Sabawedi

Bae bajangjilepi bae rechanjilene
I am not here unnecessarily

Dina adatgai kasa adatgai
To make the earth look good

Neran pandenjane kapan pandanjane
Nerandali has sent (me)

Satali Pandanjane Pditali Pandenjane
The person who gave birth has sent (me)

Sareni sajanjileye banjuri sajanjileye
Sareni has not gone there

Erek bajamai erek rechamai
Therefore I have come

Asi besnigai asi grapnigai
Telling like that

Jendawedi penu sabawedi penu
Jendawedi deity, Sabawedi deity

(76) *Eledede betaka eledede prambuka*
Hey Beta - Prambu?

Iri sareni adeye iri banjuri adeye
This will not be useful for Sareni

Puinjigutkunatali bai gutkunatali
Tip of bamboo is broken, that can't be good

Gachi duanjane sani duanjane
Orchids have grown on it

Rata mrugenjane kana mrugenjane
It has become tipless

Iri lengu ligeye iri paka ugeye
It can't be sliced

Irad dina adeye irad kasa adeye
This can't be useful (to level the earth)

Asi nache peinjane asi toe peinjane
Saying like that driving away

Eledede betaka eledede prambuka
Hey Beta - Prambu?

Bahi itelnjilen bahi rasanjilen
It was not necessary to keep it

(77) *Mio udurgai mio penargai*
With udurengad, Penarengad

Itenjiamai rasanjiamai
I have kept secured

Mio rakegai mio gurpagai
With Rake and Gurpa

Mio diagai mio urbugai
With your Vansa

Kali sirigai dana sirigai
To stich leaf plates, leaf cups

Anu itenjiamai anu rasenjiama
I have kept secured

Iramani siene ira dambi siene
I will not give this Bamboo

Asi nache peinjane asi toe peinjane
Driving him out

Tanu betamangera tanu prambu mangera
He is Betamangera, he is Prambumangera

Jendawedi kata sabawedi kata
From Jendawedi - Sabawedi

(78) *Guchel wainenje sangel wainenje*
Returning, fast leaving the place

Wenda sapangada wenda sarchangada
Returning back to Sapangada - Sarchangada

Sapangada baja sarchangada baja
On reaching Sapangada

Eledela nerandi eledela kapandi
Hey Nerandali, Kapandali

Manibati manema dambibati manema
Bamboo is there

Sareni ade injate banjuri ade injate
That can't be useful for Sareni

Lengu uge injate paka uge injate
It can't be made to blades

Kena serigaisi maka siri gaisi
For stiching leaves

Itenjia nege rasenjia nege
Have kept it

Inisina nerandi inisina kapandi
How to do Nerandi?

(79) *Inis sarenina inis banjurina*
How can Sareni be made?

Eledela nerandi eledela kapandi
Hey Nerandi-Kapandi

Nanek linganatali nanek jananatali
(The bamboo) that took birth with me

Embe dina sache embe kasa sache
To which country it went?

Kaja sajamai mada sajamai
I will follow it

Tamu kandangurad tamu nipingurad
Give me my axe

Tamu utukbilu tamu petekbilu
Give me my bow, arrow

Tamu gasangbilu tamu sembingbilu
Give me my catapult

Tamu kichangani tanu rabangani
Give me my arrows

Tamu donikeri tamu panakeri
Give me my arrow (without iron part)

(80) *Iri kandanguradi iri nepinguradi*
This is your axe

Tanu siene tanu gaspine
She gave it to him

Utukbilu siene petekbilu siene
Gave the bow, arrows

Tanu betamanger tanu prambumanger
He is Betamanger, Prambumanger

Utuk bilu aisi petekbilu aisi
Carrying the bow, arrows

Kichangani aisi rabangani aisi
Carrying arrow shafts

Kandangurad aisi nipingurad aisi
Carrying axe on shoulder

Taapuju kaja bana puju kaja
Winding up his hair

Nanek linganatali nanek janaratali
Bamboo that took birth with me

Embe dina sachena embe kasa sachena
Went to which country?

(81) *Kaja sajinenje mada sajinenje*
Going to search

Sapangada kata sarchangada kata
From Sapangada, from Sarchangada

Katamunda giriti beimunda giriti
Crossing Katamunda - Beimunda path

Sager era leika laber era leika
Like going for hunting

Puki era leika kriya era leika
Like going for honey collection

Ana banginenje gati banginenje
Crossing Ana and Gati

Sati kambanati pditi kambanati
Crossing large tree forests

Ragamara giri bichumara giriti
Crossing Ragamara - Bichumara route

Kaja sajinenje mada sajinenje
Going to search

Sitka mati giriti latpa mati giriti
Crossing muddy fields

(82) *Pidel nella giriti jadel nella giriti*
Jumping over a bamboo bush

Tedipanga giriti kudepanga giriti
Crossing Tedipanga - Kudepanga route

Duerwedi giriti angurwedi giriti
Crossing Duerwedi Angurwedi route

Kajang sajinenje madang sajinenje
Following footprints of ancestors

Talapuju kaja banapuju kaja
Following the hair that had fallen

Nanek linganatali nanek jananatali
Bamboo that was born with me

Emben dina sachina emben kasa sachina
Went to which country?

Gambar nella giriti kuja nella giriti
On the Gambar Nella route, Kuja nella route

Gdispavali giriti matpavali giriti
On the Gdispavali route, Matpavali route

Sapar nella giriti pudeni nella giriti
On Saper Nella route, Pudeni nella route

(83) *Kandavali giriti sakusivali giriti*
On Kandavali route, Sakusivali route

Galabada giriti rekibada giriti
On Galabada route, Rekibada route

Suramaru giriti atisana giriti
On Suramaru route, Atisana route

Kadapana giriti ganikuda giriti
On Kadapana route, Ganikuda route

Tanu betamangera tanu prambu mangera
He is Betamangera, he is Parambumangera

Ana banginenje gati banginenje
Crossing Ana, Gati

Sager era lega lawer era lega
Like going for bird trapping

Sinjel kaja sanenje barel kaja sanenje
Going for bamboo

Tanu jenda atanja tanu kada atanja
He the young man

Prenja nella giriti ladki nella giriti
On Prenja nella route, Ladki nella route

(84) *Kiud Bandha Giriti Kadad Bandha Giriti*
On Kiud bandha route, Kadad bandha route

Sajel kuti giriti mekad kuti giriti
On Sajel kuti route, Mekad kuti route

Wisa saburgiriti kasi sabur giriti
On Wisa sabur route, Kasi Sabur route

Pusu badi giriti sendur badi giriti
On Pusubadi route, Sendur badi route

Utumunda giriti padimunda giriti
On Utumunda route, Padimunda route

Kidepanga giriti ekapada giriti
On Kidepanga route, Ekapada route

Manavali giriti burkivali giriti
On Manavali route, Burkivali route

Bindebanda giriti sadebanda giriti
On Bindebanda route, Sadebanda route

Tera jindang ati tera gadang ati
Through Terajindong, Tera Gadang

Laka dara giriti semel dara giriti
On Laka dara route, Semul dara route

(85) *Kupa nella giriti baki nella giriti*
On Kupa nella route, Baki nella route

Nigad nella giriti taladi nella giriti
On Nigad nella route, Taladi nella route

Andarvali giriti kadakvali giriti
On Andarvali route, Kadakvali route

Gadavali giriti nagaravali giriti
On Gadavali route, Nagaravali route

Biriguda giriti masaguda giriti
On Biriguda route, Masaguda route

Penu eju giriti maju eju giriti
On Penu eju route, Maju eju route

Kangajandi giriti berengjandi giriti
On Kangajandi route, Berengjandi route

Dimbul bandha giriti rani bandha giriti
On Dimbul bandha route, Rani bandha route

Tera dibul nenenja tera atad nenenje
Reached at Dimbuli hill

Leke rindinenje luku rindimanenje
Climbed up Dimbuli hill

(86) *Mai betamangera mai prambumengera*
Our Betamangera, our Prambumangera

Erki taka tukita rapkitaka tukita
Standing in the middle of hill

Lekeri indenanga lukuri indenanga
Climbing up the hill

Tanu betamangera tanu prambumangera
He is Betamangera, he is Prambumangera

Kaja anginenje mala anginenje
Seeing with his hand on eyebrows

Nanek linga atali nanek jananatali
Bamboo that was born with me

Emben dina sachena emben kasa sachena
Went to which country?

Embe dunga sajate embe mranga sajate
Where did it hide?

Kaja anga kangari mala anga kangari
Seeing with hand on eyebrows

Saibeda repeli kangari lanju repeli kangari
Looking towards the sun setting end

(87) *Eju repeli kangari kudurepeli kangari*
Looking towards water streams

Saen dina kangari saen kasa kangari
Looking at the low lands

Sae irpu nella kangaki dantar nella kangari
Looking towards Irpu nella Dantar nella

Sreka repeni ganju rupeni kangari
Looking down towards Chara and Bhalia trees

Pujuguda erpuguda kangari
Looking towards Pujuguda, Erpuguda

Embet mani embet dambi sajate
Which way bamboo went?

Ichek kangar ichek sina wnaetedf
After viewing such places

Ate kangari sinadi manenje
Looking again

Minu kadeni jana kadeni kangari
Looking at Fish holes, crab holes

Eju kumbeli kudu kumbeli kangari
Looking at foaming water

(88) *Kanusiri mukusiri manjane*
Beyond the eye sight

Eled mani eled dambi mehene
No, can't see bamboo

Embeti sinjeli embeti bareli sajate
Where did it go?

Kaskigada tarbagada kangari
Looking at Kaskigada - Tarbagada

Kadigata karugata kangari
Looking at cattle sheds, buffalo sheds

Nejugada palugada kangari
Looking at Nejugada, Palugada

Atabata bdinjabata kangari
Looking at Atubata, Bdinjabata

Tatikena, bisaiadi kangari
Looking at Tatikena-Bisaladi

Judangadu, madangadu kangari
Looking at Judangadu - Madangadu

Sisakana, marbakana kangari
Looking at Sisakana, Marbakana

(89) *Ate bendek ate dunek kangari*
Again looking back

Wenda mdiji duna mdiji kangari
Again looking at the places he covered

Kaju mdiji mala mdiji kangari
Keeping his hand on eyebrow

Vanipatna, senapatna kangari
Looking at Vanipatna, Senapatna

Amadula, oilbata kangari
Looking at Amadula, Oilbata

Rachangsoru parangsoru kangari
Looking at Rachangsoru, Parangsoru

Wanga sirchudi, nella sirchudi kangari
Looking at Muniguda - Duikala

Muniguda, daikala kangari
Looking at Muniguda, Daikala

Ate bendeka ate duneka kangari
Looking back again

Weda dueri lanju dueri kangari
Looking towards sun door - moon door

(90) *Sarukuda, nunukuda kangari*
Looking towards Sarukuda - Nunukuda

Minu mrengi jana mrengi kangari
Looking at fish bones, crab shells

Elede mani elede dambi panene
(Perhaps) it is not possible to find bamboo

Bake baja bae recha jiteye
Unncessarily we came

Mani mepi dambi mepi silene
Can't find bamboo

Ate bendeka ate duneka kangari
Looking backwards again

Karengada bakergada kangari
Looking towards Karengada, Bakergada

Kanikanda, karanikanda kangari
Looking at Kanikada, Karnikanda hills

Deupuru, sasapuru kangari
Looking at Deupuru, Sasapuru hills

Asagada paragada kangari
Looking at Asagada, Paragada hills

(91) *Nulugda drasigada kangari*
Looking at Nulugada, Drasigada hills

Asa gurudi para gurudi kangari
Looking at duck shed, pigeon shed

Ichek kangar ichek sinad iametede
Viewing that much

Kanumunu mukumuku sarate
Beyond the eye sight

Sinjel panate barel panate
Big bamboo, small bamboo not found

Tanu kangar tanu sinad manenje
He is looking again

Sae kandawada sae bakawada gabata
Towards the low lands of Kandawada, Bakawada

Libinija bakanija manjane
There it grows, there it is

Kana kana kata kata deali
Bushy bushy looking

Kandawada, bakawada gabata
At low lands of Kandawada-Bakawada

(92) *Deusana, tumasana gabata*
At low lands of Deunsana - Tumasana

Jendalaja, kadalaja manjane
It is growing there

Nejudiyee paludiyee manjane
Massaged with oil on its body

Sikangasa, kadagasa manjane
Being chained, being bundled

Bandagasa, drahangasa manjane
Bound to each other

Arine manipa, arine drambipa
That is bamboo

Neju broi manjane palubroi manjane
Massaged bamboo with oil all over

Wanirachi padani rachi manjane
Touching heaven - the sky

Wanirachi manjane padani rachi manjane
Touching heaven, touching the sky

Tanu beta mangera tanu prambumangera
He is Betamangera, he is Prambumangera

(93) *Manimea nangani dambi mea nangani*
On seeing bamboos

Sinjel mea nangani barel mea nangani
On seeing large bamboos, small bamboos

Tanu sajimanenje tanu repimanenje
He is going, he is leaving

Tanu jenda atanja tanu kada atanja
He is an elderly man

Tera dimbul katani tera atadi katani
From Tera dimbul, Tera Atadi

Mani kaja sanenje dambikaja sanenje
Going near the bamboo

Achabonda giriti mniabonda giriti
Climbing on the hills Achabanda, Mniabonda

Piju sudi giriti bidi sudi giriti
On the Piju sudi route, Bidi sudi route

Piju mundang ati bidimundang ati
Rain and storm approaching

Sikadi nella giriti tobuli nella giriti
On Sikadi nella, Tobuli nella route

(94) *Ladu racha giriti kidadi racha giriti*
On the Ladu racha, Kidadi racha

Kakadaka giriti kidadaka giriti
On the Kakadaka route

Delkiri giriti dandakeri giriti
On the Delkiri, Dandakiri route

Kandun nella giriti palad nella giriti
On the Kandun nell, palad nella route

Kesugati giriti jarugati giriti
On the Kesugati jarugati route

Kichanjaru giriti rabanjaru giriti
On the Kichanjaru-Rabanjaru route

Apka depa giriti kamang depa giriti
On the Apkadapa-Serapati route

Kangan wali giriti serapati giriti
On the Kanganwali-Serapati route

Lidi lada giriti kdani lespa giriti
On the Lidi lada Kdani-lespa route

Akudanja giriti pdipadanja giriti
On the Akudanja-Pdipadanja route

Satradika giriti manik dika giriti
On the Satradika-manidika route

(95) *Tanu sajimanenje tanu repimnenje*
He is going, he is leaving

Mae betamangera mae prambumangera
Our Betamangera, our Prambumangera

Tade kala giriti made kala giriti
On the Tade kala - Made kala route

Isikidi giriti bimbikidi giriti
On the Isikidi - Bimbikidi route

Deusana giriti tumasana giriti
On the Deusana - Tumasana route

Kandawada nenenje bakawada nenenje
Reached at Kadawada - Bakawada

Tanu betamangera tanu prambumangera
He is Betamangera, Prambumangera

Kandawada necha bakawada necha
Reached at Kandawada, Bakawada

Tani mani basata tani dambi basata
Reached at Bamboos

(96) *Gunja gunja sanenje sucha sucha sanenje*
Going in slow steps

Gunja gunja ranawa sucha sucha anawa
Approaching in slow steps

Kandawada penu bakawada penu
Kandawada deity, Bakawada deity

Ininati tati ini puti tati
Whose grandson are you

Kaja mestanwandi mada mestanwandi
Why did you step here?

Inisiru tati inisiru tati
What surname do you have?

Palu snepinjane data snepinjane
Rubbing his teeth

Kandawada penu bakawada penu
Kandawada deity, Bakawada deity

Tinja injine gada injine
Threating to eat up

Tanu betamangera tanu prambumangera
He is Betamangera, he is Prambumangera

(97) *Eled kandadada eled bakawada*
No kandawada, no Bakawada

Inak tinji injandi inak gatainjandi
Why do you want to eat me up?

Dina adatgal kasa adatgal
For the better of the country

Anu bajamai anu rechamai
I have come here

Nai punjaele nai wenjaele
I have come in ignorance

Eren pandewane kapan pandewane
Nerandali - Kapandali has sent me

Satali pandenjane pditali pandenjane
She who took birth first has sent me

Erek bajamai erek rachamai
Therefore I have come

Saren aja sile banjuri aja sile
Sareni is not made

Siru dapi manjandi daludapi manjandi
Looking from toe to tip

(98) *Tinja injijandi gata injijandi*
Threatening to eat up

Nache peinjandi toe peinjandi
Go away from here

Manmu kandawada manmu bakawada
Halt Kandawada, Bakawada

Manmu isikidi manmu bimbikidi
Halt Isikidi, halt Bimbikidi

Guchel salisa sangel salisa
I will be far from here

Bekad salisa dana salisa
I shall go back

Nache peinjandi toe penjandi
Driving (me) out

Manmu kandawada manmu bakawada
Halt Kandawada, halt Bakawada

Parataka sa gundataka sa
I will go for rice

Sanda taka sa dana taka sa
I will go for rice flour

(99) *Tanu betamanger tanu prambumanger*
He is Betamangera, he is Prambumangera

Guchel wainenje sangel wainenje
Returning back

Kandawada kata bakawada kata
From Kandawada, from Bakawada

Deusana giriti tumasana giriti
Through Deusana - Tumasana route

Isikidi giriti bimbikidi giriti
Through Isikidi - Bimbikidi route

Wenda sapangada wenda sarchangada batere
Reached at Sapangada, Sarchangada

Nerandalani weskandi kapandalani weskandi
Reached at Nerandali, Kapandali

Ali ali nerandi ali ali kapandi
Hey hey Nerandi, hey hey Kapandi

Manibati manema dambibati manema
Bamboo is there

Chnjel bati manena barelbati manema
Large bamboo , small bamboo (there) is there

(100) *Brihanaa britate kandanaa kandate*
Demanded a lot of things

Kajumudi injate malamudi injate
Demanded finger ring

Alorbeni injate banabani injate
Demanded headlace

Talabani injate banabani injate
Demanded a lot

Tatangaju injate grumbanju injate
Demanded cock

Kujamila injate kujadali injate
Demanded small child

Aranade siasa are nade basasa
(we) will not give (him) small child

Ninge jella noana ninge baling naona
Your soul will cry

Arasiba suasa aragaspa suasa
That we can't give

Sibabati sinama gaspabati gaspanamu
Should it be given or not?

(101) *Na sananja muenje na pdinanja muenje*
No more people can take birth

Ewansiba muenje ewangaspa muenje
Later people can't offer

Sirudai tinjane darudai tinjane
(he) will hunt for the same Vansa

Arenade siasa arenade gasasa
That we can't give

Mai mani batika mai dambi batika
That is our bamboo

Paraweye siana gundaweye siana
Unnecessarily we'll give

Tamu rachangpara tamu rachangunda
Get me rice flour

Juarinja mekaa paerinja mekaa
Saluted, regarded

Irirachampara iri racha gunda
Giving rice flour

Parabati siati gundabati siati
Gave rice flour

(102) *Engamua nati legamua nati*
Person who can't climb trees

Inis aku pai inis gau pai
How did you get leaves?

Patel panje jiati sipti panje jiati
Wrapped rice with leaves

Embet aku pai embet gau pai
Where did you get leaves?

Jendawedi tai sabawedi tai
Got it (leaves) from Jendawedi Sabawedi

Asanaku adine asangau adine
Those leaves will come in use

Ini mara tai inidadi tai
Of which tree?

Ini tula tai ini mala tai
Of which creeper?

Kena tula tai maka tula tai
Of Siali (*Bauhinia vahlii*) creeper

Tanu Mniamara tai maka mara tai
Of Mniamara - Makamara

(103) *Asan aku adine asan gau adine*
Those leaves will come in use

Juerinja meka paerinja meka
Saluted

Tanu betamangera tanu prambumangera
He is Betamangera, he is Prambumangera

Dina ajayele bara ajayele
Roaming around all the day

Kichda aja ele padi aja ele
Everywhere

Mai beta sanenje mai prambu sanenje
Our Betamangera going

Liket nerand injina liket kapand injina
Nerandali thinking something

Asan sajimai asan repimai
Then I am coming

Tanu betamangera tanu prambumangera
He is Betamangera, Prambumangera

Tani rachapara tani racha gunda
That rice, that rice flour

(104) *Tedikirita Anenje Renikirita Anenje*
Carrying in his waist

Juaringagai paeringagai
For saluting

Tanu betamangera tanu prambumangera
He is Betamangera, he is Prambumangera

Sata juargai sata paergai
For saluting seven times

Kalu dapandgai bada dapandgai
Falling at feet prostrating

Parapi manenje gunda api manenje
Offering rice, rice flour

Sapangada kata sarchangada kata
From Sapangada, from Sarchangada

Ranipalu kata bendipalu kata
From Ranipalu, from Bendipalu

Para achananga gunda achananga
Taking rice flour

Ala kandawada ala bakawada
Hey Kandawada, Hey Bakawada

(105) *Nachembei manjati toembei manjati*
I have brought things for you

Para tachamai gunda tacha mai
Have brought rice, rice flour

Nai sina para nai sian gunda
Accept my offering

Juarinjanawa paerinjanawa
Saluted, took dust from foot

Manisie nichisi dambisie nichisi
(I'll) not give bamboo

Tulamasi drembamu malamasi drembamu
I'll make snakes coil around bamboos

Kambat kaju astamu kambat sipa astamu
If jungle fowl talks

Bada kanja astamu bada musu astamu
If monkey talks

Mani siene ichisi dambi siene ichisi
I'll not give bamboos

Nai sianpara nai sian gunda
I am offering rice, riceflour

(106) *Para endala gunda endala*
I will not give offerings (anymore)

Mani sie ichisi dambi sie ichisi
(if) bamboo is not got

Atede kaju endamu demala endamu
Again I am offering

Kandrasechi endamu warpu sechi endamu
Offerings given on winnow

Sata kandawada athisi sata bakawada athisi
If you are truely Kandawada - Bakawada

Deusana atisi tumasana atisi
(I) Have come through Tumasana -Deusana

Sata sianpara nai siangunda endamu
If I'm really offering

Ayi kandawada penuni bakawada penuni
To the Kandawada - Bakawada deities

Para siemai gunda siemai
Giving rice, rice flour

Ala kandawada ala bakawada
Hey Kandawada, Hey Bakawada

(107) *Sanda sienja dana sienja*
Giving offerings

Ni rapabaka ni kapabaka
Those who guard your forest

Kanjarati baka musurati baka
Monkeys guard it

Kira rati baka bale rati baka
Birds guard it

Ete machibaka dungemachibaka
What I carry with me

Parawaine Gundawaine
Offering rice, rice flour

Para sirpinja gunda sirpinja
I'm offering worship

Jakanati benjamu sipenati benjamu
All the deities above, listen

Wanisira benjamu padanisira benjamu
Listen . . . listen

Dundrukuda benjamu kudukambu benjamu
Listen . . . listen

(108) *Tanabai benjamu patabai benjamu*
Listen

Kandawada penuni bakawada penuni
Kandawada deities, Bakawada deities

Isikidi penuni bimbikidi penuni
Isikidi deities, Bimbikidi deities

Deusana penuni tumasana penuni
Deusana deities, Tumusana deities

Para siemai gunda siemai
I'm giving rice, rice flour

Asi tutelianenje asi bangelianenje
I am not telling a lie

Tibaia manenje daia manenje
I am promising, taking an oath

Mai betamangera mai prambumangera
I'm Betamangera, Prambumangera

Tiba ianangani daianangani
Promised, took oath

Juarinji manenje paerinji manenje
Saluted, fell at the feet

(109) *Para Sirpi Manenje Gundasirpi Manenje*
Offered rice offerings

Para sirjanawa gunda sirjanawa
At time of giving rice

Tulamasi bendane malamasi bendane
Snakes left bamboos

Kambatkaju aseye kambat sipa aseye
Jungle fowl stopped talking

Bada kanja aseye bada masu aseye
Monkeys stopped crying

Tanu betamangera tanu prambumangera
He is Betamangera, he is Prambumangera

Mani sianepa dambi sia nepa
For bamboo to be given

Tulamasi Bendate Malamasi Bendate
Snakes left bamboos

Tanu jende jatanja tanu kade jatanja
He is the supreme man

Mani dakit sanenje dambi dakit sanenje
Going to inspect bamboos

Mera manala atad manala
Returned back thinking inauspicious

Tiariji panganenje satariji panganenje
Came back on seeing bamboo roots

Tani mani dakini tani dambidakini
That bamboo is worshipped

Tani sinjel butani tani barel butani
That thick bamboo, that thorny bamboo

Tani mani dakita tani dambi dakita
At the bamboo root

Tanu betamangera tanu prambumangera
He is Betamangera, he is Prambumangera

Kandangurad aha nipingurad aha
Carried axe on shoulders

Dingigati inji tadangati inji
For cutting

Mani ahi inji dambi ahi inji
To cut bamboo

Dingigati manenje tadangati manenje
To cut it completely and bring

(111) *Dingigati inawa tadangati inawa*
To completely wipe out the root

Mani bdie manjane dambi bdie manjane
Felling bamboos after cutting

Liwibdie manjane bakabdie manjane
Falling down

Embed sinjeli bdiane embed kali bdiane
Which side bamboo will fall

Embeti mani bdiane embeti dambi bdiane
Which side bamboo will fall

Weda adam genawa lanjuadan genawa
Facing towards sun, facing towards moon

Weda duer gena lanju duer gena
Facing to sun door, facing to moon door

Sinje sinjelwati bare barelbati
Those thick bamboo, thorny bamboo

Mani mani bati dambi bati
This is bamboo

Ejurepel bdiane kudu repel bdiane
It will fall to the side of water stream

(112) *Liwibdie bakabdie manjane*
will fall down from base

Wanidunja bdiane padanunja bdiane
Will fall with a sound as sky bursted

Mani mani bati dambi dambi bati
Bamboos and Bamboos

Laingsapa bdiane tukingsapa bdiane
Lightly fall down, heavily fall down

Tana Drunja Lega Pata Drunja Lega
Without blowing dusts

Mani bdiangaisi dambi bdiangaisi
For bamboo to fall

Sinjel bdiangaisi barel bdian gaisi
For thick bamboo to fall for thorny bamboo to fall

Tanu betamangera tanu prambumangera
He is Betamangera, he is Prambumangera

Kata datpi manenje daki datpi manenje
Cutting the apex of bamboo

Chendangi manenje bundangi manenje
Cutting into pieces

(113) *Daki dasta nangani katadasta nangani*
Separating the base and apex

Sera manala atad manala
Cleaning the nodes

Tapenjie manenje tesanjie manenje
Cutting the branches and twigs

Atad kate nangani ganikate nangani
Cutting the nodes

Tanu betamangera tanu prambumangera
He is Betamangera, he is Prambumangera

Imban mani lesnenje imban dambi lesnenje
Who will carry bamboo

Mani mani bati dambi dambi bati
Bamboos and bamboos

Tanu betamangera tanu prambumangera
He is Betamangera, he is Prambumangera

Mani dina ade ichisi kasa ade ichisi
To which country did bamboo go

Manileja la dambi leja la
Don't climb up the bamboo

(114) *Asi tutel manenje asi bangel manenje*
He promised, took an oath

Beta kele ichisi prambukele ichisi
If not Beta Prambu then nobody (can carry)

Kanda serin pandamu nipiserin pandamu
Otherwise shoulder will be injured

Sate beta - katisi sate prambu katisi
If really Beta - Prambu has cut it

Kanda dapa dibamu nipidapa dibamu
Bamboo will be on his shoulders

Jodadapa diamu kapadapa diamu
Easily can be lifted up to shoulder

Beta kele ichisi prambu kele ichisi
If Beta - Prambu do not take

Kanda bdisi dikamu nipibdisi dikamu
May it fall down from shoulder

Asi tutelianenje asi bangelanenje
He is promising, taking an oath

Tuteliananga bangeliananga
Promised, took an oath

(115) *Tanu betamangera tanu prambumangera*
He is Betamangera, he is Prambumangera

Manidapa Lesnenje Dambi Dapa Lesnenje
Carried the bamboos

Mani dapa dibani danbi dapa dibani
Bamboo stayed right on shoulder

Kanda dapa dibani nipidapa dibani
Easily was lifted up to shoulders

Sateine betaka sateine prambuka
If I am Betamangera, Prambumangera

Sateine satana sateine pditana
If I truely have emerged out from earth

Mani dekenenga dambi dekenenga
Carrying the bamboo

Tanu waine tanu repinenje
He is coming

Kandawada kata bakawada kata
From Kandawada, from Bakawada

Isikidi kata bimbikidi kata
From Isikidi, from Bimbikidi

(116) *Deusana kata tumasana kata*
From Deusana, from Tumasana

Tanu betamangera tanu prambu mangera
He is Betamangera, he is Prambumangera

Sinjel nepchananga barel nepchananga
Returned with thick and thorny bamboos

Embe ite jiena embe kasa jiena
Where to keep

Ali ali nerandi ali ali kapandi
Hello Nerandi, Hello Kapandi

Sinjel tachamai barel tachamai
I have bought thick bamboo, thorny bamboo

Mani tachamai dambi tachamai
I have brought bamboo

Embe repchanjie embe itenjie
Where shall I keep?

Like depanjina like seka injina
A little farther?

Kandang noatede niping noatede
(My) shoulder is aching

(117) *Imba kandawadana imba bakawadana*
This is from Khandabada Bakabada

Imbe itenjie imbe rasanjie
Where shall I keep?

Teli rachat gina mali rachat gina
Should I keep it in the middle of village?

Katamundat gina beimundat gina
Should I keep near hedge?

Kumda jagdi gina mundra jagdi gina
Should I keep it near the pumpkin stage?

Bada bekat gina kata bekat gina
Should I keep in front of house?

Amba ada mue amba ranjamue
There it can't be

Mani mani batika dambi dambi batika
To keep bamboo

Nerandalan tukita kapandalan tukita
Behind Nerandali's house

Sata lalani dukita pditalalani tukita
In front yard of Satalalani (Nerandali)

(118) *Mani repi manenje dambi repi manenje*
Unloading bamboos

Kaju sala basa sipa sala basa
Near hens place

Mila sala basa dali sala basa
Where children will not go

Manirepchananga dambi repchananga
Unloading bamboo

Eledela nerandi eledela kapandi
What do you think, hey Nerandali?

Manibati toteye dambibati toteye
I brought bamboo

Sinjelbati toteye barelbati toteye
Brought thick bamboo, thorny bamboo

Nanelinganatanju nanek jananatanja
Bamboo that took birth with me

Imbe dina sachenje imbe kasa sanenje
Went to which country?

Imbe pehe siate lucha siati
Where did you drive him?

(119) *Mai kandra tada embepae, embelucha siati*
Where has gone the bamboo foiling man?

Simba gena siati eju gena siati
Didn't you give him gruel?

Ere gurtenje ere mrangi tenje
Is it that he left for not getting gruel

Nangedibotenje nangekdaba tenje
Came near me, cried

Mai aba gatali mai kaki gatali
She my sister-in-law, my aunt

Simba sia laate eju sia laate
Didn't give gruel

Saelaja laate armelaja laate
Didn't like him

Esi dinja tenje esi kdabatenje
That's why he cried at me

Anubati nerandi anubati kapandi
Because it was I who

Sara madang siteye sarakinga siteye
Gave him mere Salap toddy, Mahuli liquor

(120) *Nehi ana siteye nehi gati siteye*
Showed him the right path

Madi ana siteye madi gati siteye
Showed him the middle road

Nei bilu siteye nei ambu siteye
Gave him good bow, arrow

Deke deke treteye dunge dunge treteye
Carried him on my shoulder

Asanatisi nerandi asanatisi kapandi
Hence Nerandi - Kapandi

Inu pehenjilaya inu luchanjilaya
If it is you who drove him away

Kandrakaja punjina warpu kaja punjina
Can you identify footprint of that bamboo foiling man (kandra)?

Atalate manjina bitalache manjina
Have you measured his steps?

Kajalache manjina mada lache manjina
Have you seen his hands, legs?

Tanu nerandali tanu kapandali
She is Nerandali, she is Kapandali

(121) *Kajang lache mai tadang lache mai*
I know his foot prints, I have measured

Kandra kaja pui warpukaja pui
I know his hands

Asanatisi nerandi asanatisi kapandi
Hence, Nerandi - Kapandi

Tamu Atangila Tamu Bitangila
Bring me the measuring stick

Kajanglachi saja madanglachi sajaa
I will again measure his foot steps

Kandra kaja dakaa warpukaja dakaa
Will search for his foot steps

Tanu betamangera tanu prambumangera
He is Betamangera, he is Prambumangera

Atangila aisi bitangila aisi
Carrying the measurement of his hands and legs

Saeduki kanata mioduki kanata
Looking up, down of it

Kajangdapi manenje madangdapi manenje
Searching for his foot steps

(122) *Virapunja Kueti Balipunja Kueti*
On soil, on sand

Kajanglachi manenje madang lachi manenje
Measured his hands and legs

Embesachin kandra embesachin warpu
Where have the Kandra gone

Kajangsari manjan madang sari manjan
This is his foot step

Atangsari manjan bitang sari manjan
The land measured more

Iri udurkajapa iri penar kajapa
This is print of Udurengad - Penarenged

Iri laur kajapa iri binjar kajapa
Of other bamboo foiling men

Iri rake kajapa iri gurpa kajapa
Footprint of Rake Gurpa

Kilangsari manjan bakangsari manjan
The measure is more than the footprint

Atangsari manjan bitangsari manjan
One hand excess in measure

(123) *Iridi kajapa iri purbu kajapa*
This foot step is of others

Embe sachenje kandra embe sachinji warpu
Where has the Kandra gone?

Ate iachi manenje ate dapi manenje
Measuring again

Kila saman ajan pakang saman ajana
Foot print matched to the measurement

Kaja saman ajane mada saman ajane
Both are found equal

Iri kandra kajapa iri warpu kajapa
This is of that Kandra

Iri lengur kajapa iri pakar kajapa
This is that measuring rod

Atang saman ajate bitang saman ajate
Now it became equal

Irad sachinja kandra irad sachenje warpu
This way Kandra has gone

Tanu betamangera tanu prambumangera
He is Betamangera, he is Prambumangera

(124) *Sapangada kata sarchangada kata*
From Sapangada, from Sarchangada

Ranipalu kata bendipalu kata
From Ranipalu, from Bendipalu

Kandrakaja sanenje warpu kaja sanenje
Kandra footsteps have gone this way

Kajuangi manenje maja angi manenje
On pointing by extending hand

Kaju anginaba mala anginaba
By showing hand

Tanu kandrabadi tanu warpubadi
That Kandra, that Warpu (bamboo foiling man)

Senamuje manenje baramuje manenje
Hiding behind big grasses, bushes

Awanje kandra awanje warpu
That's the same Kandra

Kandra mehananga warpu mehananga
On seeing that Kandra

Tanu betamangera tanu prambumangera
He is Betamangera, he is Prambumangera

(125) *Kajasaji manenje mada saji manenje*
Again following his footprint

Tani sana bena tani rena bena
By the time he was moving

Kandraba wanga atati warpuanga atati
His wife was coming

Tanu achak manjane tanu duri manjane
She was surprised, thought

Kade dinang genawa lache dinang genawa
Stranger from which land

Briha dina gena jacha dina gina
If he was a beggar

Asiaji manjane asiduri manjane
Fearing like that

Tanu kandraba tanu warpu aba
She is Kandra sister-in-law (Kandra's wife)

Tanu dupi mangane tanu magi mangane
She is going to sleep

Beta kaiaje prambu kaiaje
Out of fear to Beta - Prambu

(126) *Tani Dugi Nawa Tani Mraginawa*
By time she went to sleep

Wenga nepi manenje prambu nepi manenje
Beta reached her

Abar kandraba abar warpuaba
My dear sister-in-law

Inagai ajandi inagai durandi
Don't fear me

Abaride betaka abaride prambuka
Why Beta, why Prambu?

Ninge kade dina iche lacheng dina iche
I thought you are a beggar

Eri danga aade eri kapa aade
Don't feel sorry for that

Bahe wajanjilene bahe rechanjilene
I have not come here unnecessarily

Dina adatgai kasa adatgai
The country is not levelled

Sareni saja sile banjuri saja sile
It is not Sareni operated

(127) *Neran pandejane kapan pandejane*
Nerandali has sent

Kandra tadagai warpu tada gai
For Kandra brother

Erek bateye erek reteye
So I have come

Kandra tada embe warpu tada embe
Where is Kandra brother?

Tanu kandraba tanu warpu aba
She is Kandra-sister-in-law

Eledede betaka eledede prambuka
Why Beta, Why Prambu?

Mi kandratada mi warputada
Your Kandra brother

Namber muisilenje dukumui silenje
Fever has attacked

Eled kandraba eled warpuaba
Why sister-in-law?

Tidi mua tisiba renimua tisiba
Even if waist is aching

(128) *Namber mua tisiba dukamua tisiba*
Even if fever is continuing

Tanu kandraba tanu warpuaba
She is Kandra sister-in-law

Eledede betaka eledede prambuka
Why Betaka, why Prambuka?

Mai kandratada mai warpu tada
My Kandra brother

Namber muisilenje dukamuisilenje
Even if fever is contiuning

Tanu Eled kandra aba eled warpu aba
Why Kandra sister-in-law?

Tidimua tisiba renimua tisiba
Even if waist is aching

Namber mua tisiba dukamua tisiba
Even if fever is continuing

Deke paneoi duche paneoi
I'll carry him on

Mai kandratada mai warputada
My Kandra brother

(129) *Abaride betaka abaride prambuka*
Why Betaka, why Prambuka?

Rajimujina ereka penu munu ereka
He is suffering

Erek dekenandi erek duchenandi
So you can not carry

Kandra kandra tada warpu warpu tada
Your Kandra brother

Dire wapanja kalewapanja
Let him walk slowly

Tanu kandratada tanu warputada
He is Kandra brother

Kandrakare aisi warpukare aisi
Carrying his knife

Usalaud aisi burunga laud aisi
Carrying his stick

Dire dire wanenje kale kale wanenje
Walking slowly, slowly

Kandra wainenje warpu wainenje
Kandra is coming

(130) *Wenda sapangada wenda sarchangada*
Again to Sapangada, Sarchangada

Sapangada wanenje sarchangada wanenje
On reaching Sapangada

Dire dire wanenje kale kale wanenje
Walking slowly, slowly

Sapangada waja sarchangada waja
Coming to Sapangada

Kandrawanigai warpu wani gai
For Kandra to come

Tanu betamangera tanu prambumangera
He is Betamangera, he is Prambumangera

Eledela nerandi eledela kapandi
Why Nerandi, why Kapandi?

Inu nepe echi inu lucha echi
Had driven him out?

Kandra watenje warpu watenje
The Kandra man came

Kandrawatikata warpuwatikata
From where Kandra lives

(131) *Tanu kandrawadi tanu warpuwadi*
That Kandra man

Manikape sanenje dambikape sanenje
Went near the bamboos

Manikape saja dambikape saja
On reaching the bamboos

Ekchikangari wapchi kangari
Looking up-down

Inis prikchanjie inis sisanjie
How to cut bamboos

Inis pakdi ajane inis sari ajane
How to make blades

Tani kandaguradi tani nipinguradi
He is searching for his axe

Siri kitinenje pdaka katinenje
Cutting the bamboos

Sari sirinenje sari pakadi inenje
Slicing it into four parts

Pinjatui priknenje pnasatuhi priknenje
Threw away the skin of bamboo

(132) *Pdikchanjiananga gesanjiananga*
On slicing bamboos

Sedangienenje budangainenje
On searching to polish

Ganituhi dapnenje atad tuhi dapnenje
Cleaning the nodes, internodes

Chedangiananga bendangiananga
Finishes the cutting

Tanu kandrawadi tanu warpuwadi
That Kandra man

Pendi gaspinenje garla gaspinenje
Binding them in bundles

Pendigasananga garla gasananga
Finishing the bundling

Embe legu brajane embe paka brajane
Where to put them?

Embe itenjie embe rasanjie
Where to keep them?

Karigamat genaa akari gamat genaa
Should it be kept to dry under sun?

(133) *Papi arut genaa sicheni arut genaa*
Should it be kept inside the house?

Embasa datane emba machi datane
Where it will not be dirty?

Kumda jagdita genamunda jagdita gena
Should it be kept on the pumpkin stage?

Lengu lengu wati paka paka wati
Bamboo blades, bamboo branches

Tanu kandrawadi tanu wạrpuwadi
He is Kandra man

Tadejapa sena mada japa sena
Where sago palm pith is kept to dry

Itenjienenje rasenjienenje
Keeping them there

Lengu graspinenje paka graspinenje
There keeping the bamboo to dry

Alala lengu alala paka
You bamboo

Satadina jai satabara jai
For seven days

(134) *Lengubraje gitamu paka braje gitamu*
Be here to be dried

Asitiba manenje asi dai manenje
Promising, taking an oath

Satadina ninaka satabara ninaka
After it is seven days

Tanu kandrawadi tanu warpuwadi
He is the Kandra

Lengu kadi manenje paka kadi manenje
Bringing out bamboo branches, blades

Waranitigai jagunitigai
After seven days

Lengubraji manjane praka braji manjane
It is perfectly dry

Lengu brajatgai praka brajatgai
Blades, branches dried

Inat siri nahi inati pdaka nahi
How to make thinner blades

Siripalute siridatate
Could it be with teeth

(135) *Sirinaha menenje pdaka naha menenje*
Trying with teeth

Iriba adate iriba ranjate
It can't be ok like that

Siripalu dimbate siridate dimbate
Tooth broke down

Ate akad manenje ate gangad manenje
Thinking again

Inat siri nahi inat idaka nahi
With which I will foil bamboo

Titi unga laati mati unga laati
Could it be with fingers

Sirinaha menenje pdakanaha menenje
Trying with fingers

Titi ungali dinibane mati dimbane
Trying it with little finger

Iribati adite iribati ranjite
It can't be ok like that

Ate edu manenje ate budhi manenje
Thinking for knowledge

(136) *Tanu kandrawadi tanu warpuwadi*
He is the Kandra man

Tedi tedi kangari reni reni kangari
Observing again

Tani kandra kareti tani warpu kareti
With his knife

Lengu upkinenje pakaupkinanenje
Making foils (of bamboo)

Lengu upimanjane paka upimanjane
Bringing out foils out of bamboo pieces

Nulu lega ujane drasilega ugane
Making them thin like thread

Lengu upkinenje paka upkinenje
Brought out blades

Mesa mesa inji punja punja inji
Making bundles

Lengu ukchananga paka ukchananga
After finishing foiling

Inat lengu suari inat paka suari
With which it will be ok

(137) *Inat tudul inat tuduli*
With which that will be soft

Ate akad ate gangad manenje
Thinking again

Tanu kandrawadi tanu warpuwadi
That Kandra man

Lengu suargai pakasuargai
Could the foils be made thinner

Tani jangate tani kalute
On keeping them on thigh

Siri reja menenje pdakareja menenje
Testing on pulling

Tanijanga karanenje tanikalu kranenje
Strething legs, thighs

Iriba adate iriba ranjate
How it will be ok, how it will fit?

Tanu kandrawadi tanu warpuwadi
He is the Kandra man

Kana kana kangari muju muju kangari
Looking at four corners

(138) *Tani usa laudi tani usa dengusi*
Using his walking stick

Dapangada tanenje dipingada tanenje
Bringing his walking stick

Lengusuari injika paka suari injika
To make bamboo foils thinner

Siri relpinenje pdaka relpinenje
Pulling the foils

Legusua rajane paka sua rajane
Foils became soft

Lasa lasa injisi punja punja injisi
Bound them into bundles

Iribati adite iribati ranjite
How would it be alright

Lengusuar ajate pakasuarrajate
Foils became fully soft

Inisatisi adine inisatisi ranjiine
How to do, how will it fit?

Tanu kandrawadi tanu warpuwadi
He is the Kandra man

(139) *Kandrawana ijisi warpuwana ijisi*
On seeing his face

Sache napinenje geanapinenje
Started doing for Sareni

Sache nachananga meha nachananga
Started making Sareni

Kandrawana ijisi warpuwana ijisi
Kandra is working

Murudipinenje kanadapinenje
Cutting down the nodes

Iriba adate iriba jranjate
How'd it be ok fit?

Kandrawana ajate warpuwana ajate
Kandra is working

Iati bechangra iati jarangra
In it seeds can't be kept

Ate tupkinenje ate betpinenje
Again started making

Tanu kandrawadi tanu warpuwadi
He is the Kandra man

(140) *Tupcha jiananga wetpa jiananga*
On opening out all foils

Ate edu manenje ate budhi manenje
Thinking again for knowledge

Ina baina ina saina
Which one should I do

Wanasila dinata sai sila dinata
In a land where there are no people

Tanu kandrawadi tanu warpuwadi
He is the Kandra man

Kdanibana mehisi alibana mehisi
Doing like tiger colour, bear colour

Sitadbana mehisi siadbana mehisi
On imagination of deer colour

Rada kana ijisi rada banga ijisi
Boring them, making holes

Sache napkimanenje gia napkimanenje
Started weaving the Sareni again

Penatoi manenje murutoi manenje
Weaving by pressing on toes

(141) *Kanadapi, mujudapi manenje*
Making corners

Sarikana inenje sarimuju inenje
Made four corners

Sareni atelgai sareni barelgai
For Sareni to be strong

Sirang ibki manenje nanang ibki manenje
Adding bamboo on four sides

Sirang ikchananga nanek igjananga
After making border frame

Ate sachi manenje ate gepi manenje
Started weaving again

Sache nachananga gia nachananga
Starting the work

Ate sirang idpi manenje nanang dapimanenje
For strength, adding bamboo

Sareni wespagai banjuri wespagai
For Sareni to look beautiful

Lengu utpinenje paka utpinenje
Binding the buffer foils

(142) *Lengu watchananga paka watchananga*
After joining all the foils

Iribati adite iribati ranjite
How'd it be ok fit?

Sareni bati ajate banjuribati ajate
The Sareni is made well

Sareni sariti lenguta banjur sariti lenguta
To the buffer stock of foils

Ate sachinenje ate mepinenje
Started weaving another

Dia burki randa kaha burka randa
Making a bamboo basket to measure rice

Sache napmanenje mea napi manenje
Starting to do it

Kutanaika gai lambinaika gai
For the *kutaka*

Kandraseche randa warpu sechi randa
A winnow

Ninandi suatgai adandi suat gai
For his livelihood

(143) *Sira burla randa nana burla randa*
A seed basket

Tardaibagai ladaibagai
To do work

Tarda kacha randa lada kacha randa
To make large bamboo baskets

Sira daangai danda daangai
For unmarried girls

Sajuli ita gai mekad ita gai
To keep necklace

Sajul pirchade randa mekadi pirchadi
Making a box

Kapangaud gai nepangaud gai
For the milk man

Akusatadi randa gau satadi randa
Making an umbrella

Mdika datuli randa janang datuli randa
A fishing sieve

Mnika biseri randa janang biseri randa
A basket to keep fishes, crabs

(144) *Kudagana inenje parjagana inenje*
Made of many types

Tanu kandrawadi tanu warpuwadi
He is the Kandra man

Tanu lengu bindara tanu paka bindara
He is the bamboo foiling man

Ate edu manenje ate budhi manenje
Thinking again for knowledge

Ichek kuda iteye ichek parja iteye
Made these types

Inisatisi adine inisatisi ranjine
How will it be ok, how will it fit

Iribati adite iribati ranjite
How'd it be ok fit?

Bara sachandi bihate bara gepand bihate
This time everything is finished

Sarenbati ajate banjuribati ajate
Sareni is made

Sareni atigai banjuri atigai
After finishing Sareni

(145) *Tanu nerandali tanu kapandali*
She is Nerandali, she is Kapandali

Tani barabichani tani barajarani
Her seeds of many types

Bicha tapki mangane jara tapki mangane
Carrying these seeds

Bicha take nangani jara take nangani
Carrying them on her waist

Inisgunda manjane inis duding ajane
How to grind them for flour?

Bicha bachikane jara bachikane
Drying the seeds

Yi bara bicha yi bara jara
The seeds (that are) got now

Embe gundaina imbe dudi ina
Where to make flour?

Senisila dinata kutani sila dinata
Mortar is not there, pestle is not there

Inis gunda ajane inis budi ajane
How to make flour?

(146) *Senidapimanere kutanidapi manere*
Searching for mortar, pestle

Maskakalu gena maska kuten gena
Could the mortar be of mango wood pestle

Pujukulu gena pujukuteni gena
Could it be with mahuli wood mortar and pestle?

Sena kalu gena sena kutani gena
Could it be possible to get wood mortar and pestle?

Laka kalu gena laka kutani gena
Could it be with semul wood mortar and pestle?

Are adamue are ranjamue
Those can't be

Inat kalu pani inat kutani pani
Which mortar-pestle will do?

Kaludapinanere kutanidapimanere
Bringing mortar and pestle

Sarenikalu gena sarenikutani gena
Could it be with sal mortar and pestle?

Mardi kalu gena mardi kutani gena
Could it be with asan mortar and pestle?

(147) *Embe gunda ajina embe duding ajina*
With which to grind to make flour

Embe bichang sajan embe jarang sajan
Where to make flour out of grains?

Jambukalu gena jambu kutani gena
Could it be with jamun wood mortar and pestle?

Tanu betamangera tanu prambumangera
He is Betamangera, he is Prambumangera

Kalumepi manenje kutenimepi manenje
Could see mortar and pestle

Mujekalu manenje kae kalu manenje
Got sissoo wood mortar and pestle

Arine senipa arine kutani
That can be useful

Emba bichang sajan emba jara sajan
Grains can be pestled

Ayi muje kaluta ayi bae kaluta
With this wood of sissoo

Arad bicha sajan arad jarang sajan
With that it will be ok

(148) *Muje mea nangani kaemea nangani*
On seeing sissoo tree

Muje api manenje kae api manenje
Cutting it down

Kalu api manenje kuteni api manenje
After cutting down for mortar and pestle

Kalu ahananga kutani ahananga
Cutting for mortar and pestle

Kalu bdiangai kutani bdiangai
Fell it down

Dastanjie manenje tunjaji manenje
Cut into pieces

Kandangie nanenje bendangjie manenje
Cutting it into small pieces by axe

Kandaiananga bendaiananga
Finishing the segmentation

Palapadpi nanenje pandapadpi nanenje
Removeing its bark

Pala padjananga panda padjananga
Finishing the peeling

(149) *Atad machala ganan machala*
All its nodes, internodes

Trahangati manenje trapangati manenje
Stripping them off

Tibaiananga satariananga
Made it into the desired shape

Kalutapi manenje kuteni tapi manenje
Carrying mortar and pestle

Kalu tachananga kutani tachananga
Brought mortar and pestle

Sapangada wangaota sarchangada wangaota
Reached at Sapangada

Kalukepi kutanikepi manenje
Mortar and pestle were got

Tapenjie manenje katkejie manenje
Scratching again

Kalukepi manenje kutanikepi manenje
Mortar is got, pestle is got

Tiarie manenje satarie manenje
Polishing them properly

(150) *Tiariananga satariananga*
On finishing the making

Kalubati ajate kutanibati ajatess
Mortar and pestle were made

Inati seni kundari inat kutani kunderi
Where to keep mortar and pestle?

Inali seni kundari ate inali kundari
In which hole will they fit?

Asi akad manjane asi gangad manjane
Thinking deeply

Seni kundargai kutani kundargai
For fitting the mortar and pestle (in holes)

Wae titikirini wae baireni
Hello woodpecker

Senikunderibamu kuteni kunderibamu
Come to make a hole on mortar

Asi arpimangane asi kelpi mangane
Saying like that

Seni kundargai kutani kundergai
To make a hole on mortar

(151) *Tanu titikirini tanu bairini*
It is the woodpecker

Kulidapi manjane butidapi manjane
Searching for wage earning

Eledela nerandi eledela kapandi
Why Nerandi, why Kapandi

Enge kuli siamu nange buti siamu
Would you give me wages?

Asan seni kundari asan kutani kundari
Then I would do it

Senikundargai kutani kundargai
For a round hole to be made

Kulisie manjane butisie manjane
Paying the wage

Tani titikirinie tani bairinie
To that woodpecker

Elede titikirini elede bairini
No woodpecker

Marasani nechuta dadisani nechuta
By the time of death of trees

(152) *Marapdiu tingamu dadi pdiu tingamu*
Eat up insects from tree trunks

Erini kuli erini buti
That will be your wages

Kuli sinigai butisinigai
To be a wage labourer

Tanu titikirini tanu bairini
That woodpecker

Seni kundarikane kutani kundarikane
Making a hole as a mortar

Seni kundaranaka kutani kundaranaka
After the hole was made

Senibati adate kutanibati adate
Hole is made as a mortar

Embenanga musina embenanga pakina
Where to place it

Seni embe musie kutani embe musie
Where to bury the mortar

Seni seni bati kutani kutanibati
Mortar-mortar, pestle-pestle

(153) *Tange adine basata tange ranjin basata*
In the right place

Musanjie mangane pakanjie mangane
Burying it

Nechur aru mehinsi nechur pati mehinsi
Just under the main (middle) beam of the roof

Seni suspi mangane kutani suspi mangane
Going to put the mortar in a hole

Seni gdangalega kutani gdangalega
It should not be shaken

Seni musanangani kutani musanangani
Place it properly in a hole

Iribati adite iribati ranjite
How'd if be ok-fit?

Seni anigaisi kutani anigaisi
After mortar and pestle (were) ready

Bichagrepi mangane jara grepimangane
Bringing seeds

Bicha grechanangani jaragrecha nangani
After measuring seeds

(154) *Seni kapa kikane kutanikapa kikane*
Filled the hole of the mortar

Tani barabicha tani barajara
Her mixture of seeds

Bichaji manjane jaraji manjane
Pestling them

Tade gundalega mada gunda lega
Like flour of the sago palm

Bichangpai manjane jarangpai manjane
Pestling the seeds

Glubu glubu nanga glaba glaba nanga
Hammering heavily

Gundabani lega dudingani lega
Like flour

Kalingejin lega demangejin lega
Separating the seed coats

Bichang reni lega jarangreni lega
Like powder

Bichangsai manjane jarangsai manjane
Pestled the seeds properly

(155) *Bichang senigai jarangsenigai*
When seeds were powdered

Bichagrepi mangane jara grepimangane
Bringing seed flour out

Bicha brecha nangani jaragrechananga
After bringing seed flour

Tanu sarenitali tanu banjurtali
The Sareni mother

Saiduki kanata mioduki kanata
Looking here and there

Sapangada wangawota sarchangada wangauta
At Sapangada earth, Sarchangad earth

Bichang renkela jarang renke la
Whether powder will fall or not

Sarenia mekane banjuria mekane
Observing it

Peisa mekane gadaisa mekane
To see after shaking Sareni

Bichang repi manjan jarang repi manjan
Seed flour falling down

(156) *Gundang repi manjan duding repi manjan*
Flour fell properly

Demangeji manjan kalingeji mangan
Seed coats got separated

Iribati adite iribati ranjite
How would it be good, fine?

Wari sareni sale banjuri sale
Sareni can't go alone

Wae malandali wae dupandali
Hey Malandali, hey Dupandali

Malanani atati dupanani atati
Come having fire with you

Tidependi atati sakrapendi atati
Fire with dried Tila plants

Tanu arpimangane tanu kelpimangane
She is calling, she is directing

Asi argan gaisi asi kergan gaisi
For the purpose

Tanu malandali tanu dupandali
She is Malandali, she is Dupandali

(157) *Malanani toduti dupanani toduti*
Following the lamp, following the torch

Tidependi toduti sakrapendi toduti
Following fired dry plants of Tila

Sareni navi manjane banjuri navi manjane
Sareni will move

Sapangada sareni sarchangada sareni
For levelling Sapangada, for levelling Sarchangada

Ranipalu sareni bendipalu sareni
For levelling Ranipalu, Bendipalu

Malanani toduta dupanani toduta
Following the lamp, following the torch

Pein pein sareni gada gada sareni
Sareni moving, sounding "pein pein, gada-gada"

Satikambani, pditikambani sareni
For levelling Satikambani, Pditikambani

Penakamban, majakamban sareni
For levelling Penakambeni, Majakambeni

Takamachi baradmachi sareni
For levelling Takamachi, Baradmachi

(158) *Mala ujadati dupa ujadati*
In the light of lamp torch

Sareni navi manjane banjuri navi manjane
Sareni moved slowly

Tikipadari sareni bandipadari sareni
For levelling Tikipadari - Bandipadari

Raji linga, penulinga sareni
For levelling Rajilinga, Penulinga

Sareni moved from Sapangada in the east to the following places and levelling them

Barigati sareni patagati sareni
Jendawedi sareni sabawedi sareni
Jatrukupda sareni banakupda sareni
Sarenvali sareni sagervali sareni
Virapukur sareni valipukur sareni
Pdingenella sareni gapasnella sareni

(159) *Solubiri sareni bandibiri sareni*
Gunjinanu sareni mahananu sareni
Pijubata sareni widibata sareni
Sanasella sareni rupasella sareni
Wendamniji sareni dunamniji sareni
Kalangura sareni endangura sareni
Sutagati sareni marelgati sareni
Sorudaring sareni pangadaring sareni
Nachavani sareni kangavani sareni
Kdukingnella sareni matadnella sareni

(160) *Gundangdini basata duding dini basata*
Dusting (seed powders) throughout

Nehi wanga ajane nehi nella ajane
Earth and fields became beautiful

Kaling dini basata demang dini basata
The seed coats that are falling

Ritadi wanga ajane ritadi nella ajane
Will be converted to stones

Malang dini basata dupang dini basata
Where fire falls

Urla dani ajane kapelidani ajane
Urla plant comes out

Pein pein sareni gada gada sareni
Sareni moving, sounding "pein pein"

Pidkidiji sareni kandanadidi sareni
Pitrimara sareni soari mara sareni
Kadingbarga sareni karka targa sareni

(161) *Usarena sareni baerena sareni*
Anipura sareni jadigati sareni
Katugada sareni padigada sareni
Ate bendek sareni ate dunek sareni
Wenda sapangada wenda sarchangada
(Sareni moved) through Sapangada

Sareni mnie manjane banjuri mnie manjane
Sareni moving slowly

Angasoru sareni bering soru sareni
Petavali sareni brahivali sareni
Juanbalu sareni paambalu sareni
Dapinella sareni dakudnella sareni

(162) *Depanella sareni tungarinella sareni*
Piparani sareni batarani sareni
Arikada sareni pakirada sareni
Padelpanga sareni wangapadeli sareni
Manalada sareni dariada sareni
Pukigati sareni kriyagati sareni
Ganjugati sareni srekagati sareni
Kadamnella sareni dadamnella sareni
Mele ende sareni tue enda sareni
Pite valing sareni ganivaling sareni

(163) *Tide daberi sareni sakradaberi sareni*
Anangadu sareni kenangadu sareni
Tumudibandha sareni roelbandha sareni
Wanga jelesi sareni nellajalesi sareni
Rahudi nella sareni bradanella sareni
Mundigada sareni lakagada sareni

Sachingnella sareni kudengnella sareni
Wangasandak sareni nella sandak sareni
Wanga kudeli sareni nella kudeli sareni
Wanga gareti sareni nella gareti sareni

(164) *Pein pein sareni gada gada sareni*
Sareni sounding pein-pein, gada-gada

Taka nachi sareni baradnachi sareni
Moving in a wriggling manner

Kaling dinibasa dana dinibasa
Where seed coats are falling

Ritad wanga ritad nella ajate
Stony lands come up

Gundang dudinga dinibasa
Grinding the flour

Nehi wanga ajane nehi nella ajane
Nice fields are being formed

Ate bendek sareni ate dunek sareni
Again Sareni is moving towards:

Wenda bekad sareni wenda danasi sareni
Usavali sareni dauvali sareni
Rindavali sareni duchavali sareni

(165) *Pikusnella sareni sarangnella sareni*
Dara bengeri sareni kajabengeri sareni
Germel nella sareni dipur nella sareni
Sinder soru sareni sambing soru sareni
Wanga nalaki sareni nella maleki sareni
Wanga kumudi sareni nella kumudi sareni
Wanga kanjad sareni nella kanjad sareni
Tera jindang sareni tera gada sareni
Kupa nella sareni baki nella sareni
Lakadara sareni simeli dara sareni

(166) *Niga nella sareni taladnella sareni*
Gada vali sareni nagaravali sareni
Ada gadi sareni piogadi sareni
Dimbul bandha sareni ranibandha sareni
Tera dimbul sareni tera atal sareni
Senduroti sareni dauroti sareni
Achabanda sareni mniabanda sareni
Pijumunda sareni bidimunda sareni

Pijusudi sareni bidisudi sareni
Singuli nella sareni gundeli nella sareni

(167) *Laduracha sareni kidadracha sareni*
Kakadaka sareni kidadidaka sareni
Bdelakeri sareni bandakeri sareni
Kandu nella sareni palad nella sareni
Jarugati sareni kesugati sareni
Kichang joru sareni rabang joru sareni
Rengani soru sareni rengani gati sareni
Tulangdiba sareni malangdiba sareni
Akudanja sareni pdipadanja sareni
Lidilada sareni kdanilespa sareni

(168) *Dadingbada sareni magdamada sareni*
Satradika sareni maningdika sareni
Deusana sareni tumasana sareni
Isikidi sareni bimbikidi sareni
Kandabada sareni bakabada sareni
Tiditada sareni bajargada sareni
Gunanimbar sareni gadinimbar sareni
Kriyarinja sareni pukirinja sareni
Apkadepa sareni kamangdepa sareni
Pdiudupa sareni paradupa sareni

(169) *Talabega sareni banabega sareni*
Patigdua sareni napagdua sareni
Etandudu sareni pamandudu sareni
Tanu Wendamiandina wendanian kasa
Throughout the country
Wenda mnie sareni dunamnie sareni
Sareni moves all through:
Guchka nella sareni padel nella sareni
Wangatidi sareni nellatidi sareni
Sik dandangi sareni bdeladahda sareni
Jurgabata sareni sakadbata sareni
Singavali sareni meravali sareni

(170) *Wangapita sareni nellapita sareni*
Deugara sareni sipanana sareni
Didkinella sareni dadkinella sareni
Kunadeli sareni basadeli sareni
Kachelaku sareni branjelaku sareni
Pusabadi sareni sindurbadi sareni

Tuakola sareni maskakola sareni
Wanga gardi sareni nella gardi sareni
Dumangati sareni erpugati sareni
Wanga lanja sareni nella lanja sareni

(171) *Randa dina ijisi randa kasa ijisi*
Making one country

Wendamdiji dunamdiji sareni
Moving throughout:

Kutumunda sareni patimunda sareni
Sunabangi sareni rupabangi sareni
Kinipanga sareni ekapada sareni
Manavali sareni wirkivali sareni
Rangaparu sareni pitadparu sareni
Sikerbada sareni baerbada sareni
Deri pijur sareni kagari pijur sareni
Wanga suler sareni nella suler sareni

(172) *Kanangdaka sareni katangdaka sareni*
Batipada sareni selapada sareni
Wanga brambu sareni nella srambu sareni
Basi gati sareni poegati sareni
Wendamdiji sareni dunamdiji sareni
Sativali sareni pditivali sareni
Belagada sareni raygada sareni
Alisoru sareni kdanisoru sareni
Kusumunda sareni balumunda sareni
Sechkuri aru sareni daberi aru sareni

(173) *Sekagati sareni mundigati sareni*
Siramdeu sareni bamanadeu sareni
Getavali sareni muanvali sareni
Wanga wanguri sareni nella wanguri sareni
Wanga katadi sareni nella katadi sareni
Burlubaru sareni tikerbaru sareni
Pujugati sareni irpigati sareni
Maningkeri sareni dambingkeri sareni
Miunduti sareni kanaduti sareni
Adavali sareni kanavali sareni

(174) *Kurangalu sareni baingalu sareni*
Damensoru sareni gasensoru sareni
Aling gahadi sareni kdaningahadi sareni
Wanga tengeli sareni nella tengeli sareni

Wanga pakari sareni nella pakeri sareni
Rindavali sareni duchavali sareni
Sabduni sareni baeduni sareni
Alidapa sareni artu dapa sareni
Wanga sikadi sareni nella sikadi sareni
Soru supeni sareni panga supeni sareni

(175) *Pein pein sareni gada gada sareni*
Sareni sounding pein-pein, gada-gada

Taka nachi sareni barad nachi sareni
Sareni is making, moving

Kaling dinibasa demang dinibasa
Where seed coats are falling

Ritad wanga ajane ritad nella ajane
Stoney lands are coming out

Gundang dinibasa duding dinibasa
Flour falling over places

Nehi goba ajane nehi dani ajane
Nice landscape coming up

Soru gumu panga gumu
Hills and plains

Sorubdali sareni pangabdali sareni
Deri jrameli sareni kagir jrameli sareni
Surambaru sareni atisada sareni

(176) *Bichandi nibasa sareni jarangdinibasa sareni*
Nehi wanga ajane nehi nella ajane
Nice earth, nice fields are forming

Malandinibasa dupandinibasa
Where fire falls

Urladani ajane kapelidani ajane
Urla plants come up

Sareni nabinjane banjuri nabinjane
Sareni works

Pein pein sareni gada gada sareni
Sareni makes a sound like "pein pein"

Wanga tajangi sareni nella tajangi sareni
For levelling the earth, fields

Wanga jakeri nella jakeri
For levelling Wango jakeri, Nella jakeri

Bade gati sareni tuta gati sareni
Achadiger sareni mniadiger sareni

(177) *Wendamniji sareni dunamniji sareni*
Randa dina ijisi randakasa ijisi
Making one country

Atingarada sareni gadangarada sareni
Wanga durjudi sareni nella durjudi sareni
Palki nella sareni kandam nella sareni
Sela soru sareni tatisoru sareni
Damanigata sareni kneligata sareni
Keravani sareni baivani sareni
Kamesoru sareni kamegada sareni
Tulapada sareni balipada sareni

(178) *Sareni mnienjane banjuri mnienjane*
Sareni in operation

Wendamniji dunamniji sareni
Sareni is made throughout

Wendamaidina sareni wendamakasa sareni
Throughout my country

Pein pein sareni gada gada sareni
Sareni makes a sound like "pein pein"

Lalakuti sareni surkuti sareni
Laktinella sareni runenella sareni
Lakingadu sareni pagingadu sareni
Tambadedi sareni pitaddedi sareni
Barigaba sareni sirigaba sareni
Sindingkala sareni madangkala sareni

(179) *Kinigaba sareni kinevira sareni*
Sersangada sareni baingada sareni
Wanga sarchangada sareni nella sarchangada sareni
Sana duer sareni rupaduer sareni
Judangadu sareni gedangadu sareni
Seningadu sareni kajangadu sareni
Sareni mnie manjane banjuri mnie manjane
Sareni works
Sareni nachimangane banjuri nachimangane
Sareni is shaking, moving

Mala ujadaati dupa ujadaati
In the light of a lamp - torch
Tikerpada sareni dumber guda sareni
Levelling Tikerpada, Dumberguda

(180) *Melu enda sareni knehali enda sareni*
Sinjangeri sareni grapanela sareni
Rindavali sareni duchavali sareni
Guchka nanga sareni ambadapadar sareni
Soru jaram sareni pangajoram sareni
Dupanella sareni dupapadar sareni
Janavali sareni bandugoda sareni
Sukilabata sareni oinlabata sareni
Amadula sareni bisamkata sareni
Asangsala sareni parangsala sareni

(181) *Nangelbadi sareni jualbadi sareni*
Wanga sirchudi sareni nella sirchudi sareni
Muniguda sareni daikala sareni
Ramaniguda sareni bamaniguda sareni
Tatikana sareni bisaladi sareni
Ate bendek sareni ate jonek sareni
Laurkudan sareni laurpatan sareni
Sirkibandha sareni arkabandha sareni
Wanga katadi sareni nella katadi sareni
Ajin salu sareni peransalu sareni

(182) *Surgabata sareni bechabandha sareni*
Widi-okad sareni dalangbata sareni
Randa dina ijisi randakasa ijisi
One world has been made

Barangaru sareni kapangaru-sareni
Sechkuri aru sareni daber aru sareni
Karla kudang sareni sakrakudang sareni
Tangani soru sareni tangani gati sareni
Bake laku sareni bakel padar sareni
Pusarani sareni batarani sareni
Padekanda sareni toaranja sareni

(183) *Sandili gati sareni bandiligati sareni*
Randa dina randakasa ijisi
One world is in making

Gahinvali sareni darni maska sareni
Tide kudang sareni sakrakudang sareni

Soru bareng sareni pangabareng sareni
Mundimaska sareni pingamaska sareni
Nisipidi sareni mundipidi sareni
Achangadel sareni bapangadel sareni
Basakada sareni punakada sareni
Muskasoru sareni kajangsoru sareni

(184) *Lakapaju sareni badapaju sareni*
Atadtulla sareni siadtulla sareni
Haisala sareni prapasala sareni
Gunangadu sareni ganingadu sareni
Tulampadi sareni malangpadi sareni
Bindankeri sareni satrakeri sareni
Wangapudrung sareni nellapudrung sareni
Sipangadu sareni gunagadu sareni
Tadkala sareni machadkala sareni
Rindavali sareni duchavali sareni

(185) *Jindagadu sareni markadu sareni*
Nachuladu sareni talaladu sareni
Jagadalpur sareni satanpur sareni
Sataludanja sareni kudaddanja sareni
Baliguda sareni rekigada sareni
Dadingmada sareni pipadmada sareni
Achangdeli sareni mniangdeli sareni
Sareni mniate sareni banjuri mniate sareni
Sareni moving forward

Wenda mniji sareni dunamniji sareni
Wekadmniji sareni dunamniji sareni

(186) *Achakadu sareni bananakadu sareni*
Wangabakla sareni nellabakla sareni
Pujugati sareni irpigati sareni
Soru burlang sareni pang aburlang sareni
Ukanmundi sareni berengmundi sareni
Kranjikana sareni masikana sareni
Bagamunda sareni pagamunda sareni
Takanasana sareni birmasana sareni
Bikapanga sareni nanapanga sareni
Damanvali sareni knehelipali sareni

(187) *Tanbadaku sareni dampatanga sareni*
Dundrukadu sareni petekadu sareni

Sunivali sareni sindebaru sareni
Wangapadel sareni nella padel sareni
Garanginella sareni nanangnella sareni
Damanpanga sareni kneheli panga sareni
Bilamala sareni malabila sareni
Valigati sareni jambagati sareni
Sambangsoru sareni satasoru sareni
Dudus nella sareni manusi nella sareni

(188) *Deri dengeni sareni kageri dengeni sareni*
Jambuguda sareni artaguda sareni
Sunakatak sareni rupakatak sareni
Sarenidanga sareni mardidanga sareni
Kinad nella sareni dandad nella sareni
Tidengadu sareni sakrangadu sareni
Mahavali sareni getavali sareni
Gulampanga sareni rekipanga sareni
Kanebaru sareni endabaru sareni
Wanga bangeri sareni pijubangeri sareni

(189) *Bechabandha sareni sanabandha sareni*
Sanasela sareni rupasela sareni
Nuamunda sareni purunamunda sareni
Pedem nella sareni gopas nella sareni
Wanga sikeri sareni nella sikeri sareni
Kanangadu sareni anangadu sareni
Jendawedi sareni sabawedi sareni
Sarenipunda danede banjuri punda danede
Sareni moving non-stop

Dinagunda sareni kasagunda sareni
Jatrukupda sareni banakupda sareni

(190) *Jenanguda sareni nisananguda sareni*
Rajilinga sareni penulinga sareni
Ranipalu sareni bendipalu sareni
Sapangada sareni sarchangada sareni
Dinagunda dajate kasagunda dajate
Reached Dinagunda-kasagunda

Ate bendek sareni ate dunek sareni
Tuitambu sareni darmaladi sareni
Penukala sareni majukala sareni
Rajam kala sareni sadga nella sareni
Barda gati sareni ardagati sareni

(191) *Ranimundi sareni badamundi sareni*
Mnasukeri sareni dandakeri sareni
Burlapanga sareni ardapanga sareni
Sosabata sareni pagerpadi sareni
Krichitula sareni salapadi sareni
Mundavali sareni sekavali sareni
Odavali sareni knavali sareni
Maavali sareni partivali sareni
Sirasmbar sareni baimbar sareni
Siradandang sareni sirapakar sareni

(192) *Sondekidi sareni baikidi sareni*
Dodod kalla sareni muchan kala sareni
Lakajada sareni grabajada sareni
Kranjanella sareni barinella sareni
Kutudidi sareni banangjala sareni
Tikimadar sareni bandi madar sareni
Sapangada pundadi sarchangada pundadi
Non stop movement from Sapangada

Sarenpunda ajate banjuri punda ajate
Sareni coming on, moving through:

Ate bendek ajate ate dunek ajate
Again moving ahead

Kajuger ajate baiger ajate
Reached Kajuger-baiger

(193) *Gunjigata sareni baigata sareni*
Tadengbaru sareni ardabaru sareni
Damankala sareni knelukala sareni
Meskari kala sareni miokala sareni
Sitkipanga sareni toadoni sareni
Sapar nella sareni pudeni nella sareni
Grispa vali sareni mratpavali sareni
Kujanella sareni gambar nella sareni
Duer bedi sareni anguri bedi sareni
Kude panga sareni tedi panga sareni

(194) *Kakibaki sareni barabaki sareni*
Masangdia sareni kadangdia sareni
Pidelnella sareni jadelnella sareni
Wango prieni sareni nella prieni sareni
Sitka mati sareni katpa mati sareni

Rogamara sareni bichumara sareni
Meravali sareni mnepavvali sareni
Japinella sareni pdubanella sareni
Sareni punda danede banjuri punda danede
Sareni returned covering all through

Sareni punda adate banjuri punda adate
Sareni's work is good

(195) *E sapangadata e sarchangadata*
In Sapangada, in sarchangada

Dina punda ajate kusapunda ajate
The whole country was levelled

Mai sareni tali - mai banjuri tali
Our Sareni mother

Sapangada gunjari sarchangada gunjari
Around Sapangada

Bichadia watali jaradia watali
Broadcasted seeds

Kaling iji watali dembang iji watali
Broadcasted seed coats

Dinewide watali kasawide watali
Having covered the whole country

Ana bide watali gatiwide watali
Jumping over ana-gati

Keriwide watali dandabide watali
Jumping over steep slopes, wide slopes

Mai sareni watali mai banjuri watali
Our Sareni is like that

(196) *Kelu bria watali mara bria watali*
Sareni is broken

Sro doa atali machi droa atali
Sareni has become dirty

Ikja tua tuna danjegena tuna
Should it be thrown away?

Iri itandi ade iri raspandiade
This can't be kept

E kelu britali e mara britali
Its handles are broken

Ikjanode tuasa wanjenade tuasa
We are not going to throw it away

Like sareniji tuasa like banjuri wana tuasa
Is it an ordinary Sareni?

Dina wide watali kasa wide watali
It has covered the country

Embe itenjina embe rasenjina
Here we'll keep it

Katamundat gena bei mundat gena
Should it be near a hedge

(197) *Widi okad gena kata wekad gena*
Should it be kept in the courtyard

Kumda jagdit gena mundrajagdit gena
Should it be kept under the pumpkin stage?

Sicheni arut gena papi arut gena
Should it be kept on a stage inside the house?

Emba sra datane emba machi datane
There it will be dirty

Emba lengu adane embapaka dengani
Where will it be good?

Embe pitenjina emberasanjina
Where shall we keep it?

Sare sarenbati banju banjur bati
Our Sareni

Tange abin basa tange ranjin basa
Where to keep it?

Piju pana basa bidipana basa
Where there is no rain?

Sro doabasa machidoa basa
Where there is no dust-dirt?

(198) *Kukudaha basa bumbudaha basa*
Where there is no water?

Sareni itenjina banjuri itenjina
Sareni is to be kept

Karamara pechat gena bidimara pechat gena
Should it be kept on a Kara tree, Bidi tree

Emba ada mue embà ranjamue
There it can't be

Na piju wanali na widi wanali
If rain approaches

Echkitaha nachane rapchitaha nachane
It will come back suddenly

Embe pitenjina embeparsanjina
Where shall (we) keep

Mae sarenani mae banjurani
Our Sareni?

Sareni ita gai banjuri itagai
To keep the Sareni

Tanu tiba inenje tanu bainenje
He is promising, taking an oath

(199) *Ade laka dara-ade bima dara*
Taking the names of the ancestors

Ade sara sauta ade bura sauta
Hey Sora Sauta, Bura Sauta

Ade pijubimenje ade baibimenje
Hey Lord of rain, wind

Sareni itenjie banjuri itenjie
To keep Sareni

Mera nulu siamu singanulu siamu
Give us yellow thread

Mniadara detamu patpadara detamu
Please open the door

Tanupiju gulra tanubidi gulra
He is the rain god, wind god

Tiba inigai dau inigai
Promising, taking an oath

Mnia dara denenje patpadara denenje
Opening the door

Meranulu repnenje singanulu repnenje
Yellow thread came down

(200) *Mera nulu repnaka singa nulu repnaka*
When yellow thread came down

Sareni gaspinere banjuri gaspinere
Binding Sareni

Sareni gasananga banjuri gasananga
Finishing the binding

Tanu lakidara tanu bimadara
He is the ancestor

Sareni relpinenje banjuri relpinenje
Pulling the Sareni

Pijupadi kueti bidipadi kueti
Above the rain sphere, wind sphere

Nachadanga kueti toadanga kueti
Above the slopes of heaven

Sareni rejananga banjuri rejananga
On pulling the Sareni up

Tanu itlnenje tanu respinenje
He is there

Piju pana basa bidipana basa
Where rain can't be

(201) *Sro dohabasa machidroabasa*
Where dust can't be

Kukudoa basa bubmudoa basa
Where it will not imbibe water

Sata bakridae sata perli dae
In a seven compartment house

Sareni itenanga banjuri itenanga
Sareni is kept

Atetaru tibamanere ate taru daimanere
Promising again, taking an oath again

Ade laki dara ade bima dara
Remebering the ancestors

Ade piju gulra ade widi gulara
Took name of rain god, wind god

Palas pein isa palas gada isa
Unncessarily don't let it rain (please)

Palas dundrumeta palas kudu meta
Unnecessarily don't make mist and fog

Palas janjadia palas nibadia
Unnecessarily don't make haze

(202) *Maska kala mehisi dasikala mehisi*
May rain come with mango flowers

Sachi kanduli mehisi kude kanduli meaisi
May rain come with gram flowers

Rai mande mehisi kada mande mehisi
At the time mustard, finger millet sprout

Tia paka mehisi tia junu mehisi
On seeing maize flowers, bean flowers

Embe pei istamu embe gada istamu
May rain come then

Emba taka nacha emba barad nacha
Then push it - pull it

Emba dundru metamu emba kudu metamu
When there will be fog and mist

Asi tibaia asi daia
Promising, taking an oath

Tibaiananga dai iananga
Promised, took an oath

Iribati adite iribati ranjite
How'd it be ok fit?

(203) *Sarenibaki ichite banjuri baki ichite*
Sareni is there

Iri laing ajate irituking ajate
Now it's ok, it fits

Sareni sachi bekadi banjuri sachi bekadi
After the Sareni

Tanu nerandali tanu kapandali
She is Nerandali, she is Kapandali

Tanu jendaladu tanu kasaladu
She is the central woman

Sapangada wango sarchangada wangaota
In Sapangada earth, Sarchangada earth

Sareni sachi beasi banjuri sachi beasi
Following Sareni's path

Tanu wide mepingane tanu kreje mepingane
She is roaming, observing

Sareni bati sajate banjuri bati sajate
Following Sareni's path

Iribatii adite iribati ranjite
How'd it be ok, fit?

(204) *Sareni sachi beasi banjuri sachi beasi*
Following Sareni's path

Rangan sajanjileye paber sajanjileye
Stones have not gone there

Rangan aja sile paberi aja sile
Rangan is not done

Denge denge ajane dene dene ajane
(Earth) is shaking being pushed down

Jabamera lega jaba keta lega
Like muddy lands

Kada aja manjane kutiaja manjane
Still small holes are there

Depa aja manjane tupur aja manjane
Furrows are still there

Tani kangarinawa tanisinadinawa
She is observing

Tanu nerandali tanu kapandali
She is Nerandali, she is Kapandali

Ate akad mangane ate gangad mangane
Again thinking for knowledge

(205) *Akad manjananga gangad mangananga*
After thinking

Akad machisi ade gangad machisi ade
Only thinking can't do

Wae rangan tali wae paberi tali
Hey, Rangan mother

Rangan tali paber tali atatee
Rangan mother coming

Rangani ajanjileye paberi ajanjileye
The earth is not Rangan operated

Tana ruenjileye pata ruenjileye
Earth is not properly levelled

Dili kasta mebamu budung kasta mebamu
Hammer the earth to make it plain

Sindemata ajati kajurmata atati
Date palm trees are there

Sana jatra atati rupajatra atati
Small bushes are there

Dili kastamebamu budung kastamebamu
Hammer the earth to be hard

(206) *Rangania mebamu paberia mebamu*
Make the earth plain with Rangan

Tanu Nerandali tanu Kapandali
She is Nerandali, she is Kapandali

Asiarpi mangane asi kelpimangane
Calling like that

Asi kargan gaisi asi kelgan gaisi
To tell like that

Tanu rangan tali tanu paber tali
She is Rangan mother

Rangan tali paberi tali aisi
Rangan mother came

Sindemata, kajurimata aisi
Mat weaving mother (from date palm leaves)

Sana jatra rupajatra aisi
Golden brown, silver brown sticks brought

Sapangada wango sarchangada wangawota
In Sapangada earth, Sarchangada earth

Diling gatpigane kudung gatpingane
Hammering hard

(207) *Diling gasti mangani kudung gastinangani*
Hammering to level the earth

Sapangada rangani sarchangada rangani
Making Sapangada, Sarchangada leveled

Ranipalu bendipalu rangani
Making Ranipalu, Bendipalu leveled

Pijusilat dinata widisilat dinata
In the country without rain

Sugad supi rangani noad supi rangani
Putting soil on earth

Kada atala kuti atala
Holes were made, slopes were made

Kada atibasa kuti atibasa
At the place of composting

Kalu dudi trichisi gada dudi trichisi
Removing dirt from the body (and putting it in the holes)

Tupuri atibasa depa atibasa
At upper places

Kichendui rangani rabendui rangani
Taking out earth

(208) *Dilingasti rangani kudungasti rangani*
Hammering hard

Satikambani rangani pditi rangani kambani
Making Satikambani, Pditikambani plains

Pena kambani rangani maja kambani rangani
Making Penakambani, Majakambani plains

Sapangada gunjari sarchangada gunjari
Around Sapangada, around Sarchangada

Ragamara rangani bichumara rangani
Making Ragamara, Bichumara plains

Sitakamati rangani katapamata rangani
Making Sitkamati, Katapamata plains

Pidel nella kambani, jadel nella kambani
Making Pidel nella, Jadel nella plains

Sapangada gunjari sarchangada gunjari
Around Sapangada, around Sarchangada

Ragamara rangani bichumara rangani
Making Ragamara, Bichumara plains

Rangan aai manjane paber aai manjane
Rangan is made

(209) *Tana kajat basa pata kajatbasa*
At places where earth is not levelled

Duruvali igjisi durupata igjisi
Throwing away stones

Sendurvali igjisi daurvali igjisi
Red stones thrown off

Grapki vira igjisi garli vira igjisi
Earth taken out, thrown off

Tana kajatbasa pata kajatbasa
At places of dry earth

Igja napingane kapke napingane
Throwing off and going on

Masangdia rangani kadangdia rangani
Making Masangdia - Kadangdia plains

Kudepanga rangani tedipanga rangani
Making Kudepanga, Tedipanga plains

Duerbedi rangani paberbedi rangani
Making Duerbedi paberbedi plains

Anardroha rangani kadakdroha rangani
(210) *Wango janaka rangani nella janka rangani*
Sindasur rangani madasur rangani

Susabata rangani pagarpadi rangani
Salapadi rangani krichitulla rangani

Rangan nabinjane paber nabinjane
Sapangada gunjari sarchangada rangani

Dilinggasti rangani budangasti rangani
Pijusila dinata bidisila dinata

Suptisupi rangani nawadsupi rangani
Mundavali rangani sekavali mangani

(211) *Odavali rangani knahavali ramgani*
Maa vali rangani partivali rangani

Sirambar rangani baimbar rangani
Siradandang rangani sirabakad rangani
Sindekidi bedi rangani
Dududkola rangani muchadkola rangani
Lakajada rangani brabajada rangani
Kranjanella rangani barinella rangani
Utisira rangani tangisira rangani
Kutududi rangani vanajala rangani

(212) *Nuamunda rangani purnamunda rangani*
Pijubangeri rangani bidibangeri rangani
Pedemnella rangani dasamnella rangani
Jendawedi rangani sabawedi rangani
Barigati rangani patagati rangani
Jatrukupda rangani banakupda rangani
Jenanguda rangani nisanaguda rangani
Sarenivali rangani sagerivali rangani
Hirakupur rangani valikupur rangani
Pringanella rangani gapasnella rangani

(213) *Salubiri rangani bandibri rangani*
Gunjinanu rangani mahananu rangani
Gunjervali rangani pudmavali rangani
Sandimaska rangani dedamaska rangani
Kalungura rangani endangura rangani
Majimundang rangani moelmundang rangani
Kangasoru rangani berengsoru rangani
Vira panga rangani vali panga rangani
Indira mundi rangani kadakmundi rangani
Jipkabata rangani prapabata rangani

(214) *Judhaabata rangani kelabata rangani*
Widi okadi sareni dalangbata sareni
Gumagada rangani seragada rangani
Tiki padari rangani bandipadari rangani
Rangen pudanede paber pundanede
Rangani penulinga rangani
Rangen pundadi ainjadi paberipundainjadi
Rangen doing work properly

Dina punda ainede kasa punda ainede
Ranipalu rangani bendipalu rangani
Sapangada rangani sarchangada rangani

(215) *Rangan pundadajate paberi pondadajate*
Rangan completing its work

Iribati adite iribati ranjite
How'd it be ok, how'd it fit

Ranganbati paberibati sajate
Rangan mother going

E rangan valini e paberi valini
To this rangan stone

Inisatisi adine inisatisi ranjine
How will it be ok, how will it fit

Dina rukchabatali kasaruchavatali
To make a good country

Igja gena tuna danje gena tuna
Should the stones be thrown off

Ina pdibandi ade ina raspandi ade
It will come in no use

Igjanade tuasa danjenede tuasa
No we will not throw it

Liket rangani valita liket paberi valita
Is it an ordinary stone

(216) *Dina rukuchi batali kasa rukucha*
(It) has levelled the earth

Inisina nerandi inisina kapandi
How to be done, Nerandi?

E ranganvalini e paberivalini
This Rangan stone

Imbe itanjina imbe rasanjina
Where shall we keep it?

Katamundat gena kasamundat gena
Should it be near the hedge?

Kichad pechata gena padipechat gena
In which place is it to be kept?

Amba ada mue amba ranjamue
There it can't be

Amba laingae amba tucingai
There it will not be ok, not fit

Imbe itenjina imbe rasanjine
Where shall we keep it?

Karamarat gena bidimarat gena
Should it be at Kara tree-Bidi tree

(217) *Ambaba ade ambaba ranje*
There it will not be ok, not fit

Mae rangan valini mae paber valini
Our Rangan stone

Ite njie manere rasenjie manere
Keeping it there

Na laurgai na kanjar gai
For our blacksmith

Na sasagai na gurugai
For other people

Mai rangan ualini mai paber valini
Our Rangan stone

Itenjie manere rasenjie manere
Keeping it there

Aai didki nellata aai dadki nellata
Came to Didki nella, Dadki nella

Aai deugara aai sipananata
Came to Deugara, Sipanana

Deugara wanga sipanana wangawota
In Deugara earth

(218) *Ranganvali lani paber valilani*
To this Rangan stone

Itenjie manere rasanjie manere
Keeping it there

Itenjiananga rasanjia nanga
After keeping it there

Taru tibamenere tarudaimanere
They are promising, taking an oath

Ala rangan vali ala paber vali
Hey, Rangan mother

Nasumnia gitamu duenmnia gitamu
Be here as garlic

Urkumnia gitamu arkamnia gitamu
Be here as onion

Anda mnianamu paba mnianamu
Be here as onion

Anda ajamanjamu paba ajamanjamu
After my promise

Nai tiba toduta nai dai toduta
My blacksmith will come

(219) *Na laurgai na binjargai*
For that blacksmith

Na gurugaisi na sasagaisi
For that man

Ala ranganvali ala paber vali
Hey, Rangan mother

Arka mnianjamu urku mnianjamu
Convert from stone to steel

Asitiba inenje asi dai inenje
Promising, taking an oath

Tiba iananga dai iananga
After promising, taking oath

Iribati adite iribati ranjite
How'd it be ok, fit?

Iribati laingi iribati tukingi
How'd it be ok, fit?

Rangan bati sajate paber bati sajate
Rangan stone went

Tanagati ruate patagati ruate
Earth became perfectly levelled

(220) *Kadabati munjate kutibati munjate*
Holes filled in •

Tanagati kajate patagati kajate
Gaps on earth, became full

Iribati adite iribati ranjite
How'd it be ok, fit?

Tanu nerandali tanu kapandali
She is Nerandali, she is Kapandali

Tanu jendaledu tanu kadaladu
She is the central woman

Rangan sachi beasi paber sachi beasi
Following the path Rangan moved

Sapangada wango sarchangada wangawota
In Sapangada earth, Sarchangada earth

Wide mepingane preje mepingane
Going to roam and observe

Tani bidineba tani prejineba
When she was roaming

Jin jin dewali wango wango deali
Earth was looking empty, empty

(221) *Usumai sile rumai sile*
Not crowded, not noisy

Jienanga deali wangananga dewali
Only emptyness was there

Iriba adate iriba ranjate
Now it's not ok, does not fit

Jien jien ajate wango wango ajate
Looking empty, empty

Soru ninge sile gadaninge sile
No hills, no low lands

Ara ninge sile timbaninge sile
Not a small hill (even) there

Manang sajasilu adang sajasilu
Manang is not there to make hills

Tanu nerandali tanu kapandali
She is Nerandali, she is Kapandali

Manang lachagai adanglachagai
To make Manang-Adang

Wae manandali wae adandali
Hey, Manandali, hey Adandali

(222) *Asi arpimangane asi kelpimangane*
Calling like that

Bae sra mananati matimana atati
Bring your dirty mana

Vira mana atati vali mana atati
Mana that was measuring earth, sand

Mana lache mebamu ada lache mebamu
Bring me the measuring mana

Asi inigai asi benigai
Saying like that

Tanu manandali tanu adandali
She is Manandali, she is Adandali

Manalachi mangane adalachi mangane
Measuring with mana

Sra manat maneka machimanat maneka
Measuring one mana

Vira manati maneka machi manati maneka
One mana of earth

Manang achingane adang lachinjane
Measuring with mana

(223) *Sapangada kikane sarchangada kikane*
To put it in Sapangada

Ningamu sapangada ningamu sarchangada
Grow on Sapangada, grow on Sarchangada

Taru pangi ningamu pada pangi ningamu
You grow high

Daru gachi ningamu pada gachi ningamu
Keeping your own name, grow up

Jendalije ningamu kadalaji ningamu
You grow up as a big one

Ranipalu kikane bendipalu kikane
To put it in Ranipalu, Bendipalu

Ningamu ranipalu ningamu bendipalu
Grow on Ranipalu, grow on Bendipalu

Daru gachi ningamu padagachi ningamu
Keeping your own name, grow up

Usarana kikane bearana kikane
To put it in Usarana, Bearana

Ningamu usarena grow on bearena
Grow on Usarena, grow on Bearena

(224) *Jendabedi kikane sababedi kikane*
Placed on Jendabedi, sababedi

Piju bangeri kikane bidi bangeri kikane
Placed on Pijubangeri, Bidibangeri

Ningamu piju bangeri ningamu bidibangeri
Grow on Pijubangeri, Bidibangeri

Daru gachi ningamu padagachi ningamu
Grow on Darugachi, padagachi

Dene dene ningamu denge denge ningamu
Grow fast, grow high

Kriajika lega puki jika lega
Like ant hills

Kering iji ningamu dandang iji ningamu
Grow on slopes, low-lands

Sanasela kikane rupasela kikane
Placed on Sanansela, Rupasela

Ningamu sanasela ningamu rupasela
Grow on Sanasela, Rupasela

Daru gachi ningamu padagachi ningamu
Grow up with your name

(225) *Pijubata kikane bidibata kikane*
Placed on Pijubata-bidibata

Manang started functioning. It measured earth and poured at certain places. Hills grew in such places. Manang moved around. It started working from Sapangada and followed the same path of Sareni. It covered the whole world of the Kuttia Kondh. Here, only the names of certain large hills are mentioned.

Sutagati kikane marelgati kikane
Placed on Sutagati, Marelgati

Piparadi kikane jendaradi kikane
Placed on piparadi-Jendaradi
Kenang adu kikane anangadu kikane
Dara bengeri-bija bengeri kikane
Wango sandak kikane nella sandak kikane
Wenda mniji kikane duna mniji kikane
Sika dandang kikane bdel dandang kikane
Surgabata kikane sakad bata kikane
Soru pijur kikane gada pijur kikane

(226) *Tera dimbul kikane tera atad kikane*
Ningamu tera dimbuli ningamu tera atadi
Grow on Dimbuli, grow on Tera Atadi

Darupanga ningamu padapanga ningamu
Having your name grow up

Dina panga kikane kasa panga kikane
To put it in the country

Achabanda-mniabanda-
To put it in Achabanda, Mniabanda

Ningamu achabanda ningamu mniabanda
Grow on Achabanda, Mniabanda

Betakana pihisi prambukana pihisi
In the name of Betakana, Prambukana

Kdani ana pihisi ali ana pihisi
Making tiger care, bear care

Kandum nella kikane palam nella kikane
Ningamu kandum nella ningamu palamnella
Grow on Kandum nella, Palamnella

(227) *Tiditada kikane bajargada kikane*
Placed on Tiditada, bajargada

Ningamu tiditada ningamu bajargada
Grow on Tiditada, Bajargada

Kandabada kikane bakabada kikane
Placed on Kandabada, Bakabada

Deusana kikane tumksana kikane
Puki renja kikane kriarenja kikane
Ningamu pukirenja ningamu kriarenja
Grow up like ant hills

Darugachi padagachi ningamu
Grow up with your name

Talabega kikane banabega kikane
Placed on Talabega, banabega

Ningamu talabega ningamu banabega
Grow on Talabega, Banabega

Darugachi padagachi ningamu
Grow up with your name

(228) *Wendamniji kikane dunamniji kikane*
Acha digeri kikane mnia digeri kikane
Sela soru kikane tati soru kikane
Wango durjud kikane nella durjud kikane
Manang lachi mangane adang lachi mangane
Measuring with mana

Judang nella kikane menang nella kikane
Seningadu kikane kajangadu kikane

Sana dueri kikane badadueri kikane
Wenda mdiji kikane dunamdiji kikane
Soru dapeni kikane panga dapeni kikane

(229) *Soru pokar kikane pangapokar kikane*
Wenda mai dina wenda mai kasa
To make the world good

Siramdeu kikane bamandeu kikane
Soru burlang kikane panga burlang kikane
Sra manat maneka machi manat maneka
With many measures of Mana

Vira manat kikane vali manat kikane
Manang lachi mangane adang lachi mangane
Measuring with Mana

Mana kapa kinali ada kupa kinali
Mana doing its job

Panga joru ajane panga gada ajane
Pangajoru, pangagada come up

Ninge dungu talani ninge bdesu talani
For you to see

(230) *Sapaniji ningamu briseniji ningamu*
Grow on Sapanji, Briseniji

Khali siji ninganu dana siji ningamu
Grow on Khali, Dana

Bechasiji ningamu mukisiji ningamu
Grow on Bechasiji, mukisiji

Baudiji-atadiji ningamu-
Parajati ningamu gunoajati ninganu
Ninge dungu tani ninge bdesu tani
For her to see

Mana srapad kinali adaki srapad kinali
Mana doing consistently

Lada soru ajane lada gada ajane
Lada soru, Lada gada came up

Mana nesanai ada nesa nai
By the work of Mana

Bade gati kikane tutagati kikane

(231) *Lakti nella kikane runem nella kikane*
Laki nella kikane paging nella kikane
Tanba dedhi kikane pitadi dedhi kikane
Jurgabata kikane achabanoha kikane
Darangaru kikane kapangaru kikane
Sechkuri aru kikane daber aru kikane
Pusarani kikane batarani kikane
Sandili gati kikane bandali gati kikane
Soru bareng kikane panga bareng kikane
Nisipidi kikane mundipidi kikane

(232) *Hatisada kikane prapasada kikane*
Tuitambu kikane darmaladi kikane
Sargi dongar kikane mardi dongar kikane
Kilang nella kikane bandang nella kikane
Mio dueri kikane mio banguri kikane
Wango dimuli kikane nella dimuli kikane
Manang pundadanede adang punda danede
Manang covered areas, completed work

Soru punda danede gada punda danede
Hills and slopes made properly

Dina punda danede kasa punda danede
The world making

Singa bdeu kikane mera bdeu kikane

(233) *Jendabedi kikane sababedi kikane*
Pijubangeri kikane bidi bangeri kikane
Ranipalu kikane bendipalu kikane
Sapangada kikane sarchangada kikane
Manang punda jat adang punda dajat
Manang completing its work

Soru pundadajate gada punda dajat
Completed making hills-slopes

Iribati adite iribati ranjite
How would it be ok, fit?

(234) *Manang sachi beasi adangsachi beasi*
Manang operation complete

Operation manang ceases and large hills are developed. For the erection of smaller hills, operation muting (fist) starts in the same way, begining from Sapangada to finish at Sapangada in a circular path (treyena).

Soru ningit bekati
For hills to be formed

Muting nabinjane graling nabinjane
Operation Muting was done

Mana ada sachi bekadi
For Mana Ada finished working

Lika soru lika gada gaisi
For small hills, small holes

Muting nabimanjan graling nabimanjan
Operation Muting was done

Lika soru lika gada gaisi
For small hills, small holes

Sapangada nachane sarchangada nachane
Throughout Sapangada-Sarchangada

Ranipalu nachane bendipalu nachane
Throughout Ranipalu, Bendipalu

Rajininga nachane penuninga nachane
Throughout Rajininga, Penuninga

(235) *Kranja nella nachane bari nella nachane*
Throughtout Kranja nella Bari nella

Muti baradang pinali grali barad pinali
Fistful of earth being put

Lambasoru pinali lambagati pinali
To create small hills

Kaju pechat dinali malapechat dinali
By hand it is done

Kanga tupur ajane bereng tupur ajane
Kangatupur, Berengtupur came up

Muting nachi manjane groling nachi manjane
Going on throwing fistful earth

Lika soru gai lika gada gaisi
To make small hills

Bari gati nachane patagati nachane
Earth put on Barigati, Patagati

Jatru kupda nachane banakupda nachane
Sareni vali nachane sagervali nachane

(236) *Hira pukur nachane vali pukur nachane*
Pringeri nella-gapas nella-
Solvbiri nachane bandibiri nachane
Muting mnienjane graling mnienjane
Muting in operation

Wendamniji nachane bunamniji nachane
Like sowing activity

Bekad mdiji nachane
Dangasi nachan basa Diasi nachan basa
Operation muting follows the path in which Sareni and Manang operations were made under the supervision of Nerandali. Muting made small hills which Manang did not. All the names of small hills are not listed here. The hills and planes covered by Sareni minus the hills made by Manang can give the names of the smaller hills-that are made by Muting. The following lines that are recited to give an account of the evolution of plants and trees

Tanu betamangera tanu prambumangera
He is Betamangera, he is Prambumangera

Beta saluoga prambu salugaisi
To set out on hunting expedition

Bandude kagara bandude likara
Come elder brothers, come younger brothers

Ana dia gati dia mekana
Let's go to see Ana and Gati

Soru sispinjane gada sispinjane
Hills, holes looking empty

Tanu kaga raja tanu likaraja
He, the big king, small king

Runda wainere guta wainere
Gathering at one place

Runda bajananga guta bajananga
Being gathered

Tanu betamangera tanu prambumangera
He is Betamangera, he is Prambumangera

(237) *Bandude kagara bandude likara*
Come elders, come youngers (males)

Beta sajamena prambu sajamena
Let's go for hunting games

Ana dia gati dia mekana
To see the Ana Gati

Keri bangamena danda bangamena
Crossing the steep slopes and wide slopes

Tanu kaga raja tanu lika raja
He, the big king, the small king

Beta sajiner prambu sajiner
Going for hunting

Sapangada kata sarchangada kata
From Sapangada, from Sarchangada

Ranipalu kata bendipalu kata
From Ranipalu, from Bendipalu

Teli racha kata maliracha kata
From where paths met

Lekenja sajiner lukunja sajiner
Going step by step

(238) *Aai saskinellata aai matadinellata*
Reached at Saskinella, reached at Matadinella

Mendude likara mendude kagara
Encircle elders, encircle youngers

Kdani bdaka ali bdaka jindu
Kill tigers, kill bears

Bada bdakatara bdaka jindu
Kill the games

Tanu betamanger tanu prambumanger
He is Betamanger, he is Prambumanger

Tanu udurengad tanu penarengad
He is Udurengad, he is Penarengad

Jian pine ahan pinenje
Killing and going

Kebunainere kikanainere
Howling, noising

Biwa injinere gaga injinere
Noising with huge voice

Kama putinere tutu putinere
Blowing horn pipes

(239) *Anang ratpe gating ratpe manere*
Encircle passages at Ana-Gati

Aai saskinellata aai matadinellata
Reached at Saskinella, Matadinella

Majuwa silat brahawa silat
Sambar is not there, wild boar is not there

Lakamaji silate dara maji silate
Large sambar is not there, small sambar is not there

Adebede tada adebede kaku
Hello elder brothers, hello uncles

Inisana tada inisana kaku
How to do elder brother, how to do uncle?

Emben kana sana emben muju sana
To which direction should we go?

Bandu bandu tada bandu bandu kaku
Encircle elder brother, encircle uncle

Sajanjia mena rechanjia mena
Will go there and see

Kata barta rale nanga
Made a discussion

(240) *Runda guta ajananga*
Gathering (all there)

Tanu sajinere tanu repinere
He is going, he is leaving

Beta sajinere prambu sajinere
For hunting, going

Nachikeri wangawota bindanikeri wangawota
To Nachikeri fields, Bindanikeri fields

Udugutu-brapagutu-
To Udugutu fields, Brapagutu fields

Ade bede tada ade bede kaku
Hello elder brother, hello uncle

Ananga ratpandu gatinga ratpandu
Encircle the Ana-Gati

Majumua brahamua mane
Sambar, wild boar are present

Ananga gatinga ratpandu
Encircle Anas, Gatis

Biwa inji manamu gaga inji manamu
Make huge noises

(241) *Kebuni kikani ajandnamu*
Come with a loud voice

Kagaraja lika raja nangani
Elders, youngers all will go

Tanu kebuni kikani ainere
They are howling

Kebuni na bena kiknina bena
While making noise

Aku gau mrakana bena
Nothing was there to be hidden

Seka sama dara sama sakane
Huge bison came out

Seka maju daramaju sakane
Huge sambar came out

Papa nasta mriani giriti
Who has no parents

Ananga gatinga kapa sakane
Come out covering Ana-Gati

Tanu papa mrienja
That orphan

(242) *Maju mea braha mea*
On seeing sambar, wild boar

Tanu ajinenje tanu durinenje
He is surprised, he is feared

Jella itelia kali itelia
Soul trembled

Ambu putpinenje ambunilu putcha
Took arrow on bow

Are nitine mure nitinenje
Left the arrow off bow

Nei ande nei trala mehisi
Targetted to the chest liver

Jian jia ahanjia manenje
Arrow hit the target

Ade bede tada ade bede kaku
Hello elder brother, hello uncle

Sekamaju daramaju jiami
I've killed large sambar

Jamai wahamai
Have arrowed it

(243) *Anangapa gatingapa sakate*
Sambar come out (its body fitting exactly to the size) of Ana

Tanu Satate gaisi pdiate gaisi
To come out, to emerge

Jianjia wahanjia ma
Killed with arrow

Tanujendi kaka tanu jendi kaku
He is big uncle

Inisati tada inisati kaku
How to do elder brother, uncle

Are murena nitemai
Took arrow on bow

Rakatira mepenere
Following blood drops

Iba kajanga iba madanga
Here is the foot print

Kaja lespi madalespi manere
Following foot steps

Kajamada lesananga
Following track of foot steps

(244) *Raka mehi tira mehi lesnere*
Following blood drops

Kaja kaja mada mada sanere
Going on following foot steps

Tanu saji tanu repi manere
He is going, he is leaving

Aai gunjinanu aai mahananuta
Reached at gunjinanu, mahananu

Eju gahi kudu gahi inji
To drink water

Gunginanu mahananu eju
Water of gunjinanu mahananu

Ejugapa kudugapa kurate
Sambar fell down (there) to drink

Gunjinanu mahananu dakata
Gunjinanu mahananu spring

Iride tada iride kaku
Here it is elder brother here it is uncle

Maju kurenja braha kurenja
Sambar (has) fallen, boar has fallen

(245) *A bara adite a bara ranjite*
Now it's ok, now it's fit

A bara laingi a bara tukingi
Now it's equal

Majupunde brahapunde nangani
Hunting game is done

Tanu betamangera tanu prambumangera
He is betamangera, he is prambumangera

Edu giananga budhi giananga
Thought came, knowledge came

Laud daha muchi daha mendu
Search for sticks, rods

Dekinjia duchenjia mena
Let's see the earth

Tanu Betamangera tanu Prambumangera
He is Betamangera, he is Prambumangera

Tanu Udurengad tanu Penarengad
He is Uderengad he is Penarangad

Ate edu iananga ate budhi iananga
Again thought for knowledge

(246) *Edu iananga budhi iananga*
Thought for knowledge

A bara adite a bara ranjite
Now it's ok, now it's fit

Virakali valikali daha
Worshipped earth, stones

Kiu dupinere panda dupinere
Worshipped sambar's ears

Kiudusa nangani pandadusa nangani
Finished worshipping ears

Roe tudu roe palu gatali
May more take birth at the same place

Kanudumbe mukudumbe mapali
May new games come closing their eyes

Na ana na gati dinawa
Again when to ana gati

Nae keri nae danda dinawa
While going from one hill to another

Anagapa gatigapa satalapali
May it come out as it came out

(247) *Sapangada sarchangada rasi*
Of Sapangada, of Sarchangada

Ranipalu bendipalu rasi
Of Ranipalu, of Bendipalu

Satavali murlivali rasi
Of satavali, of murlivali

Pijubangeri bidibangeri rasi
Of pijubangeri of bidibangeri

Sanasella rupasella rasi
Of sanasella of rupasella

Kudepanga tedipanga rasi
Of kudepanga of tedipanga

Kanudumbe mukudumbe mapali
May it come closing eyes

Acheka inja acheka janangani
Saying this much

A bara adite a bara ranjite
Now its ok now it's fit

Surikare gabakare aha
Taking knife, big knife

(248) *Tadengare madangare aha*
Taking salap cutting knife

Sandekacha jienere
Cutting down

Kauduju bechaduju bechinere
Cut the flesh from hind limbs

Sukja jienere make jienere
Burnt the flesh

Sukjanjia makenjia
Burning finishing

Jibangat wakangat nai
(Addressing) To hunting people

Siripalu siridata baenji
Unnecessarily to give teeth, jaws

Tani kauduju tani bechaduju
That flesh of back

Muchigrali api sienere
Giving to the hunter

Tani uju tani pdenu ignali
It's flesh, bones (he) threw

(249) *Tani kubju tani pdenu ignali*
Threw away its hind legs, forelegs

Sire wango kandek wango ajane
Became small fields

Ikja danje dupinenje
Throwing fleshes off

Sirewango kandewango ajane
Hills, fields came up

Mara linganja dadi linganja ajane
Trees took birth, leaves took birth

Kiusiri pandasiri ignali
Threw away ear pinna

Raelmara raeldadi ajate
Rael tree, rael leaves came out

Tani ande tani paje igdali
Threw its bile

Duruvali sinjavali ajate
Big stones came up

Bichavali jaravali ajate
Grainstone came up

(250) *Tani kapda tani munju igdali*
Threw its head skull

Ritod wango ritad nella ajate
Stoney earth, field came up

Tani palu tani data igdali
Threw its molar and other teeth

Darnivali jakervali ajate
Dharani stone came up

Tani buri tani gadi ditali
Threw its body hairs

Pdibalinga jadalinga ajate
Grasses, small plants came up

Tani wahen tani paja igdali
Threw its intestine

Tula linga mala linga ajate
Creepers and leaves came up

Atadi gabda paeri gabda ajate
Atadi creeper, siali creeper came up

A bara adite a bara ranjite
Now its ok, now it's fit

(251) *Mara dadi lingainjane*
Trees, leaves took birth

Edu itere budhi itere
Thought for knowledge

Inisatisi adine inisatisi rnjine
How it will be ok, how it will fit

Tanu nerandali tanu kapandali
She is Nerandali, she is kapandali

Tanu Pusarani tanu batarani
She is pusarani, she is batarani

Edu iananga budhi iananga
Thinking for knowledge to come

A bara adite a bara ranjite
Now it's ok, now it's fit

Soru usumgaisi gada usumgaisi
For hills, holes to be crowded

Mara linganjane dadi linganjane
Trees took birth, leaves took birth

Karamara linga bidimara linga
Kara tree took birth , bidi tree took birth

(252) *Lingainjane jananainjane*
Taking birth getting covered

Maralinga dadilinga aainjane
Trees and leaves taking birth

Asamara linga besamara linga ainjane
Medicine tree, poison tree took birth

Lingainjane jananainjane
Taking birth, getting covered

Sorvrete gadarete ainjane
Took birth in hills, holes

Soru usumgaisi gada usum gaisi
For hills, holes to be crowded

Soruta soruta gadata gadata
In hills, in hills, in holes, in holes

Jadita jadita, dakata dakata
In stream in stream, in fountain in fountain

Lingainjane jananainjane
Taking birth, getting covered

Mnia mara linga makumara linga
Mnia tree took birth, maku tree took birth

(253) Bbademara linga bandamara linga
Banyan tree took birth, bonda tree took birth

Eju pipadi linga kudupipadi linga
Water-peepal-tree took birth

Japi mara linga japi dadi linga
Champak tree took birth

Kadamara linga kada dadi linga
Cadamba tree took birth, cadamba leaves took birth

Saragi mara linga saragi dadi linga
Sal tree took birth, sal leaves took birth

Laka mara linga laka dadi linga
Semul tree took birth

Benger mara linga benger linga
Piasal tree took birth

Mardimara linga mardi dadi linga
Asan tree took birth

Linga ainjane jana nainjane
Taking birth, getting covered

Soru usumgaisi gada usumgaisi
For hills to be crowded

(254) *A bara adite a bara ranjite*
Now it's ok, now it fits

Jambumara linga jambudadi linga
Jamun tree, leaves took birth

Soru surgaki linga pangasurgaki linga
Amla myrobalan took birth

Linga ainjane jananainjane
Taking birth, getting covered

Bajad mara linga bajad dadi linga
Bajad tree took birth, Bajad leaves took birth

Tata mara linga gudki mara linga
Big mango, small mango tree took birth

Maska mara linga dasi mara linga
Mango tree took birth

Dengen mara linga dengen dadi linga
Dengen tree, leaves took birth

Be na mara linga be na dadi linga
Bahada tree, leaves took birth

Daman mara linga daman dadi linga
Daman tree, leaves took birth

(255) *lingainjane jananainjane*
Taking birth getting covered

Soru usumgaisi gada usumgaisi
For hills, holes to be crowded

Lingainjane jananainjane
Taking birth, getting covered

Soruta soruta gadata gadata
In hills, in holes

Jadita jadita dakata dakata
In springs, in fountains

Mara linganja dadi linganjane
Trees took birth, leaves took birth

A bara adite a bara ranjite
Now it's ok, now it fits

Jatrumara linga jatrudadi linga
Jatru tree, leaves took birth

Gambar mara linga gambar dadi linga
Gambar tree, leaves took birth

Lingainjane-jananainjane
Taking birth, getting covered

(256) *Kuen sapangadata kuen sarchangadata*
On Sapangada, on Sarchangada

Kuen ranipaluta kuen bendipaluta
On Ranipalu, on Bendipalu

Lingainjane jananainjane
Taking birth, getting covered

Maralinganja dadi linganja
Trees took birth, leaves took birth

Bajad mara linga bajad dadi linga
Bajad tree, leaves took birth

Sekchuri mara linga sekchuri dadi linga
Sekchuri tree, leaves took birth

Made mara linga made dadi linga
Mahi tree, leaves took birth

Bisamara linga bisa dadi linga
Poison tree, leaves took birth

Mara dadi usumgaisi
For trees, leaves to be crowded

Tula mala linga ajate
Creepers came out

(257) *Maranjapa dadinjapa ajate*
Coiled around trees

Mara dadi wespa gaisi
For trees, leaves to look beautiful

Soru wespa gada wespa gaisi
For hills, holes to be beautiful

Kanja musu dugagai
For monkeys to hide

Tulagenes malagenes gaisi
For squirrels to hide

Patakira gaisi
For birds

Tulamala praginjane
Creepers coiling around

Mara dadi adite
Good for trees, leaves

Tulanaka malanaka adite
Good for creepers

A bara adite a bara ranjite
Now it's ok, now it fits

(258) Edu itere budhi itere
Thinking for knowledge

Tanu nerandali tanu kapandali
She is Nerandali, she is Kapandali

Linganainjane jananainjane
Taking birth, getting covered

Soru gada usumgaisi
For hills and holes to be crowded

Soru gada wespa gaisi
For hills and holes to be beautiful

(259) Ara linga ajate dadi linga ajate
Trees came, leaves came

Aa bara adite aa bara ranjite
Now it's alright, it fits

Appendix-2
Kapaka Gaani

Tanu beta mangera tanu prambu mangera
He is Betamangera, he is Prambumangera

Ana anegati ane
Fell at the Ana-Gati

Keri bangenedanda bangenenji
Jumping the steep slopes, wide slopes

Tani kapamandatani rapamanda
He is the brave man

Dadi mrukaganegaumraku gane
Collecting leaves from trees

Bada kata katadamana kata kata
From Banyan tree, Daman tree

Tanu piapatatanu kadapata
It is singing bird

Piadapinekadadapine
Bird crying

Inakala pia inakala kada
Why do you cry bird?

(1) *Piadapinjanekadadapionjane*
The bird crying

Mrajumua sutanebrahamiua satane
Sambar, boars would come out

Kadani muni sutanealimua satane
Tiger - bear would come out

Asi ooche menenjeasitande menenje
Crying loudly, replying loudly

Kiliaitepikiaite

The birds kept quiet

Era gutirajandiera sandi aajandi
This is scolding

Ashek oochemenenjeachek tande menenje
(Both man and bird) cried loudly

Tanu beta manger tanu prambumanger
He is Betamanger, Prambumanger

Pinje bainenjegooe baine
Running fast to hide

Tani pinje banaba tani gooe banaba
When he was running

(2) *Siraaba aatalisirakaki aatali*
Came across sister-in-law, aunt

Ruda bapkimanali machi bapki manali
To throw dust, dirt

Aade aapu betaka aade aapu prambuka
Hey son

(Apu used to call to males who are younger than the person who calls)

Bilu regaseaambu regase
Keep your bow, arrows

Inakila aaba inakela kaki
Why sister-in-law, why aunt

Nenju jaka jelakia jakakali eeandi
Today to save my life?

Eledede apu eledede raji
Why son-our king

Duasikani padakara sikan pad
Gave him chewing tobacco

Kutabengi sagamu bartabeng sakamu
Talk to us and go

Me ari aatali me judi satali
Your friends were coming

(3) *Nasa mniaa manabane tunga mniaa munbane*
Came through the hamlet

Tedi kapaatali oodung kapa aatali
Have tied hair knots irregularly

Raji magani maanga penu magani gianga
The king's daughter is crying

Brapa nember diwate pira nemer diwate
Out of malaria fever, cold fever

Palu sede diwate data sete diwate
Rubbing her teeth

Raji magani gianga
The king's daughter

Peni srulu diwate peni srulu diwate
Trembling with cold

Raji magana gianga penu magani gianga
The king's daughter

Samana raji maga sanana penu maga
Do you think the king's daughter is ordinary?

Eka bedana tali ku bedanatali
She is carrying a broom

(4) *Neju dnipa trinali palu dnepatrinali*
She talks as if an oil mill

Eendinga deumaga bindinga deumaga
She talks Hindi, Telugu

Beta rajimaga kata rajimaga
She is the daughter of the king man

Sarcha sandimaga rai sandimaga
Daughter of a mustard, rape seed cultivator

Sreka neja atali ganju neju atali
Who gives massage with oil of chara and marking nut tree

Kalama kali atali rasam kadi atali
A person who uses pen and ink

Sani bangla kata sadani bangla kata
Whose house is made with resin of sain tree

Adasiskikuda kata ni bidasi kudakata
From hedges to walls of house

Kisa ranjine kana ranjimane
What is she saying?

Bala telingi atali bala malingi atali
Telugu, Malayalam speaking person

(5) *Tani kasu gunjina tani bulu gunjina*
Can you understand them?

Pui nilema wei enilega
To understand her

Bae kichenjata wae rabenjata
Why to scrach ourselves?

Laka aku atali pipada aaku atali
Person who writes on semul leaves, pipada leaves

Lire lieenji pichirelieenji
To paint (chita ?) on floor

Tanu edu mane tanu budhi mane
She is thinking for knowledge

Na wanai inasaee
Which picture is to be drawn

Tanu akadai mane gangadaee mane
Thinking with hand on forehead

Weda bana sandeka lanjubana sandeka
Separated sun, moon with a border line

Srobana sandeka machibana sandeka
Pointed with dirt, dirt of body

(6) *Ejubana sandeka kudubana sandeka*
Mixed water (with dirt)

Minubana sandeka jana bana sandeka
Painted figures of fishes, crabs

Masibana sandeka badabana sandeka
Painted figures of old snake, python

Lee relpeemane piching relpi mane
Stretching the art

Kuda gana saneka parja gana sandeka
Didn't she tell a lot !?

Sadi bana sande gua bana sande
Drawing border of printed cloth

Atibana sande gada bana sande
Separated with a borderline of elephant, horse

Kuena bana sande mnibenja bana sande
Separated the Kuena (Kuttia), spirits (ancestors)

Raji bana sande penubana sandeka
Separated king, god

Snana bana sande patu bana sande
Separated bullock, cow

(7) *Pite bana sandeka ganibana sandeka*
Separated bag, basket

Kanda bana sandeka bana bana sandeka
Separated sword, gun

Pide bana sandeka kapa bana sandeka
Separated box, bamboo box

Naki bana-jari bana sandeka
Separated big pots, small pots

Sieli wana sandeka topel bana sandeka
Separated turban, turban feather

Imbalinga bihata imba janani bihate
There she ended giving birth (to pictures)

Li biatkata pichi biatkata
Drawing the art finished

Tanu todu raji tanu todu penu
He, king's friend, god's friend

Akdai manenje gangdai manenje
Thinking deeply

Girisainji duju sainji
Shall be a street beggar

(8) *Tanu edu mane tanu budhi mane*
Thought, knowledge came

Ran ekalai ran mundelai
I will be alone

Rajinji punere penuinji punere
Nobody will know me as king, lord

Majhi bengi manenje jani bengi manenje
Called for *majhi*, *jani*

Sethi bengi nenje sani bengi manenje
Called for Pano, Dom people

Girisainji duju sainji
Shall be a street beggar

Ran mulu aene ran data aene
I will not be alone (people should follow me)

Jacha dinanja inere bria dinanja inere
I will be told as beggar

Gada damenja inere gada setenja inere
I will be regarded as Dom, Pano

Acheka tutelia acheka bangelia
Saying this much, he promised

(9) *Muluni data benge dujugiri sapinenje*
He'll leave when all are gathered

Tani sada tani gua bechinenje
Bringing out his king dress

Tani jaga tani angi medinenje
Wearing his dresses

Kalu panda gada panda medinenje
Wearing his leathers, shoes

Medenangani embakata ate tanu edumanenje
After being dressed, again he is thinking

Rajiatanja penuatanja
King's servant, lord's servant

Nain atani nain gadani arpinenje
Bring my elephant, horse

Ala tendaati ala tenda gada
Hey, my hunchback elephant, horse

Anugiri sapimai dutu sapimai
I am going to the streets

Nain dinasayee nain kasa sayee
I will go to my country, my state

(10) *Ade sika gadada ade kacha gadada*
Hey, palanguin careers

Dekul sika atati putka sika atati
Bringing Dekul sika (?), Putka (sika)

Bade kacha atati daman kacha atati
Bringing Banyan Palanguin, Daman Palanguin

Bamukanju bamu bdenju putubamu
Come Palanguin carrying people

Hatini sari gadani sari manala-a inu putbamu
Whatever (luggage) is left from elephant horse, you carry them

Ade raji ade penu
Hey king, hey lord

Piteritpi ganiritpi manenje
(We) are loading all your luggage

Atini gadani ritenje
(Everything) kept on the back of elephant

Ateni lai gadani lai ate
Loading on elephant, horse ends

Sika gadada kacha gadada puchtenje
Weight carrying people tied up everything

(11) *Siel sethi gapel sethi*
Siel sethi, gapel sethi

Tanu raji atanja tanu penu atanja
He is king man, lord man

Muluni bengi datani bengi manenje
Announcing before the mass

Aate tada aate kaku
Isn't it elder brother, uncle?

Anusaji anurepi mai
I am going, I am leaving

Nai dina nai kasa sali-ee
I am going back to my country, my state

Giridenja duijudenja ate
I have got my way

Jendalaja mache kadalaja mache
I am grown up in your place

Raji ajamache penu ajamache
I was the king, the lord here

Anu sajimai anu repinai
I am going, I am leaving

(12) *Ade tada bandu ade deku bandu*
Hey elder brother, uncle, come with me

Ala mila bandu ala dali bandu
Hey children, kids, come with me

Nange bajenbagai atendibagai
To cook for me

Nange pitipara siamu pitigunda siamu
Give me rice flour to make cakes

Anugiri sapimai duju sapimai
I am going on the road

Idanguli siamu mundaguli siamu
Give me paddy from fields

Anu sajimai anu repimai
I am going, I am leaving

Aterindimai gadarindimai
Sat on elephant, horse

Raingabanai piringabana ahi
Sat with gun in hand

Banajiji sali nali jiji sali
Going by firing from gun

(13) *Ala ilu penu ala kanda penu*
Hey home deity, Kanda (main supporting beam of roof) deity

Naneka banati bamu nanek renati remu
Who ever want to come with me come or stay back

Ala ilu pieri ala kanda pieri
Hey, home Pieri Kanda Pieri (pieri: thatching grass)

Na mila ajine na dali ajine
My children will fear

Nane jieebaiaa nane bangaba-a
Their life will be in trouble

Na randiaji na duhkhiajine
Don't come with me you all

Anu sajimai anu repimai
I am going, I am leaving

Nai senipenda nai reni pendasi
After I go back

Mila ajapai dali ajapai
May not your children fear

Randi ajapai duhkhi ajapai
May not the widows, cry

(14) *Anu sajimai anu repimai*
I am going, I am leaving

Alala raji alala penu
Hey king, hey lord

Nai ati rindinaba gada rinidinaba
At the time I ride on elephant, horse

Menangaetalamu kaniotalamu
(Elephant,horse) sat at their knees, elbows

Satarajiati satapenu atisi
Is it really the king is coming, lord is coming?

Bira matalamu bali matalamu
Threw away earth, stones

'Biwa injalamu gaga injalamu
Cried loudly (elephant / horse)

Ati kuetrindi gada kuet rindi
Sitting on elephant, horse

Raji rindi manenje penu rindi manenje
King is sitting, lord is sitting

Tani ati kueti randinaba
When he sat on elephant

(15) *Masa laingate masa duking ate*
Everything became alright

Tanu kangaramane sinadamanenje
He is looking, he is observing

Tani kangarina bena sinadina bena
At the time he was observing

Giridela laisile duju dela laisile
Nowhere a road was to be seen

Bisagiri mane kanigiri mane
(Road seems to be very narrow) road is there for flies

Naragiri mane kape girimane
Road is there for human beings

Rakasa girimane baeni girimane
Road is there for demons

Penu girimane maju girimane
Road is there for gods, sambar

Tanu kangarimane sinadi manenje
He is looking, he is observing

Tanu kangarina bena sinadina bena
At the time he was observing

(16) *Giridela laisile duju dela laisile*
Nowhere a road was to be seen

Tani saliinji reinji akadai ganga dai manenje
He is thinking to go out

Emba-a ate tanu edu budhimanenje
He is thinking for knowledge to come

Sateraji satapenu atisi
Is it really the king, lord is coming !

Bisagiri kanigiri salenje
He will not go on narrow path (fly path)

Rajidandru penudandru danenje
Searching for grand road

Mataradandu riela dandu danenje
Searching for motor road, rail track

Banagasundhi gulingasundhi manenje
Taking gun aiming at

Embakatani banangasapi gulingasapi silee
Then, no firing even after triggering

Mia eju repeli kudu repeli jinenje
He tried to fire towards the spring

(17) *Jendha wedi saba wedi jinenje*
He fired at Jendha wedi - Saba wedi

Bananga sapi sila
Gun is not firing

Guling sapi sila
Bullet is not coming out

Dina kangara kasa kangara jinenje
Firing at all corners of the country

Kata munda bei munda jinenje
Firing at the hedges

Weda dueri lanju dueri jinenje
Firing at sun door, moon door

Suru gada guna gada jinenje
Firing at Suru gada (hole of wood pecker), Guna gada

Banangsapa gulingsapa sila
Bullet not coming out even after firing

Embakatani akdai gangdai manenje
Then he is thinking deeply

Naindeena nain kasa mehene injika
I can't see my country, my state

(18) *Akdai gangdai sanenje*
Thinking deeply

Tanu todu raji tanu todu penu
He is the king, he is the lord

Bananggaspi guling aspi sila
Bullets are not coming out after tiggering

Ate bana ate nali kangara manenje
Again testing his gun

Ate weda adasi lanju adasi atenji
Again fired at sun, moon horizontally

Kaski gada, taraba gada, kadigata a, karugata
Looking towards cattle sheds, buffallo sheds

Bananga gulinga jipinenje
Firing his gun again

Kaskigada tarabagada jipinenje
Firing at kaskigada, tarbagada

Guling aspi banang aspi sil-a
Bullets not coming out after triggering

Manigada parjagada jipinenje
Firing towards crowded places, community places

(19) *Nulugada drasigada jipinenje*
Firing at Nulu gada (thread), Drasi gada

Bananga aspi sil-a
Bullet didn't come out

Eju sapi kudu sapi manjana
Water is inside the gun

Elede rajiaene penuaene andama
I can't be the king again

Ate akadaiate gangadai manenje
Again thinking deeply

Ala soru ala gada penu
Hey hill god, hole god

Isinar isidur waina
Is it I will mingle with soil

Gada sethi gada sani aina
Is it I will become Pano or Dombo

Ate akadai ate gangadai manenje
Thinking again deeply

Naingiri satali duju satali adamuda tena
Was it inauspicious to come out to road?

(20) *Regai giripanpi duju panpi silene*
I am not finding my known path

Banang aspi guling aspi sil-a
Gun is not firing

Inis jendal inis kadal aie
How can I be the king

Nanda dina nandakasa mehi ichisi
I will see my country

Na randi na ebukhi manjana
I have also suffering people

Kangari sinadi manenje
He is observing

Toduraji todupenu atanja
He is the king, lord man

Bedaraji kadaraji atanja
Felt like his hands chained

Indingdeu binding deu atanja
Hindi, Bengali speaking man

Ate banangjipi gulingjipi manenje
Again fired the gun

(21) *Tanu beta kada raji*
His hands chained

Banangaspi gulingaspi sil-a
Bullet not coming out on firing

Ejusapi kudusapi man-a
Water coming out instead of bullet

Bedadueri jinenje lanju dueri jinenje
Firing towards sun door, moon door

Suka gada tarba gada jinenje
Firing towards Suka gada, Tarba gada

Aiti jendaseine katalaene
The king gained power

Ate kangariinenje sinadiinenje
Again looking, observing

Minukada janakada jinenje
Fired towards fish hole, crab hole

Banang aasta, guling aasta
Gun fired, bullet came out

Eju kumbela kudu kumbela jinenje
Fired towards water waves

(22) *Banang sala guling sal-a*
The bullet did not come out

Ate edu manenje ate budhi manenje
Again thinking deeply

Tanu edu inali tanu budhi inali
Again thought for knowledge

Nara ajanengena dura ajanengena
Is it again I will be mingled with soil

Inagai nara bajane inagae dura bajane
Why shall I mingle with soil?

Ate edu manenje ate budhi manenje
Again thinking for knowledge

Ate banang jinenje ate guling jinenje
Again firing for bullet to come out

Ate gada gani gada jinenje
Again fired towards holes

Kaski gada tarba gada jinenje
Fired at Kaski gada, Tarba gada

Kadigata jinenje karugata jinenje
Fired at cattle sheds, buffallo sheds

(23) *Atu gata jinenje bdinja bata jinenje*
Fired at Atu gata, Bdinja bata

Aiti banang gulinga as-a
Here gun will not fire

Ate banang lespi guling lespi manenje
Again raised his gun

Piring bana rainga bana anenje
Raised his pistol, gun

Ate bana sundi guling sundi manenje
Again aiming at

Tati kana kasa ladi jinenge
Firing towards Tati kana, Kasa ladi

Ate edumanenje embeti naijendali ajane
Again thought if anybody superior than he is there

Rasi jueri bakari jueri manjane
Fired towards cattle grazing site

Nai randi nai duhkhi gada
My family place

Icheka an edu itede budhi itene
His thought said like this

(24) *Embadune dinamepi kasamepi sile ne*
From there also my place is not seen

Embe jendalai embekadalai anu
Where I was grown up

Rajipangene penupangene andama
I can't again get hold of the king's post

Tanikangarinabena sarasaki saraeski satede
When he is looking towards all corners he feels hungry

Munelbain sinelbain atede
Intestines are drying up

Wedalai lanjulai atede
Sun, moon coming out/going away

Banang aspi guling aspi manjana
Gun is not firing, bullets not coming out

Sinapura gadapura gadata
Fired at Sinapur, Gadapur holes

Asagada paragada gadata
Fired at swan, pigeon holes

Arhinandi deena andama
That is also my place

(25) *Embakatani tanukangari manenje*
Then he looked at

Rajiatanja penuatanja
He is the would-be king

Nulu gada drasi gada arinai jendali
Fired at Nulu gada - Drasi gada

Arinai katali
Is my place

Imbakatani nain dina nain kasa mete e
When would I see my place

Jendalai kadalai ranjiba
My country is there

Embakatani edusanenje gangadamanenje
Then thinking deeply for knowledge

Tanu rajiatanja penuatianja
He is the would - be king, would be lord

Nain dina nain kasa mete e
I saw my country, my state

Sinel bain sunel bain atene
Feeling very hungry

(26) *Wedalai lanjalai atete*
Time has already been due

Wajendeidi anendeide iji
Will eat after cooking

Acheka akadamanenje gangadamanenje
Thinking deeply for this

Nain atini nain gadani
My elephant, my horse

Embe gasie embe alii
Where will they drink

Tanu rajiatanja penuatanja
He is the would be king, would be lord

Duamepi manenje madamepi menenje
Looking for tree shades

Maskamara dua dasi mara dua
Shade of mango tree

Taamara dua pena a
Shade of mango tree

Iribaade e eriba ranje e
That can't be alright, does not fit

(27) *Embedasanjiri duapanene madapabene andama*
Under which shade I will tie them

Ate katamunda menenje beimunda menenje
Again testing the hedge poles

Amba atigasi gina-a gada gasi gina a
Should I tie the elephant there ?

Emba a adamue emba ranja mue
There it can't be ok, does not fit

Katajueri beijueri basa
Should I tie them at poles on the road

Ambana milabane na dalibane
Here children may come

Na hatike bhari gadake bhari ane
Breathing of elephant, horse will touch children

Ati dadu gada dadu ane
Ring worm of elephant, horse will spread

Ati kaura gada kaura hunali
Disease of elephant, horse will spread (to children)

Bapunamberi piranamberi ane
Malaria fever, cold fever will spread

(28) *Ati dadu dadu ane*
Ring worm from Elephant, horse will spread

Ambati ambagada gaspandi ate-e
Tying here won't be alright

Ate gucheli ate sangeli manenje
Taking them to another place

Ate kangari ate sinadi manenje
Again looking, again observing

Todu raji todu penu atanja
He is the would be king, lord

Ate duakangara madakangara manenje
Again looking for tree shades

Todu raji todu penu atanja
The would be king, lord

Dua kangara madakangara manenje
Looking for tree shades

Bade mara banda mara menenje
Bade tree, banda tree is there

Amba ati amba gada gasnenje
There tying elephant, horse

(29) *Amba atirete gada rete injane*
Here tying elephant, horse will be strong

Bademara basa bandamara basa
Bade tree place, banda tree place

Ambalaingajane tukingajane
There it will be ok, it will fit

Nain ati nain gada
My elephant, my horse

Tatamara gudungimara duata
Under shade of large mango trees

Atigusu gadagusu renenje
Got down from elephant, horse

Sikad rabdi manala
Cleaned the garbages there

Sikari rabani nache-e tanipitegani kepnenje
Unloaded all luggages from elephant, horse

Sieli tapeli repnenje tadinenje
Put off his turban, cap

Duagai madagai
For shade

(30) *Tani sadhi tani gua tandinenje*
Put off his clothes to surround the place

Duagai madagai atini gasnenje
Started to tie elephant, horse

Alimara ta pipadi mara ta
At mahula tree, pipadi tree

Ati tinbo gaisi
For elephant to eat

Alikena pipadikeme siinenje
Breaking twigs of mahula tree, pipada tree

Sarasaki saraeski satede
He is feeling very hungry

Sunel wainga sinel wainga atede
Intestines are drying up

Eju sila a kudu a dina ta
In the country without water

Embaoosara embabeara ate e
From where'd he fetch them

Eju delal kudu delal aisile e
Water is not seen

(31) *Embe eju embe kudu panii*
Where shall I get water

Embe eju embe kudu manjani
Where is water

Tanu todu raji tanu todu penu
He is the king, the lord

Eju kaja kudukaja saleba gabasi
To go for water

Tika bamana banabanana ejugura aisee
Water needed to cool forhead

Eju kaja kudukaja sanenje
Went in search of water

Satikambani giriti pditi kambani giriti
On the Satikambani, Pditikambani route

Penakambani giriti, majakambani giriti
On Penakambani, Majakambani route

Ejukaja sanenje, kadu kaja sanenje
Went is search of water

Ragamara ejuna bichumara ejuna
If Ragamara water, Bichumara water

(32) *Pidel nella ejuna, jadel nella ejuna*
If Pidel nella water, Jadel nella water

Ari ada mue raji tinbo ade e
That is not suitable for a king to drink

Masan gadia ejuna kadan gadia ejuna
If Masan gadia water, Kadan gadia water

Kakibaki ejuna bara baki ejuna
For Kakibaki, Barabaki water

Ari ba a ade e ari ba a ranje-e
That will not be ok, does not fit

Ari maju gatali ari braha gatali
There sambar is drinking, boar is drinking

Susabata ejuna pagaripadi ejuna
If Susabata water or Pagerpadi water

Krichitula ejuna salapadi ejuna
If Krichitula, Salapadi water

Nuamunda ejuna purna munda eju
If Nuamunda water, Purnamunda water

Ari kanja gatali ari musu gatali
There monkey's drinking

(33) *Mahabali ejuna paratibali ejuna*
If water of Mahabali or Paratibali

Siradandangi ejuna sirabakadi ejuna
If water of Siradandangi, Sirabakadi

Embe eju pani ee embe kudu pani ee
Where shall I drink water?

Sara saki satede sara eski sate-de
I am feeling very hungry

Embe eju manjane embe kudu manjane
Where is water available?

Kaja saji manenje sada saji manenje
Going in search of water

Sindekidi ejuna bambhakidi ejuna
If water of Sindekidi-Bambikidi

Dadada kala ejuna muchada kala eju
If water of dada kala-muchada kala

Laka jada ejuna braba jada eju
If water of semul pool

Kranja nella ejuna bari nella eju
If water of Kranja nella-Bari nella

(34) *Utisira ejuna tangisira eju*
If water of Utisira, Tangisira

Kutududi ejuna banajella eju
If water of Kutududi - Banajella

Nuamuna ejuna purnamunda eju
If water of Nuamuna, Purnamunda

Pijubanger ejuna widibanger eju
If water of Pijubanger, Widibanger

Ari ba-a ade-e ari ba-a ranje-e
That can't be ok, does not fit

Ari kdani gatali aligatali
There tiger is drinking, bear is drinking

Embe eju pani-ee embe kudu pani-ee
Where shall I drink water?

Pedem nella ejuna dasari nella eju
If water of Pedem nella, Dasari nella

Jenda bedi eju saba bedi eju
If water of Jenda bedi or Saba bedi

Bari gati ejuna pati gati eju
If water of Bari gati and Pati gati

(35) *Jatrukupda ejuna banakupda eju*
If water of Jatrukupda or Banakupda

Sarena bali ejuna jageri bali eju
If water of Sarena bali or Jageri bali

Rapukari ejuna bali pukuri eju
If water of diamond pond or stone pond

Ariba-a ade-e ari ba-a ranje-e
That can't be ok, can't fit

Aripata gatali arikira gatali
There bird is lying

Aririji tinbandi aripenu tinbandi thad-e
It is not worth a king, lord

Ari ado mue ari ranjo mue
That can't be ok, can't fit

Pringe nella ejuna gapas nella eju
If water of Pringe nella or Gapas nella

Salukari ejuna bandikari eju
If water of Salukari or Bandikari

Tanu todu raji tanu todu penu
He is the king man, lord

(36) *Tanutika bamana tanu bana bamana*
He wears tika on forehead, he carries gun

Gunjinanu bangawada mahananu bangawada
Gunjinanu earth, Mahananu earth

Minandula daeti janandula daeti
Under fish creeper, crab creeper

Tanukangira nenje tanu sinari nenje
He is looking, he is observing

Sisisidi tenjali nungununguri tenjali
Looking glittering, transparent

Kejel daki daeti rachal daki daeti
Under roots of kejel grass bush

Aripena eju aripena kudu
This is king's water, lord's water

Tanutodu raji tanutodu penu
He is the king, he is the lord

Ejukape-e sanenje kudukape-e sanenje
Going nearer to the water

Tanu tiba manenje tanudai manenje
He is promising, taking an oath

(37) *Sate raji atisi sate penu atisi*
If I am truly the king, the lord

Kejeldaki renawa rachelidaki renawa
On uprooting the bushes

Kajunibada satamu malanibadi satamu
May water come out

Raji ele ichisi penu ele ichisi
He can't become the king

Eju sata sea kudu satase-a
Water didn't come out

Sate raji atisi sate penu atisi
If he is really the king

Panda basi satamu drangasi satamu
Water will come out in flush

Asitiba manenje asidai manenje
Again he is promising, taking an oath

Acheka tibbai-a acheka dai-a
Taking an oath to this much

Kejel daki renenje rasel daki renenje
Again tried to uproot the kejel bushes

(38) *Tani renabena tani tadinaba*
At the time he was uprooting

Patke minu dai barul minu dai
Bush came out with fishes

Andira gasi satane dra-a gasi satane
Water came out

Enda minu mesa bdasa minu mesa
With fishes swimming in water

Bandagasi satane drangasi satane
Water flew on embankments

Satene raji satene penu
Really he will be the king, the lord !

Tanu todu raji tanutodu penu
He will be the king!

Eju satat gai kudu satat gai
For water to come out

Eju pdupkinenje kudu pdupki nenje
Water flows on

Eju pdukcha nanga kudu pdukcha nanga
Bringing water

(39) *Eju miee manenje kudu miee manenje*
Taking water bath

Eju mia nanga kudu mia nanga
After taking water bath

Jiri jayee manenje ganda jayee manenje
Washing the clothes

Jirajamucha gandajamucha
After washing the clothes

Tanutodu raji tanutodu penu
He is the king, the lord

Ejudeki manenje kududeki manenje
Taking water

Eju tapi manenje kudu tapi manenje
Water is flowing

Gunjinanu kata mahananu kata
From Gunjinanu, Mahananu

Tanutodu raji tanutodu penu
He is the king, the lord

Tanutika bamana tanubana bamuna
He is wearing tika on forehead, carrying gun

Ejutacha nanga kudu tacha nanga
After bringing water

Tanu akad manenje tanu gangad manenje
He is thinking deeply

Embebajendi-ee embe atendaji-ee
Where to cook?

Eju paha atena kudu paha atena
Water is got

Bani sila dinata jui sila dinata
There is no fire

Inatnani nani-ee inatijui nani-ee
Where to get fire?

Badapaka tanenje damani paka tanenje
Brought banyan sticks, daman sticks

Tanurache menenje tanutere menenje
Rubbed the sticks to each other

Nani saidi sile-e jui sapi sile-e
There is no fire

Drambitula tanenje drambimala tanenje
Brought drambi creeper

(41) *Tere mepi manenje rache mepi manenje*
Again rubbed the sticks

Nani sapi sile-e jui sapi sile-e
There is no fire

Tanutodu raji tanutodu penu
He is the king, the lord

Ate akadai manenje ate gangadi manenje
Again thinking deeply

Raji raji bati penu penu bati
He has become the king (in oath)

Nani kilanga adi jui kilanga adi
Brought his match box, fire box

Nanitpati manenje juitpati manenje
Rubbing sticks to get fire

Nanibati riate juibati riate
(Sticks) caught fire

Ina beramu mrasina ina aku mrusina
Which wood is to be burnt

Tanu todu raji tanu todu penu
He is the king, the lord

(42) *Mujeberamu tanenje kaeberamu tanenje*
Brought Sissoo wood, dry wood

Nani mruspi manenje jui muspi manenje
Added to fire

Mergu musa nangani akumusa nangani
Wood caught fire

Nanibati riate juibati riate
Fire is caught

Ina wajendii inaatendii
What to cook?

Inasalu ee inadeba ee
Where to make hearth?

Mera dekna tanenje keta dekda tanenje
Should crop field soil be brought?

Eri ba-a ate-e eri ba-a ranje-e
That can't be

Ate akada manenje ate gangadi manenje
Again thinking deeply

Tanu todu raji tanu todu penu
He is the king, the lord

(43) *Raji raji bati penu penu bati*
He is the man to be king, be lord

Mendakati manenje katakati manenje
Digging pits to make earth

Kanda katenenga katakate nenga
After digging the pits

Saludae nani ebkimanenje
Put fire inside hearth

Jui ebki manenje nani ebki manenje
Went to fire it properly

Eju katpi manenje kudu katpi manenje
Putting water pot over fire

Eju kandimana kudu kandimana
Water came to boiling point

Eju kanditgai kudu kanditgai
For water came to boiling point

Pranga ki manenje para ki mane
Put rice in water

Tanu todu raji tanu todu penu
He is the king, the lord

(44) *Bidibajenanga paga bajenanga*
Cooked rice

Bidi beimane paga beimane
Rice was cooked

Bidi biatgai paga biatgai
After finishing cooking rice

Bidi espinenje paga espimane
Brought down rice (from fire)

Tanu akadmanenje gangada manenje
He thought deeply

Ina akupanine inagau panine
Where to get leaves?

Rajirajibati penu penubati
He is the would be king, lord

Ooshatade laku mata tadelaku
Banana leaves are right

Jendika ta sha jendi kana ta
The foliage leaf of banana

Dingigate tanenje toda gate tanenje
Cut it and brought

(45) *Aku paegai gau pai gai*
After getting leaves

Bidi bapki manenje pagabapki mane
Brought rice on leaves

Bidi bapchananga pagabapchananga
After bringing rice (on leaves)

Jau bajagai jakana bajagai
For dal to be cooked

Ate eju kapti manenje kudukapti manenje
Again put water over fire

Eju kandidgai kudu kanditigai
For water to be boiled

Brihangdali kinenje mugangdali kinenje
Put black gram, green gram in

Masangdali kinenje kradang dalikine
Put Cajanus gram

Minu ujukine jana ujukine
Put a piece of fish

Asauju metnenje paiuju metne
Put flesh of swan

(46) *Kaju uju metnenje melu metnenje*
Put fowl meat, peacock meat

Meragunda kinenje sringamunda kinenje
Put turmeric powder

Ulimundi kinenje nasunimundi kinenje
Put onion, put garlic

Pularsaru kinenje pulanunu rinenje
Put salt

Rajirajeni kinenje penu rajeni kinenje
Put big chilly

Nasuni ine pueni ra mane
Roasted it

Like todu raji like todu penu
Is he an ordinary king

Randaruda tinenje randa paja tinenje
(Who) will eat with one item only

Tanu todu raji tanu todu penu
He is the king, he is the lord

Bidi tinbogai paga tinbogai
For rice to eat

(47) *Bidi baramanenje pagabara manenje*
Brought water

Tanu todu raji tanu todu penu
He is the king, the lord

Bidi tinbogai pagatinbogai
For rice to eat

Kaju nabginenje mala nabgine
Washed his hands

Tanu todu raji tanu todu penu
He is the king , the lord

Tinjai-inji gadha ji-inji
To eat

Raji tinjimanenje penu tinjine
King is eating, penu is eating

Raji tinjimanawa penu tinjimanawa
After eating up

Tanu salek sethi tanu gapel sethi
He is Salek Sethi, Gapel Sethi

Merang denenanga adang denenanga
Carrying turmeric

(48) *Dagang sajimanenje miring sajimanenje*
Passing through that way

Ade salek sethi ade gapel sethi
Hey Salek Sethi, Gapel Sethi

Naing tinjimanawa naing gapi manawa
When I am eating

Raji-inji gunana penu inji gvnana
Don't you know the king is eating

Nange bangi manjande nange dei manja
Passing in front of me

Abade raji abare de penu
Why king, why lord?

Minge punjala adene metalaatane
I couldn't recognise you

Erek kapa-a erek danga-a
Don't feel otherwise

Juaride raji juaride penu
I salute you king, lord

Tanu todu raji tanu todu penu
He is the king, the lord

(49) *Tani tinjimachala-a megimachala-a*
He finished eating

Ade salek sethi ade gapel sethi
Hey Salek Sethi, Gapel Sethi

Nai tudijuta nai tudi kata
My left over food

Tinjimunjin sethi tintimunjin saan
Will you eat Sethi ?

Abaride raji abarede penu
Why king, why lord?

Gada kaka pada guda kaka pada
I am like crow who eats here and there

Sitapekjandinana para pekjandinana
I eat on picking up what is left

Tanu salek sethi tanu gapel sethi
He is Salek Sethi, Gapel Sethi

Raji tutala-a penu tutala-a
The king's left over

Tanu tinjimanenje tanu gopi mane
He is eating

(50) *Tinjajiananga giajiananga*
After he ate up

Rajitichikali penu tichikali
To the king's leaf plates

Tanu salek sethi tanu gapel sethi
That Salek Sethi, Gapel Sethi

Kali apimanenje dana apimanenje
He is taking leafplates, cups away

Naki apimane jari apimane
To throw in stream

Tanu sate ejue sete kudu e
To water places

Naki rachine manenje jari rachimanenje
Washing the pots, (utensils)

Tanu salek sethi tanu gapel sethi
He is Salek Sethi, Gapel Sethi

Tani kalila ani tani dana la-ani
Bringing his leaf plates, cups

Tani teli nandi tani mali nandi
Threw in Teli river

(51) *Kali pandimane dana pandi manenje*
Throwing the leaf plates in water

Jana unasata minu unasata
To fish house, crab house

Sae teli nandiamu mali nandiamu
Take them to Teli river, Mahanadi river

Eju se-embi akang kudu se-embi akang
May it be tortoise in water

Tani bidipara ditali pagapara ditali
That left over rice

Enda minu akamu krasa minu aka
May it be fishes

Mera paluri ditali stinga palari dinali
The turmeric peels

Kanja bes akamu musu beska akamu
May it be algae

Achek tutelianangа bange liananga
Telling this much

Tanu salek sethi tanu gapel sethi
He is Salek Sethi, he is Gapel Sethi

(52) *Rajibasa manenje penu basa manenje*
Went to the king, the lord

Tanu todu raji tanu todu penu
He is the king, the lord

Bada biji sanere sada biji sanere
Returned to the king, the lord

Ade salek sethi ade gapel sethi
Hey Salek Sethi, Gapel Sethi

Ra mera tanati ra stinga tanati
Taking only one turmeric

Shae asugada sae brinja gada
Go to the low countries

Nulu kadi sagamu drasi kadi sagamu
To buy threads

Kara kadi sagamu luga kadi sagamu
Go to buy clothes

Kanganakaru kadamu kekanakaru kadamu
Go to buy bullocks, buffalloes

Debari ee mangamu banajii mannga
Go to do a business there

(53) *Ra mera tanati ra stinga tanati*
Taking only one turmeric

Kade ninali pane-e ahe ninanipane-e
Nothing much can be bought

Bandik kiche manala latat kite manala-a
What they would be keeping in pots

Mashalacha lapa ada lacha lapa
Bring from them on measuring

Adek tuteli izee sanere bankelizi sanere
Promise this much

Salmu nede sethi salmu nede sani
Go down Sethi

Inubaad razi inubaad penu
You are the right king, right lord

Ni sanigiri ni renigiri
On your path

Kadi saji manabara lani saja manabara
People might be making problems

Ani thajamanaba benithajamanaba
Might have been cut, murdered

(54) *Kati saja manabara jiee saja manabara*
If they have murdered one

Kadi se e ne mu lachi se e nemu
Demand bribes from them

Mila puri nemu dali panji nemu
May you help the children, kids

Mana rupe panga mana taka pangamu
You will get measures of money, paise

Asi badabaji sanera sada biji sanera
Go like that

Todu rajimesa todu penu mesa
With the would be king, lord

Badabisanera sada biji sanera
They went

Rizisazinenje penu sajimanenje
The king is going

Raji sachikata penu sachikata
After the king, the lord

Sethi sajinenje sani sajinenje
Sethi is going

(55) *Rajikata bihit penukata bihit*
The king's tale ends

Iribati adite iribati ranjite
Now it's ok, its alright

Tanu akad manenje tanu gangad manenje
Again he is thinking deeply

Isi akat machis ade e gangad
It will not be, if only thoughts

Tanu edu manenje tanu budhi manenje
He is thinking deeply

Ini satisi adine inisatisi ranjine
How to do, how it will fit

Daen sapangada daen sarchangada
Under Sapangada, under Sarchangada

Weda siladae lanju siladae
Where there is no sun, no moon

Sataandaradae sata kada kdae
In full darkness

Bira mugurdae bali mugurdae
Into the earth

(56) *Malasila dae dupasila dae*
Where no lamps, no torch

Pae ranipalu daen bendipalu
Under the Ranipalu-Bendipalu

Daen bangadae daen neladae
Under the earth

(57) *Daen darni dae daen jaker dae*
Under the darni

1. A Kuttia Kondh man climbing up a sago palm tree to collect toddy.

2. A combination of swiddens at different stages of cultivation (i) little millet on the swidden (ii) adjoined by seven years fallow land which is further continued to (left) two years fallow swidden and (right) four years fallow swidden on the same hill; and the far off hill is not cultivated for sacred purposes.

8. A swidden plot near a 5 year-fallow forest. The swidden plot shows cultivation of little millet and pigeon pea and a watch hut where people stay to safeguard the crops.

7. Plain land is very precious for the Kuttia Kondh. To clear a patch of forest they do not fell big trees. Trees are girdled at the base; then the tree withers and finally the forest department fells it. The picture shows a girdled *Sal* tree.

6. In the foreground near the sago palm tree terraced paddy fields and in the background the elongated hill alternately show the paddy with crops under cultivation and with fallow patches (5 years). In between the paddy field a dwarf variety of banana plantation has been grown which is surrounded by some economic trees like mango and sago palm.

5. In the Kuttia Kondh habitat the elongated hill at the backdrop shows a 5 year-fallow swidden. Its foothill is marked by paddy cultivation. In between the two paddy fields tender *sal* trees are left for growing. In the foreground, little millet is cultivated in the swidden of another hill.

4. In the foreground castor plants are grown on the swidden which is clearly separated from another swidden by a line of dry grasses. The background hill shows on the right side a three-year fallow swidden and an uncultivated hill top.

3. Two adjacent fields with the crop of alasi (*Guizotia abyssinica*) and mustard during November. The field is protected by a strong fence made of wooden logs and planks of *sal*. In the background, the village school is surrounded by *sal* and jack fruit trees.

9. Withered trees as an effect of tree girdling by the Kuttia Kondh. The plain land cultivated with alasi (*Guizotia abyssinica*).

10. Tuleni and Katani type forest — A restricted forest near the village and agricultural land due to the location of a graveyard.

11. A carefully preserved Kambani type *sal* forest in the Kuttia Kondh habitat near Belghar. The site is not suitable and economic to be converted to swidden plots as it would require enormous human labour to clear the patch.

12. A virgin Bamanadeu Dongar, not cleared for fear of forest deities' anger, close to the Kuttia Kondh village of Madalakuna.

13. A totally virgin forest near village Rangaparu, a Kuttia Kondh village. The forest is not cut because it is a restriction by Kulibandhu Penu. The nearby pond is named Kulibandha.

14. A scene of village Rangaparu — a typical Kuttia village, houses are arranged linearly with a long street (Rachagiri) in between. At the center, a small jackfruit tree — under which Dharani Penu is located and Karumunda is erected. Kitchen gardens are to be seen at the background of the village .

15. A distant view of Rangaparu village showing its water resource (deified) surrounding crop fields, kitchen garden, foot hill or plain lands and the uncultivated hill (because of its sacredness).

16. Entrance of village Burlubaru. Women are fetching water from the streams in the morning hours.

17. A Kuttia Kondh man and a Kuttia Kondh woman trodding little millet panicles for grains.

18. A Kuttia old man carrying *siali* (*Bauhinia vahlii*) for sale in the weekly market.

19. A lonely Kuttia child guarding little millet from the reach of livestock.

20. A Meriah pole in Kuttia Kondh village Rangaparu.

21. A Kuttia woman with her children returning to the village after bathing in the stream and fetching water.

22. A Kuttia Kondh woman in her kitchen garden.

23. From village to work place (forest). Kuttia women leaving for their swidden. In the background the hill closest to village Burlubaru showing virgin and fallow forest.

24. A Kuttia Kondh woman attempting to carry a pole for house building.

25. A retiring moment: Kuttia Kondh after returning from their worksites.

26. The grief of parting from her dear ones after marriage:
A Kuttia young lady crying before leaving for her in-law's house.

32. Kuttia Kondh women bringing loads of little millet from the hill to home. The crop is received by the family head. The women are usually more hardworking than the men.

31. The profile of a Kuttia house and the pigshed showing the use of wood and logs.

30. Cattle shed at the backyard of a Kuttia Kondh house. The quantity of wood used for making cattle sheds and fencing is to be imagined. In the background a cleared patch for swiddening is flanked by fallow lands.

29. An old Kuttia Kondh lady during her swidden clearing time.

28. A Kuttia Kondh man making a cow bell and winding a rope with which the bell is tied.

27. Village Burlubaru: Kuttia children enjoying sweets that the grandmother bought for them from the weekly market.

33. A Kuttia man shaping a *sal* log for making a plough. At the background a pile set for the pigs has been constructed utilizing a lot of wooden poles. The fence of the kitchen garden is also partly seen which is made of wooden logs.

34. Kuttia agricultural implements are mostly made out of *sal* wood.
In view are: plough, yoke, harrow, axe, sickle, leveller.

35. Kuttia Kondh going to the weekly market.

36. Kuttia Kondh waiting to collect rice and kerosine from the mobile van of State Civil Supplies Corporation.

37. Kuttia women sharing dua (chewing tobacco) in a market place. Dua is an offering on formal and informal occasions that indicates good hospitality.

38. A market scene at Belghar. The earthen pots are purchased by Kuttia from the Pano.

39. A Kuttia Kondh girl picking up lice from her mother's head — A leisure time activity.

40. Kuttia children in village Burlubaru.

41. A successful game hunt of Sambar followed by the post hunt ritual performed by the participants with twigs of *Emblica officinalis*, *Thysanolaena maxima*, egg, rice, etc. One of the researchers is seen with a red towel.

42. Three Kuttia belles in the traditional attire in the village Burlubaru with the Bamanadeu hill in the background marked by swidden plots and fallow patches.

43. A Kuttia belle adorned with traditional costume and ornaments.

44. An old Kuttia lady carrying her grandson in front of her house.

45. A Kuttia Kondh priest with the traditional dagger.

46. A line tattoo design on the face of a Panga Kondh woman (Pangaliadu) at the Belghar market place.

47. The oldest lady called Dutali (grand mother) in Burlubaru village: The living legend of Kuttia knowledge and an important source of Kui Gaani.

48. Kuttia village deserted in the day time. When everybody leaves for the forest and swiddens, children are only left to guard the livestock and the houses.

49. Village Rangaparu: The biggest Kutia Kondh village in Belghar area.

50. Village Burlubaru: Mother is away, so father has to look after the kids.

51. Village Burlubaru: Kuttia women sitting in front of their houses.

52. Siram Deu.

53. Field preparation for swiddening.

54. Watch-hut in a swidden.

55. Deukuda Penu.

56. Ritual for proliferation of game: Maju Penka Dakina offered to Gopal Penu performed by Kutaka (magician-astrologer). Materials used include a symbolic bamboo umbrella covered with leaves of *Bauhinia vahlii*, slippers made of *Lannea coromandelica* bark, brush sticks and leaves of *Shorea robusta* and a palanquin made of *Grewia tiliaefolia* rods.

Bibliography

(References and related titles used as background literature)

Agarwala, V.P., 1990, *Forests in India — Environmental and Production Frontiers*, New Delhi: Oxford & IBH Publishing Co.

Ali, A., 1979, "Health and Genetic problems of Kuttia Kondh of Burlubaru village, Phulbani district, Orissa". *Adibasi* vol. XVIII, nos. 1-4, Tribal and Harijan Research cum Training Institute, Bhubaneswar, Orissa, pp. 56-62.

Ali, A., 1983, "Health problems of primitive tribal communities of Orissa". *Adibasi* vol. XXIII, no.2, Tribal and Harijan Research cum Training Institute, Bhubaneswar, Orissa.

Areeparampil, M., 1992, "Forest policy and denial of tribal rights". In: Fernandes, W. (ed.), *National Development and Tribal Deprivation*, New Delhi: Indian Social Institute, pp. 148-174.

Atran, S., 1993, *Cognitive Foundations of Natural History Towards an Anthropology of Science*. Cambridge: Cambridge University Press.

Ayensu, Edward, S., 1983, "A reader for health administrators and practitioners". In: Bannerman, R.H., Burton, J., Wen-Chieh, C., (eds.), *Traditional Medicine and Health Care Coverage*, Geneva: WHO.

Bailey, F.G., 1960, *Tribe, Caste and Nation — A Study of Political Activity and Political Change in Highland Orissa*, Manchester.

Bailey, F.G., 1963, *Politics and Social Change*, Orissa in 1959, Berkeley and Los Angeles: University of California Press.

Ballée, W., 1994, *Footprints of the Forest, Ka'apor Ethnobotany — the Historical Ecology of Plant Utilization by an Amazonian People*. New York: Columbia University Press.

Barnes, T.J., Duncan (eds.), 1992, *Writing Worlds: Discourse, Text and Metaphor in the Representation of Landscape*, London: Routledge.

Behera, B.K., 1996, *Tribal Culture, Modernisation and Development. A Study of Kondh Tribe*, New Delhi: Khama Publishers.

Behura, N.K., 1990, "Shifting Cultivation — A Cause for Environmental Degradation". *Adibasi*, vol. XXX, no. 4, December.

Berlin, B., 1992, *Ethnobiological Classification, Principles of Categorization of Plants and Animals in Traditional Societies*, Princeton: Princeton University Press.

Bertalanffy, L.V., 1949, *Das Biologische Weltbild*, vol. I Die Stellung des Lebens in Natur und Wissenschaft, Bern: Francke.

Bhai, N., 1997, "Towards a new forest policy". In: Mohapatra, P.M., Mohapatro, P.C. (eds.), *Forest Management in Tribal Areas. Forest Policy and Peoples' Participation*. New Delhi: Concept Publishing Company, pp. 60-64.

Biswas, P.K., 1988, "Sociological Issues in Forestry". *The Indian Journal of Social Science*, vol. 1, no. 2, New Delhi: Sage.

Boal, Barbara M., 1978, "Centuries of change and resistance to change among the Konds of Orissa", In: Moser, R.R., M. K. Gautam (eds.), *Aspects of Tribal Life in South Asia I*, Strategy and Survival. Berne: University of Berne, Inst. Of Ethnology, pp. 135-151.

Boal, B.M., 1984, *The Konds*. Bhubaneswar: Modern Book Depot.

Brush, S.B., Stabinsky, D. (eds.), 1996, *Valuing Local Knowledge. Indigenous People and Intellectual Property Rights*. Washington DC: Island Press.

Burman, P.D., 1986: "Disease: Is it individual or societal"? In: Choudhury, B. (ed). Tribal Health. *Socio-Cultural Dimensions*. New Delhi: Inter-India Publications.

Caietan, Th., 1959, *The Analogy of Names and the concept of being* (De nominum analogia). Pittsburgh: Duquesne University Press (reprint).

Chakraborty, M., 1996, An Analysis of the Causes of Deforestation in India. In: Brown, K., Pearce, D.W. (eds.), *The Causes of Tropical Deforestation, The Economic and Statistical Analysis of Factors Giving Rise to the Loss of the Tropical Forests*. London: UCL Press, pp. 226-239.

Chaudhuri, B., Maiti, A.K. (eds.), 1989: *Forest and Forest Development in India*. New Delhi: Inter-India Publications.

Choudhury, B., 1986, "Medical Anthropology in India with special reference to Tribal population". In: Choudhury, B. (ed)., *Tribal Health: Socio-Cultural Dimensions*. New Delhi: Inter-India Publications.

Choudhury, B.S., 1986: "Tribal Health, Disease and Treatment, A review study". In Choudhury, B. (ed.), *Tribal Health, Socio-Cultural Dimensions*. New Delhi: Inter-India Publications.

Cobden-Ramsay, L.E.B., 1982, *Feudatory States of Orissa*, (Bengal Gazetteers). Calcutta: Firma KLM. (reprint of 1910 ed.)

Conklin, H.C., 1961, The Study of Shifting Cultivation, *Current Anthropology*, vol. 3, (February), pp. 27-61.

Davis, S.H. (ed.), 1993, *Indigenous Views of Land and the Environment*. World Bank Discussion Papers 198, Washington D.C.

Deeney, J., Fernandes, W., 1992, "Tribals: their dependence on forests, their traditions and management systems". In: Fernandes, W. (ed.), *National Development and Tribal Deprivation*, New Delhi: Indian Social Institute, pp. 49-75.

Desai, V., 1991, *Forest Management in India. Issues and Problems*. Bombay: Himalaya Publishing House.

Driesch, H., 1945, *Der Mensch und die Welt*. Zurich: Rascher, 2nd ed., 1945 (first ed. 1928).

Driesch, H., 1909, *Philosophie des Organischen*, Leipzig: Engelmann. 2 vols.

Duncan, J., Lay, D. (eds.), 1997: *Place/Culture/Representation*, London: Routledge.

Dunn, F.L., 1977, "Traditional Asian Medicine and Cosmopolitan Medicine as Adaptive System". In : Leslie, Ch. (ed.), *Asian Medical Systems*, Berkeley: University of California Press.

Dupré, L., 1993, *Passage to Modernity. An Essay in the Hermeneutics of Nature and Culture*, New Haven: Yale University Press.

Ellen, R., 1993, *The Cultural Relations of Classification — An Analysis of Nuaulu Animal Categories from Central Seram*, Cambridge: Cambridge University Press.

Ellen, R., Fukui, K. (eds.), 1996, *Redefining Nature: Ecology, Culture and Domestication*, Oxford: Berg.

Elwin, V., 1963, *A new deal for tribal India*, New Delhi: Ministry of Home Affairs.

Fernandes, W., 1988, *Shifting Cultivation, Deforestation and Technical Changes*, Indian Association of Social Science Institution (unpublished).

Fernandes, W., 1992a, "Forest Policy, A solution to tribal deprivation?" In: Fernandes, W. (ed.): *National Development and Tribal Deprivation*, New Delhi: Indian Social Institute, pp. 229-253.

Fernandes, W., 1992b, "National development and tribal deprivation, an introduction". In : Fernandes, W. (ed.), *National Development and Tribal Deprivation*, New Delhi: Indian Social Institute, pp. 1-18.

Fernandes, W. (ed.), 1992c, *National Development and Tribal Deprivation*, New Delhi: Indian Social Institute.

Fernandes, W. (ed.) 1996a, *The Emerging Dalit Identity, The Re-Assertion of the Subalterns*, New Delhi: Indian Social Institute.

Fernandes, W. (ed.) 1996b, *Drafting a People's Forest Bill, The Forest Dweller — Social Activist Alternative*, New Delhi: Indian Social Institute.

Fernandes, W., Menon, G. (eds.), 1987, *Tribal Women in Forest Economy*, New Delhi: Indian Social Institute.

Fernandes, W., Menon, G., Viegas, Ph., 1988, *Forests, Environment and Tribal Economy, Deforestation, Impoverishment and Marginalisation in Orissa*, New Delhi: Indian Social Institute, Tribes of India Series, No. 2.

Foster, George M., 1983, "An Introduction to Ethnomedicine". In: Bannerman, Robert H. *et al.* (eds.), *Traditional Medicine and Health Care Coverage, A Reader for Health Administrators and Practitioners*. WHO Geneva.

Fuchs, Stephen, 1973, *The Aboriginal Tribes of India*, New York.

Fürer-Haimendorf, Chr. v., 1967, "The Position of the Tribal Populations in Modern India". In: Mason, Ph. (ed.), *India and Ceylon: Unity and Diversity*, A symposium, London: Oxford University Press.

Fürer-Haimendorf, Chr. v., 1991, *Tribes of India, The Struggle for Survival*, Delhi: OUP.

Gadgil, M., Guha, R., 1995, *Ecology and Equity, The use and abuse of Nature in Contemporary India*, London/New York: Routledge.

Gadgil, M., Prasad, N., Ali, R., 1987, "Forest management and forest policy in India: a critical review". In: Fernandes, W., Menon, G. (eds.), *Tribal Women in Forest Economy*, New Delhi: Indian Social Institute.

Gerber, J., 1997, "Beyond dualism — the social construction of nature and the natural and social construction of human beings". *Progress in Human Geography* 21, 1:1-17.

Girach, R.D., Ahmed, A., Ahmed, I., 1987, "Importance of some folk plant names". *Adibasi*, vol. XXVII, Nos. 2 & 3 (June-Sep.), *Tribal and Harijan Research cum Training Institute*, Bhubaneswar, Orissa, pp. 41-46.

Godbole, A., Sarnaik, J., 2004, *Tradition of Sacred Groves and Communities Contribution in their Conservation*, Pune: Applied Environmental Research Foundation.

Gosden, C., 1994, *Social Being and Time*, Oxford: Blackwell.

Government of India, n.d., *Report on MAB Research Project Sanctioned by Department of Science & Technology*, Government of India, New Delhi.

Government of India, 1980, *Forest Conservation Act* (FCA). Government of India, New Delhi.

Government of India, 1988, *Report of the Commissioner of Scheduled Castes and Scheduled Tribes*, 28th report (1986-87), Government of India, New Delhi.

Government of India, 1990, *Report of the Commissioner of Scheduled Castes and Scheduled Tribes*, 29th report (1987-89), Government of India, New Delhi.

Government of India, 2005, *The Draft Scheduled Tribes (Recognition of Forest Rights) Bill 2005*, Government of India, New Delhi.

Guha, R., 1989, *The Unquiet Woods, Ecological Change and Peasant Resistance in the Himalaya*, Delhi: OUP.

Guha, R., Gadgil, M., 1996, What are forests for? In: Fernandes, W. (ed.) 1996b, *Drafting a people's forest bill, The Forest Dweller-Social Activist Alternative*, New Delhi: Indian Social Institute, pp. 33-67.

Hadley, M., Schreckenberg, K., 1995, "Traditional Ecological Knowledge and UNESCO's Man and the Biosphere (MAB) Programme". In: Warren, D.M. *et al., The Cultural Dimension of Development, Indigenous Knowledge Systems*, London: Intermediate Technology Publications, p. 464-74.

Haines, H.H., 1921-25, *The Botany of Bihar and Orissa*, London: Abelson & Co.

Horigan, S., 1988, *Nature and Culture in Western Discourses*. London: Routledge.

Ingold, T., 1992, "Culture and the perception of the environment". In Croll, E., Parkin, D. (eds.), Bush Base, *Forest Farm — Culture, Environment and Development*, London: Routledge, pp. 39-56.

Ingold, T., 1996, "Hunting and gathering as ways of perceiving the environment". In: Ellen R., Fukui, K. (eds.), *Redefining Nature: Ecology, Culture and Domestication*, Oxford: Berg, pp. 117-55.

IUCN, 1995, *Inter-Commission Task Force on Indigenous Peoples, Indigenous Peoples and Sustainability*, A Call To Action, (Review draft, Dec. 1995).

Jeffery, R. (ed.), 1999, *The Social Construction of Indian Forests*, New Delhi: Manohar Publishers, second ed.

Jeffery, R., Sundar, N. (eds.), 1999, *A New Moral Economy for India's Forests? Discourses of community and participation*, New Delhi: Sage Publications.

Jena, M. K., Pathi, P., Dash, J., Patnaik, K.K., Seeland, K., 2002, *Forest Tribes of Orissa*, vol.1, *The Dongaria Kondh*, Man & Forest Series vol. 2, New Delhi: D.K. Printworld.

Jena, M. K., Seeland, K., 2003, "Animals used in folk medicine of Kutia Kondh and Gond". *The Tradition — International Quarterly*, vol.1, no.1 (April 2003), pp.10-16.

Kachroo, J.L., Kachroo, V., 1990, *General Sociology*, New Delhi: Cosmos Bookhive.

Kaith, D.C., 1958, *Shifting Cultivation Practices in India*, New Delhi, ICAR Review Series No. 24.

Kannan, K.P., 1982, "Forests for Industry's Profit". *Economic and Political Weekly*, XVII (23), June 5, pp. 936-38.

Kant, S., Singh, N.M., Singh, K.K., 1991, *Community Based Forest Management Systems* (Case Studies from Orissa), New Delhi: Indian Institute of Forest Management/Swedish International Development Authority/ISO/Swedforest.

Lal, J. B., 1992, "Economic Value of India's Forest Stock". In: Agarwal, A. (ed.), *The Price of Forests*, New Delhi: Centre for Science and Environment.

Mac Pherson, Samuel C., 1846, Report upon the Khonds of the District of Ganjam and Cuttack. *Calcutta Review* VI/11, pp. 45-108.

Mac Pherson, Samuel C., 1852, An Account of the Religion of the Khonds of Orissa, *Journal of the Royal Asiatic Society of Great Britain and Ireland*, Series 1, vol. XIII, pp. 216-74.

Mahapatra, L.K., 1953, *Shifting Cultivation in Orissa, Report of the Second Conference for Tribes and Tribal (Scheduled) Areas*, Lohardaga.

Mahapatra, L.K., 1983, "Swidden Cultivation in India", In: *Swidden Cultivation in Asia*, vol. 1, UNESCO.

Mahapatra, L.K., 1990, "Ecology and Technology of Livelihood as Determinants of Tribal Economy in Eastern India". *Adibasi*, vol. XXX, no. 2 & 3. Tribal and Harijan Research cum Training Institute, Bhubaneswar, Orissa.

Mahapatra, L.K., 1992, "Development for whom? Depriving the dispossessed tribals". In: Fernandes, W. (ed.): *National Development and Tribal Deprivation*, New Delhi: Indian Social Institute, pp. 131-47.

Mahapatra, S., 1974, "The Meriah Sloka, Songs of the Kondh accompanying the rite of human sacrifice". *Man in India* 54/1, pp. 73-82.

Mann, R.S., Mann, K., 1986, "Religious Attributes and Cure in Tribal India" In: Choudhury, B. (ed.), *Tribal Health: Socio-Cultural Dimensions*, New Delhi: Inter India Publications.

Mazumdar, B.C., 1932, The Kui or the Kondh people, *Man in India*, vol. XII, no. 4, pp. 245-52.

McNeely, J.A., 1995, IUCN and indigenous peoples, "How to promote sustainable Development". In: Warren, D.M. *et al., The Cultural Dimension of Development, Indigenous Knowledge Systems*. London: Intermediate Technology Publications, pp. 445-50.

Metha, J.L., 1970, Heidegger and the comparison of Indian and Western philosophy, *Philosophy East and West* 20/3, pp. 303-17.

Metha, J.L., 1976, *Martin Heidegger, The Way and the Vision*, Honolulu: University Press of Hawaii.

Metha, J.L., 1987, Heidegger and Vedanta, Reflections on a questionable theme, In: Parkes, G. (ed.), *Heidegger and Asian Thought*, pp. 15-45, Honolulu: University of Hawaii Press.

Mishra, H.K., n.d., *Working Plan for the Reserved Forests of Balliguda Division,*1981-82 to 2000-2001, Part I and Part II.

Mishra, N., 1978, *Handbook of Botanical cum Oriya Names of Some Common Plants*, Berhampur: House of Life.

Mishra, N., Mishra, M.K., 1985, *Udvida Parichaya Taratarini Pustakalaya*, Barax, Berhampur.

Mishra, P.K., Samal, J.K. (eds.), 1997, *Comprehensive History and Culture of Orissa*. vol. 2, part 1 and 2, New Delhi: Kaveri Books.

Mohapatra, K., Debi, K., 1974, "Shifting cultivation in Orissa". *Adibasi*, vol. XIV, no. 4 (1972-73), Tribal and Harijan Research cum Training Institute, Bhubaneswar, Orissa, pp. 11-28.

Mohapatra, P.M., Mohapatro, P.C. (eds.), 1997, *Forest Management in Tribal Areas, Forest Policy and Peoples' Participation*, New Delhi: Concept Publishing Company.

Mohanty, G., 1989, "Genesis of land reforms in Orissa". *Adibasi*, vol. XXIX, no.1 (Mar.) Tribal and Harijan Research cum Training Institute, Bhubaneswar, Orissa, pp. 12-19.

Mohanty, R.P., 1991, "Deforestation in Eastern Ghats and its Bio-social Impact on the Tribal Population of Orissa". *Adibasi*, vol. XXXI, nos. 3 & 4 (Sep.-Dec.) Tribal and Harijan Research cum Training Institute, Bhubaneswar, Orissa, pp. 45-52.

Mohanty, S.C., 1993, "Social position and property right of Kuttia Kondh women". *Adibasi*, Tribal and Harijan Research cum Training Institute, Bhubaneswar, Orissa, vol. XXXIII, No. 2, (16-21).

Mooney, H.F., 1950, *Supplement to the Botany of Bihar and Orissa*, Ranchi.

Niggemeyer, H., 1964, *Kuttia Kond, Dschungel-Bauern in Orissa*, Frankfurt/ Main: Klaus Renner Verlag.

Oberdiek, U., 1991, *Kontinuität und Wandel, Die Staatliche Integration Der Indischen Stämme*. München.

Olsson, G., 1988, *Employment and Income Generation in Social Forestry, A Case Study from Orissa*, Geneva: International Labour Office.

Padel, F., 1995, *The Sacrifice of Human Being, British Rule and the Konds of Orissa*, Delhi: OUP.

Padhi, S.C., 1987, "Forest Management and Tribal Development". *Adibasi* vol. XXVII, no.1 (Mar.) Tribal and Harijan Research cum Training Institute, Bhubaneswar, Orissa, pp. 10-12.

Pal, D.C., Bhattacharjee, A.K., Guha, A., 1986, "Perspectives of Tribal Concept about disease — Traditional systems". In: Choudhuri, B. (ed.), *Tribal Health: Socio-Cultural Dimensions*, New Delhi: Inter-India Publications.

Panda, S., 1969/70, "Demography of Kondh village". *Adibasi*, vol. XI, no. 3, Tribal and Harijan Research cum Training Institute, Bhubaneswar, Orissa, pp. 27-35.

Pandey, D.N., 1998, *Ethnoforestry. Local Knowledge for Sustainable Forestry and Livelihood Security*, Udaipur/New Delhi: Himanshu Publications.

Parkin, R., 1997, "Tree Marriage in India". In: Seeland, K. (ed.), *Nature is Culture, Indigenous Knowledge and Socio-Cutural Aspects of Trees and Forests in Non-European Cultures*. London: Intermediate Technology Publications, pp. 51-56.

Pathak, A., 1994, *Contested Domains, The State, Peasants and Forests in Contemporaray India*, New Delhi: Sage Publications.

Patnaik, N., 1993, *Swidden Cultivation Amongst two Tribes of Orissa*, CENDERET, Xaviers Institute of Management, Bhubaneswar.

Patnaik, N., 1996, *Understanding Tribal Life and Culture in India*, Geneva: International Labour Office.

Patnaik, N., 2003, *Essential Forest Produce in Orissa*, Man & Forest Series, no. 4, New Delhi: D.K. Printworld.

Patnaik, N., 2005, *Primitive Tribes of Orissa and their Development Strategies*, New Delhi: D.K. Printworld.

Patnaik, N., Das Patnaik, P.S., 1982, *The Kondh of Orissa*, Bhubaneswar: THRTI.

Patnaik, U.N., 1984, "Kui Kondh — observations of an administrative officer in the Kondh hills in the early forties". *Adibasi*, vol. XXIV, nos. 1 & 2 (Apr.-Jul.) Tribal and Harijan Research cum Training Institute, Bhubaneswar, Orissa, pp. 1–29.

Peterson, R.B., 2000, *Conversations in the Rainforest, Culture, Values, and the Environment in Central Africa*, Boulder: Westview Press.

Plessner, H., 1928, *Die Stufen des Organischen und der Mensch*, Berlin: de Gruyter,

Poffenberger, M., McGean B. (eds.), 1996, *Village Voices Forest Choices*, Joint Forest Management in India.

Posey, D.A., (ed.), 1999, *Cultural and Spiritual Values of Biodiversity*, London: Intermediate Technology Publications/UNEP.

Prabhakar, V.K., 1998, *Social and Community Forestry*, Delhi: Indian Publishers Distributors.

Praharaj, D.M., 1988, *Tribal Movements and Political History in India. A case Study from Orissa, 1803-1949*, New Delhi: Inter-India Publications.

Prasad, M., 1987, *Tribes, Their Environment and Culture*, Delhi.

Ramakrishnan, P.S. *et al.*, 1982, *Ecological Implications of Jhum Cultivation on the Ecosystem Functions of Sub-Tropical Humid Forest Stands.*

Ramnath, M., 1998, *People, Politics and Forest Management in India: An Ethnobotanical Perspective*, Unpubl. Manuscript.

Reddy, B.S., 1986, "An approach to the integration of Traditional Medicine and Modern Medicine — A hypothetical Model". In : Choudhury, B. (ed.), *Tribal Health: Socio-Cultural Dimensions*, New Delhi.

Rout, S., 1964/65, "Dom exploitation in the Kondha villages of Koraput district". *Adibasi* vol. I, no.1, Tribal and Harijan Research cum Training Institute, Bhubaneswar, Orissa, pp. 21-28.

Routray, J.K., 1984, "Approaches to backward district planning, case study of the Boudh Khondamals District in Orissa". *Adibasi*, vol. XXIV, nos. 1 & 2 (Apr.-Jul.), Tribal and Harijan Research cum Training Institute, Bhubaneswar, Orissa, pp. 37-44.

Roy Burman, B.K., 1959, "Problem of Integration of the Tribals in Indian Society". *Adibasi*, vol. III, nos. 3&4 (August 1958-January 1959) Tribal and Harijan Research cum Training Institute, Bhubaneswar, Orissa, pp. 9-16.

Sabat, K.R., Dash, N.C., 1996, "Socio-economic and demographic profile of a Kandh village of Eastern Ghats, Orissa". *Man in India*, vol. 76, no. 2, pp. 127-40.

Sachchianand, 1987, "Tribe-Caste Continuum, A case study of the Gond in Bihar". In : Prasad, M. (ed.), *Tribes — their Environments and Culture*, Delhi: Amar Prakashan, pp. 43-79.

Sahlins, M., 1977, *The Use and Abuse of Biology, An Anthropological Critique of Sociobiology*, Ann Arbor: The University of Michigan Press, 3rd ed.

Salmond, A., 1982, "Theoretical Landscapes — On Cross-Cultural Conceptions of Knowledge". In: Parkin, D. (ed.), *Semantic Anthropology*, London: Academic Press, pp. 65-87.

Samal, J., 1997, "Role of forest in a poor resource base tribal economy, a micro analysis". In: Mohapatra, P.M., Mohapatra, P.C. (eds.), *Forest Management in Tribal Areas, Forest Policy and Peoples Participation*, New Delhi: Concept Publishing Company, pp. 105-24.

Saraswati, B., (ed.), 1991, *Tribal Thought and Culture, Essays in Honour of Surajit Chandra Sinha*, New Delhi: Concept Publishing Co.

Sarma, K., 1979, *The Konds of Orissa*, New Delhi: Concept Publishing Co.

Satapathy, G.C., 1981, "Plants and magico-religious beliefs of tribals — a field study in Kalahandy District". *Adibasi*, vol. XX, nos. 1-4, Tribal and Harijan Research cum Training Institute, Bhubaneswar, Orissa, pp. 73-80.

Savyasaachi, 1999, "Sapangada: A Kuianka living space". In : Jeffery, R., Sundar, N. (eds.), *A New Moral Economy for India's Forests? Discourses of Community and Participation*, New Delhi: Sage Publications, pp. 130-50.

Scott, C., 1989, "Knowledge construction among Tree Hunters: Metaphors and literal understanding". *Journal de la société des Americanistes* 75, pp. 193-208.

Seeland, K. (ed.), 1997, *Nature is Culture, Indigenous Knowledge and Socio-Cultural Aspects of Trees and Forests in non-European Cultures*, London: Intermediate Technology Publications.

Seeland, K., 1997, "Indigenous knowledge of trees and forests in non-European societies". In: Seeland, K. (ed.), Nature is Culture, *Indigenous Knowledge and Socio-cultural Aspects of Trees and Forests in non-European Cultures*, London: IT Publications, pp. 101-12.

Seeland, K., 1998, *Interkultureller Vergleich, Eine Theorie der Weltaneignung nach Heidegger*, Würzburg: Königshausen & Neumann.

Seeland, K., 2000, "What is indigenous knowledge and why does it matter today?" In: Seeland, K., Schmithüsen, F. (eds.), *Man in the Forest, Local Knowledge and Sustainable Management of Forests and Natural Resources in Tribal Communities in India*, Man & Forest Series, vol. 1, New Delhi: D.K. Printworld, pp. 33-47.

Seeland, K., 2003a, "Indigenous Knowledge and Tribal Forest Life in Orissa". In: Seeland, K., Schmithüsen, F. (eds.), *Indigenous Knowledge, Forest Management and Forest Policy in South Asia*, Man & Forest Series, vol. 5, New Delhi: D.K. Printworld, p. 13-25.

Seeland, K., 2003b, "Indigenous Knowledge, environmental perception and tribal management of forests in Orissa". In : Mohapatra, S. (ed.), *Rethinking of Indian Culture — Challenges and Responses*, Cuttack: Institute of Oriental and Orissan Studies, pp. 283-91.

Seeland, K., Schmithüsen, F. (eds.), 2000, *Man in the Forest, Local Knowledge and Sustainable Management of Forests and Natural Resources in Tribal Communities in India*, New Delhi: D.K. Printworld.

Seymour-Smith, C. (1992), *Macmillan Dictionary of Anthropology*.

Sharma, B.D., 1995, *Globalisation, The Tribal Encounter*, New Delhi: Har-Anand Publications.

Singh, B., 1987, "Forest policy and tribal development". *Adibasi*, vol. XXVII, no.1 (March) Tribal and Harijan Research cum Training Institute, Bhubaneswar, Orissa, pp. 5-9.

Singh, C., 2000, *India's Forest Policy and Forest Laws*, Dehra Dun: Natraj Publishers.

Sivaramakrishnan, K., 1999, *Modern Forests, Statemaking and Environmental Change in Colonial Eastern India*, Stanford: Stanford University Press.

Sivaraman, M.S., 1953, *Swidden Cultivation Amongst Two Tribes of Orissa*. CENDERET, XIM, Bhubaneswar.

Soper, K., 1995, *What is Nature? Culture, Politics and the Non-Human*, Oxford: Blackwell.

Spurgeon, D., 1982, "Making the Most of Forests". *SPAN* XXIII, pp. 10-12.

Srivastava, V.C., 1972, *Sun-Worship in Ancient India*, Allahabad: Indological Publications.

Swain, J., 1968/69, "The Kondh Pantheon and their (sic) Social Significance". *Adibasi*, vol. X, Nos. 3 & 4. Tribal and Harijan Research cum Training Institute, Bhubaneswar, Orissa, pp. 33-39.

Tansley, A.G., 1935, "The Use and Abuse of Vegetational Concepts and Terms". *Ecology*, vol. 16, no. 3 (July), pp. 284-307.

Thakur, D., Thakur, D.N. (eds.), 1994, *Tribal life and Forests*, New Delhi: Deep & Deep Publications.

Tripathy, S.N., 1989, "Tribal Development Programmes in Phulbani, Orissa: A Review". *Adibasi*, vol. XXIX, no.2 (June) Tribal and Harijan Research cum Training Institute, Bhubaneswar, Orissa, pp. 23-26.

Vivelo, F.R., 1988, *Handbuch der Kulturanthropologie*, München.

Vidyarthi, L.P., Rai, B.K., 1977, *The Tribal Culture of India*, Delhi: Concept Publishing Company.

W.H.O., 1978, *The Promotion and Development of Traditional Medicine*, WHO, TRS No. 622, Geneva.

Wilson, E.O., 1988, "The Current State of Biodiversity". In: Wilson, E.O., Peter, F.M. (eds.), *Biodiversity*, Washington DC: National Academy Press, pp. 3-18.

World Bank, 1991, *The Forest Sector: a World Bank Policy Paper*, Washington DC.

Worster, D., 1993, *The Wealth of Nature, Environmental History and the Ecological Imagination*, New York: OUP.

Index

Acacia pinnata, 155-56
Acculturated tribal communities, 33
Adivasis, 33
Agarwala, V.P., 8n, 10n, 29
Agency Marketing Co-operative Society (AMCS), 37, 90, 95, 278
Agricultural Development, 91, 94
Agricultural Extension Office, 94
Ali, A., 259-60, 268n, 269
Animals,
- aquatic, 206
- directing of, 255-56
- domestic, 205
- hunting practices in forests, 200-01
- in dreams and religious belief, 204-08
  - Ada (goat) and Sheep, 208
  - Kadi and Kadinga (cattle), 207
  - Kaju (fowl), 208
  - Nakudi (dog), 208
  - Paji (pig), 206-07
  - Poda (buffalo), 207-08
- related deities, 205-06
- sacrifices to satisfy Penuni, 209
- Sambar hunting, 202-04
- trees, human linkages, 212-13
- wild, 205

Anthropogenic ecosystems, 20
Areeparampil, 5n, 286
Artisans, 32
Arundo donax, 156
Atran, S., 27
AWARE, Belghar, 37, 94

Bagad, layout of crops in, 167-68
Bailey, F.G., 43n
Ballee, W., 16
Bamboo, 199-200
Bambusa sps, 156
Barnes, T.J., 27
Bates, C., 34
Belghar Village Panchayat, 36-37, 95

Bertalanffy, Ludwig von, 20
Bicha Supinere festival, 144
Bicker, A., 98
Boal, B., 34, 36-37, 40
Boas, F., 21
Brassica campestris L., 165
Brown, K., 8n
Brundtland Report, 6
Burlubaru village, 36
Burnt cultivation, 154

Caietan, 18
Cajanus cajan, 164
Central Arid Zone Research Institute, Jodhpur, 2
Chakraborty, M., 8n, 9, 10n
Choudhury, B., 258-59
Clans of Kuttia Kondh, 43-54
- Andanga clan, 45, 49
- Atarnaka clan, 51
- Bangura clan, 52
- Damanaka clan, 45, 50
- Diatrelu clan, 51
- evolution of system of, 52
- Gunjika clan, 45, 47-49
- *jani* clan, 44, 54
- *majhi* clan, 44, 54
- Makapuja clan, 51
- Meragundanja clan, 5[illegible]
- Mindanga clan, 45, 49
- myth about, 45
- Nondruka clan, 45-46, 52-53
- origin of, 44-45
- Pajibandi clan, 51
- Pangalienja clan, 51
- Sanderlienja clan, 51
- Saraka clan, 45, 47, 53
- Sarasambu clan, 51
- Suidedhinja clan, 51
- Sukhbichaka clan, 45, 49
- Sukuka clan, 45, 49
- Talajetinga clan, 51
- Timaka clan, 45-47, 52
- Urlaka clan, 45, 50
- Wikajudanja clan, 51
- Wisangurada/ wisanga clan, 51

Clements, F.E., 21, 22n
Cobden-Ramsay, L.E.B., 39
Collective rights, 7
Commissioner for Scheduled Castes and Scheduled Tribes, 4
Co-operative labour, 76, 2[illegible]2
Council of Cultural Growth and Cultural Relations, Cuttack, 2
Cultivated land layout, 103-09
Cultural anthropology, 21
Cultural landscape, recognition of, 8
Cultural property rights, 7
Culture, fragmentary approach to, 22-24
Curcuma longa, L., 166-67

Customary law and practice, recognition of, 8

Dalberghia sissoo, 155

Davis, S.H., 6

Dera Salla Hill, 147-49

Deutsche Gesellschaft fur Technische Zusammenarbeit (GITZ), 2

Development, right to, 7

Dillenia pentagyna, 155-56

Dimbuli Soru Hill, 145-47

Dioscorea alata L., 165-66

Diospyros melanoxylon, 155

Disease,
- concept of, 256
- folk medicine, 257-58
- herbal medicine, 266-67
- natural diseases, 259-60
- omens and beliefs associated with, 261-65
  - Dakandi pdukandi, 262
  - Dolai, 263-64
  - Eju penu dakina, 265
  - Jaka dakandi, 264-65
  - Wechinja, 262-63
- related to socio-economic relations, 260-61
- spiritual diseases, 258-59
- traditional medicine, 267-70
- treatments, 265-66

Dongria Kondh, 34

Dravidian language, 33-34

Driesch, Hans, 20

Duncan, J., 26-27

Dunn, F.L., 268

Ecological hermeneutics, 17

Ecosystem, 20-22
- theory of, 21-22

Edu, concept of, 99

Eickstedt, E.V., 34

Eleusine coracana, 163

Ellen, R., 18, 26

Empiricism, 17

Environmental integrity right, 7

Esoteric knowledge, 19

Fernandes, W., 6n, 35, 89, 97, 284

Five Year Plan, India, 13

Flora and fauna, 15

Folk medicine, 257

Folk taxonomy, 19

Forest Department, 91-94, 97, 156-58, 169, 187, 289

Forest Law (1865), 5

Forest management, future of, 6

Forest policy (1854), 5

Forests,
- as world of representation, 284-85

- classification of area under, 8-9
- clearing of, 158-62
- culture, 16-20
- definition of, 8-9
- development of area in India, 7-8
- human activity influence on, 16
- in Orissa, 29
- indigenous knowledge of, 2, 11-12, 27
- legislation in India, 286
- management, 286
- modern policy in traditional cultural setting, 285-87
- protected, 8-9, 29, 169, 187, 289
- reserved, 8-9, 29, 169, 186-87, 289
- unclassified, 8-9, 29, 289
- vedic tradition and, 18

Frobenius Expedition to India, 283

Fuchs, S., 33-34

Fuel wood, 11

Fukui, K., 18

Furer-Haimendorf, C.V., 4

Gandhism, 4

Gerber, J., 27

Gmelina arborea, 155

Godbole, A., 281

Gond tribe, 35

Grewia tiliaefolia, 155

Guha, R., 5, 34

Guizotia abyssinica, 165

Guna Village Panchayat, 36

Gyana Mandir, 96

Hati Salla Hill, 149-50

Heidegger, M., 17

Herder, J.G., 20

Hills,
- as realms of Gods, 133-34
- forests and, 121-23
- god appearance in dreams, 134-41
  - Bangeri Penu, 136
  - Dharani Penu, 137-39
  - Digerisoru Penu, 137
  - Gadabali Penu, 137
  - Gangi Penu, 139-40
  - Kama Penu, 139
  - Keri Penu, 140
  - Kidi Penu, 139-40
  - Kutti Penu, 140-41
  - Lakuti Penu, 136
  - Mardi Penu, 139
  - Rupasella Penu, 135-36
  - Sandhi Penu, 140-41
  - Sandili Penu, 136
  - Sunasella Penu, 135
  - Tambadadi Penu, 136
- Gods and, 124-29, 133

Achanjala Penu, 129
Adagadi Penu, 128
Bade Gati Penu, 127
Bakabada Penu, 127
Bamanadeu Penu, 128-29
Bichabari Penu, 125
Daramaru Penu, 126
Dhumamaska, 126
Donade Penu, 127
Gunangi Penu, 125
Jindangi Penu, 128
Kamei Penu 127
Kandabada Penu, 127
Katamunda Penu, 128
Kitangi Penu, 125
Maunli Penu, 127
Murjikeri Penu, 128
Murlivali Penu, 125
Nisipidi, 126
Padekanda Penu, 126
Pudrung Penu, 127
Pusarani Penu, 126
Raji Dandra Penu, 126
Rupapata Penu, 128-29
Sasadanga Penu, 128
Sechakuriaru Penu, 128
Senduroti Penu, 127
Sikadi Bandha Penu, 128
Sonadueri Penu, 127
Talabega Penu, 125
Tundabata Penu, 126
Widiokadi Penu, 126
great hills of Kuttia Kondh,
Dera Salla, 147-49
Dimbuli Soru, 145-47
Hati Salla, 149-50
Sapangada, 141-45
Siram Deu, 147-49
Kuttia Kondh's perception of, 123-24
Manang, 121-22
Mooting, 122-23
mythical origin of, 121-23
parts of, 124
Soru Nede, 131
Soru Panga, 131-33
Soru Penu, 133-34
Soru Tude, 130-31
Soru/ Gati Jaka, 129-33
Hill-Tracts Agency, 40
Horigan, S., 21
House,
construction, 116-19
death of, 119
patterns, 115-16
Human rights, 7
Hunter gatherers, 31
Hunting, 5, 24, 39
Husserl, E., 17

Indigenous people, traditional knowledge of, 14
Industrial workers, 32
Integrated Tribal Development Agency (ITDA), 185
Intellectual property rights, 7
Ipomoea batatas L., 166

Jella and Palla, 194
Jena, M.K., 34
Jhiripani Village Panchayat, 36

Kachroo, J.L./V., 250
Kalahandi Anchalika Gramya Bank, 37
Kannan, K.P., 4, 13n
Kant, S., 29
Kapaka Gaani, 241
Kdu Pata worship, 202
Kinadi village, 36
Kinship relations, 23
Koesing, M.F., 250
Kondh tribe, 14
Kroeber, A.L., 20
Kui Gaani, 121, 151, 177, 191, 194, 196, 199-200, 202, 241, 243, 281
Kui language group, 34
Kuiladu, 34
Kuneja, 34
Kutaka,
  directing animals, 255-56
  fear of revenge due to marriage disputes, 254-55
  power and influence, 254
  responsibilities of, 251-54
  thief identification, 255
Kuttia Kondh Development Agency (KKDA), 36-37, 91, 94-96, 261, 269
Kuttia Kondh tribe,
  acculturated communities, 33
  administrative setting of area of, in pre-colonial, colonial and independent period, 39-41
  agricultural calendar, 79-80
  agricultural economy, 75-76
  agricultural work, 77-78
  animals and hunting practices in forests, 200-01
  area, 36-39
  barter system, 88-91
  clans, 43-54
  classification of, 31-33
  communities based on patterns of life, 32-33
  crops grown by, 162-68
  cultural identity, 295
  deforestation and, 91-93
  deities associated with sacred environment of, 141
  development in area with, 93-96
  diseases and their treatment, 256-70
  employment opportunity, 291
  environmental and spatial concept of, 101-02
  ethnic and cultural identity, 287
  everyday routine of work, 76-79

exploitation, 292
expropriation and pauperization of, 294
familial relation with trees and plants, 192
folk taxonomy of trees in, 191
forest culture, 16-20
formal group, 62-63
fragmentary approach to tribal culture, 22-24
gender relations, 54-57
government development programme, 275-79, 290-92
great hills of, 141-52
health care and traditional medicines, 267-70
herbal medicine, 266-67
hermeneutic approach to study life-world of, 16-18, 24
hill god appearance in dreams, 134-41
hills and forests, 121-52
home, habitat and placement of deities, 113-15
houses, 115-19
hunter gatherers, 31
hunting practices, 200-01
in transition, 293-94
inaccessibility of forests, 91-93
informal group, 62-63
intoxicants and stimulants, 214-19
knowledge of work tradition, 293
languages, 33-34, 279
life cycle rituals, 63-73
life in forest, 271-81, 285
magic and magicians, 250-56
marriages among, 67-72
material culture, 44, 213-24
names of trees relevant to, 198
nature relationship, 288
nutrition, 80-84
omens and beliefs associated with diseases, 261-65
Pano among, 59-62, 273-74
peasants, 31
plants cultivated by, 170-76
population, 29-30
preservation and conservation of forests, 280-81, 288-89
primitive communities, 32-33
primitive-modern continuum, 290
productivity in swiddens, 168-77
reciprocal relationship with nature, 244-45
religious events, 245-50
religious life, 54
resources in economy of, 84-88
resource-use crisis, 91-93
rights and demands on forests use, 271-72
sacred landscape of, 135-41
seasonal food pattern, 80-84
semi-tribal communities, 33
settlements, 103-13
shifting cultivation, 153-87, 276

shifting cultivators, 31
socialization of, 272
society, 43-73
socio-cultural aspects of plants, animals and humans, 189-239
socio-cultural development, 96-98
socio-economic change, 93-96
space, environment and village settlements concepts, 99-119
tribal-non-tribal interface, 273-81
use of prominent tree and plant species, 225-39
view of forest life, 194-96
village trade, 88-91
women's role in, 54-57
work pattern on social events, 78
youth, 57-59
Kuttia Kondh tribe, 2, 14

Lal, J.B., 10n
Land and territorial rights, 7
Landscape, 15
Lanja Saora tribe, 2
Large-sized Agricultural Multi-purpose Cooperative Society (LAMPCS), 37, 94
Ley, D., 26
Life cycle rituals,
birth ritual, 63-64
Daru itina ceremony, 64-66
death ritual, 72-73
marriages, 67-72
menstrual cycle ritual, 66-67
name giving ceremony, 64-66
Local Additional Primary Health Center (LAPHC), 261, 269

MacPherson, S.C., 40
Magic and magician,
directing animals, 255-56
fear of revenge due to marriage disputes, 254-55
identifying thief, 255
kutaka, 251-56
Mahapatra, L.K., 154
Majumdar, D.N., 31n
Malinowski, B., 250
Manihot esculenta, crantz, 166
Marriage among Kuttia Kondh,
by capture, 68-69
by elopement, 67-68
by negotiation, 69-72
sororate and levirate, 69
Material culture of Kuttia Kondh,
articles to keep clothes, 220-21
household articles, 219
household equipment, 224
intoxicants and stimulants, 214-19
Katul, 218

kitchen equipment, 219
mada (toddy), 214-17
mahula liquor, 217-18
mara and mraka, 213-14
miscellaneous artefacts, 224
musical instruments, 222-23
sleeping furniture, 221-22
storing articles, 222
water storing articles and eating vessels, 220
Mehta, J.L., 17
Minor forest produce, 5
Mixed-cropping pattern, 83

Nation-building, process of, 3-4
Natural diseases, 259
Natural human environment, protection of, 13
Natural resources, 25-26
Nature and natural resources, 287-95
Nature vs. culture dichotomy, 18
Nature-culture continuum, 18
Nehru, Jawaharlal, 4
Niggemeyer, Hermann, 34, 36, 38-40, 43-44, 47, 53-55, 59, 133, 209n, 283
Nomadic groups, 32
Non Governmental organization (NGOs), 96, 98, 284, 287
importance in tribal development, 5-6

Oberdiek, U., 31
Oil Orissa, 94-95
Orissa,
administrative hierarchy in, 41
administrative setting in, 39-41
animal species in, 38-39
challenges for modern forest policy in traditional cultural setting, 285-87
climate, 37
forest area, 29
Kuttia Kondh area, 36-39
natural environment, 35-36
population, 29
soil, 37
species of forests, 38
tribes of, 29-35
Oryza sativa L., 162-63
Other Backward Classes, 30

Padel, F., 39-40
Panicum miliare, 163
Pano community, 59-62, 273-74, 283
Parkin, R., 189
Pathak, A., 5, 9n, 13n
Patnaik, N., 31n, 186n, 286
Pearce, D.W., 8n
Peasants, 31-32
Pennisetum typhoides, 163
Phaseolus mungo, 164
Phillips, J., 22

Phoenix acaulis, 156

Phoenix sylvestris, 156

Plants,
  genealogy of, 19
  see, Trees and plants

Plessner, Helmuth, 20

Podu Prevention Scheme, 91, 93, 185, 275

Poffenberger, M., 10, 29

Polysemy, 26-27

Posey, D.A., 288

Positivism, 17

Praharaj, 5n, 39, 286

Primary Health Centre, 95

Primitive communities, 32-33

Protected forest, 8-9, 29, 169, 187, 289

Protection of cultural heritage, right to, 7

Pterocarpus marsupium, 155

Rai, B.K., 31n, 269

Rangaparu village, 36

Reddy, B.S., 257-58, 268

Religious events,
  Badbinere, 246-49
  Basa dakina, 249-50
  Dasehra kandanga dakina, 249
  Meriah festival, 246
  Puni kalu, 245-46

Religious freedom, right, to, 7

Research method, 17

Reserved forest, 8-9, 29, 169, 186-87, 289

Resource rights, 7

Ricinus communis, 164-65

Ricoeur, Paul, 27

Rigveda, 18

Roy Burman, B.K., 31n

Sachchidanand, 31

Salmond, A., 85

Samal, J., 283

Sambar hunting, 202

Saora tribe, 2

Sapangada Hill, 141-45

Sarnaik, J., 281

Saru-Siru-Soru linkages, 212-13

Scheduled Castes and Scheduled Tribes, 4, 30, 283-84
  expropriation of, 4, 294
  income by sale of locally available items, 11
  poverty alleviation, 3
  tribal advancement and, 3

Scheduled Tribes (Recognition of Forest Rights) Bill 2005, 286

Seeland, K., 17-18, 24, 98, 190

Self-determination, right of, 7

Self-reliance, political concept of, 4

Self-rule, concept of, 5

Semi-tribal communities, 33
Settled cultivation, 75
Settlements, *see*, Spatial concept
Seva Mandir, Udaipur, 2
Seymour-Smith, C., 154
Sharma, B.D., 4
Shifting cultivation,
- among Kuttia Kondh, 153-87
- Bicha Supandi Dakina, 181-82
- Burlanga Kalu, 182-84
- clearing of forest for, 158-62
- critics on, 153
- cultural core configuration, 179-80
- cycle of, 157
- Dulu Dakina, 184-85
- layout of crops, 167-68
- myth about, 177-85
- Nella Dakina, 180-81
- Neri, Nedi, Nella 179-80
- policy measures to control, 185-87
- productivity in, 168-77
- site selection, 156-58
- Taka Kalu, 184
- Wango Dropondi, 181

Shifting cultivation, 5, 25, 31, 75, 289
Shifting cultivators, 31
Shorea robusta, 155-56
Silitoe, A., 98
Singh, C., 284
Siram Deu Hill, 147-49
Sivaraman, M.S., 186n
Slash and burn agriculture, 153
Social resources, 25-26
Society, ethno-biological approach to, 26-27
Soil Conservation Department, 91
Solanum tubersosum, L., 166
Sorghum vulgare, 163
Spatial concept,
- change of settlement, 112-13
- cultivated land layout, 103-09
- environment and, 101-02
- preconditions for settlement, 109-10
- religious background of, 102-03
- religious sanctioning of new settlement site, 110-11
- size of settlement, 111-12
- village settlement layout, 103-09

Spiritual diseases, 258-59
Spurgeon, David, 177
Srivastava, V.C., 84
Sudha Saora tribe, 2
Sunken metaphor, 27
Swaraj, concept of, 5
Swidden agriculture, 153, 289
Swiss Federal Institute of Technology (ETH), Zurich, 2

Tansley, A.G., 20-22

Terminalia tomentosa, 155-56

Thysanolaena maxima, 156

Timber production, 10-13

Trees and plants,
- *Achyranthes aspera* L., 225
- animal, human linkages, 212-13
- *Arundo donax* L., 225
- Bamboo, 199-200
- *Bambusa* SP., 225-26
- *Bauhinia vahlii*, 226-27
- *Bombax malabaricum*, 227-29
- botanical names of, 191-92
- *Caryota urens* L., 229-30
- *Cassia fistula*, 229
- *Cissampelos pareira*, 230
- Daka-Daki-Dakina, 210-12
- *Dalbergia sissoo*, 238-39
- *Diospyros melanoxylon* Roxb., 239
- *Emblica officinalis*, 230
- *Eulaliopsis binata*, 239
- familial relations with, 192-94
- *Ficus scandens* Roxb, 231
- folk taxonomy of, 190-91
- Gochchi (disease), 210
- *Grewia tiliaefolia*, 231-32
- *Holarrhena antidysenterica*, 232
- *Lagenaria vulgaris*, 232-33
- life cycle of, 194-96
- *Madhuka longifolia*, 233
- *Mangifera indica*, 233-34
- *Michaelia champaca*, 239
- *Musa paradisiaca*, 234-35
- mythical evolution of, 196-99
- names of relevant trees, 198
- *Ocimum basilicum*, 235
- prominent species, 225-39
- *Pterocarpus marsupium*, 238
- *Shorea robusta* Gaertn, 235-37
- socio-cultural aspects of, 189-200
- spiritual nature, 210-12
- *Terminalia tomentosa*, 237
- *Themda arundinacea*, 238
- *Thysanolaena maxima*, 237-38
- use of, 225-39
- *Xylia xylocarpa Jaub*, 238

Tribal Development Co-operative Corporation, 90

Tribal Development Cooperative Society (TDCS), 95, 278

Tribal forest economy, 11

Tribal life, methodological approach to, 17-19

Tribals,
- methodological approach to life of, 17-19
- non-tribals interface, 273-81
- place in Hindu hierarchy, 33-35

Tribes,
- caste continuum, 31
- concept of, 30

of Orissa, 29-35
see also, Kuttia Kondh tribe

UN Commission on Sustainable Development, 1
UN Conference on Environment and Development, Rio de Janeiro (1992), 13
UN Conference on Environment and Development, Stockholm (1972), 1, 13
Unclassified forest, 8-9, 29
Utkal Navajeevan Mandal, 37, 96

Vico, G.B., 20
Vidyarthi, L.P., 31n, 269
Vigna indica, 164
Village settlements, 103-09

Weber, Max, 250
WHO, 267
Women's role and gender relations, 54-57
Worster, Donald, 20

Youth,
dormintories, 57-58
life of, 57-59

Zea mays L, 162